MULTICULTURAL PERSPECTIVES IN CRIMINAL JUSTICE AND CRIMINOLOGY

MULTICULTURAL PERSPECTIVES IN CRIMINAL JUSTICE AND CRIMINOLOGY

Edited by

JAMES E. HENDRICKS, PH.D.
Criminal Justice and Criminology
Ball State University
Muncie, Indiana

and

BRYAN BYERS, PH.D.
Sociology
Valparaiso University
Valparaiso, Indiana

CHARLES C THOMAS • PUBLISHER
Springfield • Illinois • U.S.A.

Published and Distributed Throughout the World by

CHARLES C THOMAS • PUBLISHER
2600 South First Street
Springfield, Illinois 62794-9265

ISBN 0-398-05926-8

Library of Congress Catalog Card Number: 94-21027

With THOMAS BOOKS *careful attention is given to all details of manufacturing and design. It is the Publisher's desire to present books that are satisfactory as to their physical qualities and artistic possibilities and appropriate for their particular use.* THOMAS BOOKS *will be true to those laws of quality that assure a good name and good will.*

Printed in the United States of America
SC-R-3

Library of Congress Cataloging-in-Publication Data

Multicultural perspectives in criminal justice and criminology / edited by James E. Hendricks, Bryan Byers.
p. cm.
Includes bibliographical references and index.
ISBN 0-398-05926-8
1. Criminal justice, Administration of—United States. 2. Multiculturalism—United States. 3. Discrimination in criminal justice administration—United States. I. Hendricks, James E. (James Earnest) II. Byers, Bryan.
HV9950.M85 1994
364.973—dc20 94-21027
CIP

ABOUT THE EDITORS

James E. Hendricks, Ph.D. holds a doctorate from Southern Illinois University at Carbondale and is currently a professor of criminal justice and criminology at Ball State University. He has also served on the University of Tennessee and Southern Illinois University faculties. While at Southern Illinois University he taught courses on effective interpersonal relations, conflict resolution, and counseling methods. His field experience includes serving as a police officer, chief deputy sheriff, deputy coroner, director of a victim advocate program, correctional counselor, and mental health worker. In addition, Dr. Hendricks served as a combat marine corpsman in the Vietnam war. His publications are numerous and include three books and thirty articles in the areas of crisis intervention, law enforcement, and victim advocacy. He is the author of *Crisis Intervention* (Charles C Thomas, 1985), the editor of *Crisis Intervention in Criminal Justice/Social Service* (Charles C Thomas, 1991), and the coeditor of *Adult Protective Services: Research and Practice* (Charles C Thomas, 1993). His most recent research has focused on cultural sensitivity issues in the delivery of death notifications by law enforcement personnel. He is a diplomate and certified crisis intervener of the American Board of Examiners in crisis intervention. He is also a member of the Education and Training Committee of the International Association of Chiefs of Police (IACP).

Bryan Byers, Ph.D. holds a doctorate from the University of Notre Dame and is currently an assistant professor of sociology and criminology at Valparaiso University. He has also served on the faculties of the University of Notre Dame and Saint Mary's College. Dr. Byers' field experiences include positions as a prosecutor's special investigator, adult protective services investigator, deputy coroner, mental health liaison, juvenile corrections worker, criminal justice trainer, and researcher. He has published ten articles, three book chapters, and three previous books in the areas of sociology, criminology, and crisis intervention. He is the editor of *Readings in Social Psychology: Perspective and Method* (Allyn and Bacon, 1993) and the coeditor of *Adult Protective Services: Research and Practice* (Charles C Thomas, 1993). His most recent research has focused on hate crime events and offenders. He is also the coauthor of the forthcoming book *A Flavor of Social Psychology: Focus on Diversity* (Allyn and Bacon) and is an Associate Editor of the journal *Teaching Sociology* published by the American Sociological Association.

CONTRIBUTORS

James S. Arnott, M.A.
Agnes L. Baro, Ph.D.
Michael P. Brown, Ph.D.
Steven M. Chermak, Ph.D.
Myrna Cintron, Ph.D.
Charles J. Corley, Ph.D.
Helen M. Eigenberg, Ph.D.
James N. Gilbert, Ph.D.
Stephen M. Hennessy, Ed.D.
Mark S. Kiselica, Ph.D.
Jerome McKean, Ph.D.
Janet Mullings, M.A.
Laura B. Myers, Ph.D.
Dennis M. Rome, Ph.D.
Kathryn E. Scarborough, M.A.
Kurt D. Siedschlaw, J.D.
Geneva Smitherman, Ph.D.
Lori A. Spillane, J.D.
Timothy F. Wynkoop, Ph.D.

The editors would like to provide the reader with a brief biographical sketch which includes the outstanding qualifications and accomplishments of each author. Assembled within this volume are some of the most qualified authors available within the areas of multiculturalism, criminal justice, and criminology.

James S. Arnott, M.A. is an organizational development and training specialist with a major interest in organizational communication. Arnott is a senior consultant and principle of the Twin Cities consulting group Leadership of the Twin Cities. His specialties include managing change and improving organizational development. During the last several years, Jim has worked closely with issues concerning cultural diversity. With this interest he has worked with city governments, urban police departments, state criminal justice agencies, and sheriff and police departments as a trainer and consultant. Recently, he collaborated on a book to train cultural diversity trainers. He presents nationally for the International Association of Chiefs of Police.

Agnes L. Baro, Ph.D. holds a doctorate from the College of Criminal Justice at Sam Houston State University. She also attended the Cambridge University Institute for Criminology in Cambridge, England. Dr. Baro is currently an associate professor in the School of Criminal Justice at Grand Valley State University. Her field experiences include positions as a probation and parole officer, a corrections specialist, and researcher. Dr. Baro is the author of numerous articles in criminal justice and is currently conducting research in the areas of gender and criminal justice and corrections.

Michael P. Brown, Ph.D. is an assistant professor of criminal justice and criminology at Ball State University. He holds a doctorate from Western Michigan University in Sociology and has also taught at Utica College. Dr. Brown's interest in criminal justice and criminal justice education has led to involvement as a program evaluator and in academic program assessment. In addition to criminal justice education and program assessment, he also has research interests in community based corrections and intermediate sanctions.

Steven M. Chermak, Ph.D. earned his doctorate at the State University of New York at Albany in criminal justice. He is currently an assistant professor of criminal justice at Indiana University—Bloomington. Dr. Chermak's primary research interests have been in victimology, qualitative and quantitative research in criminal justice, and the role of the news media in the perception of crime and victimization. His contribution to this anthology focuses on the depiction of race in news stories.

Myrna Cintron, Ph.D. holds a doctorate from the School of Criminology at Florida State University and received her M.A. and B.A. in Puerto Rico from Inter-American University and the University of Puerto Rico, respectively. Dr. Cintron is currently an assistant professor in the College of Criminal Justice at Sam Houston State University. Her field experiences include serving as a researcher, presentence investigator, and court investigator. Her current research interests are in the areas of criminal justice decision making and vocabularies of motive.

Charles J. Corley, Ph.D. holds a doctorate from Bowling Green State University and is currently on faculty at Michigan State University. He has field experiences in community corrections, juvenile justice, and research. Dr. Corley has written extensively in the fields of juvenile delinquency, minorities in criminal justice, drugs and society, and the family. His research and teaching interests include race relations, Black history, and ethnic studies.

Helen M. Eigenberg, Ph.D. is Chairperson and professor of sociology and criminal justice at Old Dominion University. Dr. Eigenberg holds a doctorate from the College of Criminal Justice at Sam Houston State University. The author of numerous publications and presentations, her primary areas of specialization are violence against women, women and the criminal justice system, institutional corrections, and victimology. Her most recent interests and research have focused on the depictions of women in criminal justice literature, gender issues in corrections, and women in criminal justice higher education.

James N. Gilbert, Ph.D. holds a doctorate from the University of Southern Mississippi where he concentrated on the police training needs of the Choctaw Indians, Mississippi Band. He is currently serving as professor and chair of the Department of Criminal Justice, University of Nebraska at Kearney. He is the author of two books, *Criminal Investigation* (Macmillian, 1993) and *Criminal Investigation: Essays and Cases* (Charles E. Merrill Publishers, 1990) as well as numerous articles and book chapters. Dr. Gilbert has served as a trainer for special agents of the Federal Bureau of Investigation and the State of Florida. In addition, he has served as a consultant on Native American issues with the Bureau of Indian Affairs and the Nebraska Indian Commission.

Stephen M. Hennessy, Ed.D. holds his doctorate from the University of St. Thomas. He is a former Special Agent with the Federal Bureau of Investigation. He is currently with Leadership, Inc. in Scottsdale, Arizona and an administrator with the Phoenix Regional Police Training Academy. Dr. Hennessy's work with Leadership, Inc. involves the publication of cultural awareness training manuals. In addition, he has participated in cultural awareness training throughout the nation. With the Phoenix Regional Police Training Academy, he develops training courses and is involved in curriculum evaluation. Dr. Hennessy works extensively with the International Association of Chiefs of Police.

Mark S. Kiselica, Ph.D. earned his doctorate in counseling psychology from The Pennsylvania State University and is currently an assistant professor of counseling psychology at Ball State University. Within this capacity he is also the director of the Master's Programs in School and Community Counseling. Dr. Kiselica has had numerous experiences in community mental health, school psychology, and counseling. He has published in the areas of multiculturalism, diversity, and psychology. Dr. Kiselica's current research focuses on adolescents, children and parents, gender, and the multicultural counseling concerns.

Jerome McKean, Ph.D. is an assistant professor of criminal justice and criminology at Ball State University and holds a doctorate in criminology from Florida State University. His primary areas of specialization include juvenile justice and research methodology. He is the coauthor (with James E. Hendricks) of *Crisis Intervention: Contemporary Issues for On-Site Intervenors,* Second Edition (Charles C Thomas, forthcoming) and various articles and presentations in the areas of juvenile justice, minorities, and criminal justice.

Janet L. Mullings, M.A. holds a Master's degree from Sam Houston State University's College of Criminal Justice and is currently a doctoral fellow in criminal justice. Her primary research interests are in the areas of prison boot camps, gender and stress, multiculturalism, gender and occupations, race, and domestic violence. She has published and presented in the fields of probation, graduate education, and gender and corrections.

Laura B. Myers, Ph.D. holds a doctorate in criminology from Florida State University and is currently an assistant professor of criminal justice in the College of Criminal Justice at Sam Houston State University. Dr. Myers' primary interests are in Latinos and criminal justice, ethics, criminal justice education, research methods, statistics, program evaluation, and the courts. She has published in the areas of intermediate sanctions, criminal justice program evaluation, and cross-national research having appeared in the *International Journal of Comparative and Applied Criminal Justice.* She is also the coauthor (with Sue Titus Reid) of *The Correctional System,* Second Edition (Harcourt Brace Jovanovich, forthcoming).

Dennis M. Rome, Ph.D. holds a doctorate from Washington State University and is currently an assistant professor of sociology and Afro-American Studies at Indiana University—Bloomington. Dr. Rome has extensive professional experience in the areas of multiculturalism and diversity in the areas of race and society, policing, and minority professionals. In addition, he has published and presented widely in the areas of race, ethnicity, and crime. He has served on staff of the American Sociological Association and is currently an Associate Editor of the journal *Teaching Sociology.*

Kathryn E. Scarborough, M.A. holds a Master's degree in applied sociology from Old Dominion University and is currently a doctoral fellow in the College of Criminal Justice at Sam Houston State University. She has served as a police officer, a chemical dependency technician, and a naval hospital corpsman. Her primary areas of research expertise include policing, gender and race issues in criminal justice, and criminal justice education.

Kurt D. Siedschlaw, J.D. holds his Juris Doctor from the University of South Dakota School of Law. He is currently an Associate Professor of Criminal Justice at the University of Nebraska at Kearney. The author of several papers and articles on Indian affairs and issues, Kurt Siedschlaw has also served as a multicultural assessment seminar trainer and as a special investigator for a commission on Indian affairs. Additionally, Siedschlaw has provided expert testimony to various groups and organizations on Native American issues and related social policy matters.

Geneva Smitherman, Ph.D. holds a doctorate from the University of Michigan and is presently the University Distinguished Professor of English and the Director of the African American Language and Literacy Program at Michigan State University. Dr. Smitherman has also held visiting professorships in Pan African Studies and English at California State University, at the Institute for African Studies at Oxford, and has also held the Martin Luther King-Cesar Chavez-Rosa Parks Visiting Professorship at Michigan State University. She has conducted research and training on interpersonal violence for the Detroit Police Department, on Black child abuse for the U.S. Department of Health and Human Services, and on police-community relations for the city of Detroit. Dr. Smitherman is the author of numerous articles, book chapters and books including *Educating African American Males: The Malcolm X Academy Solution* (Third World Press, forthcoming), *Black Talk: Words and Phrases from the Hood to the A-Men Corner* (Houghton Mifflin, 1994), and the editor of *Anita Hill/Clarence Thomas: Race, Class, Gender* (Wayne State University Press, 1994).

Lori A. Spillane, J.D. holds a Juris Doctor from the Saint Louis University School of Law. She practices law in the state of Indiana and is a member of the Indiana and Missouri Bar. She is presently serving as a deputy prosecuting attorney in the state of Indiana. Her teaching experience includes serving as an adjunct instructor of criminal justice and criminology at Ball State University where she teaches courses in criminal law, criminal processing, and women and crime. She has also served as an assistant prosecuting attorney, a law clerk, and a faculty research assistant.

Timothy F. Wynkoop, Ph.D. holds a doctorate in counseling psychology from Ball State University and is with the Psychology Department at the U.S. Medical Center for Federal Prisoners. He also served with the Texas Department of Corrections in the provision of outpatient psychological services to inmate populations, as a probation officer, and in residential treatment. Dr. Wynkoop has published extensively on psychology and psychiatry and has most recently written in the areas of diversity and conducted training in multicultural counseling.

To my daughter Kacey.
***To I** 3/5/1-69.*
J.E.H.

To my daughter Leah Marie and my son Adam Edward Rhea.
B.B.

To all who know the pain of cultural insensitivity.
J.E.H.
B.B.

INTRODUCTION

Multiculturalism, Criminal Justice, and Criminology

The present work, *Multicultural Perspectives in Criminal Justice and Criminology*, addresses cultural diversity, criminal justice, and criminology. As an edited anthology, this book represents the work of national scholars who have expertise in criminal justice issues and multicultural contexts. This coupling is both necessary and timely. In recent years, there has been increasing attention given to the themes of multiculturalism and cultural diversity in society and the criminal justice system. For instance, the theme for the March 1993 national meeting of the *Academy of Criminal Justice Sciences* was "Race, Class and Gender." This theme, and the sessions organized and attended by national experts in criminal justice, attests to the emphasis placed on this area. Regionally, a conference was held in the fall of 1993 by the *Western and Pacific Association of Criminal Justice Educators* entitled "Multiculturalism and the Criminal Justice System." Additionally, social science journals have devoted special issues to this area in order to meet the needs of academicians addressing diversity topics and practitioners working with diverse groups. The present volume adds to these efforts.

Multicultural Perspectives in Criminal Justice and Criminology is as diverse as the field of study it represents. This volume includes original work addressing such diversity issues as gender, race, ethnicity, and sexuality in criminal justice and criminology. In addition, types of crime, juvenile justice issues, training, and college curricula are also addressed. Taken together, the volume couples the discussion of important multicultural groups within society with critical issues facing criminal justice and criminology within a multicultural society. The main thrust of the project is to bridge theory and practice in this important area for criminal justice and criminology.

More specifically, this volume attempts to accomplish three objectives. First, we attempt to introduce the reader to the topic of multiculturalism, criminal justice, and criminology. Second, the volume attempts to demonstrate the role and function of multicultural perspectives in criminal justice theory and practice. Third, we attempt to highlight various multicultural perspectives within the fields of criminal justice and criminology. An important consideration for the reader, relevant to the third objective, is that each author represents a unique perspective in bridging multiculturalism, criminal justice, and criminology. At times, the authors may seem to agree on topics and issues pertinent to this important area, while at other times the perspectives may seem divergent. This, we believe, adds significance to our emphasis on *perspectives.*

Other books have also been published in this area, but none with the broad-based approach inherent here or with an emphasis on criminal justice. While there have been books published on cross-cultural perspectives in criminal justice and such areas as policing, there has not been, to date, any book which attempts to examine the multifaceted nature of the criminal justice system as a whole with a focus on multiculturalism. Within criminal justice practice, one of the most influential, if not the most influential, factors currently at work is to promote cultural sensitivity. This text promises to bridge the gap between research and practice in the area of promoting cultural awareness and sensitivity.

Taken together, we believe the present volume adds to the existing body of knowledge within this topical area. There are several specific contributions made. First, it is the first book to attempt a comprehensive examination of multiculturalism within the criminal justice system, its implications, and system wide responses. Second, we hope this volume not only provides valuable information for criminologists, criminal justice scholars and practitioners, but also encourages others to pursue knowledge within the field. Third, we hope the book provides students, academicians, and practitioners with insight into the theory and practice of criminal justice multiculturalism.

This book should appeal to those teaching undergraduate or graduate courses in criminal justice or criminology. It should also be of particular interest to criminal justice personnel, criminologists, and students of criminal justice/criminology with an interest in diversity issues. It may also be of interest to those instructors teaching in African-American Studies, Ethnic Studies, or Women's Studies programs at various schools or within related courses in multiculturalism.

Chapters and Contents: Multicultural Perspectives

As stated earlier, the present volume is as diverse as the field it represents. There are at least two ways in which this book represents this diversity. First, the anthology addresses important groups and subcultures in society. In particular, groups such as women, African-Americans, Asian-Americans, Latinos, Native Americans, and gays and lesbians are all represented in varying ways within chapters. While there may be the absence of a particular chapter on a certain group (e.g., Asian-Americans), this does not necessarily mean the group has not been represented. The second manner in which the anthology represents diversity within society has to do with the varying topics discussed and perspectives represented. Practitioner, academician, and trainer are merely three identifiers which characterize the diverse and expert collection of individual authors featured. Together, the topics, issues, perspectives and diverse writers add to the theme of *multicultural perspectives.* It is truly an honor for us to edit this anthology of superb scholars.

Chapter 1, "Multicultural Perspectives and Issues," by Drs. Timothy F. Wynkoop and Mark S. Kiselica provides the reader with a comprehensive overview of multiculturalism, diversity, definitional issues, and practice perspectives. The chapter, broad in its content, lays an important foundation for subsequent works featured within the volume. While broad-based, it is also comprehensive in its treatment of important concepts, definitions, practice issues, and service delivery to diverse groups within the criminal justice system. Wynkoop and Kiselica challenge the reader to question his/her own perspectives and paradigms in attempt to highlight the importance of multicultural perspectives and issues.

Chapter 2, by Dr. Helen M. Eigenberg, Janet L. Mullings, and Kathryn E. Scarborough, entitled "Gender, Feminism, and Criminology" addresses the important role feminist scholarship has within the field. Within this piece, the authors highlight their research, from a feminist methodological perspective, and its implications for criminal justice and criminology. This chapter makes a significant contribution in helping the reader to understand the significance of gender and feminist for the complimentary fields of criminal justice and criminology. The chapter is thought provoking and critical whereby it provides a unique and valuable contribution to the present volume.

Jerome McKean, Ph.D., in Chapter 3 entitled "Race, Ethnicity, and Criminal Justice" focuses on criminal justice statistics and the nature of crime and victimization. Dr. McKean, like the authors in the previous chapter, forces the reader to examine crime data and presumed crime prevalence more critically. It is also a significant contribution within the field of criminal justice and criminology given the emphasis on patterns of victimization, explanations, and the treatment, albeit often the mistreatment, of Hispanic- and African-Americans by the criminal justice system.

Chapter 4, "Native Americans in Criminal Justice" by Drs. Kurt D. Siedschlaw and James N. Gilbert, not only provides for the reader historical and social accounts of minority mistreatment and their implications for criminal justice, but the chapter also highlights an important, and often forgotten, social group within American society and the criminal justice system. There seems to be at least two contemporary reasons for this neglect.

First, reservation living means social and physical segregation from the dominant Anglo society. Second, Native American reservation criminal justice has been separate from the traditional conceptualization of the "criminal justice system" given its distinct historical and social roots and contemporary structure. Drs. Siedschlaw and Gilbert provide us with an important glimpse into the world of Native American criminal justice.

Chapter 5, by Drs. Laura B. Myers, Myrna Cintron, and Kathryn Scarborough entitled "Latinos: The Conceptualization of Race," like Chapter 4 provides us with an examination of a social group which is all too often forgotten in traditional criminal justice and criminology scholarship. The authors aptly point out the methodological, and corresponding policy implications, relevant to Latinos, as an important social group within criminal justice scholarship. Drs. Myers, Cintron and Scarborough make a significant contribution to not only our understanding of Latinos as a social group, but also the issues surrounding criminal justice scholarship and the conceptualization of Latinos as a racial group.

Drs. Dennis Rome and Steven M. Chermak in Chapter 6 "Race in Crime Stories," provide the reader with an additional point of conceptualization. As a point of reality construction, the mass media determines, to a large extent, how we define events within the social milieux of society. Drs. Rome and Chermak demonstrate how race influences the crime news production. As a conceptual and analytical piece, the chapter provides the reader with a lucid presentation of this important relationship between the media and our perceptions of crime.

Chapter 7 by Dr. James S. Arnott entitled "Gays and Lesbians in Criminal Justice" also addresses the issue of perception and provides us with a challenge. The challenge is to consider gays and lesbians as viable and contributing members within the criminal justice system. Dr. Arnott specifically focuses on gays and lesbians within the strong subculture of law enforcement and discusses some of the special issues and concerns which these individuals may face within the vocation. Within the piece, critical issues such as myths, phobias and the human costs of prejudice are examined. The author also provides important policy implications for gays and lesbians in law enforcement. Taken together, and much like Chapter 4, Chapter 7 addresses an often forgotten group within criminal justice.

Lori A. Spillane, J.D., in Chapter 8 entitled "Hate Crimes: A Legal Perspective" addresses a topic of critical concern within criminal justice and criminology. Hate crimes have existed for some time but the terminology, or criminal justice parlance, of "hate crime" is a recent development. It is within this context that the present chapter addresses this important topic for criminal justice. Attorney Lori Spillane provides the reader with an overview of the problem of hate crime from a legal perspective and includes important case law directly germane to this phenomenon.

Chapter 9, "Juvenile Justice: Multicultural Issues" by Drs. Charles J. Corley and Geneva Smitherman, addresses yet another, and often neglected, area of criminal justice and criminology: juvenile delinquency and justice. Drs. Corley and Smitherman present important theoretical, methodological, and research information pertinent to the practice of juvenile justice within a multicultural society. The authors address important areas such as disparate treatment, rates of offending, and delinquency treatment and prevention. Drs. Corley and Smitherman provide an important step toward our understanding of juvenile justice and multiculturalism.

Also providing an important step toward understanding, Drs. Helen M. Eigenberg and Agnes L. Baro in "Invisibility and Marginalization of Women of Color" (Chapter 10) address the absence and misrepresentation of women of color in academic textbooks within the fields of criminal justice and criminology. Much like the subtle nature that the media shapes our perceptions of others in the creation of crime news which Drs. Rome and Chermak demonstrate in Chapter 6, Drs. Eigenberg and Baro analyze the patterns, prevalence and implications of depictions of women of color within the texts via content analysis. The chapter challenges many of our notions of representativeness and offers the reader an alternative perspective on the oft taken-for-granted belief in equity and inclusion.

Chapter 11, "Criminal Justice Curricula" by Dr. Michael P. Brown, also addresses an important issue within the academic fields of criminal justice and criminology. Like Chapter 10, Dr. Brown not only addresses an issue of educational importance but also gathers original data. Using a survey methodology, the chapter attempts to uncover support and uses of multicultural perspectives within criminal justice education. The piece makes a significant contribution to the book via its methodology, findings, and pedagogical implications.

Pedagogy is also the thrust of Chapter 12, "Cultural Sensitivity Training," by Stephen M. Hennessy. Dr. Hennessy assists the reader in understanding the important role and function of teaching tolerance in law enforcement training. Given the level of contact law enforcement officers maintain with the public, this is of vital importance as society moves more toward the recognition of cultural pluralism and diversity so common today. Dr. Hennessy's contribution is an important one for the future of law enforcement, criminal justice, and criminology within a multicultural society.

We believe the theme and contributions to this anthology, consistent with the theme of *multicultural perspectives,* provides the reader with an introduction to multiculturalism within the companion fields of criminal justice and criminology. Further, we believe the volume demonstrates the place of multicultural perspectives in theory and practice. Moreover, we are confident the anthology provides exposure to convergent and divergent multicultural perspectives within criminal justice and criminology.

James E. Hendricks, Ph.D.
Bryan Byers, Ph.D.

ACKNOWLEDGMENTS

A project such as this is only possible due to the contribution of many individuals. Therefore, we would like to thank those individuals who have made this project possible, for their assistance, guidance, feedback, and support.

First, we would like to especially acknowledge and thank Charles C Thomas Publishers for their confidence in our ideas and this project and the fine editorial assistance we received. In particular, we would like to thank Payne and Michael Thomas for the generosity of their time, energy and assistance. Special thanks to Marilyn Ginter for her ever faithful assistance.

Second, we would like to acknowledge and thank each of the contributors to this anthology. Without their commitment and dedication to multiculturalism, diversity, criminal justice, and criminology this project would not have been possible. Thank you all for your fine contributions.

Third, thanks to the Department of Criminal Justice and Criminology at Ball State University and the Department of Sociology at Valparaiso University for support of this project. Such projects are only possible through strong institutional support, and we greatly appreciate this commitment to scholarship. Dr. Byers would also like to especially thank Dr. Peter J. Venturelli, Dean Philip Gilbertson, and Dr. Susan Kenyon of Valparaiso University for their moral support and commitment to multiculturalism which helped to make this project possible.

Finally, both of us would like to thank special people in our lives. James Hendricks would like to thank the following individuals. To Gary Webb for his kindness and generosity and to Michael Brown for his depth of character and emotional support, both who gave of themselves during my time of grief. Bryan Byers would like to thank his spouse Dr. Peggy Byers for her unending support and love. He would also like to thank his parents, Dean and Clarisse Byers, for teaching him the lessons in life which make a person capable of completing a project of this nature. Finally, Dr. Byers would like to acknowledge and thank two new friends, Jimmy Santiago Baca and Deborah Stein, for their works and creativity which have so inspired him.

ACKNOWLEDGMENT
FOR
SPECIAL EDITORIAL ASSISTANCE

The Editors would like to express their genuine and heartfelt appreciation to Traci Thomas for her editorial assistance with this project. Without her commitment, dedication and hard work, this project would not have been possible. Thank you Traci.

CONTENTS

MULTICULTURAL PERSPECTIVES IN CRIMINAL JUSTICE AND CRIMINOLOGY

CHAPTER ONE

MULTICULTURAL ISSUES AND PERSPECTIVES

Timothy F. Wynkoop and Mark S. Kiselica

INTRODUCTION

A White inmate is being harassed by a group of three African-American inmates. Their goal is to extort him for money and sexual favors. The White inmate enters into a fight with them. A group of Chicano inmates observes the happenings. The Chicanos intervene after some time of the White inmate being beaten, but still fighting back.

What does this scenario mean? A working knowledge of multicultural issues in criminal justice is necessary to clarify the issues involved. Incarcerated Chicanos have been known to align themselves with Whites, against African-Americans, under certain circumstances. In this instance, they were waiting to see whether the White inmate would display machismo in his dealings with the African-American inmates. In other words, was the White inmate worthy of their intervention in the situation? In not so fictitious words to the African-American inmates, the Chicanos state, "he's shown you that he's not a punk, he's a man, so leave him alone." This is but one of the more blatant examples of the cross-cultural workings that may be observed within the criminal justice systems of the United States (U.S.). There are many more.

Multicultural issues have been of increasing concern to researchers in the social sciences for the past three decades. This interest has seemed to coincide with the emergence of the civil rights movement in the U.S. Much has been written on the provision of services to ethnic minorities and other culturally defined groups (e.g., women, elderly). The area remains, however, under-researched, with much of what has been written being in the form of theory, opinion, and/or political posturing. Specific to criminal justice, multicultural issues (aside from accounting for numbers and trends in numbers) have been given little attention in the literature. This is quite perplexing, when one considers the representation and concentration of multicultural groups within the criminal justice systems of the U.S.

Multiculturalism in criminal justice refers to the crossing of cultural boundaries in the provision of services to victims and offenders. It implies the need for training in sensitivity to, and respect for, the cultural values and mores of others (see Kiselica, 1991). It is the provision of criminal justice services across cultural boundaries that is the focus of this text. Traditionally, the provision of human services (including criminal justice services; see Whitehead, 1989) in a cross-cultural context has been perceived as being from the majority (as the service provider) to the minority (as the receiver of services). Such cultural boundaries have included gender (i.e., males providing services to females) and age (e.g., youth and elderly being serviced by young to middle-aged adults). While it may be the case that minority groups receive many of their services from the majority, there is growing recognition in the literature that preparation for crossing cultural boundaries in service provision needs to become more inclusive (e.g., minority to majority, minority to different minorities).

This chapter will consider broad philosophical and academic underpinnings of multiculturalism in criminal justice. The intent of this chapter is to provide students with the requisite knowledge and personal reflection necessary to allow them to be able to fully comprehend the more specific content areas of the subsequent chapters. In essence, this chapter will provide a foundation in general multiculturalism upon which the later, more specific, chapters will build. It will introduce text readers to the relevance of multiculturalism to criminal justice, requisite definitions, cross-cultural perceptions (including stereotypes and multicultural identity development), the philosophy of multiculturalism, models of cross-cultural service delivery, and a systematic means of examining behavior in the cross-cultural context.

Because multiculturalism in criminal justice is under-researched, this chapter will, by necessity, need to rely on information from behavioral science disciplines other than criminal justice (e.g., psychology; in particular the disciplines of Social Psychology and the multicultural movement within organized Counseling Psychology). The information from these related behavioral science disciplines will be applied to work in criminal justice. Empirical research will be given first priority in the chapter, with anecdotal experience provided where the research is weak and/or where appropriate for clarification of concepts. Ample illustrations, including real life examples from criminal justice work, will be provided.

Before proceeding, it may be prudent to explain what is meant by *criminal justice professional* and *client,* terms that will be used throughout this chapter. Criminal justice professional is applied broadly to mean anyone who performs duties in any capacity with a criminal justice function. This would include personnel involved in police functions (officers, investigators), courts (e.g., judges, prosecuting attorneys, defense attorneys, bailiffs), forensic evaluations (e.g., psychologists, psychiatrists, social workers, support staff, guards), corrections (including community programs, half-way houses, jails, and prisons; e.g., correctional officers, probation and parole officers, mental health staff, medical staff, managerial staff), and even legislation (state and federal legislators who construct the laws that the criminal justice system endeavors to enforce). The term client refers to those persons who receive services from the criminal justice system. Such services could include arrest, prosecution, evaluation, incarceration, community monitoring (e.g., probation, parole, mandatory supervision, house arrest), and victim restoration.

THE RELEVANCE OF MULTICULTURALISM TO CRIMINAL JUSTICE

If there exists a need for multicultural training in the provision of human services, perhaps nowhere else in our society would such training be as germane as it is in criminal justice. This is due to at least two factors. First, is that the philosophy that underlies our system of justice is a melting pot of ideals, analogous to the melting pot that is our society. Second, is the high concentration of diverse cultural groups in the criminal justice systems of the U.S.

Philosophy of Criminal Justice in the United States

As world history has evolved it is clear that American law has had its roots in the laws of other great civilizations (e.g., Mid-Eastern, North African, European) which preceded it. One is hard pressed, however, to find minority clients of the criminal justice system who do not take the position that they are subject to an Anglo system of justice (discounting any other cultural influences), and are, therefore, somehow being inherently unjustly treated by that system. Nonetheless, upon examination of the foundations for justice in the U.S., one is struck by the cultural hybrid of traditions that form the philosophical basis for our system of justice. The U.S. system of law and justice has its roots in the British (i.e., Anglo) tradition. It also, however, has roots in the philosophies of other societies. For example, some of the writers of the U.S. Constitution (e.g., Jefferson) were students of French and Italian philosophy, and applied French and Italian concepts in their writing of the Constitution (Allen & Simonsen, 1986). Additionally, the concept of punishment for wrongs done (a mainstay of the U.S. system of justice), is a concept that existed long before the rise of the Anglo civilizations of Europe. In fact, such a concept was formalized in the Sumeritan (approximately 1860 B.C.) and Hammurabian (approximately 1750 B.C.) codes, and was also well established in the Old Testament law of the Hebrews. The Greeks, and consequently the Romans, borrowed from the legal codes of these earlier civilizations in the formulation of their own laws. As the Roman empire conquered the ancient lands and spread throughout northern Europe, its concepts of law touched those peoples who would later pass their own legal concepts on to the Americas (i.e., the Anglos).

This is not to say that the western style of law and order is non-Eurocentric. What, of course, distinguishes a society's system of justice is its underlying value structure, and the values of main-stream U.S. are those of Anglo Europe. The values upon which a system of justice are predicated may not, however, be solely a function of the culture in which the system exists, but may rather be a function of the sheer complexity of the society (in terms of size of population, industrialization, means of barter, etc.) which the law is intended to serve and to protect. This would imply a natural evolution of basic rules and restrictions that serve to protect the societal structure necessary for any large group of people, such as the U.S., to function together. This would provide an explanation for the basic rules of conduct that most complex civilizations have historically embraced (e.g., prohibitions against rape, murder, and treason; Allen & Simonsen, 1986).

In addition to the suggestion that non-Anglo influences underlie the philosophy of U.S. criminal justice, there are also some public opinions relevant to criminal justice that may be perceived as minority agendas, but which actually have their roots in Anglo thought. For example, the notion of prevention, in terms of changing social conditions as a means of fighting crime, was not new with liberal and/or minority social reformers of this century, as might be assumed. This philosophy, though rejected at the time, was heralded in English print by Sir Thomas Moore during the reign of King Henry VIII (Allen & Simonsen, 1986).

In short, the issue of what is Eurocentric and non-Eurocentric with regard to criminal justice (e.g., policy, public opinion) in the U.S. can be confusing. What may appear as Anglo may not be so Anglo after all, and visa versa. This is an important discovery, one that will help to challenge exaggerated perceptions of Eurocentrism in U.S. criminal justice, and, thereby, will allow minority individuals to share a sense of investment in the system.

Multicultural Populations in Criminal Justice

It is most likely that the criminal justice professional will encounter individuals from cultures (in the traditional sense) other than his or her own during the performance of his or her duties. This is because the U.S. criminal justice system brings together mixtures of cultures that are more highly concentrated than they are in society at large. For example, in U.S. society it is quite possible for a Caucasian therapist in private practice to operate an entire professional career and to never provide services to a minority client. This is due, in large measure, to the low base rate of minorities in particular regions of the U.S.. (There is an acknowledgement that minority base rates are increasing and may become higher than the base rate of Caucasians in the U.S. in the not too distant future; Ponterotto & Casas, 1991). The base rate of American minorities is much higher in the criminal justice system, making the chances of avoiding other cultures in criminal justice employment highly unlikely. It is this cultural mixture that underscores the need for multicultural training of the criminal justice professional. A comparison of racial, or ethnic (the difference between these two terms will be discussed later), base rates in the U.S. general population with those in the criminal justice system will serve to illustrate the point further.

The latest census data (i.e., 1990) indicate that Caucasians account for approximately 75.6% of the U.S. general population, African-Americans 12.1%, Hispanics 9.0%, Asians or Pacific Islanders 2.9%, and a residual category of others 3.9% (overlap in the data accounts for the addition of all categories equalling 103.5%; U.S. Department of Commerce, 1992). Additionally, women comprise 51.3% of the general U.S. population, while men account for 48.2% (rounding of percentages accounts for the error in addition). In terms of crimes in which there is a direct victimization of an individual (see Priest, Kordinak & Wynkoop, 1991, for a definition of offense categories), victims report that Whites (including White Hispanics) account for 63.7% of lone victimizers, Blacks (including Black Hispanics) 27.9%, others 7.0%, and unidentified 1.4% (Bureau of Justice Statistics [BJS], 1992). Males account for 85.0% of such victimizations. Reports of victimizations by multiple offenders (groups of two or more) indicate that groups of Whites alone account for 34.8% of victimizations, groups of Blacks alone 37.5%, all others 7.9%, mixed races 16.0%, and not identified 3.9% (BJS, 1992). Male offenders are involved in 93% of offenses perpetrated by multiple offenders (82.9% male only, 10.1% male and female), while groups of females account for only 4.9% of such victimizations. In terms of adult arrests for all types of offenses, Whites account for 68.5%, Blacks 29.6%, Native Americans (including Alaskan natives) 1.1%, and Asians (including Pacific Islanders) 0.8%. Males account for 81.3% of arrests, and females account for 18.7%. In terms of incarcerated offenders (state and federal), Whites account for 46.7% of inmate populations, Blacks 48.0%, Native Americans 0.9%, Asians 0.4%, and unknown 4.0%. Males account for 94.4% of state and federal prison inmates, while females account for 5.6% (BJS, 1992).

These numbers suggest that the criminal justice professional would find it quite difficult to operate in the field for any length of time without encountering individuals from outside of his or her own race or ethnicity. Such cross-cultural contact is just as likely for professionals from minority groups as it is for professionals from the majority group. The likelihood of cross-cultural contact in the criminal justice setting underscores the desirability for multicultural training of criminal justice professionals. This issue will be re-visited in more depth later, after the readers have acquired some requisite knowledge in the area. Training in cross-cultural issues would naturally begin with definitions of relevant terms.

Definitions

There are several terms with which the reader should become familiar. These are terms that are encountered throughout the multicultural literature. They will also be terms that will be encountered throughout the rest of this chapter and the text.

Race and Ethnicity. Race refers to genetic or biological differences between groups (Atkinson, Morten, & Sue, 1983). There are three broad racial groups identified in the literature: Caucasoid, Black, and Mongoloid (Atkinson, Morten, & Sue, 1979). Ethnicity refers to within race distinctions between groups in terms of customs, language, religion, and behavior (Pedersen, 1988). Ethnic behaviors are learned as opposed to biological. A common example of the use of the term ethnicity in criminal justice is the consideration of Hispanics as an ethnic subgroup of the White race. In addition, distinctions can be made among the various Caucasoid groups in the U.S. (e.g., Irish, Italians, English).

Race and ethnicity have often been used synonymously in the professional literature. Some authors, as well as some criminal justice systems (e.g., U.S. Bureau of Prisons), however, treat the two terms as different (e.g., Pedersen, 1988; Ponterotto & Pedersen, 1993; along with our personal observations). When used as synonyms, race and ethnicity address group differences on the basis of genetic, or biological distinctions; in other words on the basis of the common definition of race (see Atkinson, Morton & Sue, 1983). Common racial/ethnic classifications in corrections would be Caucasian, Black (or African-American), Hispanic, Asian-American, and Native American.

The ways in which some criminal justice agencies report ethnic distinctions can be confusing. For example, the criminal justice statistics reported earlier in this chapter were not as consistent across categories as would have been desired. This was because of the way in which they were reported by the government (see BJS, 1992). (This also accounted for the use of the terms Black and African-American in the same paragraph. While at the present African-American is the preferred societal term, the inclusion of other Blacks in some of the statistics reported by the BJS [e.g., Black Cuban immigrants, Blacks from U.S. territories who may not refer to themselves as African-American] necessitates the use of both terms for technical and social accuracy). Sometimes the categories represented are racial. Other times they are ethnic. In some instances Hispanics are granted their own category (an ethnic distinction) while at other times they are collapsed across the other racial groups (namely White and Black; a racial distinction). Another anomaly in the criminal justice literature is the application of the racial distinction Hispanic to many Mexican-Americans who might be more properly referred to as Indian (a Mongoloid race). Additionally, the Mexican population is comprised of Hispanics and Italians as well as Indians, and terms such as Latino and Chicano are bantered about in the literature without clear definition as to what authors mean by them. This caveat is an admonition to the student of criminal justice to be careful in interpreting criminal justice data. It is also an admonition for future criminal justice researchers and policy makers to practice clarity in the reporting of data. In this chapter, race and ethnicity will be used as different terms.

Culture. Culture can be defined as a collection of those values, attitudes, and ways of behaving that distinguish one group from another (Grunlan & Mayers, 1979). Though culture can be a correlate of race, it is not considered genetic, or biological. Rather, cultural characteristics are considered to be learned. This is evident in those instances in which differing cultural groups have arisen out of the same gene pool (e.g., differing White ethnic communities). Cultural distinctions can also be applied to ethnic subtypes, or subcultures (e.g., Hasidic Jews) (see Ponterotto & Pedersen, 1993). At present, experts in multiculturalism (e.g., Pedersen, 1990, 1991; Sue et al., 1982) define the concept of culture broadly. Included are ethnicity, gender, age, sexual orientation, socioeconomic status (SES), religious orientation (Casas, 1985a, 1985b; Hills & Strozier, 1992; Lorion & Parron, 1985; Sue et al., 1982; Sundal-Hansen, 1985), the disabled (e.g., Copeland, 1982; Gliedman, 1979; Hills & Strozier, 1992), Caucasian subgroups within the U.S. (e.g., Amish, rural Appalachians, Jews; APA, 1993; Pedersen, 1988), teenage fathers (Kiselica, in press), and farmers (Hills & Strozier, 1992). In effect, the concept has evolved to include diversity in just about any area. The number of categories has grown to such an extent that an individual can find him/herself as a member of several cultural groups at any given time.

Salience. Salience refers to the central, or prominent, cultural role that the individual assumes at any given time (see McCall & Simmons, 1966; Stryker & Serpe, 1982; Thoits, 1983, 1992; Weigert, Teitge, & Teitge, 1986). In other words, a role is salient if it is the prominent role for the individual at the moment. At various times, and under various circumstances, the groups to which the individual belongs will change their position in the *salience hierarchy* (i.e., the level of importance to the individual). This is considered to be a dynamic process in that the individual can actually shift roles as the environment dictates (e.g., from criminal justice professional to mother). Consider, for example, a middle-aged Native American female from an upper SES. In this instance, the individual belongs to no less than four cultural groups. At any given time, one cultural membership will be more prominent for this individual than will be the others. Additionally, an individual can experience identity development (to be discussed later) in any number of cultures on an almost simultaneous basis (e.g., Chan, 1989).

Multiculturalism. The defining construct of multiculturalism, as Sue et al. (1982) proposes, is the provision of human services to persons outside of one's own culture, or group. In this definition, the criminal justice professional can be of any diverse group (not necessarily the majority group) as long as the professional and the client are from different cultural groups. In fact, as will be discussed later, any encounter between a criminal justice professional and a criminal justice client can be considered as cross-cultural (by virtue of the distinctions between these groups).

Minority and Majority. The term minority originated in the historical context of racial distinctions, where it was an accurate reflection of numerical inferiority. Accompanying the numerical distinction was the notion of oppression (Wirth, 1945). Current usage of the term includes any group that has a history of oppression by the majority, whether or not it is numerically inferior (Ponterotto, Lewis, & Burlington, 1990; Ponterotto & Pedersen, 1993). For example, females, even though in the numerical majority, are considered to be a minority due to a history of oppression by males in the U.S.

Majority, like minority, had a numerical reference in the historical context. Whites were (and still are) the largest numerical group in the U.S.. As the term has evolved, however, it has come to refer to White middle class males, even though they do not represent the numerical majority (Ponterotto & Pedersen, 1993). In this sense, the term has come to denote what is perceived as the amount of power and influence that the group can wield within the society at large (Ponterotto & Pedersen, 1993). The assumption inherent in this evolved definition is that White males are dominant in the U.S. in terms of power, and that they tend to discriminate against other groups to maintain control. The terms minority and majority will be used with regard to their current meanings throughout this chapter.

Prejudice and Ethnocentrism. Prejudice has traditionally referred to the negative attitudes that one has toward members of other groups, which are generalizations typically based on limited information about those groups (Allport, 1954; Baron & Byrne, 1991). In the racial/ethnic arena, the term has been applied to the negative attitudes that one holds toward racial and ethnic groups other than one's own. As the usage of the term has evolved, however, it has been taken to mean attitudes held toward just about anything, including one's own group (evidence the minority identity development models to be discussed later), and does not necessarily need to be negative (i.e., it can be positive; see Ponterotto & Pedersen, 1993). One of the primary difficulties in dealing with prejudice is its resistance to change (a fact that will be discussed later in terms of the literature on stereotypes).

Ethnocentrism (i.e., judging other cultures against the values of one's own culture) is a term that is related to prejudice. It implies a sense of superiority of one's own culture over the culture of others. Examples include Eurocentrism (judging other cultures on the basis of European values) and Afrocentrism (judging other cultures on the basis of African values) (see Wrenn, 1962).

Discrimination and Racism. Discrimination is the behavioral component that sometimes accompanies prejudice. It is as an outgrowth of prejudice. It refers to negative actions toward members of a particular group because of their membership in that group (Baron & Byrne, 1991). Racism is discrimination in the context of race (see Ponterotto & Pedersen, 1993). Given the broad definition of culture, it has become more efficient to speak in terms of discrimination, rather than in terms of racism.

Discrimination can be discussed in terms of three distinct contexts (discussed in terms of racism by Jones, 1981). The first is *individual discrimination,* in which the individual acts out of his or her prejudice to the detriment of someone from another group. The second type of discrimination is *institutional discrimination.* In this type of discrimination, institutions are seen as fostering and/or perpetuating discrimination (sometimes inadvertently; e.g., college admission requirements, NCAA grade and test score policies for college athletes, disproportionate percentages of arrests and incarceration of minorities). The third type of discrimination is *cultural discrimination.* This type of discrimination is inherent in societal systems in which a particular culture forces its values on other cultures (an outgrowth of ethnocentrism). In North America, the White culture is often perceived as forcing its values on other cultural groups (on and off the North American continent).

There are authors who propose that racism, or discrimination, can be committed inadvertently by non-racist (or non-prejudiced) persons in a non-prejudicial context (e.g., Ridley, 1989). Such a position, however, places the definition of discrimination on the shoulders of the perceived injured party, and, thus, lacks a sense of objectivity. With a history of oppression against minorities in the U.S., it is not surprising that certain instances of equal treatment are misinterpreted by minority individuals as instances of discrimination. Such misperceptions, however, lend themselves to a sense of helplessness on the part of minority individuals regarding discrimination, and on the part of well meaning persons from the majority who feel as though they can do nothing right when it comes to minority issues (e.g., "why even try?").

Pluralism and Assimilation. Pluralism refers to the existence of multiple cultures coexisting within the same society. It is perhaps best understood in contrast to cultural assimilation. Historically, the U.S. has been perceived as a melting pot of cultures, to which persons from other societies immigrated and became part of the U.S. society via assimilation. In assimilation, the immigrating culture (or individual) loses its distinctiveness as it fades into, and takes on the characteristics of, the new society. In recent years there has been a growing emphasis on cultural distinctiveness within the U.S. (evidenced in part by the ethnic pride festivals held in many of our major cities). Thus, the U.S. public has become more tolerant of diversity, and in the process has moved toward pluralism (i.e., allowing differences between groups).

The current emphasis on pluralism and multiculturalism in our society has placed an emphasis on cultural boundaries, and, therefore, on the limited exchange of information between groups. Limiting the exchange of information between groups can have the effect of exaggerating intergroup differences, and can increase the probability of cross-cultural conflict. This provides a segue into the next section on cross-cultural perceptions.

PERCEPTIONS ACROSS CULTURES

Cross-cultural perception refers to the way in which members of a particular cultural group are perceived by others not of that group. Social psychology has much to offer in discussions relevant to perceptions across cultures. In fact, researchers in social psychology have studied and written on biases in social judgement as far back as the 1920's (e.g., Lippmann, 1922). One of the most significant contributions of social psychology to our understanding of cross-cultural perceptions and relations is in the area of stereotyping.

Stereotypes

Stereotypes are schemata of (i.e., ways of perceiving) members of other groups (Forsyth, 1990) that are resistant to change (Lippmann, 1922). Stereotypes are a fact of everyday life (see Lesko, 1991). Research has demonstrated that stereotypes do exist, that they can be called into working memory by environmental cues, that individuals are aware of their existence, and that what differentiates prejudiced individuals from non-prejudiced individuals is the way in which they are challenged once accessed from memory (Devine, 1989). A common misconception of stereotypes is that they should be eradicated. While eradication of stereotypes is perceived as being for the social good, this presupposes that such an eradication is somehow humanly possible. To the contrary, there are indications that it may not be possible for humans to function without information management systems such as stereotypes.

The existence of stereotypes is presented in this section from a scientific perspective. The content of stereotypes is not endorsed, merely acknowledged. The focus of this section of the chapter is to discuss the existence and nature of stereotypes in light of human neuroanatomical function, and information processing and management. The supposition of this chapter is that individuals who harbor stereotypes are not evil, but are rather subject to natural biological and cognitive processes. Because stereotypes are a category of schemata (categorized on the basis of their content), it is appropriate to discuss them in terms of schemata.

Schemata

Schemata aid in information processing, storage, and retrieval relevant to social cognition (Baron & Byrne, 1991). Schemata are not information themselves. Rather, they are frameworks, or storage racks (to use a metaphor), upon which information is stored and used. In effect, they provide an efficient means of managing large amounts of simultaneous information. The moment to moment operations of being human, including our perceptions of, and interactions with, others is governed by this system of information management.

Biological Basis for Schemata

The brain is neuroanatomically divided into two hemispheres, each specializing in particular functions. For example, the right side of the brain (or right hemisphere) controls the motor movement of the left side of the body. Likewise, the left hemisphere controls the motor function of the right side of the body (Kolb & Wishaw, 1990). In addition to the lateralization of motor functions is the lateralization of the processing of sensory information, cognitions, and emotions. In our discussion of schemata, we are most concerned with the processing of cognitive information. Cognitive information is believed to be processed differently in each hemisphere. The left hemisphere in the right handed individual (handedness is an important concept in discussions on neuroanatomical function which is beyond the scope of this text) tends to be more involved in the processing of verbal/sequential information. The right hemisphere in the right handed individual tends to be more involved in the processing of spatial/simultaneous information. It is the ability to process a group of data, or a high amount of information, simultaneously that accounts for the ability and the necessity to form schemata. There would appear, then, to be a biological basis for the type of information processing that we term as schemata (i.e., a right hemisphere phenomenon; see Kolb & Wishaw, 1990).

Schemata, including stereotypes, are stored out of consciousness, analogous to information on a computer disk. The information stored in a particular schema can be called into working memory (i.e., consciousness) either voluntarily, or by environmental cuing (e.g., seeing someone of a different race; Devine, 1989). Stereotypes are typically called up into working memory with accompanying emotions (e.g., disgust, revulsion). In theories of emotion and behavior that are considered cognitive-behavioral there is a clear causal connection between cognitions, or thoughts, and resulting emotions (i.e., thoughts create emotions; Beck, Rush, Shaw, & Emery, 1979; Ellis, 1973; Maultsby, 1984; Michenbaum, 1977; Wynkoop & Gerstein, 1993). This would appear to account for the negative emotions that seem to be called up simultaneously with stereotypes. In addition to the cognitive-emotive connection, there may also be an anatomical explanation of the connection between thoughts and emotions, particularly in the case of stereotypes. Neuroanatomically, the simultaneous processing of high amounts of information and the emotions that accompany this information are believed to be right hemisphere phenomena (Kandel, 1991; Kolb & Wishaw, 1990) (the location of emotion is currently being revisited by the neurosciences, yielding some conflicting conclusions). Hence (as things stand currently in the neurosciences), there may be a biological link between the content and emotion of a stereotype without the need for the cognitive processing as proposed by the cognitive-behavioral theories. In other words, when a stereotype is activated the accompanying emotional content may be activated simultaneously via biological means. The link between schemata and emotion, regardless of its origins, is an important fact to keep in mind when considering the difficulty that individuals experience when attempting to modify their feelings about others. It can be a difficult process.

Formation and Maintenance of Stereotypes

Development and maintenance of stereotypes are related phenomena. Stereotypes are formed quickly and with typically little information (information which can be quite inaccurate). Their content can be quite tenacious. Prejudice can, and often does, flourish in the presence of seemingly contradictory information. This section will examine how this is possible. To do so, it will examine some of the processes thought to underlie the formation of stereotypes (i.e., first impressions, heuristics) and how stereotypes are reinforced and maintained (i.e., confirmatory biases, in-group/out-group phenomena, attributional errors).

Formation of Stereotypes: The processing of simultaneous information (i.e., schemata) is not the only means of information processing, storage, and management. There is also the processing and storage of sequential information (you will recall this to be a left hemisphere function). The use of sequential information processing is typically more labor intensive than that of simultaneous processing. Thus, we tend to avoid its use.

We are what is referred to in the literature as *cognitive misers* (Baron & Byrne, 1991; Fiske & Taylor, 1984), being chintzy with our cognitions and taking the path of least resistance to arrive at a conclusion. Schemata, as compared to sequential processing, provide this path of least resistance. Two phenomenon are relevant to our proclivity for economy of psychic effort. First, is that gaps in schematic information are "filled in" by assumptions about the person, place, or thing that is being contemplated. Second, is that the information upon which schemata are based may, by a series of cognitive processing difficulties, be faulty (both the information received from the senses as well as the information constructed to fill in the gaps). This forms a prelude to a discussion on heuristics and first impressions.

Heuristics. Heuristics can be described as mental shortcuts that allow the user to make sense out of a situation (person, place, or thing) with relative ease. In simplistic terms, heuristics allow us to skip from point A to point C (or points beyond) without needing to analyze point B (or any other points in between), including gaps in information. They allow us to make snap judgements with limited information. The use of a heuristic is analogous to cutting across the lawn of a home on a corner lot (rather than staying on the sidewalk). This action might get the individual to his or her destination quicker than remaining on the sidewalk, but it can also lead to undesirable consequences (e.g., violating the rights of others, being fined for trespassing).

If the reader is not sure that this phenomenon is at work in everyday life, then consider the following. The presence of heuristics forms the theoretical basis for a criminal defendant getting a hair cut, a shave, and dressing-up to appear in court. It is easier for the judge and/or jury to believe the innocent plea, or the argument for extenuating circumstances, of someone who "looks," or who fits the stereotype of, innocent (i.e., clean-cut, polite), than it is for the judge and/or jury to believe a similar plea from someone who does not look innocent.

First Impressions. A process that depends on heuristics is at work in the development of first impressions. This process is known as the primacy effect (Baron & Byrne, 1991; see also Asch, 1946). The *primacy effect* refers to the tendency to judge others based on our very first impression(s) of them, which is often resistant to change. In a seminal study (Asch, 1946) on the effect of first impressions, two groups of subjects were provided with two different lists, each containing six personal traits, or adjectives, describing the same hypothetical person: Intelligent, industrious, impulsive, critical, stubborn, and envious. The only difference between the lists was the order of presentation of the words on the list. In one list, the more desirable traits were presented first (as above). In the second list, the negative traits were presented first (in opposite order from above). The subjects were told that these traits described an individual and were asked to render an opinion as to their impression of the individual. Even though both lists contained identical information, those subjects who received the list with the positive traits presented first were more favorably disposed toward the individual than were those subjects who received the list with the negative traits presented first. This study demonstrated just how quick people are to form opinions, or judgements, about others, and also how difficult it is to modify these initial opinions even in the face of contradictory information. The results of the Asch (1946) study appear to be robust. It is quite interesting to replicate the experiment in the classroom and to view the reaction of students to their ratings and to the accompanying explanation.

The tendency to take the quickest route to a conclusion, via heuristics, allows for the formation and tenacity of first impressions. In essence, what happens is that once an impression is formed all subsequent information received about the individual is colored by that impression. When impressions are made, they become stereotypes and are difficult to modify. In fact, in light of relevant research, it may be that stereotypes are not unlearned per se, but may only be modified via addition of new content, or by the construction of competing stereotypes (see Devine, 1989). The next section will present a discussion about how stereotypes, once formed, are maintained.

Maintenance of Stereotypes: There are several forms of information distortion that can account for the preservation of the functional capacity of a stereotype in the face of contradictory information. The mechanisms that are employed in the maintenance of stereotypes fall under the rubric of confirmatory bias.

Confirmatory Bias. Confirmatory bias is a psychological construct that is used to explain the maintenance of stereotypes. As humans, we appear to have a tendency to attend to information that reinforces our stereotypes of others, while also tending to dismiss information that is contrary to our stereotypes. It requires work to challenge stereotypes. Therefore, challenging stereotypes is a process that is antithetical to their nature of improving the speed of information processing. We are, after all, cognitive misers. Behaviorally, challenging a stereotype slows down the processing of information, making the processing of information more laborious and less reinforcing (i.e., punishing; see Watson & Tharp, 1993 for a discussion on the suppression of behavior by the use of punishment). Two ways in which erroneous information about persons from other groups can be maintained, while contradictory information is dismissed, is by the in-group/out-group phenomenon and by attributional errors.

In-Group/Out-Group Phenomenon. The in-group/out-group phenomenon refers to the formation of attitudes toward others not of one's own group. The tendency is to perceive others and their groups as inferior. The boundaries of what constitutes an in-group and/or an out-group are defined egocentrically by the individual making the judgement. An in-group is the salient group to which the individual belongs at the moment, while the out-group is any other group. The options are almost limitless, and incorporate all of the cross-cultural groups discussed in this text (e.g., race, ethnicity, gender, sexual orientation, SES) and more (e.g., grade point average, eye color, musical preference). The in-group/out-group phenomenon is not static, and is complicated by constantly changing group memberships, constant restructuring and evolution of groups, and multiple group memberships.

The notion of in-group superiority over that of other groups is a central theme in stereotyping. The notion of in-group superiority is maintained by several sources of confirmatory bias (Forsyth, 1990), including complexity bias, extremity bias, out-group homogeneity bias, and in-group heterogeneity bias. *Complexity bias* is the tendency to simplify one's view of the out-group while maintaining a complex view of the in-group. It is related to the *out-group homogeneity bias,* which is the tendency to overlook the variability of the characteristics of individuals in the out-group. The *in-group heterogeneity bias* refers to the tendency to view the members of one's own group as varying in characteristics. In short, the tendency is to perceive members of the out-group as being more characteristically homogenous than the members of the in-group (Judd & Park, 1988; Park & Rothbart, 1982; Simon & Brown, 1987). The *extremity bias* refers to the tendency to polarize perceptions of individuals in the in-group and the out-group, working favorably for the in-group and unfavorably for the out-group (Forsyth, 1990).

In short, to maintain stereotypes via the in-group/out-group phenomenon, it is required that the individual perceive the out-group as limited in variability (e.g., all Whites are racist) so that the stereotype is not challenged by disconfirming information (e.g., while there are some Whites who are racist, there are many Whites who are not racist). There is also a need to perceive members of the in-group as varying in characteristics (e.g., Whites vary greatly with regard to the amount of prejudice held toward others), so that the illusion can be maintained that the in-group is somehow not subject to stereotyping by others (i.e., it is too multidimensional for such a thing as stereotyping).

Attributional Errors. Closely related to the in-group/out-group phenomenon are attributional errors. In the development of a schema, or stereotype, of another person, there is a tendency to attribute negative behavioral outcomes to situational or dispositional causes (Heider, 1958). *Situational attributions* are those in which environmental influences are credited with the negative consequence(s) of a particular behavior, while *dispositional attributions* are those in which individual characteristics are credited with the negative consequence(s) of a particular behavior (see Hamachek, 1982). For example, landing a job with the Federal Bureau of Investigation could be due to a high level of intelligence (a dispositional attribution), or to luck (a situational attribution). In the development of pejorative schemata, or stereotypes, there is typically an error involved in the attributional process. There are three principle types of attributional errors: Fundamental attribution error, the actor-observer effect, and self-serving bias.

In *fundamental attribution error,* the tendency is to attribute dispositional causes to the negative behavioral outcomes of others (Milgram, 1974; Sabini & Silver, 1983). The *actor-observer effect* is similar to the fundamental attribution error. It speaks to negative outcomes as the result of behavior of others (actors) or of the self (observer). In the case of others, the attribution is to dispositional causes. In the case of the self, the attribution is to situational causes (Jones & Nisbett, 1971; Peterson, 1980). *Self-serving bias* pertains to attributions of the self: Behavior with a positive outcome is attributed to dispositional causes, while behavior with a negative outcome is attributed to situational causes (Miller & Ross, 1975; Baumgardner, Heppner, & Arkin, 1986). In addition to attributional errors of individual behavioral outcomes, there is also an attributional process known as *group-attribution error.* In this type of attributional process, one attributes a decision made by another group (out-group) to all members of that group, negating variability in the members' attitudes toward the group decision (Allison & Messick, 1985; Worth, Allison, & Messick, 1987). An example would be the assumption that all Germans in Hitler's Germany were anti-semitic and wanted to exterminate Jews. Group attribution error is related to the out-group homogeneity bias discussed previously.

How do attributions reinforce stereotypes? Quite simply, they allow us to confirm our beliefs about others by discounting information that is contrary to the stereotype. In general, when discussing attributions, theory suggests that people tend to be kind to themselves and their in-group while being much more harsh toward others. Consider the following example. You have just received the score on your midterm examination in the class in which you are using this text. You find out that you and another student in the class were at the bottom of the curve for the examination (heaven forbid!). According to attribution theory, you will likely attribute your score to situational variables (e.g., being ill, not having enough time to study, instructor prejudice; i.e., the actor-observer effect, self-serving bias) while attributing the score of your classmate also to dispositional variables (e.g., stupid, lazy; i.e., actor-observer effect). The attributional process does sometimes go awry, as in certain forms of depression in which the sufferer is more harsh in his or her attributions toward the self (Beck et al., 1979). Having examined the formation and maintenance of stereotypes, it may be beneficial to examine briefly how one can proceed with the conscious modification of undesired stereotypes.

Challenging Stereotypes

In the introduction to this section (on stereotypes) there were research findings presented which suggested that the non-prejudiced individual is one who, by definition, has challenged his or her stereotypes of the reference group in question. The basic assumption of this proposition is that everyone possesses stereotypes. It is not the possession of stereotypes per se that accounts for prejudice, but rather what is done with them (e.g., believed, challenged). Challenging stereotypes requires conscious consideration of competing (i.e., realistic, convincing) information. Take, for example, the stereotype of African-American females as unproductive employees. This stereotype is called into question by several personal observations in corrections as well as by the results of a local Federal Bureau of Prisons personnel study which indicated that employee retention rates were highest among African-American females (in comparison to White males, White females, and African-American males; Bascom, 1982). Poor work productivity and high retention rates are not entirely synonymous. The non-prejudiced person will remind him/herself of this fact whenever the stereotype of poor work productivity of African-American females is accessed.

The development of realistic schemata (or a schema) to compete with, and to modify, an existing stereotype can be effortful at first, particularly given the forces that work against such a lack of cognitive efficiency (as discussed in this section). As with any behavior (including cognition), however, the more that it is practiced, the easier (i.e., more efficient, more habitual) that it becomes. In essence, individuals who do not hold prejudicial attitudes are those who have successfully developed realistic schemata to compete with the negative stereotypes that they possess.

Interim Summary

This discussion on schemata and stereotypes was presented to reinforce the notion that they are a fact of every day life. Most schemata are good and help us to function. Unfortunately, however, with the good that schemata bring also comes some bad. For those individuals who hold prejudicial attitudes, stereotypes can create functional problems. It is not necessarily the existence of stereotypes that is the problem. It is what is done with stereotypes that can result in prejudice, and what is done with prejudice that can result in discrimination. Stereotypes are a personal phenomenon, but they are not developed in a vacuum. They are developed in relation to others and their cultures. They are also developed in relation to a sense of self. The next section will consider the broader context of a sense of the self within one's culture.

SELF-PERCEPTIONS

Cultural identity development refers to the development of a sense of self within the cultural context. The formation of cultural identity serves to shape one's world view. *World view* is the outlook that colors one's perceptions of life and of the world. An understanding of the client's world view in relation to that of the professional's is crucial in determining how the client will likely react to the professional. Therefore, an understanding of the development of a sense of self (i.e., identity) within the cultural context can be beneficial to the professional who provides services across cultures.

Identity Development Models

There have been several attempts at describing identity development within one's culture. Cultural identity development models have included those for African-Americans (Cross, 1971, 1991; Hall, Cross, & Freedle, 1972; Jackson, 1975; Thomas, 1971; Vontress, 1981), Mexican-Americans (also referred to as Chicano; Arce, 1981), Cuban-Americans (sometimes referred to as an Hispanic model; Szapocznik & Kurtines, 1980), Asian-Americans (Sue & Sue, 1972), and Gays and Lesbians (Cass, 1979, 1984; Gonsiorek & Weinrich, 1991; Troiden, 1989). Though underdeveloped, there have also been identity development models proposed for women (Ivey, Ivey, & Simek-Morgan, 1993; see also Delworth, 1989; Gilligan, 1982), Japanese-American women (often referred to as an Asian-American model of identity development; Kim, 1981), and Viet Nam Veterans (Ivey et al., 1993). Gaining increased attention, are hybrid (or generic) models of minority identity development (Atkinson, Morten, & Sue, 1979, 1993; Phinney, Lochner, & Murphy, 1990; Ponterotto & Pedersen, 1993), and models of White identity development (Hardiman, 1982; Helms, 1984, 1990; Ponterotto, 1988; Sabnani, Ponterotto, & Borodovsky, 1991). The interested reader can consult the various primary references for detailed information. The models of cultural identity development are stage models, which implies that the individual must progress successfully through a series of sequential stages in the development of a cultural identity. Many are extensions of an earlier model of Black (African-American) identity development (Cross, 1971).

The exploration of identity development by multicultural theorists was strongly influenced by the work of Erikson (1963, 1968, 1982). In his eight stage model of identity development, Erikson proposed that ego identity was shaped by crises throughout the life cycle, beginning with trust issues in infancy, and continuing through life introspection (in retrospect) in old age. The formation of non-White identity development models was in response to the notion that the existing models (e.g., Erikson's) were based on White development, and were, therefore, not applicable to non-White groups.

There are four models of identity development with which the criminal justice professional should become familiar. These models will be presented briefly here. They pertain to minority identity development, White identity development, identity development of women, and the development of an identity as a criminal justice professional. These four models were selected for review because they represent the majority of cross-cultural encounters for the criminal justice professional.

The *Integrative Model* of minority identity development (Ponterotto and Pedersen, 1993, p. 44) is a four stage qualitative compilation of the main themes of other, more specific, models of minority identity development. The model also takes into account the generic work of Atkinson et al. (1979, 1993) and Phinney et al. (1990). It is predicated on the notion that minority identity development evolves in reaction to prejudice and discrimination by the dominant White culture. In the first stage, *Identification With the White Majority,* the minority individual may operate from a White frame of reference, identifying him/herself with the White majority, and even harboring prejudice toward his or her own group. In the second stage, *Awareness, Encounter and Search,* the minority individual begins to question his or her ethnicity in relation to the White majority, and issues of discrimination become prominent. In the third stage, *Identification and Immersion,* the minority individual rejects what is perceived as the White establishment. There may also be a heightened amount of anger toward Whites and toward what are perceived to be White values. In the final stage, *Integration and Internalization,* the minority individual has come to grips with his or her own ethnic/cultural identity and is comfortable with the culture of others, including the White culture. The minority individual in this stage has developed a "bicultural, or multicultural identity" (Ponterotto & Pedersen, 1993, p. 61).

The *White Racial Identity Development* model of Sabnani et al. (1991) consists of five stages. The model is specific to professionals who provide human services in a cross-cultural context. In the first stage, *Pre-exposure/Pre-contact,* there is a lack of awareness of multicultural issues. In the second stage, *Conflict,* there is conflict between the pressure to espouse White values and the pressure to be non-racist. In the third stage, *Pro-minority/Anti-racism,* there is an inclination to forsake one's Whiteness out of a sense of guilt for White discriminatory practices, and an inclination to "save" minority individuals. In the fourth stage, *Retreat Into White Culture,* the individual has returned to the safety of his or her own culture. This is a reaction to rejection by Whites and non-Whites in the previous stage. In the final stage,

Redefinition and Integration, the individual resolves the conflict of the earlier stage, is able to accept his or her Whiteness, and is comfortable with the cultural differences of others.

The increasing presence of women in criminal justice necessitates a discussion on the identity development of women. Though there are no well developed models, Ivey et al. (1993, p. 103) present a brief model applied to women as an extension of Jackson's (1975) model of Black (African-American) identity development. This model of identity development is comprised of five stages (Jackson, 1975). In the first stage, *Naivete,* the woman is not aware of the existence of gender issues. In the second stage, *Acceptance,* the woman may become aware that gender issues exist, but may lack an awareness of systemic issues in this regard. She may buy into the system, or accept the status quo. In the third stage, *Naming and Resistance,* the woman becomes aware of oppression based on gender. There may be a reaction of anger, and of behavior to promote social change. In the fourth stage, *Redefinition and Reflection,* the female develops a sense of pride in her identity as a woman. She may immerse herself in being woman, and may separate herself from men in the process. In the final stage, *Multiperspective Internalization,* the woman is able to accept inter-male variability (i.e., not all males are the same), and can conceptualize male and female relationships in an historical perspective.

It is apparent that cross-cultural encounters create unique problems in interpersonal interaction. It is less evident, however, that similar problems can arise in intra-cultural interactions with individuals at differing levels of identity development. Consider, for example, the interpersonal difficulties that may arise between an African-American law enforcement officer in the Identification With the White Majority stage (Ponterotto & Pedersen, 1993) and another African-American, in the officer's custody, who is in the Identification and Immersion stage (Ponterotto & Pedersen, 1993). Consider, also, the cultural differences between the criminal justice professional (as a distinct identity that cuts across other cultural boundaries) and that of the criminal justice client (another distinct identity). Even if the client and criminal justice professional are from the same racial group, conflicts can, and do, arise.

Identity Development of the Criminal Justice Professional

In addition to the cultural identity development of ethnic minorities, Whites, and women, criminal justice employees also appear to pass through a series of stages as they develop an identity as a criminal justice professional. Though a voluntary identity, being a criminal justice professional does set the individual apart from other members of U.S. society. The criminal justice professional has an identity bestowed upon him or her from within (i.e., the individual's perception of what it means to him or her to be a criminal justice professional), and from without (i.e., from those with whom the professional comes into contact including clients, family members, friends, citizens in general). He or she is granted favorable accord from segments of the society who respect law and order, and who perceive the system as a source of protection and help. Conversely, there are segments of society which perceive the criminal justice system, and anyone associated with it, with a certain amount of mistrust and/or destain (e.g., many criminals, some ethnic groups). Such a distinction between the self and others lends itself to the formation of an identity within the profession. The development of a healthy identity as a criminal justice professional is essential to perform one's duties with congruity and integrity (i.e., not violating one's own values in the process). We have not found any criminal justice identity development models in the literature, so we propose the following.

The criminal justice Professional Identity Development (PID) model proposes analogous to the minority development models, that it is the interpersonal contact with others (i.e., primarily criminals, secondarily society) that appears to form the basis for the development of a separate identity as a criminal justice professional. The model is comprised of six stages. It was developed qualitatively, out of our experiences in a variety of criminal justice settings.

Pre-contact. The individual has an interest in becoming a criminal justice professional, but has not had much, if any, contact with criminal justice clientele. Much of what has been learned about offenders has come about from isolated personal experiences (e.g., personal victimization, a significant other as an offender), or from observation (e.g., media, witness of a crime). The individual has developed "ideal" opinions (based on stereotypes) about crime, criminals, victims, and the criminal justice system, which may predispose him or her to prejudice (on a continuum from positive to negative). In other words, the individual may be predisposed to identify with victims, or with offenders. The potential criminal justice professional may not yet fully comprehend the magnitude of his or her decision to enter the field.

Preparation. The individual acts upon his or her desire to become a criminal justice professional. He or she may attend college, or may initiate preparation for employment with a criminal justice agency. There may be an internal conflict over whether this is the right decision. Additionally, there may be familial conflict generated by the decision (e.g., family members concerned about the safety of the future criminal justice professional). This familial conflict may signal the onset of the separation from others (sometimes subtle, sometimes obvious) that the criminal justice professional will experience throughout his or her career.

Contact/Conflict. Contact with criminal justice clientele (particularly offenders) creates the conflict produced in this stage. The "ideals" of the pre-contact stage are now challenged by the reality of the criminal justice system and its clientele. The individual's sense of naivety is challenged as he or she is exposed to the sometimes gruesome realities of crime and punishment (e.g., various offense types, bizarre rituals, sexual abuse, psychosis and murder; see Priest, Kordinak, & Wynkoop, 1991; Wynkoop, 1993; Wynkoop, in press; Wynkoop & Priest, 1986). It is at this point that the individual is directly confronted with the reality of his or her decision to become a criminal justice professional. Prior to this exposure, it was impossible for the individual to realize the full impact of his or her career choice decision. The conflict generated by this initial contact may help to account for the resignation of most correctional officers (of those who eventually leave correctional employment) within the first year (most often within the first six months) of employment (Bascom, 1982).

Boundary Issues. Work with criminal justice clientele raises issues of self-esteem for the worker, as well as issues regarding his or her ability to form appropriate interpersonal boundaries in relation to clientele. Based on the conflict generated by the contact in the previous stage, there appear to be three general directions (lying on a continuum) in which the new criminal justice professional will proceed (dictated to an extent by previously held beliefs, values, and stereotypes). In essence, there is a continuum of adjustment to the culture of criminal justice (i.e., rescuer to professional to punisher), and those at either end of the continuum pose a threat to themselves (in terms of employment and physical safety) and to those around them.

Rescuer. There may be an enmeshment with clientele, or an over-identification with the "oppressed" (i.e., victims, offenders). There is a tendency to believe whatever is said by a client, and to go-to-bat for clients without exploring all sides of the issue at hand.

Punisher. This individual makes a personal crusade out of punishing offenders. In a sense, there is an over-identification with the "oppressor."

Both of these reactions can have undesirable consequences. In the case of the rescuer, the individual leaves him/herself open to manipulation by clientele (which can have physically dangerous consequences). In the case of the punisher, there is the danger of physical aggression by the worker, or of provoking aggression by the client. Both reactions are detrimental to the operations of the criminal justice system in which the individual is employed.

Professional. The individual is able to separate personal issues from the performance of his or her professional duties. There are also few problematic issues related to interpersonal boundaries and self-esteem in relation to clientele. Those personal issues that do arise as a function of the job are addressed and resolved by the individual. This individual takes the time to ponder, and challenge, previously held "ideals" and stereotypes of offenders, victims, and of the criminal justice system.

Resolution/Adjustment. For those who successfully negotiate the previous stage (i.e., emerge as a professional), there is a sense of comfort with one's own identity as a criminal justice professional. This comfort will exist in relation to the clientele served (e.g., the professional does not take personal offense to the attempts of a client to manipulate his or her situation) as well as to the community (including the professional's family). There is an awareness and an acceptance that others may perceive the professional in a stereotypical manner as a function of his or her career identity.

Integration. The criminal justice professional is able to move into and out-of cultural roles in his or her daily life. The identity of being a criminal justice professional is always present, but this identity does not assume prominence in all areas of the individual's life. He or she is able to allow other roles (e.g., mother, husband) to come to the fore as required by the necessities of life. In other words, the criminal justice professional at the integration stage has mastered the ability to leave the job at the job, and to leave the family and bills behind when on the job.

The models of identity development presented here can help the criminal justice professional to consider his or her own cultural identity development in relation to the identity development of others with whom he or she will come into contact in the performance of his or her duties. This is pertinent to contact across cultures as well as to contact within cultures. Now that the readers have been educated on the complexity of some of the issues involved in cross-cultural contact, it would be beneficial to re-visit the matter of the necessity of training in multiculturalism for criminal justice professionals.

NECESSITY OF TRAINING IN MULTICULTURALISM

Previously, an argument was made in favor of multicultural training for criminal justice professionals on the basis of the concentration of multicultural groups in the criminal justice system. This topic is now re-visited with a deeper examination of the philosophy that forms the basis for formal training in multicultural issues. While appearing on the surface to be a simple matter, the philosophy underlying training in multiculturalism for criminal justice professionals can be quite complex. The purpose of this section is to challenge the student to examine his or her own personal philosophy on the matter. The pragmatic importance in such an examination is found in the fact that one's philosophical basis of multiculturalism will mould the way in which one approaches the delivery of criminal justice services in the cross-cultural context. In fact, this discussion will culminate in a presentation of models of cross-cultural service provision (in the next section). These are difficult issues, confounded by some authors who have political, rather than service, agendas.

The necessity of training in multiculturalism for providers of human services, including criminal justice professionals, is predicated upon differences between the groups to which the service provider and recipient belong. In other words, diverse groups differ on various dimensions, and service providers need to have an understanding of these differences to adequately serve members of other groups. Without these differences, cross-cultural training would be of limited value. It comes as no surprise, therefore, that those who promote cross-cultural training also promote inter-group differences, sometimes at the expense of existing similarities. It is the average difference between groups, rather than the variability within groups, that is often compared in discussions promoting multiculturalism. This is tantamount to a simple comparison of group means as opposed to an analysis of variance in the examination of between group differences (see Howell, 1987 for a discussion of statistical analysis). There are arguments that attempt to counter the emphasis on inter-group differences. Such arguments take into account the likelihood of large intra-group variability as compared to inter-group variability.

Doctrine of Differences

To examine the impact that the evolution of multiculturalism may have on the provision of criminal justice services, a discussion of the impact of multiculturalism on a related field (i.e., professional psychology) will be presented. Multicultural training in professional psychology began to receive much attention in the late 1960's (Bernal & Padilla, 1982). By 1973, there was documentation that organized psychology (i.e., National Institute of Mental Health, American Psychological Association [APA]) had decided to formalize standards of multicultural training in professional psychology curricula. The culmination of this formalization was the inclusion of multicultural training in APA accreditation criteria for doctoral programs in professional psychology (in 1979; Bernal & Padilla, 1982) (the APA is the accreditation authority for doctoral training programs in professional psychology at the present; see Wynkoop & Dixon, 1994b). In addition, committees addressing multicultural issues have been established at the national level in APA to encourage multiculturalism in psychology (Wynkoop & Dixon, 1994a).

It used to be the case that color blindness was the standard for multiculturalism (Thomas, 1985). This has changed in recent times toward the recognition of cultural differences (Thomas, 1985). In fact, differences between cultures (or diverse groups) appears to be the bulwark of the current multicultural movement (see the content of Casas, 1985; Ivey, 1987; Sue,

Akutsu, & Higashi, 1985; Sue & Sue, 1990; Thomas, 1985; Wehrly & Watson-Gegeo, 1985). The movement toward an emphasis on differences (i.e., a doctrine of differences) between groups is so strong that it can appear to the onlooker as if the similarities among groups is being overlooked, or even negated. Indeed, difference has become such an integral issue in multiculturalism that minority authors have begun to express animosity toward those authors/researchers of the majority who choose to write in the multicultural arena (Mio & Iwamasa, 1993). The basis for such an argument is that no one from outside of a particular culture can ever come to a full understanding of that culture. While compelling to an extent, this argument has drastic consequences. Group separation, as you may recall, produces an out-group phenomenon, which lends itself to a lack of informational exchange between groups. It has been acknowledged that typical cross cultural problems (e.g., negative stereotyping, prejudice) are fueled by a lack of reciprocal knowledge between groups (Sue & Sue, 1990).

A Voice of Opposition

Arguments against the strict multicultural position have concentrated on the likelihood that the average differences that exist between groups are often less in magnitude than are many of the individual differences that exist within groups. In effect, when the distributions of a particular trait are plotted, there would likely be a great deal of overlap of the distributions between groups. Therefore, the service provider may do more harm than good by assuming that because a client is a member of a particular group, that he or she will display certain behaviors, or will harbor certain beliefs, characteristic of that particular group. One example of this position is that of Lloyd (1987a, b). It was his opinion that there is so much intragroup variability among persons (implying similarity across groups), that application of group information in service provision, even if positive, might miss the concerns, or the particular frame of reference, of the individual client. In effect, it is the individual who is being treated, not his or her culture, and to confuse the focus of therapy (i.e., to treat the culture instead of the client) can be detrimental to the client. Lloyd's (1987a, b) views, though predicated upon cross-cultural service (e.g., Lloyd, 1987c), have been debated and summarily dismissed by other writers (Hood & Arceneaux, 1987; Ivey, 1987; Parker, 1987). The primary criticism of his work has been that even if the counselor does not use the training in cultural differences, he or she would still benefit clientele by possessing a working knowledge of the intergroup differences that do exist (a position promoting difference over similarity).

An additional argument against training in multiculturalism is the notion that such training can cause the creation of new stereotypes, which, while perhaps kinder to the group under consideration, may be just as inaccurate as the original stereotype(s) (and just as disruptive to the provision of human services in the cross-cultural context). Spiegel (1979), for example, argued that specialty training in women's issues may serve to instill new stereotypes that could be based upon faulty information. Her position was that womens' issues had not yet been thoroughly researched, and that training human services providers how to treat women may lead to faulty or inappropriate treatment. Spiegel's argument, though dated, may still be applicable today. To date, much of what has been written regarding women has been qualitative in nature (i.e., scientific knowledge in the area has not expanded much over the past 15 years). Similar can be said of research on other cultural groups.

An inspection of the arguments for and against specialty training in multiculturalism for human services providers reveals a common ground. In their attempt to pursue polarity, both sides have been relegated to a univariate course (one in group differences, one in nondifference). In other words, they have neglected the possibility that cross-cultural differences may be multivariate (see Casas, 1985; see also the content of Bascom, 1982). In effect, they do not appear to recognize that while groups, or cultures, can differ significantly in certain respects, they can also be very similar in others, and that these similarities can be the basis for social healing.

Promoting Similarity Within Diversity

Maintaining a posture of difference, at the expense of a balance between difference and similarity, creates a situation in which cultural groups are separated, at least cognitively and emotionally, and cannot, therefore, exchange accurate information reflective of their members. This serves to isolate groups from one another and allows for the spread of misinformation, perhaps resulting in the creation and/or perpetuation of negative stereotypes and of out-group paranoia.

It is widely held, that individuals tend to like those with whom they find similarity (Forsyth, 1990). It is also widely held that the most efficient means of combating negative stereotypes is to provide conflicting information that cannot be ignored or reasoned away by the receiving person. In fact, Devine's (1989) research showed that those persons who were not considered to be prejudiced were those who had developed schemata contrary to their stereotypes of a particular out-group.

Perhaps the basis for the development of competing schemata is that there is some amount of perceived similarity between the individual battling the negative stereotype and the group, or individual, that is the focus of the stereotype. This would allow for a certain amount of empathy to be expressed toward the out-group. A real-life example is found in work with criminal offenders. A key element in the commission of violence toward another person, or his or her property, is a lack of empathy on the part of the perpetrator toward the victim(s) (see Wynkoop & Priest, 1986). In training offenders in empathy, it is often beneficial to encourage a sense of similarity between themselves and their victim(s). It is difficult to empathize with someone with whom no similarity with oneself can be recognized. It may well be that the ability to empathize (on a continuum from none to great) is positively correlated with perceived similarity (also on a continuum of none to great) between the offender and victim.

It is clear from this discussion that the ends will suggest the means when it comes to multiculturalism. In other words, if the goal is inter-group conflict, then promoting difference at the expense of similarity will be the most efficient approach. On the other hand, if the goal is social healing, then promoting similarity between individuals within the different groups would be the most effective course of action. A consequence of the promotion of similarity between cultures could be that cultural distinctiveness would be lost. This is, however, a unidimensional conceptualization of a multidimensional issue. There is no law of culture that dictates that communication and recognition of similarities between groups needs to result in the disintegration of one culture or the other. To the contrary, the recognition of similarities between groups may be a way to also recognize and appreciate, rather than despise, the differences between them.

CRIMINAL JUSTICE SERVICE DELIVERY

To this point, the readers have been sensitized to various multicultural issues. In an attempt to integrate these issues, this last content section will discuss how to incorporate multicultural information into criminal justice service. This will be accomplished by a discussion of models of cross-cultural service delivery and the presentation of a model for evaluating behavior in the cross-cultural context.

Paradigms of Cross-Cultural Service Provision

The ultimate goal of examining and debating the theory of multiculturalism is to arrive at certain conclusions as to how best to deliver criminal justice services in the cross-cultural context. Given that this is the goal, it may be beneficial to briefly examine the types of service delivery that result from the differing theoretical positions presented in the previous section (i.e., difference versus similarity). Three of the more noteworthy models (see Kiselica, in press) will be presented in brief.

The first is the *Culture Specific Model* (Pedersen, 1988). This paradigm, or model, is an outgrowth of the doctrine of differences discussed previously. It calls for specific training on cultural differences and how to approach individuals based on their cultural background. A difficulty with this position, as previously discussed, is that within group variation may be overlooked (Pedersen, 1991; Speight, Myers, Cox, & Highlen, 1991). The second paradigm, the *Universal Model* (Patterson, 1986; Pedersen, 1991), proposes that there is enough commonality among humans that cross-cultural differences can somehow be transcended (Kiselica, in press; Vontress, 1988). This position promotes the similarities between individuals in various groups, rather than emphasizing differences. The final paradigm, Pedersen's *Generic Model* (Kiselica, in press; Pedersen, 1990, 1991), is a hybrid model which incorporates elements of the previous two models. Pedersen (1990, 1991) defines culture broadly (as we have in this chapter), and, therefore, conceptualizes human service provision in all contexts as multicultural (see also Ivey et al., 1993). The benefit of this perspective is that it acknowledges the common sense notion that cultures do have differences. It also, however, keeps these differences in perspective (i.e., in relation to individual differences within cultures and individual similarities across cultures).

It would appear reasonable to assume that the type of paradigm employed in the delivery of services in the cross-cultural context would be determined by the cultural make-up of the society in which the services were being delivered. For example, in a society that requires assimilation of its immigrants, the Universal Model would be the most relevant perspective. Along similar lines, in a society that requires gross cultural and/or class separation, the Culture-Specific Model would be the most sensible approach. The U.S., on the other hand, is neither a society of assimilation, nor of separation (in their pure forms). While there are many nationalities represented in the population of the U.S., their distinctiveness is diluted somewhat by survival needs and with the passage of time. The result is a blending of sorts, with the retention of a certain amount of distinctiveness between groups. Therefore, of the three models presented, the more general Generic Model would appear to provide the best conceptual fit with U.S. society.

Evaluation of Behavior in the Cross-Cultural Context

The evaluation and explanation of behavior across cultures necessitates the simultaneous consideration of several interpersonal, cultural, and demographic variables. The *Cultural Grid* (Pedersen, 1985, 1988) provides a systematized approach to the evaluation of behavior in the cross-cultural context. The Cultural Grid can help the criminal justice professional to separate individual variability in behavior from the cultural context in which the behavior occurs. Its intent is not to provide global explanations for behavior, but to explain a particular behavior committed by a particular individual in the context of his or her salient culture. The Cultural Grid, while allowing that there are environmental influences on behavior, perceives of culture as "being within the person" (Pedersen, 1988, p. 69). It is the interaction between culture and environment that accounts for behavior according to this model of behavioral evaluation.

The Cultural Grid seeks to explain behavior within four interpersonal contexts bounded by *expectations* and *behaviors* (Pedersen, 1985, 1988). The contexts include those in which participants from different cultural backgrounds have similar expectations and behaviors (*Type I relationships*), those in which the participants have similar expectations, but different behaviors (*Type II relationships*), those in which the participants have similar behaviors, but different expectations (*Type III relationships*), and those in which the participants differ on both expectations and behaviors (*Type IV relationships*) (Pedersen, 1988). The ideal cross-cultural relationship would, of course, be a Type I relationship.

In the Cultural Grid, the expectations and behaviors of the type of relationship are evaluated in relation to the *social/cultural* variables of *ethnographic* information (i.e., nationality, ethnicity, language, religion, other relevant factors), *demographic* variables (e.g., age, gender, marital status, children, place and type of residence), *status* (e.g., level of income and education, political), and *affiliation* (i.e., formal, informal) (Pedersen, 1988). In effect, a grid is constructed to examine behavior in terms of the type of helping relationship, with the individual variables along one axis and the social/cultural variables along the other axis. The interested reader is directed to Pedersen (1985, 1988) for a more detailed account of the use of the Cultural Grid in multicultural relationships. What is most relevant for the student at this point, is to understand that examination of behavior in the cross cultural context takes into account a myriad of individual and social/cultural variables.

An example of the use of the Cultural Grid would be the examination of the behavior of a White inmate who has been refusing to wash himself for some time, and has recently begun to defecate on himself. The criminal justice professional in this hypothetical case is an Hispanic male. The expectation of the professional is that the inmate is likely psychotic, in need of antipsychotic medications, and in need of intervention into his personal hygiene. The expectation of the inmate is not to allow this. The behavior of the professional is cordial, but authoritative. The inmate is resistant to the authority of the professional, whom he feels does not understand his situation. This results in a Type IV relationship. Further, the inmate is young, from a middle SES environment, and this is his first incarceration. The inmate is accustomed to solving problems without reliance on others. The professional is more relational in his interpersonal approach, and cannot understand why the inmate has no associates in the prison environment. Consideration of the inmate's behavior in terms of his cultural background, expectations, and values (i.e., digging for information) reveals that he has been approached for sexual favors by a group of African-American inmates, and having limited coping abilities in the prison environment (i.e., no associates to rely on, limited physical skills, little knowledge of how to avoid such advances) he has adopted a strategy of making himself less attractive to them. What may have appeared initially as psychotic behavior is quite explainable, and even rational, given the circumstances and the alternatives. The solution is no longer antipsychotic medication, but a resolution of the problem of sexual harassment (e.g., a move to a different part of the institution, lessons in prison survival skills).

CHAPTER SUMMARY

This chapter has been broad in its content. It has attempted to provide a context for subsequent chapters, which will emphasize specific multicultural issues in criminal justice. Culture was defined broadly, as diversity in almost any sense of the word (e.g., race, ethnicity, gender, sexual orientation, employment). Also discussed were the philosophical bases for multiculturalism in criminal justice, definitions of several key terms used in multiculturalism, stereotypes as a fact of life, cultural identity development, and paradigms of cross-cultural delivery of criminal justice services. It was concluded that perhaps no where else in our society is there so much cultural diversity in such concentration as in criminal justice.

Much time was spent on stereotypes. It was concluded that stereotypes, as schemata, are a fact of everyday life. It was also concluded that there is nothing inherently evil about stereotypes (or the persons who possess them), but rather what is done with them that makes the difference between prejudice and non-prejudice. Students of criminal justice, like anyone else, possess schemata and, therefore, stereotypes. This may not be readily apparent to the student, but it is the case just the same. This goes for members of minority groups as well as for those of the majority group.

The student of criminal justice who wishes to be sensitive to stereotypes in his or her own life will take time to examine his or her views toward various out-groups. An exercise in which the student could engage would be to construct a list, in private, of the first things (i.e., adjectives) that come to mind when thinking of a particular cultural group, without censoring any negative thoughts. Then, after leaving the list for a while, the student could consciously contemplate and challenge its content with accurate information that may not be reflected in the stereotype. One method of challenging the content of one's own stereotypes toward another group may be to make contact with that group (e.g., going to a gay bar with some friends, attending a particular type of religious service), as well as reminding oneself that members of the particular out-group may have as much difficulty in understanding the student as the student has understanding them. Cross-cultural understanding is a two-way street. The subtle danger of stereotypes is ignorance of their existence. They exist. They do not go away. They can, however, be modified.

The remainder of the text will present some unique information to students of criminal justice. Discussed will be victimization in terms of race and ethnicity, Native Americans in American criminal justice, hate crimes, multicultural issues from a juvenile justice perspective, race and the media, cross-cultural victim/offender reconciliation programs, competence in multicultural affairs, and multicultural training in undergraduate criminal justice programs. These topics will prove to be quite practical for the student of criminal justice in the development of a professional identity as a provider of services in a cross-cultural context.

REFERENCES

Allen, H. E., & Simonsen, C. E. (1986). *Corrections in America: An introduction.* New York: Macmillan.

Allison, S. T., & Messick, D. M. (1985). The group attribution error. *Journal of Experimental Social Psychology, 21,* 563–579.

Allport, G. W. (1954). *The nature of prejudice.* Reading, MA: Addison-Wesley.

American Psychological Association. (1993). Guidelines for providers of psychological services to ethnic, linguistic, and culturally diverse populations. *American Psychologist, 48*(1), 45–48.

Arce, C. A. (1981). A reconsideration of Chicano culture and identity. *Daedalus, 110,* 177–192.

Asch, S. (1946). Forming impressions of personality. *Journal of Abnormal and Social Psychology, 41,* 258–290.

Atkinson, D. R., Morten, G., & Sue, D. W. (1993). A minority development identity development model. In D. R. Atkinson, G. Morten, & D. W. Sue (Eds.), *Counseling American minorities: A cross-cultural perspective* (4th ed.). Dubuque, IA: W. C. Brown.

Atkinson, D. R., Morten, G., & Sue, D. W. (1983). *Counseling American minorities: A cross-cultural perspective* (2nd ed.). Dubuque, IA: W. C. Brown.

Atkinson, D. R., Morten, G., & Sue, D. W. (1979). Proposed minority identity development model. In D. R. Atkinson, G. Morten, & D. W. Sue (Eds.), *Counseling American minorities: A cross-cultural perspective.* Dubuque, IA: W. C. Brown.

Baron, R. A., & Byrne, D. (1991). *Social Psychology: Understanding human interaction.* Boston: Allyn and Bacon.

Bascom, N. B. (1982). *Retention study of new hires at FCI, Lexington.* Unpublished manuscript, Federal Bureau of Prisons, Federal Correctional Institute, Lexington, KY.

Baumgardner, A. H., Heppner, P. P., & Arkin, R. M. (1986). Role of causal attribution in personal problem solving. *Journal of Personality and Social Psychology, 50,* 636–643.

Beck, A. T., Rush, A. J., Shaw, B. F., & Emery, G. (1979). *Cognitive therapy of depression.* New York: Guilford.

Bernal, M. E., & Padilla, A. M. (1982). Status of minority curricula and training in clinical psychology. *American Psychologist, 37,* 780–787.

Bureau of Justice Statistics. (1992). *Sourcebook of criminal justice statistics.* Washington, DC: Author.

Casas, J. M. (1985a). A reflection on the status of racial/ethnic minority research. *The Counseling Psychologist, 13*(3), 581–598.

Casas, J. M. (1985b). The status of racial- and ethnic-minority counseling: A training perspective. In P. Pedersen (Ed.), *Handbook of cross-cultural counseling and therapy.* Westport, CT: Greenwood Press.

Cass, V. C. (1979). Homosexuality identity formation: A theoretical model. *Journal of Homosexuality, 4*(3), 219–235.

Cass, V. C. (1984). Homosexual identity formation: Testing a theoretical model. *Journal of Sex Research, 20*(2), 143–167.

Chan, C. S. (1989). Issues of identity development among Asian-American lesbians and gay men. *Journal of Counseling and Development, 68*(1), 16–20.

Copeland, E. J. (1982). Minority populations and traditional counseling programs: Some alternatives. *Counselor Education and Supervision, 21*(3), 187–193.

Cross, W. E. (1991). *Shades of black: Diversity in African-American identity.* Philadelphia: Temple University Press.

Cross, W. E. (1971). The negro-to-black conversion experience: Towards a psychology of black liberation. *Black World, 20,* 13–27.

Delworth, U. (1989). Identity in the college years: Issues of gender and ethnicity. *Journal of the National Association of Student Personnel Administrators, 26,* 162–166.

Devine, P. G. (1989). Stereotypes and prejudice: Their automatic and controlled components. *Journal of Personality and Social Psychology, 56,* 5–18.

Ellis, A. (1973). *Humanistic psychotherapy.* New York: McGraw-Hill.

Erikson, E. H. (1963). *Childhood and society* (2nd ed.). New York: Norton.

Erikson, E. H. (1968). *Identity: Youth and crisis.* New York: Norton.

Erikson, E. H. (1982). *The life cycle completed.* New York: Norton.

Fiske, S. T., & Taylor, S. E. (1984). *Social cognition.* Reading, MA: Addison-Wesley.

Forsyth, D. R. (1990). *Group dynamics* (2nd ed.). Pacific Grove, CA: Brooks/Cole.

Gilligan, C. (1982). *In a different voice: Psychological theory and women's development.* Cambridge, MA: Harvard University Press.

Gliedman, J. (1979, August). The wheelchair rebellion. *Psychology Today, 13,* 59–101.

Gonsiorek, J. C., & Weinrich, J. D. (1991). *Homosexuality: Research implications for public policy.* Newbury Park, CA: Sage.

Grunlan, S. A., & Mayers, M. K. (1979). *Cultural Anthropology.* Grand Rapids, MI: Zondervan.

Hall, W. S., Cross, W. E., & Freedle, R. (1972). Stages in the development of black awareness: An exploratory investigation. In R. L. Jones (Ed.), *Black psychology.* New York: Harper & Row.

Hamachek, D. E. (1982). *Encounters with others: Interpersonal relationships and you.* New York: Holt, Rinehart and Winston.

Hardiman, R. (1982). White identity development: A process model for describing the racial consciousness of white Americans. *Dissertation Abstracts International, 43,* 104A.

Heider, F. (1958). *Psychology of interpersonal relations.* New York: John Wiley.

Helms, J. E. (1990). Toward a model of white racial identity development. In J. E. Helms (Ed.), *Black and white racial identity: Theory, research, and practice* (pp. 49–66). New York: Greenwood Press.

Helms, J. E. (1984). Toward a theoretical explanation of the effects of race on counseling: A black and white model. *The Counseling Psychologist, 12,* 153–165.

Hills, H. I., & Strozier, A. L. (1992). Multicultural training in APA-approved counseling psychology programs: A survey. *Professional Psychology: Research and Practice, 23*(1), 43–51.

Hood, A. B., & Arceneaux, C. (1987). Multicultural counseling: Will what you don't know help you? *Counselor Education and Supervision, 26*(3), 173–175.

Howell, D. C. (1987). *Statistical methods for psychology*(2nd ed.). Boston: Duxbury Press.

Ivey, A. E. (1987). Cultural intentionality: The core of effective helping. *Counselor Education and Supervision, 26*(3), 168–172.

Ivey, A. E., Ivey, M. B., & Simek-Morgan, L. (1993). *Counseling and psychotherapy: A multicultural perspective* (3rd ed.). Boston: Allyn and Bacon.

Jackson, B. (1975). Black identity development. *Journal of Educational Diversity and Innovation, 2,* 19–25.

Jones, E. E., & Nisbett, R. E. (1971). *The actor and the observer: Divergent perceptions of the causes of behavior.* Morristown, NJ: Erlbaum.

Jones, J. M. (1981). The concept of racism and its changing reality. In B. J. Bowser & R. G. Hunt (Eds.), *Impacts of racism on white Americans* (pp. 27–49). Beverly Hills, CA: Sage.

Judd, C. M., & Park, B. (1988). Out-group homogeneity: Judgements of variability at the individual and group levels. *Journal of Personality and Social Psychology, 54,* 778–788.

Kandel, E. R. (1991). Brain and behavior. In E. R. Kandel, J. H. Schwartz, & T. M. Jessell (Eds.), *Principles of neural science* (3rd ed.). Norwalk, CT: Appleton & Lange.

Kim, J. (1981). *Process of Asian-American identity development: A study of Japanese-American women's perceptions of their struggle to achieve positive identities.* Unpublished doctoral dissertation, University of Massachusetts, Amherst.

Kiselica, M. S. (in press). *Counseling teenage fathers: A multicultural perspective.* Newbury Park, CA: Sage.

Kiselica, M. S. (1991). Reflections on a multicultural internship experience. *Journal of Counseling and Development, 70*(1), 126–130.

Kolb, B., & Wishaw, I. Q. (1990). *Fundamentals of human neuropsychology* (3rd ed.). New York: W. H. Freeman.

Lesko, W. A. (1991). *Readings in social psychology.* Boston: Allyn and Bacon.

Lippmann, W. (1922). *Public opinion.* New York: Harcourt & Brace.

Lloyd, A. P. (1987a). Multicultural counseling: Lloyd's reply. *Counselor Education and Supervision, 26*(3), 181–183.

Lloyd, A. P. (1987b). Multicultural counseling: Does it belong in a counselor education program? *Counselor Education and Supervision, 26*(3), 164–175.

Lloyd, A. P. (1987c). Counselor Education in Malaysia. *Counselor Education and Supervision, 26*(3), 221–227.

Lorion, R. P., & Parron, D. L. (1985). Countering the countertransference: A strategy for treating the untreatable. In P. Pedersen (Ed.), *Handbook of cross-cultural counseling and therapy* (pp. 281–289). Westport, CT: Greenwood Press.

Maultsby, M. C. (1984). *Rational behavior therapy.* Englewood Cliffs, NJ: Prentice-Hall.

McCall, G. J., & Simmons, J. L. (1966). *Identities and interactions.* New York: Free Press.

Michenbaum, D. (1977). *Cognitive-behavior modification: An integrative approach.* New York: Plenum.

Milgram, S. (1974). *Obedience to authority.* New York: Harper & Row.

Miller, D. T., & Ross, M. (1975). Self-serving biases in the attribution of causality: Fact or fiction? *Psychological Bulletin, 82,* 313–325.

Mio, J. S., & Iwamasa, G. (1993). To do, or not to do: That is the question for white cross-cultural researchers. *The Counseling Psychologist, 21*(2), 197–212.

Park, B., & Rothbart, M. (1982). Perception of out-group homogeneity and levels of social categorization: Memory for the subordinate attributes of in-group and out-group members. *Journal of Personality and Social Psychology, 42,* 1051–1068.

Parker, W. W. (1987). Flexibility: A primer for multicultural counseling. *Counselor Education and Supervision, 26*(3), 176–183.

Patterson, C. H. (1986). Culture and counseling in Hong Kong. *Chinese University Education Journal, 14,* 77–81.

Pedersen, P. (1985). *Handbook of cross-cultural counseling and therapy.* Westport, CT: Greenwood Press.

Pedersen, P. (1988). *A handbook for developing multicultural awareness.* Alexandria, VA: American Association for Counseling and Development.

Pedersen, P. (1990). The multicultural perspective as the fourth force in counseling. *Journal of Mental Health Counseling, 12,* 93–95.

Pedersen, P. (1991). Introduction to the special issue on multiculturalism as a fourth force in counseling. *Journal of Counseling and Development, 70*(1), 4.

Peterson, C. (1980). Memory and the "dispositional shift." *Social Psychology Quarterly, 43,* 372–380.

Phinney, J. S., Lochner, B. T., & Murphy, R. (1990). Ethnic identity development and psychological adjustment in adolescence. In A. R. Stiffman & L. E. Davis (Eds.), *Ethnic issues in adolescent mental health* (pp. 53–72). Newbury Park, CA: Sage.

Ponterotto, J. G. (1988). Racial consciousness development among white counselors' trainees: A stage model. *Journal of Multicultural Counseling and Development, 16,* 146–156.

Ponterotto, J. G., & Casas, J. M. (1991). *Handbook of racial/ethnic minority counseling research.* Springfield, IL: Charles C Thomas.

Ponterotto, J. G., Lewis, D. E., & Burlington, R. (1990). *Affirmative action on campus.* San Francisco: Jossey-Bass.

Ponterotto, J. G., & Pedersen, P. B. (1993). *Preventing prejudice: A guide for counselors and educators.* Newbury Park, CA: Sage.

Priest, B. J., Kordinak, S. T., & Wynkoop, T. F. (1991). Type of offense and level of moral development among adult male inmates. *Journal of Addictions and Offender Counseling, 12*(1), 2–11.

Ridley, C. R. (1989). Racism in counseling as an adverse behavioral process. In P. B. Pedersen, J. G. Draguns, W. J. Lonner, & J. E. Trimble (Eds.), *Counseling across cultures* (3rd ed., pp. 55–77). Honolulu: University of Hawaii Press.

Sabnani, H. B., Ponterotto, J. G., & Borodovsky, L. G. (1991). White racial identity development and cross-cultural counselor training: A stage model. *The Counseling Psychologist, 19,* 76–102.

Sabini, J., & Silver, M. (1983). Dispositional vs. situational interpretations of Milgram's obedience experiments: "The fundamental attribution error." *Journal for the Theory of Social Behavior, 13,* 147–154.

Simon, B., & Brown, R. (1987). Perceived intragroup homogeneity in minority majority contexts. *Journal of Personality and Social Psychology, 53,* 703–711.

Speight, S. L., Myers, L. J., Cox, C. I., & Highlen, P. S. (1991). A redefinition of multicultural counseling. *Journal of Counseling and Development, 70*(1), 29–36.

Spiegel, S. B. (1979). Separate principles for counselors of women: A new form of sexism. *The Counseling Psychologist, 8*(1), 49–50.

Stryker, S., & Serpe, R. T. (1982). Commitment, identity salience, and role behavior. In W. Ickes & F. S. Knowles (Eds.), *Personality, roles, and social behavior* (pp. 199–218). New York: Springer-Verlag.

Sue, A., Akutsu, P. D., & Higashi, C. (1985). Training issues in conducting therapy with ethnic-minority-group clients. In P. Pedersen (Ed.), *Handbook of cross-cultural counseling and therapy.* Westport, CT: Greenwood Press.

Sue, D. W., Bernier, J. E., Durran, A., Feinberg, L., Pedersen, P., Smith, E. J., & Vasquez-Nuttal, E. (1982). Position paper: Cross-cultural counseling competencies. *The Counseling Psychologist, 10*(2), 45–52.

Sue, D. W., & Sue, D. (1990). *Counseling the culturally different.* New York: John Wiley.

Sue, D. W., & Sue, S. (1972). Counseling Chinese Americans. *Personnel and Guidance Journal, 50,* 637–645.

Sundal-Hansen, L. S. (1985). Sex-role issues in counseling women and men. In P. Pedersen (Ed.), *Handbook of cross-cultural counseling and therapy* (pp. 213–222). Westport, CT: Greenwood Press.

Szapocznik, J., & Kurtines, W. (1980). Acculturation, biculturalism and adjustment among Cuban Americans. In A. Padilla (Ed.), *Acculturation: Theory, models and some new findings.* Boulder, CO: Westwood Press.

Thoits, P. A. (1983). Multiple identities and psychological well-being: A reformulation and test of the social isolation hypothesis. *American Sociological Review, 48,* 174–187.

Thoits, P. A. (1992). Identity structures and psychological well-being: Gender and marital status comparisons. *Social Psychology Quarterly, 55*(3), 236–256.

Thomas, C. W. (1971). *Boys no more.* Beverly Hills, CA: Glencoe.

Thomas, C. W. (1985). Counseling in a cultural context. *The Counseling psychologist, 13*(4), 657–663.

Troiden, R. R. (1989). The formation of homosexual identities. *Journal of Homosexuality, 17*(1–2), 43–73.

U.S. Department of Commerce. (1992). *1990 Census of population: General population characteristics, United States.* Washington, DC: Author.

Vontress, C. E. (1981). Racial and ethnic barriers in counseling. In P. Pedersen, J. Draguns, W. Lonner, & J. Trimble (Eds.), *Counseling across cultures: Revised and expanded edition* (pp. 87–107). Honolulu: University of Hawaii Press.

Vontress, C. E. (1988). An existential approach to cross-cultural counseling. *Journal of Multicultural Counseling and Development, 16,* 73–83.

Watson, D. L. & Tharp, R. G. (1993). *Self-directed behavior: Self-modification for personal adjustment* (6th ed.). Pacific Grove, CA: Brooks/Cole.

Wehrly, B., & Watson-Gegeo, K. (1985). Ethnographic methodologies as applied to the study of cross-cultural counseling. In P. Pedersen (Ed.), *Handbook of cross-cultural counseling and therapy.* Westport, CT: Greenwood Press.

Weigert, A. J., Teitge, J. S., & Teitge, D. W. (1986). *Society and identity: Toward a sociological psychology.* Cambridge, UK: Cambridge University Press.

Whitehead, J. T. (1989). *Burnout in probations and corrections.* New York: Praeger.

Wirth, L. (1945). The problem of minority groups. In R. Linton (Ed.), *The science of man in world crisis* (pp. 347–372). New York: Columbia University Press.

Worth, L. T., Allison, S. T., & Messick, D. M. (1987). Impact of a group decision on perception of one's own and others' attitudes. *Journal of Personality and Social Psychology, 53,* 673–682.

Wrenn, C. G. (1962). The culturally encapsulated counselor. *Harvard Educational Review, 32,* 444–449.

Wynkoop, T. F. (1993). Differential diagnosis of adolescent satanic cult dabblers: A critique of Moriarty. *Journal of Mental Health Counseling, 15*(2), 184–189.

Wynkoop, T. F. (in press). Psychiatric symptomatology and type of treatment in Wilson's disease: A retrospective case analysis. *Medical Psychotherapy: An International Journal.*

Wynkoop, T. F., & Dixon, D. N. (1994a). Organizational and political issues in counseling psychology: An accounting of the Georgia conference recommendations. *The Counseling Psychologist, 22*(2), 342–356.

Wynkoop, T. F., & Dixon, D. N. (1994b, April). *The APA, APS, and organized counseling psychology.* Paper presented at the 1994 APA Division 17 Great Lakes Regional Conference, Notre Dame, IN.

Wynkoop, T. F., & Gerstein, L. H. (1993). Staff burnout in adult protective services work. In B. Byers & J. E. Hendricks (Eds.), *Adult protective services: Research and practice* (pp. 191–229). Springfield, IL: Charles C Thomas.
Wynkoop, T. F., & Priest, B. J. (1986, October). *Sex offender treatment at the Huntsville Unit of the Texas Department of Corrections.* Presented twice at the Texas Association for Counseling & Development Annual Convention, Waco, TX.

Disclaimer: The opinions expressed in this chapter have been those of the authors and do not necessarily reflect those of the U.S. Department of Justice or of the Federal Bureau of Prisons.

CHAPTER TWO

FEMINISM, GENDER AND CRIMINOLOGY

HELEN EIGENBERG, JANET L. MULLINGS AND KATHRYN E. SCARBOROUGH

INTRODUCTION

American society continues to struggle with structural discrimination that affects a variety of disenfranchised people including women; people of color; gays and lesbians; people of different ethnicity; and poor people. One way which society tries to address some of this discrimination is through multiculturalism.

Multiculturalism is having an important influence on campuses and curriculums nationwide. As universities strive for more racial and gender diversity in terms of both faculty and students, other intellectuals within many disciplines are also struggling to ensure that the knowledge in the field reflects a broader reality. In essence, these scholars are insisting that disenfranchised people be represented—be visible—in the body of literature that is considered "critical" in a discipline. In most disciplines, including criminology, that body of literature or the "core knowledge" usually has consisted of an overabundance of information that is based upon the experiences of economically privileged, European, white men.

Thus, multiculturalism is a battle for inclusion as disenfranchised groups continue to fight for representation in academia. However, multiculturalism also challenges the fundamental root of all power in academia: the power to define what is and is not "knowledge" in a discipline. In other words, multiculturalism asks "*whose* social reality is worthy of description and explanation, and *who* can be trusted to get it right" (Daly & Chesney-Lind, 1988, p. 500).[1] This central power struggle is at the root of all the controversy surrounding multiculturalism; however, this battle is not a new one. Feminists (along with other perspectives in the academy) already are challenging criminology to be more inclusive and are working toward the transformation of the discipline.

This chapter argues that multiculturalism is similar to feminism because both perspectives challenge what we think we know about criminology. Both perspectives argue that disenfranchised groups have been excluded from criminology in a variety of ways. Both perspectives pose epistemological challenges to existing bodies of literature. In other words, they ask "how do we know what we think we know about this subject?" As a result, both perspectives challenge the social construction of knowledge and threaten to change the very way in which we "do" criminology. *Thus, feminism and multiculturalism deal with two common themes: 1) the exclusion of disenfranchised groups and 2) transformation of the discipline through an examination of the social construction of knowledge.*

This chapter examines the exclusion of women in criminology and discusses some ways in which feminist scholarship has challenged traditional assumptions about women and their role in criminology and the criminal justice system. It identifies a key feminist epistemological challenge in each of the following categories pertaining to gender and: theories of criminality, victimization, the response of the criminal justice system, and occupations in the criminal justice system. Finally, this chapter argues that multiculturalism, like feminism, will experience resistance because it challenges the very intellectual traditions that have contributed to the marginalization of disenfranchised groups in criminology (such as women) in the first place. It concludes by focusing on the need for future theoretical development and argues that the links between multiculturalism and feminism need to be made more explicit.

FEMINIST CRIMINOLOGY

It is a misnomer to talk of "feminism" as if it were a monolithic approach or perspective, and this statement also is true of feminist criminology (Daly & Chesney-Lind, 1988; Renzetti, 1993). Instead, there are multiple feminist perspectives sometimes called socialist, marxist, liberal, moderate or radical feminist: all of which are represented in the criminological literature. It also is possible for an individual, male or female, to be a feminist and do feminist research. People may consider themselves feminist activists, but not "do" feminist research. Scholars may conduct feminist research, but may not be involved in activist politics. Professors may teach feminist scholarship, even if they do not participate in feminist research. There are many ways to be a feminist or do feminist work (Daly & Chesney-Lind, 1988).

There are, however, some central tenants or common assumptions that can be used to "classify" feminist scholarship (Daly & Chesney-Lind, 1988). At its heart, feminist scholarship assumes that gender and gender distinctions are a product of socialization, rather than biology. Gender is a central organizing aspect of our society and all social interactions are affected by gender. Furthermore, our society is organized asymmetrically with respect to gender; men are presumed to be the norm and women are compared to them as the "other." Thus, from this perspective, men are considered "superior" and accorded more power in our culture and the social structure continues to maintain definitions of masculinity and feminity that maintain a system of oppression based on gender. Furthermore, this system of gender oppression affects all aspects of our lives, including the production of knowledge and the way we do science.

We are clearly a culture that glorifies science and the use of the scientific method (Harding, 1986). This situation occurs in large part, because science is, theoretically, insulated from social influences. The scientific method supports value neutrality and the collection of objective, scientific facts. Scientists observe, theorize, and then attempt to predict phenomenon. The process is, supposedly, the epitome of rationality and objectivity.

Feminists have disputed these assumptions (Harding, 1986, 1987; Keller, 1983; Kitzinger, 1987; Ladner, 1987; Millman & Kanter, 1987; Nebraska Feminist Collective, 1983; Spender, 1981, 1983; Stacey & Thorn, 1985). They argue that science is *not* "value free" and note that a researcher's assumptions, beliefs, and values influence her/his work. In sum, feminists have elaborated on the many ways in which women and their concerns have been ignored in the pursuit of "normal" science, thereby making women invisible in the discipline.

Criminologists have offered empirical documentation of the exclusion of research on and by women. Women clearly are underrepresented as scholars in the field. While precise data are difficult to obtain, current evidence suggests that only 15 to 20% of criminologists are women (Eigenberg & Baro, 1992; Gerwerth & Bachand, 1993). Furthermore, some research (Eigenberg & Baro, 1992) shows that female scholars are less apt to produce knowledge since women are less apt to publish in criminal justice journals than are men (proportionate to their numbers in the field).[2] In addition, women rarely are represented in important editorial positions of journal publications (Eigenberg & Baro, 1992). Furthermore, journals that consistently exclude women from the editorial process are less likely to publish articles written by women (Eigenberg & Baro, 1992). Women also seldom author introductory textbooks (Eigenberg & Scarborough, 1994).

Research also shows that women rarely are discussed in introductory textbooks. Several studies (Eigenberg & Scarborough, 1994; Garrison, McClelland, Dambrot, & Casey, 1992; Wonders & Caulfield, 1993) report that one to eight percent of the total pages in introductory criminal justice texts discuss "women and women's issues." Other studies (Wright, 1987, 1992) show that introductory criminology texts devote about 4% of the text to women. Furthermore, all of these studies suggest there has not been an increase in the number of textbook pages devoted to women in the past twenty years, even though the number of journal publications on women and crime has increased (Wright, 1987). Finally, other research (Baro &

Eigenberg, 1993) shows that only 19% of the individuals portrayed in pictures in introductory criminology and criminal justice texts include women.

These studies indicate that women are ignored as subjects of inquiry and excluded from research studies. However, women also are excluded as the "knowers" or as those who produce knowledge. In other words, the discipline ignores women in general and feminist scholarship in particular. Feminist criminology is viewed as an "alternate" (read extra) perspective. Courses and material dealing with feminism are described as peripheral (read unnecessary). Feminist scholarship argues that this exclusion is not accidental, but that it occurs because the production of knowledge is gendered. In other words, feminist scholars are not on a level playing field. The odds are stacked against them in a social structure where gender is used to perpetuate oppression.

For example, published journal articles in refereed journals reflect new, cutting edge knowledge in a discipline. To publish a journal article, a paper is submitted to the editor who sends it to two or three people who read it. These reviewers then suggest changes and advise the editor to accept or reject the paper for publication. In essence, an author must generally "please" these reviewers to get the paper published. Theoretically, this process is a blind review, meaning that the reviewers are not supposed to know who the author of the paper is, nor does the author know the identity of the reviewers. Likewise, authors supposedly can choose to ignore the reviewers "suggestions" if they believe that these "compromises" are incorrect or violate some sense of scientific integrity. Realistically, however, many potential authors are under great pressure to publish as a means to get tenure and/or other professional rewards that accompany a prolific publishing career.

This peer review system, theoretically, guards against biases; however, this system may be undermined (Nebraska Feminist Collective, 1983; Spender, 1981). Editors may select reviewers who are predisposed to recommend against certain perspectives—such as feminist scholarship. Furthermore, the more specific and famous the work is, the more likely it is that the reviewers know the identity of the author which may affect decisions about publication since professional networks are often very small within a discipline. Thus, those people who hold the power to decide what gets published generally are white males (numerically speaking—see Eigenberg & Baro, 1992) and their view of criminology may be different from those held by other groups of people. In essence, these world views may be so different that it may be difficult for anyone to agree on the "scientific criteria" which should be used to determine whether a body of work qualifies as "knowledge." Thus, those in power may use the process to discourage certain perspectives by refusing to publish these papers and by labeling these works as peripheral, unscientific, or biased during the review process. Ask any feminist researcher about their experiences getting published and one is likely to stumble across any number of documented incidents of sexism evident in the scientific, value-neutral, peer review system.

Bowker (Bowker, Arbitell, & McFerron, 1988) has discussed this issue. He has published in several fields and reports that 54% of his feminist papers are published compared to 85% of his non-feminist papers. He also can document that the publication process can be manipulated by editors. A feminist article that he wrote on child abuse was submitted to a journal in early 1985. The editor informed Bowker that there were two reviewers and they had "'very divergent opinions'" (p. 172). A third review was sought. Bowker was informed that this review was negative and that the article had been rejected. However, "the editor (or his secretary, most probably) slipped and enclosed, by mistake, a copy of the real third review and an illegitimate, secret fourth review" (p. 172). Of the third and fourth review, one was favorable and one was not. Furthermore, the correspondence showed that the third review had recommended publication. Thus, the editor who apparently was predisposed against publication, then sent the paper out for a fourth review and got the intended result: a recommendation against publication. Bowker argues that there are many academicians "in the world of scholarship whose professionalism is insufficient to keep their anti-feminist attitudes in check" (p. 173).

Summary of Feminism and Criminology

Feminist scholarship has documented the exclusion of women and argues that "women should be at the center of intellectual inquiry, not peripheral, invisible, or appendages to men" (Daly & Chesney-Lind, 1988, p. 504). It challenges some of the most deeply held assumptions of the discipline by asking two questions. First, are gender and the effects of gender socialization examined in this study or theoretical discussion? And second, would the answer to this research question be the same if gender was included in the analysis? In other words, feminist scholarship asks how gender affects a particular concept, research, theory, or typology. It also examines how gender affects the practice of arrest, conviction, and/or imprisonment. At the same time, it offers a more profound challenge to traditional criminology and argues that gender affects all social relationships including the creation of knowledge. It argues that the process of producing knowledge itself is sexist and serves to maintain gender oppression. It seeks to point out biases in existing literature and demands that future research attend to the effects of gender and gender socialization.

Feminist scholarship, then, challenges conventional, mainstream (sometimes referred to as malestream) criminology; however, it is not without its weaknesses. Feminist scholarship has itself, too frequently, concentrated on the concerns of middle class, white women and has ignored the contributions and experiences of many women. While feminism espouses a philosophy of inclusiveness, it often falls short of these goals; however, feminist scholarship, at its best, recognizes that oppressions *of all kinds* are interactive and additive. For example, women of color experience both racism and sexism. Thus, race and gender are not variables that can be considered separately for women of color. Likewise, feminist scholarship notes that classism and heterosexism are other types of oppression that lead to exclusion. Thus, while feminist scholarship focuses on gender, it attempts to include other types of exclusion into a conceptual scheme that continues to struggle with the complex nature of multiple layers of oppression. However, this task is not an easy one.

In sum, then, feminism, like multiculturalism, challenges the traditional knowledge base of criminology, but it also attempts to transform the pursuit of knowledge itself. The prior section has developed that argument. The remainder of the chapter reviews four broad areas of literature. In each of these areas we examine how feminist scholarship has pointed to the exclusion of women and we discuss some feminist challenges to conventional wisdom that have the potential to transform "knowledge" in these particular subject areas.

We are forced to be overly brief and reductionistic in our review of the literature. Despite resistance, there has been a proliferation of feminist scholarship in the past two decades. Thankfully, it no longer is possible to sum up all of what is known about women and feminist scholarship in criminology in one short, tidy, little chapter.

We consulted the empirical studies on textbooks to help us narrow down our subject matter. These studies (Eigenberg & Scarborough, 1994; Garrison et al., 1992; Wonders & Caulfield, 1993; Wright, 1992) suggest that certain "women's topics" are most often discussed in introductory criminology and criminal justice texts (in the few meager pages devoted to women). First, most texts examine gender differences in crime rates and the theoretical explanations for this difference. Second, they look at gender differences and victimization, especially as it pertains to rape. Third, they give some attention to women and their experiences with the criminal justice system to determine if women receive chivalrous treatment. Fourth, texts often discuss women in their roles as police and correctional officers. Thus, this chapter concentrates on those areas of literature that students have had or are likely to have at least minimal exposure to in an introductory criminology or criminal justice course. Key feminist epistemological challenges in these areas examined and we encourage students to think about the ways in which their textbooks examine these topics.[3]

GENDER AND THEORIES OF CRIMINALITY

Feminist scholarship has challenged our theoretical understanding of crime. It argues that conventional, mainstream, criminological theories have critical "scientific" defects because they are unable to account for female criminality. *In sum, two problems confront criminologists who work in the area of theoretical development: 1) the generalizability problem and 2) the gender ratio problem* (Daly & Chesney-Lind, 1988). Each will be discussed in detail in the following section.

The Generalizability Problem

Studies of crime generally have been authored by white men and concentrate on male criminality (Daly & Chesney-Lind, 1988; Gelsthorpe & Morris, 1990; Heidensohn, 1985; Klein, 1973; Moyer, 1992; Smart, 1977). For example, none of the traditional, sociological theories of crime (e.g., Anomie, Differential Association, Social Control) examine female criminality in any significant way. These theories were derived from studies that failed to include female criminals and/or delinquents in the samples. However, this bias was obscured throughout most of the historical evolution of the field. In other words, intellectual traditions made it seem "normal" to study men and generalize these findings to women. As a result, assumptions about male criminality became the basis for all knowledge about crime and criminality, ignoring female criminality.

Feminist scholars have discussed this bias and argued that studies using male subjects cannot be generalized to female subjects, hence the generalizability problem. And while it is possible that similar patterns of criminality may be present—that some findings are generalizable across gender—it is an empirical question that requires research using female criminals as research subjects. While some studies suggest that elements of theories apply to female criminality, other studies report that there are serious problems that confront these theories when they are applied to female criminality (see Smith & Paternoster, 1987). Thus, it is impossible to make a definitive conclusion at this time with respect to the generalizability problem.

The Gender Ratio Problem

In essence, the gender ratio problem discusses the obvious and points to the vast discrepancies in crime rates for men and women. In other words, feminist scholars have noted that any valid criminological theory must explain why women commit so much less crime than men.

Estimates of female crime vary; however, it is clear that women are arrested and convicted of considerably fewer crimes than men. Uniform Crime Report data report that women account for only 18.7% of all arrests in 1991, and for a mere 11.6% of violent crime. Women are most apt to be arrested for larceny (shoplifting) but even then women represent only 32% of all arrests in this category (Federal Bureau of Investigation, 1992, p. 220). Historically, these figures have remained fairly constant and they are similar to those in other Western nations as well (Chapman, 1980; Dahl & Snare, 1978; Edwards, 1984; Glick & Neto, 1982; Heidensohn, 1985; Mann, 1984).

Thus, feminist scholarship again highlights an important challenge to the scientific legitimacy of any theory on crime. If these theories cannot account for the vast differences in crime rates by gender, then they cannot claim to explain criminality. Thus traditional criminological theories managed to maintain their scientific legitimacy even though they were unable to address either the gender ratio problem or the generalizability problem. This fundamental flaw has been obscured because: 1) traditional theorists managed to dismiss female criminality as unimportant and trivial; 2) they defined female criminality using biological explanations for gender; and 3) they equate crime with masculinity.

Dismissing Criminality as Trivial

From the beginning, criminologists have dismissed female criminality as unimportant or trivial. They argued that female crime occurs infrequently and is "statistically irrelevant." Thus, female criminality is viewed as residual or peripheral to the "real" (male) crime problem. So by making female criminality invisible, theorists were not forced to explain why women commit so little crime or to test their theories on female subjects because women's invisibility was made to seem normal.[4]

This statement particularly is true for women of color. Few studies break down female crime rates by race (Durant, 1993). There has been little research on the criminality of women of color as they have been made invisible by the interactive effects of both race and gender (Arnold, 1994; Greene, 1981; Mann, 1989; Young, 1986; Young & Sultan, 1991).

Biological Definitions of Gender and Theoretical Development

Historically, criminological theories have relied upon common sense, sexist, assumptions about the nature of women. These theories focus on the nature of individual women, and ignore other theoretical considerations such as race, class, and other sociological factors commonly considered with regard to male criminality (Klein, 1973; Simon, 1975). Many of these theories attribute differences in men and women's behavior to biological differences while ignoring the importance of gender socialization.

While biology determines such functions as menstruation, pregnancy, and ejaculation; socialization identifies behavior which is associated with feminity or masculinity in any given culture at any given time in history. For example, women bear children, but men can nurture children. However, in most societies "childrearing is assigned to females and becomes central to the female gender role, with the result that childrearing is treated as if it were a biological imperative for females" (Lipman-Blumen, 1984, p. 2). In criminology, theorists have consistently and determinedly focused on the biological basis for characteristics which are socially defined as masculine or feminine. This trend began with Cesare Lombroso, sometimes referred to as the "father" of criminology.[5]

In 1903, Lombroso and his son-in-law (G. Ferrero) published the first major work devoted solely to the study of female criminality: *The Female Offender.* Similar to his earlier studies of male prisoners, this work expanded his notion of the atavistic, or born criminal, through the measurement of cranial features of women prisoners (Klein, 1973). Lombroso argued that women were genetically less advanced than men. Because of their lower state of evolution, women should be more criminal if Lombroso's theory was correct, but his data demonstrated that women were not more inclined to commit crime than were men. Thus, he argued that other factors (such as motherhood, piety, and sexual coldness) usually kept women from acting consistent with their evil (criminal) nature. But, when these inhibitors fail, watch out because "the innocuous semi-criminal present in the normal women must be transformed into a born criminal more terrible than any man" (Wolfgang cited in Mannheim, 1973, p. 152).

Lombroso's work was the beginning of a long line of theoretical work which stressed the sexual deviancy of women while simultaneously noting their evil nature. It also is interesting that Lombroso's ideas were embellished in subsequent theories on female criminality, long after his work was rejected as it applied to male criminality (Bowker, 1981).

The biological legacy continues to be present in contemporary criminological thought. For example, Wilson and Hernstein (1985) suggest that female offenders are more deviant (atypical) than their male counterparts due to their inherently diminished capabilities for aggression. They also support a theory which advocates premenstrual syndrome as a cause for crime despite meager evidence. In addition, they note that female offenders "have higher Paranoia scores than male offenders, expressing a more intense feeling of being misunderstood and of being different," and conclude "that female offenders often have even stronger psychotic tendencies than male offenders" (p. 116–117).

Wilson and Hernstein also demonstrate that psychological theories of criminality have relied upon biological determinism. These perspectives make stereotypical assumptions about the psychological nature of men and women, and attribute gender differences to biological factors. In other words, they fail to acknowledge that men and women act different because they are socialized to behave differently. This critical shortcoming is evident in many criminological theories on female criminality including work by W.I. Thomas (1967), the Gluecks (1934), Healy (1926), Konopka (1966), and Pollak (1950).[6] Furthermore, these theories also assume that crime is masculine behavior; they assign gender to a social problem without an adequate theoretical explanation of gender and gender roles.

Equating Crime with Masculinity

Criminologists also have avoided the gender ratio and generalizability problem by focusing on the masculine nature of criminality. Since men commit more crime, theorists have assumed that crime is masculine behavior. Therefore, they argue that female criminals are more masculine than "normal" women. While male criminals also (usually) are labeled as deviants, these theories assume that this form of deviance is as least more "normal" for men than women. When women commit crime, they are viewed as "double deviants." They are deviant because they are criminals, but they are also labeled gender deviants because they are presumed to be more masculine than normal women because criminality is viewed as a masculine activity.

One might expect that sociological theories would challenge this fundamental assumption because sociological theories moved beyond individual or biological explanations for male criminality. However, sociological theories also ignored female criminality (Daly & Chesney-Lind, 1988; Klein, 1973; Leonard, 1982; Smart, 1977) and failed to address the gender ratio or the generalizability problem. Furthermore, while biological and psychological theorists were more explicit in asserting that women committed crime because they were "too masculine," sociological theories endorsed a similar perspective. This approach is evident in sociological theories which linked female criminality to women's liberation.

Women's Liberation Theories

In the 1970s, Freda Adler (1975) and Rita Simon (1975) received a great deal of notoriety for their theories which linked the women's movement to female criminality. Both theorists predicted that increased equality for women would result in greater criminal participation. Adler argued that women would become more like men—more aggressive and violent—as they became liberated. Crime was a new career opportunity. Simon argued that women had been confined to the home where there was little opportunity to commit crime. As women moved into positions of financial responsibility, and attained greater equality with men, Simon asserted that they would have more opportunity to commit crime. Simon, unlike Adler, however did not predict that women would become more violent.

Both these theories have generated a great deal of debate and both have weaknesses. It is erroneous to assume that women have had equal access to criminal subcultures or that they have been successful in gaining equal acceptance in illegitimate markets. For example, autobiographical accounts of professional and street criminals suggest that traditional sex role attitudes are more pervasive within criminal subcultures (Smart, 1979). There also was no evidence to suggest that lower class women were seeking career opportunities in crime. In fact, such an assumption suggests that as women enter the "masculine" world, they must emulate male values, goals, and behavior in both legitimate and illegitimate avenues. Furthermore, the authors were criticized on empirical grounds. Several researchers (Mukerjee & Fitzgerald, 1981; Smart, 1977; Steffensmeier, 1978, 1979) have shown that there have been many temporary fluctuations in female crime rates during this century and that increases in crime during the 1970s were related to property crime. As such, women apparently did not become more violent ("more masculine") as they became more liberated.

In spite of the many criticisms the women's liberation thesis incurred, Simon and Adler's arguments led to an examination of new theoretical approaches to female criminality. Most importantly, they examined gender within a sociological context; however, by asserting that women would commit more crime as they became more "masculine" they reinforced traditional approaches to the study of female criminality (Daly & Chesney-Lind, 1988). It also is interesting that Adler and Simon examined female criminality because they believed it was rising. "It is indeed astounding to find Lombroso in the 1890s, W.I. Thomas in the 1920s, Pollak in the 1950s and Adler in the 1970s all discussing a **new** social problem, namely the increase in female crime" (Smart, 1977, p. 109). It appears that female criminality is most important when female crime rates go up (or when there is the perception that they are rising).

Summary on Gender and Theoretical Development

Traditional criminological theories are deficient because they cannot address either the generalizability or the gender-ratio problem. These theories ignore women or mistakenly rely upon stereotypical, biological explanations of gender. They assume that crime is masculine behavior. Feminist scholars have been critical of theoretical development in criminology and argue that new theories should attend to the power of gender stratification in our society. They argue that gender socialization is central to our understanding of crime. As Gelsthorpe and Morris (1990) note: "Despite the fact that its primary subject matter is male offenders, [criminology] focuses hardly at all on *men* and *masculinity*. It deals with men without acknowledging this and hence creates theories about criminals without a conceptualization of gender. For feminists this is a key concept" (p. 3).

Feminist scholars try to transform criminological theory by attending to the ways in which our social structure makes gender a central organizing feature of daily life for both men and women. Feminist scholarship poses a more complex examination of gender and extends way beyond asking how women fit into a particular theory. It "raises questions about how gender organizes the discipline of criminology, the social institutions that fall within its scope, and the behavior of men and women" (Daly & Chesney-Lind, 1988, p. 527).

GENDER AND VICTIMIZATION

Prior to the 1970s, very little criminological literature examined how gender influenced victimization. Furthermore, the field ignored those crimes which women most frequently experience: rape, woman battering, child sexual assault, and sexual harassment. There has been a tremendous increase in research on women and victimization; however, most of the field has remained insulated from this proliferation of knowledge. For example, of those crimes most experienced by women, rape is one most frequently covered in current criminology and criminal justice texts. Even so, only about 1 to 3% of the total pages in textbooks are devoted to rape (averaging 6–8 pages per book; Wonders & Caulfield, 1993; Wright, 1992). None of these texts discuss battering, sexual harassment, or child sexual assault in any significant way.

This chapter examines women's victimization with respect to rape since this is the area most apt to be discussed in textbooks. It uses the topic of rape to demonstrate how women's victimization is made invisible. It argues that official estimates of rape have been constructed in such a way as to minimize women's victimization. It provides alternative data and discusses feminist challenges to interpretations of the data.

There are three general sources of data which allow us to estimate the extent of rape in this country: 1) the Uniform Crime Report (UCR), 2) older, longitudinal data from the old National Crime Survey (NCS),[7] and 3) other independent research studies. A fourth source of data will be available for analysis soon. This data comes from the newly re-designed NCS—now called the National Crime Victimization Survey (NCVS).

UCR Data

The Uniform Crime Report (UCR) was established in 1930. It records official crime statistics and has several shortcomings. Most importantly, it only tabulates crimes known to the police; therefore, it tends to underestimate crime in general and rape in particular because many victims fail to report rape to the police. UCR data for 1991 show that 42.3 of every 100,000 people are victims of attempted or completed rape; however, that figure rises to 83 when the rape rate is reported as per 100,000 *women* (Federal Bureau of Investigation, 1992, p. 23 and 24). It also is interesting to note that the UCR data is presented in such a way as to maximize the textual coverage of the lower rate. This figure is highlighted and presented in a box with only a couple of lines of text on one page. In contrast, one must read through the text to find the rate calculated for women's risk of victimization. And while it is important to recognize and study male victims of rape, this type of presentation further minimizes the risk of rape that women face.

NCS Data

Just how much crime goes unreported to the police, however, remains unknown. As a result, researchers have relied upon victimization surveys like the NCS. The NCS was established in 1972. It gathers data from 60,000 households nationwide which amounts to about 132,000 respondents age 12 or older. Current NCS data for 1991 show that 1.4 of every 1000 women (or 140 per 100,000 women) are victims of attempted or completed rape (BJS, 1992, p. 5). And while it is difficult for methodological reasons to make direct comparisons, estimates based on NCS data show that rape is about twice as common as estimates derived from the UCR. It has been common to assume that the NCS rate is more reliable because a high percentage (between 40 and 45%; BJS, 1992, p. 102) of rape victims in the NCS state that they did not report their victimization to the police. Thus, researchers who were interested in a variety of research questions on rape began to publish findings based on the NCS data (Eigenberg, 1990). However, these publications fail to note a critical problem in the rape data; NCS respondents were never directly asked whether or not they had been victims of attempted or completed rape (Eigenberg, 1990; Koss, 1992).

The NCS used 13 initial screening items to determine whether or not respondents had been victimized (Bureau of Justice Statistics [BJS] 1989a, p.

100). They asked respondents whether someone had tried to take something from them, rob them, beat them up, attack them with a weapon, or steal things from them. *None of these questions asked whether someone had raped or tried to rape them.* The question that was supposed to elicit rape asked: "Did anyone TRY to attack you in some other way? (other than any incidents already mentioned)" (BJS, 1989a, p. 100). Thus, respondents were expected to make the connection between a vague reference to attacks and report rapes to interviewers. Respondents were unaware that additional screening questions would fail to target rape and they may have skipped this question and waited for a question on rape. Or, respondents may also have inferred that they were not supposed to talk about rape or that the researcher was not interested in that type of crime since it was not mentioned directly.

It appears that the NCS excluded a specific rape question because of the topic was deemed too sensitive (Eigenberg, 1990). "More explicit wording was rejected as not appropriate for a Federal agency to use and likely to be offensive to respondents" (Dodge & Turner, 1981, p. 3). Given the "sensitive nature" of the issue, one could argue that responding yes to a question such as "Have you been raped in the past six months?" is less stressful for victims than asking them to volunteer that information in response to a vague question. Regardless, the poor operationalization of rape makes the NCS data tainted and the representativeness of the sample is questionable. Given these concerns, it is difficult to assess the reliability of the NCS rape data; however, there is evidence that the NCS rape rate underestimates the amount of rape in this country.

In fact, an early pre-test of the NCS (conducted in 1971) first pointed to this problem (Turner, 1981). A sample of known victims was selected from police files and respondents were interviewed to determine the validity of the NCS instrument. Only about two-thirds of the rape victims who had their rapes reported to the police subsequently revealed their victimization to interviewers.

Other studies on rape also suggest that the NCS underestimates the amount of rape, but the majority of these studies have relied upon convenience samples (most of which have been drawn from populations of college students; see Eigenberg, 1990). However, a few other studies have used random samples and have computed statistics which can be compared to the NCS.[8] All of these studies explicitly asked respondents about rape.

Other Research Studies which Estimate Rape

Russell (1984) used a random probability sample of women in San Francisco. Data were gathered in 1978 from 930 women. Forty one percent of her sample reported that they had experienced at least one completed or attempted rape.[9] Half of these women had been raped more than once. These figures, however, reflect prevalence rates not incident rates. Prevalence rates establish the percentage of women who have been raped sometime in their lives. Incident rates, like those figures from the NCS, establish victimization over a discrete time frame. Russell was able to calculate incident rates for her sample. She claims that her rape rate is 13 times higher than the UCR and 7 times higher than the NCS reports for San Francisco for the same year (p. 47).

Koss and her associates (Koss, Dinero, Seibel & Cox, 1988; Koss, Gidycz & Wisniewski, 1987) surveyed 3187 female college students nationwide. They used a stratified sample to select universities and then randomly selected classes. All students in the classes were then surveyed.[10] The Koss study found that 27.5% of the women reported that they experienced rape or attempted rape. Furthermore, Koss reports that the incidence rate in her study is 10 to 15 times greater than that of the NCS.[11]

Moriarty and her associates also examined this issue (1994). Over 6,152 female residents of North Carolina were either interviewed over the phone or completed a survey by mail. Their data suggest that rape in North Carolina is seven times that which is reported in the UCR and 15 times that reported by the NCS.

Other data on the relationship between the rapist and victim also question the validity of the NCS rape data. The NCS reports that the majority of the rapes revealed to interviewers are committed by strangers, while these other studies suggest that the majority of rapes are committed by acquaintances. They also suggest that victims are more apt to define the experience as rape and to report it to the police when they are victimized by strangers.

The existing evidence, then, suggests that there are serious questions about the validity of the NCS rape data. It appears that the NCS underestimates the amount of rape and that this problem is more pronounced in cases of acquaintance rape. However, current changes in the NCS may help address some of the prior shortcomings.

NCVS

The NCS has a new design and a new name: the NCVS. The redesign is the result of an extensive planning project which began in the late 1970s. Input was solicited from universities, private research firms, governmental agencies, and private consultants. Some changes were introduced in 1986, but most changes, including those affecting rape, were phased in gradually beginning in January, 1989. By July of 1993, the entire sample received the new questions and data are expected to be available in Fall of 1994.

The NCVS has added a specific screening question on rape.[12] The question begins by advising respondents that unwanted sexual acts are often hard to talk about. It then asks respondents whether they have been forced or coerced to participate in unwanted sexual acts by: someone they did not know, an acquaintance, or someone they knew well. Interviewers are also given an explicit definition of rape that can be read to respondents.

Ultimately, the NCVS will most likely provide the best evidence to confirm that the NCS has underrepresented rape. After some time, researchers will be able to examine the data and determine its strengths and weaknesses. Hopefully, the NCVS will be vastly improved and allow researchers to revisit a host of empirical questions. Because of the unknown amount of error in the NCS we cannot have much confidence in the rape data. Perhaps, in 1994, we may have, *for the first time,* a national data set which will begin to provide us with information about the prevalence of rape in this country.

It is critical that we establish an accurate estimate of rape. The NCS reports much more rape than does the UCR, but their estimates are still relatively low. Low estimates of rape reinforce the myth that rape is a rare occurrence and data which points to the risk posed by strangers reinforces traditional stereotypes about what type of men victimize women. Improvements in the NCVS are an important step forward. However, we cannot ignore the harm that has been done over the past twenty years. Despite major social efforts to de-stigmatize rape, our society continues to refuse to talk about rape or, in the case of the NCS, to even utter the very word. As Schechter notes, the shame "has been bred into our bones" (1982, p. 36).

The field of criminology has not acknowledged the problems with the NCS design and its poor operationalization of rape. There is a tremendous amount of literature which discusses the deficiencies of the NCS, but most of it fails to discuss the problems with the rape question (see Eigenberg, 1990). Other researchers use the NCS data on rape to examine specific research questions but never specifically mention this particular operational deficiency or discuss its possible impact upon their findings (see Eigenberg, 1990). Textbooks have failed to incorporate this critical deficiency into their literature reviews.

As a result, it is important that the weaknesses associated with the NCS design are made more widely known as studies using the data from the original survey will be published for quite some time and because comparisons between data from the NCS and the NCVS are inevitable. Thus, it is imperative that information about the screening questions be incorporated into the basic knowledge base of the discipline.

Summary of Gender and Victimization

Even though feminist criminology has made its most significant impact upon the area of victimization, this material is still largely disregarded by mainstream criminology. This section has used the subject of rape to demonstrate why feminists challenge the value neutrality of science. It is not accident that our science minimizes and obscures women's victimization. A society based on gender oppression has little vested interest in producing data which accurately reflect the nature and extent of men's violence against women. And while women are taught to fear strangers in the bushes, it is those we know and love who most often victimize us. A society built on gender oppression encourages this type of gender domination, but it functions more effectively if this type of victimization is invisible. Therefore, it is unlikely that a patriarchal social structure will encourage documentation of this type of victimization.

GENDER AND THE CRIMINAL JUSTICE SYSTEM

The criminal justice system is composed of a variety of smaller parts, each of which have considerable impact upon an offender who is being processed by the system. Decisions to arrest, prosecute, grant bail, reduce charges, convict, sentence and incarcerate an individual are affected by a variety of variables. Before the 1970s, very little literature examined whether there were gender differences in these various decision making phases as women were excluded from the research. More recently, several studies have examined these issues, although most of these studies are atheoretical and descriptive. In other words, most of this literature does not examine gender and gender socialization in any complex theoretical fashion. Instead, it describes gender differences in the outcomes of decisions at various points throughout the system to determine whether men and women are treated equally.

However, feminist scholarship has made at least one important epistemological challenge in this area. The traditional criminological literature has argued that women receive preferential or chivalrous treatment by the criminal justice system because of their gender. Pollak first made this argument in the 1960s and it was widely accepted in the discipline despite meager (or no) empirical support (Chesney-Lind, 1986). Feminist scholarship has challenged the *chivalry hypothesis* and points to evidence which suggests that women are treated more poorly by the system.

This section of the chapter describes gender differences in the criminal justice system response to female offenders in terms of each subsystem: the police, courts, and corrections. It also reviews literature which examines whether women are treated the same as men to determine whether there is evidence to support the chivalry hypothesis.

Police Response

While the majority of gender disparity research has centered on the judicial process, some studies have examined whether police officers treat men and women differently when making decisions about arrests. Hindelang (1979) examined data from the NCS from 1972 to 1976 and compared data to arrest data to find out whether police officers appeared to treat women more leniently. His research found that women were overrepresented in arrest data for aggravated assault and robbery which suggested that women received harsher treatment for at least two types of criminal behavior. Similarly, Moyer (1982) found that police officers rejected chivalrous attitudes. However, Visher (1983) observed police-citizen interactions and reported that women who fit the stereotypical ideal of womanhood (white, older, and passive) received chivalrous, or preferential, treatment.

Other literature suggests that the chivalry hypothesis may be more relevant for some women than others: that arresting officers extend preferential treatment only to particular women (Bernstein, Nagel, Kick, Leung, & Schultz, 1977; Chesney-Lind, 1986; DeFleur, 1975; Johnson, Pettisen, & Wallis, 1977). White, middle class women, who commit property offenses are much more likely to benefit from paternalistic attitudes; however, women who violate traditional sex-role behavior expectations are treated harshly.

Chesney-Lind (1989, 1986, 1973) was one of the earliest feminist scholars to challenge the chivalry hypothesis with respect to juvenile delinquency. She reports that girls are much more likely to be arrested for status offenses such as running away. In particular, girls are more apt to be found incorrigible or in need of supervision. However, these girls frequently are arrested and convicted for being sexually promiscuous or for running away even when these girls are being sexually assaulted in the home. She argues that girls' crimes are *sexualized* and that young girls are treated much more harshly than boys when they violate the sexual norms of our culture. In contrast to the chivalry hypothesis, this research asserts that, girls are treated more harshly for minor offenses.

Some textbooks also imply that female crime rate is rising faster than the male crime rate due to a decline in chivalry. Immarigeon and Chesney-Lind (1993) suggest that the female crime rate is increasing due to changes in law enforcement, judicial decision making, and drug legislation. These changes could represent a decline in chivalry. In addition, some authors assert that women are being arrested more frequently because of changes in our social structure and views about gender. In other words, because women have become more liberated and challenged stereotypical definitions of gender, they may get more equal treatment from a criminal justice system which fails to offer them the chivalrous treatment experienced in earlier times. However, it is impossible to determine whether this hypothesis is correct because researchers do not agree on the significance of the rise in arrests for women.

At different times it appears that the female crime rate is rising faster than the male crime rate, although the data must be evaluated cautiously. It is popular to discuss the crime rate as a percentage increase by gender. For example, from 1990 to 1991 the female crime rate increased .4% compared to the 1.9% decrease in male crime rates (FBI, 1992). These figures are misleading because of gross differences in sample sizes. In other words, because women commit so much less crime to begin with, any increase in the number of crimes will exaggerate the rise in female criminality when it is presented in this manner. More accurate portrayals of criminality result when comparisons focus on the rate of criminality per 100,000 people.

Clearly there has been a rise in the number of women arrested in the last decade. Between 1982 and 1991, there has been a 35.9% increase in arrests for women (FBI, 1992). However, experts do not agree about the significance of these increases (see Moyer, 1993). First, it is difficult to determine if crime is rising when it is examined over a short time, especially given the small magnitude of the increases (statistically speaking). Thus, it is possible that what appears to be a 10-year rise in female criminality may just be a small statistical fluctuation that will disappear shortly. In other words, the rise may be random as the figures will never stay the same due to changes in demographics and other related variables. Therefore, for the time being, it appears premature to link rises in crime rates with the death of chivalry, although a more complex theoretical examination of this relationship would help us understand these issues better.

Response by the Courts

Researchers also have examined gender disparity in the courts. Bernstein et. al. (1977), for example, found that men fared better at the plea negotiation stage than did women and concluded that women who violated gender norms were treated more harshly in the charge bargaining stage.

Most of the research on gender disparity in the courts has concentrated on sentencing outcomes to determine whether chivalry results in more lenient sentences for women. The findings from these studies are mixed. Early studies found that women were treated considerably more leniently by the courts than were men. Baab and Ferguson (1967) analyzed data collected from twenty-seven Texas courts and found that women were more likely to receive suspended sentences and less apt to be sentenced to incarceration than were men. Similarly, other research has discovered that marital status plays an important role for women in the sentencing process. Nagel and her colleagues (1983) found that married women received preferential treatment, while marital status had less impact for men. Daly (1989) takes this research a step further and argues that gender differences can be explained by the defendant's familial relationships. She contends that judges are reluctant to sentence parents to prison because of the impact upon the children and that this pattern is strongest for African-American defendants of both gender. Crew (1991) found that men and women were treated similarly in sentencing, however, women who occupied traditional female roles were beneficiaries of greater leniency than women who did not.

Nagel and Weitzman (1971) reported that women were more apt to be released on bail before trial, have their cases dismissed, and be the recipient of probated or suspended sentences than were men. Kruttschnitt (1984) found that women were more likely to remain free than men prior to and after adjudication, although gender differences were not reported in the amount of bail when bail was allowed. Daly (1989) found that women with dependent children were treated more leniently by the sentencing judge than men with dependent children. Frazier, Bock, and Henretta (1983) found that women were treated more favorably by probation officers in their pre-sentence reports and were more often recommended for non-incarcerative punishment than were men.

In contrast, other research contends that gender differences disappear when other factors are considered (Hagan, 1974; Uhlman and Walker, 1979; Steffensmeier, Kramer, & Streifel, 1993; Steury and Frank, 1990). Parisi has reviewed these studies and points out that many of the studies that support the chivalry hypothesis are critically flawed because they fail to control for seriousness of offense. In other words, it appears that women receive more lenient treatment because they commit less serious offenses.

Thus, while the results are mixed, it appears most women do not benefit from chivalrous treatment from the courts. There also is evidence to suggest that this statement is equally true for corrections.

Correctional Response

The literature on women in prison also is affected by the gender ratio problem. Once again, women have been excluded from inquiry and the subject was ignored by criminologists who argued that there were too few women in prison to warrant meaningful examination.

Women and girls clearly represent a small proportion of the individuals under correctional supervision. Women represent only about 5% of prisoners in state and federal institutions (BJS, 1989b), and 9% of jail inmates (BJS, 1990b, p. 2). They are approximately 13% of those being supervised on electronic monitoring (National Institute of Justice, 1989, pp. 1–4) and 16% of those on probation (Rogers, 1992, p. 132). And while, there are relatively few women in prison, rises in incarceration rates, like arrest rates, have been used to argue that women are receiving less chivalrous treatment due to social attitudes about gender.

There is no question that there has been an absolute increase in the number of women incarcerated in the past decade. This increase in prison population is related to an increase in the arrest rates in the past ten years (as discussed earlier). In addition, a greater proportion of women who are arrested are being sent to prison. In 1981, 12 of every 100,000 women were incarcerated and that figure has risen to 34 in 1991 (BJS cited in Maguire, Pastore, & Flanagan, 1993, p. 608). However, like arrest rates, there has been relatively small increases in incarceration rates for women but reporting the data in this manner exaggerates the effect. Here again, it is possible that the death of chivalry is producing higher incarceration rates. Yet it appears premature to make this type of conclusion for the same reasons discussed previously with respect to the arrest data. Experts do not agree on the nature or the significance of the increase.

Nevertheless, criminologists have made it seem normal to focus on men and their involvement in the correctional system and to ignore women because there were so few of them. It also is interesting to note that while corrections involves numerous levels of supervision ranging from probation to incarceration, most of the research has concentrated on women in prison. This topic deserves serious attention, but it is ironic that the research concentrates on women's incarceration when most women (like men) who are subject to some form of correctional supervision are placed on probation. Thus, when women are studied in relation to corrections, they are examined in their most rare form: as incarcerated felons. Although less women than men are incarcerated, few studies have examined disparity in time served in prison. One Alabama study found that after controlling for offense, women paroled in 1970 served less time relative to men (Moseley and Gerould, 1975). However, a Texas study revealed that women served slightly more time than males when the effects of prison overcrowding policies are taken into consideration (Mullings, 1994). These mixed findings suggest a need for further research in this area.

The literature on women in prisons suggests that they have not benefited from chivalrous treatment. In contrast, scholars have pointed to the ways in which women inmates generally are treated more poorly than male inmates. This trend also has been evident throughout time.

In the 1800s, there were no women's prisons and women were housed in local jails or special sections of male prisons where male guards stood watch over them. These women were often mistreated; they were neglected, physically assaulted, and raped (Rafter, 1985). In the mid 1800s, reformers began to insist for separate women's prisons for white women, although African-American women continued to be housed in male facilities where they were abused. As time passed, this situation changed and it is rare to find women housed in men's prisons in the United States today. However, much evidence suggests that the conditions in women's prisons are still inferior to men's prisons.

For example, because female prison populations are small and because there are fewer correctional facilities, women are more likely to be incarcerated in institutions which are far from their communities (Simon, 1975; Moyer, 1993). Most states operate only one adult female prison facility and they usually are located in isolated rural areas, while the residents generally come from urban locales. This problem is exaggerated when one considers that most women in prison are mothers who have sole support of their children (Baunach, 1985; Chapman, 1980; Moyer, 1984), which means that it is difficult for female inmates to maintain regular contact with their children through visits.

Other researchers also note that women's facilities are poorly funded. These institutions offer fewer educational and vocational programs which also tend to have poor quality when compared to programs in men's prisons (Baunach, 1985; Goetting & Howsen, 1983; Hancock, 1986; Leonard, 1982; Moyer, 1984; Rafter, 1985). In addition, these programs tend to reinforce traditional gender role stereotypes as women in prison are trained for "female" occupations in a variety of fields such as cosmetology, domestic service, food service, housekeeping, and clerical services (Moyer, 1993). Thus, programs are selected which conform to social expectations about what types of jobs women should aspire to. And like men in prison, we assume that the role of education for people in prison is to provide vocational training as a means to financial security and not other types of education such as college. However, it is ironic that the correctional system prepares women to assume low-paying jobs which have little potential for advancement when the data demonstrate that most of these women are providing the sole means of financial support for both themselves and their children. Although men in prison also suffer from inadequate programming, the jobs they are prepared for (plumbing, heating and air conditioning, auto mechanics) are much more apt to ensure a salary which will provide for themselves and/or a family.

Other literature discusses the inadequacy of health care services for women in prison. Like all prisons, medical care in women's prisons is less than perfect because it is extremely expensive; however, some literature suggests that women have less access to services which are provided by less experienced medical personnel (Moyer, 1993). Furthermore, women report that gynecological problems are common and that many pregnant women fail to get adequate prenatal care (Moyer, 1993).

Studies also have looked at the special problems that occur when society incarcerates mothers. While children also suffer when fathers are incarcerated, more women than men are sole caretakers of their children. There have been some attempts to develop policy initiatives which address this difference (Moyer, 1993). Some states have weekend visits for children and mothers. Other prisons have nurseries so that pregnant women can have time to bond with their children if they deliver the baby in prison and some prison programs address parenting skills.

It also is important to note that the current overcrowding problem exaggerates the inequitable living conditions experienced by women in prison (Chesney-Lind & Rodriguez, 1983). States and the federal government continue to incarcerate larger and larger numbers of offenders which have pushed all prison capacities to their maximum at a time when states are experiencing critical budget shortfalls. Hence, smaller amounts of money are needed to maintain an increasingly overburdened prison system and women's prisons receive less resources because of the relatively smaller numbers of female inmates and because they cause less problems when they are ignored. In other words, female inmates are less likely to riot to protest prison conditions and they are less litigious (Alpert, 1982).

Thus, the field of criminology has failed to study women under correctional supervision. There is little information on gender and its affect upon probation and parole outcomes, although at least one study on parole suggests that women do not benefit from chivalrous treatment (Erez, 1992). There also is substantial evidence that women suffer from discriminatory rather than preferential treatment in prison. While conditions for women in prison have improved, administrators must ensure that women's facilities receive adequate funding so that women do not bear more than their share of the burden as resources become scarce. Feminist scholarship also points out that the supposed advantages of chivalry have been emphasized in the discipline while the discriminatory treatment has been obscured.

For example mainstream literature which addresses women in prison describes women's facilities as less secure and emphasizes the cottage system of architecture, describing women's prisons as castles, hospitals, college campuses, and motels (see Moyer, 1993). What is omitted is that these facilities generally are old and often have deteriorated faster than male facilities due to lack of financial support for upkeep. In addition, researchers also fail to connect the cottage architecture to the relationship between severity of crime, level of violence, and need for institutional security.

Women tend to commit fewer violent crimes and pose much less of a threat to society than do men; therefore, they require less secure facilities. More recently, states have been building more women's prisons and these new facilities tend to be secure facilities, like their male counterparts. Thus, women are increasingly being subjected to more institutional control even though there is little evidence to indicate that women pose a more severe threat to society than they did a few decades ago (Hawkes, 1991).

Summary of the Literature of the Criminal Justice System Response

Most of the literature indicates that women and girls do not receive more chivalrous treatment in the correctional system at least with respect to some aspects of incarceration. There is limited support for the idea that chivalry may work to help some women in the sentencing process, but not others. And there is little evidence that women are likely to escape arrest because of chivalry.

In other words, the literature has identified two competing hypotheses: 1) females are treated paternalistically because of chivalry and receive preferential treatment by the criminal justice system; and 2) females who violate their gender norms and commit criminality are treated more harshly than men. Both hypotheses are consistent with a feminist understanding of gender socialization. Women who more closely resemble our social definition of femininity (those who are passive and who are involved in property crime) and who possess other types of cultural privilege (those who are white and middle class) are not treated the same as those who challenge definitions of femininity and masculinity by behaving in gender "inappropriate" ways.

Additional research is needed badly in this area and more attention needs to be devoted to theoretical development. As it is, intellectual traditions prevail in this area and very little attention is paid to gender differences in the response of the criminal justice system. At best, gender is treated as a variable in statistical procedures without benefit of a theoretical framework which addresses the concept of gender. At worst, gender is totally ignored as studies fail to consider this topic significant enough to study.

GENDER AND OCCUPATIONS IN THE CRIMINAL JUSTICE SYSTEM

There is a growing body of literature developing on female attorneys, although most of it is being generated and discussed within legal circles and little of it is included in the mainstream criminological literature. There also is some literature developing on women as scholars in criminology. However, we know very little about women in a vast number of positions, including the entire field of probation and parole. We also know virtually nothing about women who hold supervisory and administrative jobs in all occupations in the criminal justice system. The one area where texts have concentrated reflects the biases in the field. Most occupational literature has examined female police and correctional officers. These areas appear to be of great interest because they are the most non-traditional fields for women.

Women in Non-Traditional Occupations

There is a growing body of literature which examines gender roles and the gender socialization process and its effects upon occupational experiences. Many of these studies focus on women in "non-traditional" occupations: those jobs which historically have been dominated by men.

This literature contends that society establishes rigid gender roles and that individuals are socialized to behave consistently with these roles both in and out of the workplace. Thus, gender segregation in the work place occurs because men and women select (or are pushed into) certain jobs which are consistent with stereotypical definitions of masculinity and femininity.

For example, women are socialized to be caretakers in our culture; they are supposed to be nurturing, supportive, and warm. These gender role stereotypes then are used to explain the high proportion of women in a variety of low paying service jobs such as social work; elementary and secondary education; and nursing.[13] In contrast, men are socialized to be the providers; they are to be powerful and in control. They are strong, and brave, and fearless which makes them particularly well suited for such "tough" and "exciting" jobs in fields like policing and corrections.

Thus, people act consistent with their gender roles as defined by the larger social structure, but gender roles also affect definitions of appropriate employment for men and women. In other words, some jobs have been defined as "women's work" and others as "men's work" according to the tasks which are thought to define them and comprise a majority of the work (Berg & Budnick, 1986; Broverman, 1972; Kanter, 1977; Reskin & Roos, 1990). Furthermore, women experience role conflict when they enter non-traditional occupations. They are supposed to act consistent with their gender role and at the same time they are supposed to meet the expectations associated with the job which requires masculine traits.

Reskin and Roos (1990) argue that women are tolerated in masculine occupations as long as some form of sex differentiation is maintained. The following sections demonstrate that both female police and correctional officers were ignored in the literature until they began to enter more traditional (masculine) aspects of the occupation. Once women began to perform police patrol functions and started to work as correctional officers in adult, male facilities, researchers began to take notice and study these groups of employees. Furthermore, these studies suggest that women are competent in these occupations, but that male officers in both fields believe that female officers are ineffective because of physical limitations.

Policing as a Masculine Occupation

In 1893, Los Angeles and Chicago both appointed the first female police officers (Koenig, 1978). Duties for women included supervising and enforcing laws concerning dance halls, skating rinks, and theaters. They also monitored billboard displays, located missing persons, and maintained a general information bureau for women seeking advice (Higgins, 1951). Thus, early female police officers were limited to social work functions. They worked mainly with juveniles and female offenders which theoretically allowed women to exercise their nurturing and caretaking abilities (Berg and Budnick, 1986). In other words, women were restricted to tasks which are consistent with a feminine gender role, while they were restricted from participating in real (male) police work such as walking a beat. Women continued to be encouraged to work in policing as long as they performed gender appropriate tasks. In fact, they were recruited because of their gender. For example, in 1933, female police officers were required to have experience in social work, a pleasant personality, and a positive attitude in dealing with the problems of young women. They were expected to be tolerant, sympathetic and emotionally stable (Hutzel, 1933). Twenty years later, in 1953, a police woman was to be well-adjusted, dignified, tactful and sympathetic. She was supposed to have a neat personal appearance, and to be more interested in others than herself (Tenney, 1953).

Women began to work on patrol after Title VII of the Civil Rights Act of 1964 was amended in 1972 to include public employees. Thus it no longer was legal to prevent women from performing these jobs. However, once women entered the male realm of patrol, female officers were advised to gain respect from their peers while simultaneously maintaining their femininity (Koenig, 1978). In other words, women were to manage two competing roles.

Martin (1980) describes the role conflict that occurs when women enter fields that assume that masculinity is required for adequate job performance. Martin argues that female officers adapt in two general ways. Some female officers, *police*women stress achievement and conformity to rules. They strictly adhere to the requirements of the occupational role. These women attempt to identify with policemen by being aggressive, "street-smart", and sometimes even macho. Other female officers, police*women,* emphasize conformity to gender role norms and appropriate "feminine behavior." These women focus on service activities, seeking assignments which have been typically given to women. They are not very aggressive and rarely seek out criminal activity. Martin suggests that most female police officers make a series of compromises and fall between the extreme of either role. However, the conceptual scheme helps explain the problems female police officers face when they assume an occupational role that conflicts with their gender role.

It is interesting that the earliest studies of women in policing began by studying women's competency. As long as female police officers were doing what was considered gender appropriate, criminological studies did not focus on their abilities and their competency was not questioned. However, when women entered patrol work, their performance was questioned because their gender role was no longer consistent with the definition of policing as a masculine occupation.

When women began to enter patrol work in the 1970s, most of the research on women in policing was initiated. These studies examined whether women were capable of performing the job (Ayoob 1978; Bartlett and Rosenblum, 1977; Bloch and Anderson, 1974; California Highway Patrol, 1976; Hickman, 1983; Rutland, 1978; Sherman, 1975). These studies have compared male and female police officers and evaluated their performance on a variety of criteria and conclude that female police officers are as competent as male police officers.

A great deal of research suggests that many gender differences may be beneficial (Balkin, 1988; Bartol, Bergen, Volckens, & Knoras, 1992; Bell, 1982; Christopher et. al., 1991; Hale & Wyland, 1993; Johnson, 1991; Morash & Greene, 1986; Sherman, 1975; Weisheit & Mahan, 1988; Wexler, 1985). In essence, this literature suggests that female police officers act consistent with their gender role and emphasize service functions. It also indicates that women use different problem solving skills to resolve conflict and that they rely more upon interpersonal communication skills to achieve resolution. As a result, women are less prone to use police brutality.

In other words, some literature suggests that women do the job differently and some of these differences are beneficial. The research indicates that women do the job as well as or better than men. However, the research also suggests that male police officers continue to *believe* that female officers are ineffective and incompetent (Balkin, 1988; Bartol et. al., 1992; Flynn, 1982; Koenig, 1978; LaBeff & Williams, 1982; Lord, 1986; Martin, 1990, 1980; McGeorge & Wolfe, 1976; Price & Gavin, 1982; Scarborough & Eigenberg, 1993; Remmington, 1983; Wexler & Logan, 1983).

Many of these studies demonstrate that male police officers focus on women's physical strength and assert that female police officers jeopardize the safety of others. Block, Anderson, and Gervais (1973), for example, report that male officers feel that they can handle violent situations better than females and that male officers prefer not to work with female officers. Balkin (1988) reports that police officers have negative attitudes toward female police officers and that these attitudes reflect concerns about female officers lack of physical strength. Martin (1980) indicates that most male police officers emphasize the law enforcement aspect of the work and oppose women in policing because they believe that female officers are physically weak, unreliable, and passive. Further studies (Hindman, 1975; Linden, 1983; Vega & Silverman, 1982) find that some male police officers believe that female police officers are not aggressive enough for police work. These attitudes about physical strength also appear to relate to attitudes about safety.

It is often assumed or implied that female police officers compromise the safety of others because of their relative lack of physical strength (see Charles & Parsons, 1978; Koenig, 1978). the logic of this argument is as follows: Policing is supposedly a violent occupation, and because of the potential for danger, officers need to be physically large and strong to handle physical confrontations. Women, for the most part, are not as strong as men; therefore, they are unable to control and manage violent situations which threaten the safety of citizens, offenders, fellow officers, and female officers themselves. However, there are several problems with this argument.

First, the overwhelming majority of police work consists of calls for service (90%), which are non-criminal in nature (Talney, 1969). Second, the literature suggests that women perform the job differently (Bloch & Anderson, 1974; Davis, 1984; Homant & Kennedy, 1985; Martin, 1980; Sherman, 1975), but that they do not compromise the safety of others.

It appears, however, that it is important that male police officers maintain negative attitudes toward female police officers in order to maintain gender differentiation. Because if women perform the job adequately, perhaps even superior to males in some respects, the entire system of male domination is jeopardized. Not only would men loose the advantages they have in policing, but undermining the power of gender roles also would serve to diminish gender stratification in the larger social structure.

The same domain assumptions discussed in the policing literature also are present in the correctional literature. Here again, women were tolerated as long as they performed roles that were consistent with their gender roles. When they began to work as correctional officers in male facilities, however, women also challenged traditional stereotypes about the masculine nature of the job. As a result, the research focused on their competency and argued that women's lack of physical strength compromises the safety of other officers and inmates.

Corrections as a Masculine Occupation

Historically, women were housed in men's facilities and were guarded by men. And while there were a few female matrons in the early 1800s, there were few opportunities for women to work in corrections prior to the establishment of women's prisons in the late 1800s and early 1900s (Morton, 1991; Rafter, 1985; Zupan, 1992). When women were employed, they were restricted to working with other women and juvenile offenders. However, there was resistance by male administrators because they believed that "women were not suited for controlling criminals of any kind" (Weisheit & Mahan, 1988, p. 155).

Like police officers, women began to work as guards in male facilities after Title VII was amended in 1972 to include public employees. Thus, female correctional officers began to work in male facilities because male administrators could no longer legally exclude them from working in most male facilities (Morton, 1991).

It is interesting to note that women were ignored in the correctional literature until they began to work in male prisons. In contrast to policing, however, very little research has empirically examined whether female correctional officers perform the job effectively. One comprehensive study (Holeman & Krepps-Hess, 1979) found no gender differences using a variety of performance criteria (e.g.: evaluations, reprimands, or use of sick leave) and another study reported that men and women were equally likely to write incident reports for inmate misconduct (Simon & Simon, 1993). There also is a growing body of literature which examines gender differences in a variety of work related attitudes (Zupan, 1992). Most of this research finds that women are similar to men in most of these attitudes (see Philliber, 1987). In addition, a great deal of literature examines male correctional officers reactions to female officers.

Like female police officers, female correctional officers face opposition from their male co-workers who *believe* that female officers are incompetent (Bowersox, 1981; Crouch, 1985; Holeman & Krepps-Hess, 1979; Petersen, 1982; Pollack-Byrne, 1990; Simpson & White, 1985; Townsend, 1992; Zimmer, 1986, 1987). Many male officers oppose female officers because they think women lack the physical strength to perform the job adequately thereby threatening their own safety, as well as that of other officers and inmates (Jurik, 1985; Parisi, 1984).

For example, male officers believe that female officers may be reluctant to participate in confrontations where physical violence is present. However, some research indicates that female officers are not allowed to participate in physical altercations because supervisors assign women to posts where they have limited contact with inmates based on their beliefs about the physical limitations of female officers. Some research suggests that female officers internalize these attitudes and report that they have little confidence in their ability to handle physical confrontations (Kissel & Katsampes, 1980); although, women may feel less confident because they lack experience due to their limited exposure. In other words, their confidence might increase with more experience. Other research (Bowersox, 1981) finds that women believe that they can defend themselves and they resent the protectionist attitudes displayed by male officers. Furthermore, some research reports that women are less apt than men to be assaulted by inmates and that the number of assaults on male officers does not increase when women are employed as female officers (Shawver & Dickover, 1986). Thus, male officers' fears about the competency of female officers appears unwarranted.

In addition, research indicates that male officers believe that women's sexuality compromises the security of the institution (Crouch, 1985; Jurik, 1985; Owen, 1985; Petersen, 1982; Pollack-Byrne, 1990; Potter, 1980; Zimmer, 1986, 1987). Male officers believe that female officers will compromise institutional security by having sex with inmates. Or, female officers may be reluctant to go places where men are nude or perform duties that require physical contact (pat searches) which could compromise security. Male officers also argue that women increase the sexual frustration of inmates which jeopardizes the safety of the female officers themselves.

These ideas were legitimized in a Supreme Court case (Dothard v Rawlinson, 1977). The Court concluded that women, merely by their presence, could entice sexual violence, thereby compromising the security of the institution. Hence, The Court held that employers could restrict women from working in contact positions in maximum security, male facilities. Fortunately for women, this case has not severely restricted their employment opportunities as the lower federal courts have used a narrow interpretation of the case. The lower courts note that the specific Alabama prison in the Dothard case was in terrible condition and out of control; therefore, they have ruled that women may work in most male correctional facilities (Collins, 1991). The case is interesting, however, because it demonstrates that our culture is willing to believe that women cannot work in male prisons because they might be raped. This stereotype is quite ironic as there is no empirical data which suggests that female officers are raped with any frequency. In fact, most officers who are raped in prison appear to be male officers who are hostages.

It is ironic that some literature asserts that women threaten the security of the institution, because other work indicates that female officers improve the prison environment because they "normalize" the prison. This literature asserts that prisons become more normal when female officers work there because the environment is gender integrated. Furthermore, some authors indicate that female officers have a calming influence on male inmates and that they are less apt to act aggressively toward female officers (Johnson, P., 1991; Kissel & Katsampes, 1980).

Thus, like policing, the literature on female correctional officers suggests that women may do the job differently and that some of these differences are advantageous. Furthermore, the correctional literature also indicates that male officers express concerns about the effectiveness of female officers and that many of these reservations are linked to attitudes about gender roles.

Our society dictates that corrections, like policing, is a masculine occupation because we assume that it takes big, strong men to enforce order in prisons and to physically confront dangerous, male criminals. Thus, female correctional officers did not threaten the masculine definition of the occupation as long as they remained in "female" roles (working with other women or juveniles). But if women could guard male inmates, then one could no longer assume that only men could be correctional officers in male facilities.

However, unlike the policing literature, there have been few studies which have empirically examined the competency of female correctional officers. There is a need for additional research on this topic. This type of data is needed because male correctional officers and administrators continue to believe that female officers are incompetent and ineffective. Unfortunately, the research on policing suggests that "facts" may not eliminate these stereotypes and that male officers will continue to oppose gender integration in the workplace because female officers challenge the masculine (macho) definition of the job. And if masculinity is not a prerequisite for the job, then men may lose their (almost) exclusive control of yet another occupation.

Thus, female correctional officers, like female police officers face numerous obstacles from their male counterparts who fail to believe that women can do the job. Women are underrepresented in both fields and experience substantial harassment and discrimination (Jurik, 1985; Martin, 1980; Petersen, 1982; Zimmer, 1986).

Women represent about 10% of police officers nationwide (Police Foundation, 1990, p. 31; Bureau of the Census, 1991, p. 397). Women comprise 23% of all officers in jails (BJS 1990a), 28% of officers in adult facilities, and 40% of officers in juvenile institutions are women (American Correctional Association, 1991, p. xii, xiii); however, women represent only about 12.9% of the correctional officers in male facilities (Morton, 1991, p. 20). Furthermore, the data indicate that women's participation in these occupations has leveled off despite affirmative action efforts. It is possible that women's numbers are not increasing because the number of women applying for these positions has leveled off. However, it also is possible that more women are being hired but that departments fail to retain these women—that structural discrimination and sexual harassment are driving women out of the fields.

Summary of Occupations in Criminal Justice

Women have had a difficult time breaking through male resistance as both police and correctional officers. It appears that gender integration will continue to be resisted by some male police officers who, like most of society, continue to believe that these jobs belong to men. Perhaps the most recent changes in federal civil rights legislation will increase the number of sexual harassment suits which may force administrators to take sexual harassment more seriously as they face greater financial penalties today than ever before. However, it appears that basic social attitudes must change before women will be accepted in these fields.

CONCLUSION

This chapter has shown that women were excluded from criminology and criminal justice throughout the history of the discipline. Generally speaking, they were ignored. Feminist scholarship has made this exclusion visible; however, it also has made fundamental challenges to a variety of traditional assumptions. This chapter has reviewed the exclusionary practices and discussed some epistemological challenges made by feminist criminology. It has demonstrated that feminist scholarship asks different questions, from a different perspective. It has examined how the production of knowledge itself is affected by gender. It has argued that feminism has much in common with multiculturalism.

None the less, this chapter is less inclusive than it should be. We can provide the traditional explanation and argue that "space" limitations prevent a more detailed discussion. It is true that there are entire books devoted to feminist scholarship in criminology and the various sub-topics thereof; it also is true that it is becoming more difficult to maintain areas of expertise in academia as the amount of knowledge continues to grow at a tremendous pace. Although, in the final analysis we all are forced to make choices about what is considered important. For example, then, our inadequate coverage of the intersection of race and gender also is related to the fact that all three authors of this chapter are white women. And while we attempt to be attentive to other areas of exclusion, we still have much to learn.

In many respects, feminism at its best attempts to be inclusive to a variety of intersecting oppressions and has the same goals as multiculturalism. However, there is a need for theoretical work in this area. Multiculturalism is based on the foundation that we come from a variety of cultures and that we must learn to recognize and respect the diversity of these cultures. Gender is usually considered in multiculturalism, but not always. Furthermore, gender is not a culture and the presentation suffers from poor conceptual links. More attention should be given to presenting the links between a variety of oppressions and the focus on "culture" in multiculturalism may not be broad enough. A variety of perspectives in criminology have examined issues of inclusiveness. For example, critical criminologists have focused on class issues and point to structural inequalities based on economic status. Afrocentric criminology has pointed to the racial biases in criminology, especially as they apply to African-Americans. Feminist criminology attends to gender socialization and its impact upon criminology. Multiculturalism may offer us the opportunity to unite these perspectives; however, much theoretical work must be done before we can clearly assess how this new perspective will transform criminology.

Some may believe that a book such as this one, in some ways, continues to perpetuate specific biases in the traditional literature. By dividing the effects of multiculturalism into different types of exclusion based on gender, class, ethnicity, race, and sexual orientation, written by experts in various specialty areas reinforces the idea that categories of oppression are separate and distinct instead of interactive and additive. However, this type of presentation also reflects that most of us still think by dividing oppressions into separate categories. As a result, there is much work to do before we can truly begin to understand criminology without dividing it into separate "isms." And while multiculturalism attempts to attend to various types of oppression, all of us are bound by traditional ways of thinking and we must fight against the intellectual training of the discipline. It is a struggle to continue to try to redefine criminology. However, in the end, multiculturalism should provide us with interesting new ideas as criminology continues to be transformed. New voices, new experiences, and fresh approaches should produce research findings that challenge us to think in different ways.

ENDNOTES

1. The authors in the quotation are discussing feminism, although we believe the statement is equally accurate for multiculturalism.
2. We acknowledge that surveys tend to report that gender does not predict publication productivity (cites); although, the study cited in this chapter looked at the numbers of publications which actually appear in journals. Thus, it is possible that men and women who respond to surveys (and response rates tend to be low) are those who are productive—who have succeeded in this process—and report less differences in the number of publications authored.
3. It also is important that students understand that not all of this literature in this

review is, necessarily, feminist scholarship according to the definition discussed previously. Some literature was included for mere informational purposes as a way to familiarize students with the literature on women even if it is not necessarily feminist. It was included as a first step toward that broader feminist goal of changing the study of criminology itself.

4. We are not arguing, necessarily, for some type of conspiracy theory. Instead, we assert that economically, white men were working from their realities. In other words, that all knowledge is situated and that their privilege did not allow for them to conceptualize more complex understanding of gender and crime.

5. Notice that most disciplines fail to have any "mothers" in their respective fields.

6. These theories are reviewed in detail in several classic works (Klein, 1973; Smart, 1976) and we have insufficient space in this paper to devote further elaboration to these perspectives.

7. We realize that it is becoming commonplace to call the previous NCS the NCVS. While the NCVS has been re-named, we feel that is misleading to refer to the old survey by the new name. Doing so minimizes the differences in the studies and tends to add to the confusion in interpreting the data.

8. Comparisons between studies using different populations are always precarious due to problems associated with generalizability. Nonetheless, comparisons between the NCS and other sources appear warranted given the paucity of data on rape and in light of the flaws in the NCS design.

9. These figures do not include marital rapes. When including marital rape, 24% of the women reported at least one completed rape and 31% report one attempted rape. When combined, 44% of the women report at least one attempted or completed rape.

10. They also surveyed male students and examined their willingness to commit rape and other sexually aggressive acts. These data are not relevant to this paper.

11. Koss did use a broad definition of rape including 1) women who had sexual intercourse when they did not want to because they were given alcohol or drugs; 2) women who had sexual intercourse because they were threatened or had some degree of physical force used against them; or 3) women who had been forced to participate in other sexual acts against their will (i.e., oral or anal sex, or penetration with something other than a penis). This definition is consistent with newer broader definitions of rape or sexual assault (Searles & Berger, 1987).

12. It is important to note that the redesign addresses problems with rape, but that the redesign was not initiated merely to accomplish this purpose. These alterations were incorporated in a larger redesign project.

13. Despite recent increases in the salary of nurses, it is still safe to conclude that historically, women in nursing have been drastically underpaid and undervalued when compared to the status of physicians which are predominantly male.

REFERENCES

Adler, F. (1975). *Sisters in Crime.* Prospect Heights, Illinois: Waveland Press.

Alpert, G. P. (1982). Women prisoners and the law: which way will the pendulum swing? *Journal of Criminal Justice, 10,* 37–44.

American Correctional Association. (1991). *Directory of juvenile and adult correctional departments, institutions, agencies and paroling authorities.* Laurel, Maryland: American Correctional Association.

Arnold, R. (1994). Black women in prison: The price of resistance. In M. Zinn and B. Dill (Eds.) *Women of Color in U.S. Society* (pp. 171–184). Philadelphia: Temple University Press.

Ayoob, M. F. (1978). Perspectives on female troopers. *Trooper, 3,* 32–35, 99–101, 103.

Baab, G.W., and Ferguson, W.R. (1967). Texas sentencing practices: a statistical study. *Texas Law Review, 45* (February), 471–503.

Balkin, J. (1988). Why policemen don't like policewomen. *Journal of Police Science and Administration, 16* (1), 29–38.

Baro, A. and Eigenberg, H. (1993). Images of gender: A content analysis of photographs in introductory criminology and criminal justice textbooks. *Women and Criminal Justice, 5* (1), 3–36.

Bartlett, H., and Rosenblum, A. (1977). *Policewomen effectiveness.* Denver, Co.: Civil Service Commission.

Bartol, C., Bergen, G. Volckens, J. and Knoras, K. (1992). Women in smalltown policing: Job performance and stress. *Criminal Justice and Behavior, 19* (3), 240–259.

Baunach, P. J. (1985). *Mothers in Prison.* New Brunswick, NJ: Transaction Books.

Bell, D. J. (1982). Policewomen: myths and reality. *Journal of Police Science and Administration, 10,* (1), 112–120.

Berg, B. L. & Budnick, K. (1986). Defeminization of women in law enforcement: A new twist in the traditional police personality. *Journal of Police Science, 14*(4), 314–319.

Bernstein, A., Nagel, I., Kick, E., Leung, J. T., & Schultz, B. (1977). Charge reduction: an intermediary stage in the process of labeling criminal defendants. *Social Forces, 56,* (2), 362–384.

Bloch, P., & Anderson, D. (1974, May). *Policewomen on patrol final report.* Washington, D.C.: Police Foundation.

Bloch, P., Anderson, D., & Gervais, P. (1973, February). *Policewomen on patrol.* (Major findings: First Report, Volume 1). Washington, D.C.: Police Foundation.

Bowersox, M. (1981). Women in corrections: Competence, competition, and the social responsibility norm. *Criminal Justice and Behavior, 8,* 491–499.

Bowker, L. (1981). *Women and crime in America.* New York: Macmillan.

Bowker, L., Arbitell, M., & McFerron, R. (1988). On the relationship between wife beating and child abuse. In K. Yllo and M. Bograd (Eds.)., *Feminist perspectives on wife abuse.* Beverly Hills: Sage, pp. 158–174.

Broverman, I. K., et al. (1972). Sex role stereotypes: A current appraisal. *Journal of social Issues, 28,* 59–79.

Bureau of Justice Statistics. (1989a). *Criminal victimization in the United States, 1987.* Washington, D.C.: U.S. Department of Justice.

Bureau of Justice Statistics. (1989b). *Correctional populations in the United States: 1989.* Washington, D.C.: U.S. Department of Justice.

Bureau of Justice Statistics. (1990a). *Census of local jails.* Washington, D.C.: U.S. Department of Justice.

Bureau of Justice Statistics. (1990b). *Jail inmates, 1990.* Washington, D.C.: U.S. Department of Justice.

Bureau of the Census. (1991). *Statistical abstract of the United States: 1991.* Washington, D.C.: U.S. Department of Commerce.

Bureau of Justice Statistics (1992). *Criminal Victimization 1991.* Washington, D.C.: U.S. Department of Justice.

California Highway Patrol. (1976). *Women traffic officer project-final report.* Sacramento: author.

Chapman, J. (1980). *Economic realities and the female offender.* Lexington, MA: Lexington Books.

Charles, M. T. & Parsons, K. (1978). Female performance in the law enforcement function: a review of past research, current issues and future potential. *Law and Order, 26*(1), 18–74.

Chesney-Lind, M. (1973). Judicial enforcement of the female sex role: The family court and the female delinquent. *Issues in Criminology, 8*(2), 51–39.

Chesney-Lind, M. (1987). Women and crime: The female offender. *Signs, 12*(1), 78–96.

Chesney-Lind, M. (1989). Girls' Crime and Woman's Place: Toward a Feminist Model of Female Delinquency. *Crime and Delinquency, 35*(1), 5–29.

Chesney-Lind, M. & Rodriguez, N. (1983). Women under lock and key: a view from the inside. *Prison Journal, 63*(2), 47–65.

Christopher, W., Arguelles, J. S., Anderson, R., Barnes, W. R., Estrada, L. F., Kantor, M., Mosk, R. M., Odin, A. S., Slaughter, J. B., & Traquada, R. E. (1991). *Report of the Independent Commission on the Los Angeles Police Department.* Los Angeles, CA:

Collins, W. (1991). Legal issues and the employment of women. In J. Morton (Ed.). *Change, Challenge, Choices: Women's Role in Modern Corrections.* Laurel, MD: American Correctional Association. pp. 13–19.

Crew, B. K. (1991). Sex differences in criminal sentencing: chivalry or patriarchy? *Justice Quarterly, 8*(19), 59–83.

Crouch, B. (1985). Pandora's box: Women guards in men's prisons. *Journal of Criminal Justice, 13,* 535–548.

Dahl, T. & Snare, A. (1978). The coercion of privacy: A feminist perspective. In C. Smart and B. Smart (Eds.)., *Women, Sexuality and Social Control.* London: Routledge & Keagan Paul.

Daly, K. (1989). Rethinking judicial paternalism: gender, work-family relations and sentencing. *Gender and Society, 3*(1), 9–36.

Daly, K. & Chesney-Lind, M. (1988). Feminism and Criminology. *Justice Quarterly, 5*(4), 497–535.

Davis, J. A. (1984). Perspectives on policewomen in Texas and Oklahoma. *Journal of Police Science and Administration, 12*(4), 395–403.

DeFleur, L. B. (1975). Biasing influences on drug arrests records: implications for deviance research. *American Sociological Review, 40,* 101.

Dodge, R. and Turner, A. (1981). Methodological foundations for establishing a national survey of victimization. In R. Lehnen and W. Skogan (Eds.), *The national crime survey: Working papers, Volume I: Current and historical perspectives* (pp. 2–6). Washington, D.C.: U.S. Department of Justice.

Dothard v Rawlinson (1977). 433 U.S. 321.

Durant, T.J. Jr. (1993). The changing complexion of female crimes: a sex and race comparison. In C. Culliver (Ed.) *Female Criminality: The state of the art.* New York: Garland Publishing Company, Inc.

Edwards, S. (1984). *Women on Trial.* Dover, NH: Manchester University Press.

Eigenberg, H. (1990). The National Crime Survey and rape: The case of the mission question. *Justice Quarterly, 7* (4), 655–672.

Eigenberg, H. and Baro, A. (1992). Women and the publication process: A content analysis of criminal justice journals. *Journal of Criminal Justice Education, 3* (2), 293–314.

Eigenberg, H. and Scarborough, K. (1994). *A Content Analysis of Criminology and Criminal Justice Texts.* Unpublished manuscript.

Erez, E. (1992). Dangerous men, evil women: Gender and parole decision-making. *Justice Quarterly, 9* (1), 105–126.

Federal Bureau of Investigation. (1992). *Crime in the United States—1991.* Washington, D.C.: Government Printing Office.

Flynn, E. (1982). Women as Criminal Justice Professionals: A challenge to change tradition. In N. Rafter and E. Stanko (Eds.) *Judge, Lawyer, Victim, Thief: Women, Gender Roles, and Criminal Justice* (p. 305–340). Boston: Northeastern University Press.

Frazier, C., Bock, E. W., and Henretta, J. C. (1983). Role of probation officers in determining gender differences in sentencing severity. *Sociological Quarterly, 24* (Spring), 305–318.

Garrison, C., McClelland, A., Dambrot, F., and Casey, K. (1992). Gender balancing the criminal justice curriculum and classroom. *Journal of Criminal Justice Education, 3* (2), 203–222.

Gelsthorpe, L. and Morris, A. (1990). *Feminist Perspectives in Criminology.* Milton Keynes, PA: Open University Press.

Gerwerth, K. and Bachand, D. (1993). Workload and compensation among criminal justice faculty members: A national survey. *Journal of Criminal Justice Education, 4* (1), 43–64.

Glick, R. and Neto, V. (1982). National study of women's correctional programs. In B. Price and N. Sokoloff (Eds.) *The Criminal Justice System and Women* (pp. 141–154). New York: Clark Boardman Company.

Glueck, S. and Glueck, E. (1934). *Five Hundred Delinquent Women.* New York: Knopf.

Goetting, A. and Howsen, R. (1983). Women in prison: A profile. *Prison Journal, 63* (2), 27–44.

Greene, H. (1981). "Black women in the criminal justice system." *The Urban League Review, 6* (1), 54–61.

Hagan, J. (1974). Extra-legal attributes and criminal sentencing: an assessment of a sociological viewpoint. *Law and Society Review, 8,* 357–383.

Hale, D. and Wyland, S. (1993). Dinosaurs and dragons: the plight of patrol women. *Police Forum 3* (2), 1–6.

Harding, S. (1987). *Feminism and methodology.* Bloomington, Indiana: University of Indiana Press.

Harding, S. (1986). *The science question in feminism.* Ithaca, New York: Cornell University Press.

Hawkes, M. (1991). Women's changing roles in corrections. In J. Morton (Ed.) *Change, Challenge, and Choices: Women's Role in Modern Corrections* (pp. 100–110). Laurel, MD: American Correctional Association.

Healy, W. (1926). *Delinquents and Criminals: Their Making and Unmaking.* New York: Macmillan and Company.

Heidensohn, F. (1985). *Women and Crime: The Life of the Female Offender.* New York: New York University Press.

Hickman, K. G. (1983). Measuring job performance success for female officers of the Los Angeles police department. Unpublished doctoral dissertation, Claremont Graduate School, Los Angeles.

Higgins, L. (1951). Historical background of policewomen's service. *Journal of Criminal Law, Criminology and Police Science, 41,* 822–833.

Hindelang, M. J. (1979). Sex differences in criminal activity. *Social Problems, 27* (2), 143–156.

Hindman, R. E. (1975). A survey related to use of female law enforcement officers. *Police Chief 42* (4), 58–60.

Holeman, H. and Kress-Hepps, B. (1979). *Women Correctional Officers in California.* Sacramento, CA: Final Report of Research Contractors to the Department.

Homant, R. & Kennedy (1985). Police perceptions of spouse abuse: a comparison of male and female officers. *Journal of Criminal Justice, 13,* 29–49.

Homant, R. J. & Kennedy, D. B. (1984). A content analysis of statements about policewomen's handling of domestic violence. *American Journal of Police, 3,* 265–283.

Hutzel, E. L. (1933). *The policewomen's handbook.* New York: Columbia University Press.

Immarigeon, R. & Chesney-Lind, M. (1993). Women's prisons: overcrowded and overused. In R. Muraskin and T. Alleman (Eds.). *It's a Crime: Women and Justice.* Englewood Cliffs, NJ: Regents/Prentice Hall. pp. 242–259.

Johnson, L. B. (1991). Job strain among police officers: gender comparisons. *Police Studies, 14,* 12–16.

Johnson, P. (1991). Why employ women. In J. Morton (Ed.). *Change, Challenge, and Choices: Women's Role in Modern Corrections.* Laurel, MD: American Correctional Association. pp. 6–12.

Johnson, W., Pettisen, R., & Wallis, L. (1977). Arrest probabilities for marijuana users as indicators of selective enforcement. *American Journal of Sociology, 83,* 681–699.

Jurik, N. (1985). An officer and a lady: Organizational barriers to women working as correctional officers in men's prisons. *Social Problems, 32* (4), 375–388.

Kanter, R. M. (1977). *Men and women of the corporation.* United States: Basic Books.

Keller, E. (1983). Feminism and science in E. Abel and E. Abel (Eds.) *The Signs Reader: Women, Gender, and Scholarship.* Chicago: University of Chicago Press.

Kissel, P. and Katsampes, P. (1980). The impact of women corrections officers on the functioning of institutions housing male inmates. *Journal of Offender Counseling, Services, and Rehabilitation, 4* (3), 213–231.

Kitzinger, C. (1987). *The social construction of lesbianism.* Beverly Hills: Sage.

Klein, D. (1973). The Etiology of Female Crime: A Review of the Literature. *Issues in Criminology, 8* (3), 3–30.

Koenig, E. J. (1978). An overview of attitudes toward women in law enforcement. *Public Administration Review, 38* (3), 267–275.

Konopka, G. (1966). *The Adolescent Girl in Conflict.* New Jersey: Prentice-Hall.

Koss, M. (1992). The underdetection of rape: Methodological choices influence incidence estimates. *Journal of Social Issues, 48,* 61–75.

Koss, M., Dinero, T., Seibel, C. and Cox, S. (1988). Stranger and acquaintance rape: Are there differences in the victim's experience. *Psychology of Women Quarterly, 12,* 1–24.

Koss, M., Gidycz, C., and Wisniewski, N. (1987). The scope of rape: Incidence and prevalence of sexual aggression and victimization in a national sample of higher education students. *Journal of Consulting and Clinical Psychology, 55,* (2), 162–170.

Kruttschnitt, C. (1984). Sex and criminal court dispositions: the unresolved controversy. *Research in Crime and Delinquency, 21* (3), 213–232.

LaBeff, E. & Williams, L. (1982). Male officer reactions to females in patrol: The case of a small city. *American Journal of Police, 2* (1), 73–89.

Ladner, J. (1987). Introduction to tomorrow's tomorrow: The black woman. In S. Harding (Ed.). *Feminism and methodology.* Bloomington, Indiana: University of Indiana Press. pp. 29–36.

Leonard, E. (1982). *Women, Crime and Society.* New York: Longman, Inc.

Linden, R. (1983). Women in policing—a study of lower mainland royal Canadian Mounted Police detachments. *Canadian Police College Journal, 7,* 217–229.

Lipman-Blumen, J. (1984). *Gender Roles and Power.* Englewood Cliffs, NJ: Prentice Hall.

Lombroso, C. & Ferrero, G. (1916). *The Female Offender.* New York: D. Appleton and Co.

Lord, L. K. (1986). A comparison of male and female peace officers' stereotypic perceptions of men and women peace officers. *Journal of Police Science and Administration, 14* (2), 83–97.

Maguire, K., Pastore, A. L. & Flanagan, T. J. (1993). *Sourcebook of Criminal Justice Statistics, 1992.* U.S. Department of Justice, Bureau of Justice Statistics. Washington, D.C.: U.S. Government Printing Office.

Mann, C. (1984). *Female Crime and Delinquency.* University of Alabama Press.

Mann, C. (1989). Minority and female: A criminal justice double bind. *Social Justice, 16*(4), 95–114.

Martin, S. E. (1980). *Breaking and entering: Policewomen on patrol.* Berkeley: University of California Press.

Martin, S. E. (1990). *On the move: The status of women in policing.* Washington, D.C.: Police Foundation.

McGeorge, J. & Wolfe, J. (1976). A comparison of attitudes between men and women police officers: a preliminary analysis. *Criminal Justice Review, 1* (2), 21–33.

Millman, M. & Kanter, R. (1987). Introduction to another voice: Feminist perspectives on social life and social science. In S. Harding (Ed.). *Feminism and methodology.* Bloomington, Indiana: University of Indiana Press. pp. 29–36.

Morash, M. & Greene, J. (1986). Evaluating women on patrol: a critique of contemporary wisdom. *Evaluation Review, 10,* (2), 230–255.

Morton, J. (1991). *Change, Challenge, Choices: Women's Role in Modern Corrections.* Laurel, MD: American Correctional Association.

Moseley, W. H. & Gerould, M. H. (1975). Sex and parole: a comparison of male and female parolees. *Journal of Criminal Justice, 3,* 52–54.

Moyer, I. (1993). Women's Prisons: Issues and controversies. In R. Muraskin and T. Alleman (Eds.). *It's a Crime: Women and Justice.* Englewood Cliffs, NJ: Regents/Prentice Hall. p. 193–210.

Moyer, I. L. (1984). Deceptions and realities of life in women's prisons. *The Prison Journal, 64* (1), 45–56.

Moyer, I. L. (1992). *The Changing Roles of Women in the Criminal Justice System.* Illinois: Waveland Press.

Mukerjee, S. & Fitzgerald, R. (1981). The myth of rising female crime. In K. Mukherjee & J. Scutt (Eds.). *Women and Crime.* Boston: George Allen and Unwin. pp. 51–69.

Mullings, J. L. (1994). *Gender disparity and time served in prison: the Texas prison system 1980-1991.* Unpublished Master's Thesis. Huntsville, TX: Sam Houston State University.

Nagel, I. H. & Hagan, J. (1983). Gender and crime: Offense patterns and criminal court sanctions. In M. Tonry and N. Morris (Eds.). *Crime and Justice: an annual review of research.* Chicago: University of Chicago Press. pp. 91–144.

Nagel, S. & Weitzman, L. J. (1971). Women as litigants. *Hastings Law Journal, 23,* 171–198.

Nebraska Feminist Collective. (1983). A feminist ethic for social science research. *Women's Studies International Forum, 6* (5), 535–543.

Owen, B. (1985). Race and gender relations among prison workers. *Crime and Delinquency, 31,* 147–159.

Parisi, N. (1984) The female correctional officer: Her progress toward and prospects for equality. *The Prison Journal, 64* (1), 92–109.

Petersen, C. (1982). Doing time with the boys: an analysis of women correctional officers in all-male facilities. In B. Price and N. Sokoloff (Eds.). *The Criminal Justice system and Women.* New York: Clark Boardman. pp. 437–460.

Philliber, S. (1987). Thy brother's keeper: A review of the literature on correctional officers. *Justice Quarterly, 4* (1), 9–37.

Police Foundation. (1990). *On the move: the status of women in policing.* Washington, D.C.: Police Foundation.

Pollack-Byrne, J. (1990). *Women, Prison and Crime.* Pacific Grove, CA: Brooks/Cole Publishing.

Pollak, O. (1950). *The Criminality of women.* Philadelphia: University of Philadelphia Press.

Potter, J. (1980). Should women guards work in prisons for men? *Corrections Magazine, 6,* 30–38.
Price, B., & Gavin, S. (1982). A century of women in policing. In B. R. Price and N. J. Sokoloff (Eds.). *The criminal justice system and women.* New York: Clark Boardman. pp. 399–412.
Rafter, N. (1985). *Partial Justice: Women in State Prisons 1800-1935.* Boston: Northeastern University Press.
Remmington, P. (1983). Women in police: integration or separation? *Qualitative Sociology, 6,* (2), 118–135.
Renzetti, C. (1993). On the margins of the malestream (or they *still* don't get it do they?): Feminist analyses in criminal justice education. *Journal of Criminal Justice Education, 4* 92), 219–234.
Reskin, B. & Roos, P. (1990) *Job queues, gender queues.* Philadelphia: Temple University Press.
Rogers, J. W. (1992). Probation, parole, power, and women offenders: From patriarchal paramenters to participatory empowerment. In Imogene Moyer (Ed.). *The Changing Roles of Women in the Criminal Justice System.* (2nd ed.). Prospect Heights, Ill.: Waveland Press.
Russell, D. E. H. (1984). *Sexual exploitation: rape, child sexual abuse and workplace harassment.* Beverly Hills: Sage.
Rutland, C. M. (1978). *Comparative analysis of the relationship between social background factors and training performance of male and female security specialists.* Master's thesis. California State University, Sacramento.
Scarborough, K. & Eigenberg, H. (1993). An empirical analysis of women in policing: Perceptions of competency versus effective performance. Paper presented at the American society of Criminology Meeting in Phoenix, Arizona. October, 1993.
Schechter, S. (1982). *Women and male violence: The visions and struggles of the battered women's movement.* Boston: South End Press.
Searles, P. & Berger, R. (1987). The current status of rape reform legislation: An examination of state statutes. *Women's Rights Law Reporter, 10* (1), 25–43.
Shawver, L. & Dickover, R. (1986, August). Research perspectives: Exploding a Myth. *Corrections Today.* pp. 30–34.
Sherman, L. J. (1975). An evaluation of policewomen on patrol in a suburban police department. *Journal of Police Science and Administration, 3* (4), 434–438.
Simon, R. J. (1975). *Women and Crime.* Massachusetts: D. C. Heath and Co.
Simon, R. & Simon J. (1993). Female guards in men's prisons. In R. Muraskin and T. Alleman (Eds.). *It's a Crime: Women and Justice.* Englewood Cliffs, NJ: Regents/ Prentice Hall. pp. 226–241.
Simpson, S. & White, M. F. (1985). The female guard in the all-male prison. In I. L. Moyer (Ed.). *The Changing Roles of Women in the Criminal Justice System.* Prospect Heights, IL: Waveland. pp. 276–300.
Smart, C. (1977). *Women, Crime and Criminology: A Feminist Critique.* London: Routledge and Kegan Paul.
Smith, D. A. & Paternoster, R. (1987). The Gender Gap in Theories of Deviance: Issues and Evidence. *Journal of Research in Crime and Delinquency, 24* (2), 140–172.

Spender, D. (1981). The gatekeepers. In H. Roberts (Ed.). *Doing feminist research.* Boston: Routledge and Kegan Paul.

Spender, D. (1983). Editorial. *Women's Studies Ineternational forum, 6* (5), 467.

Stacey, J. & Thorn, B. (1985). The missing feminist revolution in sociology. *Social Problems, 32* (4), 310–316.

Steffensmeier, D. (1978). Crime and the contemporary woman: An analysis of changing levels of female property crime, 1960–1975. In L. Bowker (Ed.). *Women and Crime in America.* New York: Macmillan. pp. 39–58.

Steffenmeier, D. (1979). Trends in female crime: It's still a man's world. In B. Price and N. Sokoloff (Eds.). *The Criminal Justice System and Women.* New York: Clark Boardman Company. pp. 117–129.

Steffensmeier, D., Kramer, J., & Streifel, C. (1993). Gender and imprisonment decisions. *Criminology, 31* (3), 411–444.

Talney, R. (1969). Women in law enforcement: an expanded role. *Police, 14,* 49–51.

Tenney, E. (1953). Women's work in law enforcement. *Journal of Criminal Law Criminology and Police Science, 54* (2), 239–246.

Thomas, W. I. (1967). *The Unadjusted Girl.* New York: Harper and Row.

Townsend, W. (1992). *An Empirical Assessment of Attitudes toward Female Correctional Officers among Jail Employees.* Unpublished Master's Thesis. Norfolk, VA: Old Dominion University.

Uhlman, T. & Walker, N. (1979). A plea is no bargain: the impact of case disposition on sentencing. *Social Science Quarterly, 60* (3), 218–234.

Vega, M., & Silverman, I. J. (1982). Female police officers as viewed by their male counterparts. *Police Studies, 5,* 31–39.

Visher, C. A. (1983). Gender, Police Arrest Decisions and Notions of Chivalry. *Criminology, 21* (1), 5–28.

Weisheit, R. & Mahan, S. (1988). *Women, crime, and criminal justice.* Cincinnati, OH: Anderson Publishing Company.

Wexler, J. (1985). Role styles of women police officers. *Sex Roles, 12,* 749–755.

Wilson, N. (1991). Feminist pedagogy in criminology. *Journal of Criminal Justice Education, 2,* (1), 81–94.

Wilson, J. Q., & Hernstein, R. J. (1985). *Crime and Human Nature.* New York: Simon and Schuster.

Wolfgang, M. E. (1961). Cesare Lombroso. In H. Mannheim (Ed.). *Pioneers in Criminology.* (2nd ed.). Montclair, NJ: Patterson Smith.

Wonders, N. & Caulfield, S. (1993). Women's work? The contradictory implications of courses on women and the criminal justice system. *Journal of Criminal Justice Education, 2* (1), 79–100.

Wright, R. (1987). Are "sisters in crime" finally being booked? The coverage of women and crime in journals and textbooks. *Teaching Sociology, 15,* 418–422.

Wright, R. (1992). From vamps and tramps to teases and flirts: Stereotypes of women in criminology textbooks, 1956 to 1965 and 1981 to 1990. *Journal of Criminal Justice Education, 3* (2), 223–236.

Young, V. (1986). Gender expectations and their impact on black female offenders and victims. *Justice Quarterly, 3* (3), 305–327.

Young, V. & Sulton, a. T. (1991). "Excluded: The current status of African-American scholars in the field of criminology and criminal justice." *Journal of Research in Crime and Delinquency, 28* (1), 101–116.

Zimmer, L. (1986). *Women Guarding Men.* Chicago: University of Chicago Press.

Zimmer, L. (1987). How women reshape the prison role. *Gender and Society, 1* (4), 415–431.

Zupan, L. (1992). The progress of women correctional officers in all male prisons. In I. Moyer (Ed.). *The Changing Roles of Women in the Criminal Justice System.* Prospect Heights, IL: Waveland. pp. 323–343.

CHAPTER THREE

RACE, ETHNICITY, AND CRIMINAL JUSTICE

JEROME MCKEAN

INTRODUCTION

In this chapter, the author will attempt to: (1) describe patterns of victimization as they are influenced by the variables of race and ethnic identity; (2) assess explanations for variations in rates of African-American criminal victimization among American cities; (3) review the literature on differential treatment of offenders due to the racial or ethnic identity of the victim; (4) review the literature on the influence of the racial or ethnic identity of the victim on the response to victims by agents of criminal justice; (5) discuss, based on the literature, how agents of criminal justice might improve their response to victims by developing an approach that is sensitive to multicultural considerations.

To keep the chapter to a manageable length, the author will concentrate on the *criminal* victimization of *adults,* with emphasis on violent crime. Specifically, the chapter deals with variations in criminal victimization among cities and neighborhoods. Yet criminal victimization cannot be studied apart from three other forms of mistreatment which are also often characterized as victimization: (1) the effects of oppression—or oppressive conditions such as relative deprivation, social isolation, and social disorganization as causes of criminal victimization, (2) the mistreatment of crime victims by criminal justice practitioners, and (3) any additional mistreatment of minority victims by criminal justice practitioners, such as devoting fewer resources to prosecuting those who prey on minority victims than prosecuting those who prey on European-American victims.

A consideration of these issues will allow us to conclude by addressing the broad question of whether criminal justice agencies *prevent* or *promote* criminal victimization by their practices and policies.

PATTERNS OF VICTIMIZATION

There is a great deal of information available on patterns of criminal victimization for the nation as a whole. The data indicate that African-Americans suffer from higher rates of personal victimization than white or "other" Americans, and are at greater risk of victimization over their lifetimes (Koppel, 1987). African-Americans are also more likely to suffer injury from victimization (Harlow, 1989). Available data also suggests that Hispanic-Americans experience higher rates of victimization than non-Hispanics (Bastian, 1990).

Categorizing Victims by Race and Ethnicity

The primary source of information on criminal victimization in the United States is the National Crime Victim Survey (NCVS). The National Crime Victim Survey categorizes persons as Black, White, or "other" under the heading of race. Under the heading of ethnicity, the categories are Hispanic and non-Hispanic (Bastian, 1993). The term, "Hispanic," can include persons of any race. No distinction is made among Hispanics on the basis of national origin, although that is often a very important badge of identity for persons in this category (Bastian, 1990).

Crime data compiled by the Federal Bureau of Investigation may also be used to explore patterns of victimization, especially for homicide. The FBI does not categorize the population as Hispanic or non-Hispanic. The racial categories are also white, black, and other. The "Other" category includes American Indians, Alaskan Natives, and Asian and Pacific Islanders (Federal Bureau of Investigation, 1993).

These or similar categories are often used in government statistics and social scientific research, and they may seem unexceptional. But the categories themselves reveal something about what aspects of race or ethnicity are regarded by researchers as significant. After all, racial and ethnic categories are *social constructions,* and are arbitrary from a biological point of view (Georges-Abeyie, 1989; Lynch & Patterson, 1991). Even anthropologists disagree about criteria for classifying races, although major groupings—Negroid, Mongoloid, Australoid, Caucasoid, and Indic—are commonly recognized (Hacker, 1992).

The "official" racial and ethnic categories of the Department of Justice and other agencies seem to be largely based on skin color. A gross distinction is made between "white" and other sorts of persons, which suggests a racial homogeneity that neither "whites" nor "non-whites" always exhibit. Similarly, the only criteria for dividing persons by ethnicity have at least some basis in skin color, although, as we shall see, most Hispanics do not describe themselves as having a race or describe themselves as white.

As Hacker (1992) notes, successive waves of immigrants had to learn to conform to Anglo-American norms to gain "admission" into the white "club." Those who were not Protestants, such as the Irish and the Italians, were assimilated at a slower pace than other groups. Some members of the white club still regard Jews as a separate race. Currently, upwardly mobile Arab-Americans and Hispanic-Americans are at least granted probationary membership, depending, of course, on their willingness and ability to conform to the expectations of the club's earlier members.

The perceived necessity for categorizing a group as other than white, then, may reflect both a sense of "the way things are" and *expectations* about the behavior of members of the group. As Georges-Abeyie (1989) notes, such categories sometimes denote the "social distance" between groups. Social distance is defined by Parrillo (1985) as "the degree of closeness or remoteness one desires in interaction with members of a particular group" (p. 491). Georges-Abeyie (1989) cites perceptions of physical differences, cultural differences, differences in "intrinsic worth," differences in threat to the social order, differences in criminality, and other perceived social and cultural differences as factors contributing to social distance (1989, p. 38).

As Georges-Abeyie's analysis suggests, social distance may be related to perceived differences in criminality. The Governor's Task Force on Bias Related Violence for the State of New York (1988) suggests: "The idea that being of white, Northern European descent constitutes a normal state of existence from which various groups of people deviate is pervasive in this society" (cited in Bailey, 1991). The Task Force writers go on to note that being a European-American is not perceived as constituting an ethnicity.

These considerations suggest the hypothesis that *the social distance between groups determines whether a group will be identified as a separate category in descriptions of deviant behavior.* Groups who have little political power, and low social status, yet who are socially distant from the groups who have power and status, are hypothesized to be more likely to be placed in a "non" or "minority" category for such purposes. Despite their lack of power and status, such groups are perceived as threatening. The hypothesis would require historic and cross-national data to verify.

The hypothesis suggests that the decision about which ethnic or racial "markers" to use in categorizing crime victims or offenders depends on how the markers denote the social distance between the victims or offenders and the groups with the authority to make such a decision. It is possible to identify a number of ethnic markers for "white" groups that connote a criminal tradition, such as place of birth, ancestral country of origin, and identification with a particular subculture. Examples are the assumptions that Italian ancestry is associated with involvement in organized crime, or that Irish-Americans and Anglo-Americans from rural Appalachia (so-called "White Trash") are members of a "subculture of violence." These markers are rarely employed in either official or unofficial research, although they may sort persons by their risk of victimization or propensity to criminal behavior just as effectively as do markers derived from skin coloration.

In support of the social distance hypothesis, note that early studies of race or ethnicity and crime relied on official data in which a sharp distinction was made between native-born and foreign-born persons. The categories used in official statistics may reflect the changing inclusiveness of the "white" category in official statistics. A study by Work (1913) makes use of data on prison commitments by nationality in 1904 to show that Mexican, Italian, Austrian, French, Canadian, and Russian nationals all had higher rates of imprisonment than African-Americans. In his classic study of American race relations, Myrdal presents official data in which white prisoners are only divided into native-born and foreign-born (Myrdal, 1944). Prisoner data from recent years makes no such distinction.

In addition to neglecting ethnic differences within the white population, official categories ignore differences within minority populations. For example, Americans of Hispanic, Chicano, or Latino origin may or may not regard themselves as having a "race." In the 1990 census, over half the Americans with such origins chose to identify no race at all (Hacker, 1992, p. 6). Many Hispanic persons feel that their national identities are of greater relevance. Native Americans distinguish themselves by the Nation to which they belong, tribal identity, and in some cases by clan within a tribe.

The categorization of persons as "Black," "African-American," or even as persons of color may also obscure distinctions based on national origin, religion, skin tone—color and hue, and geographic location (Georges-Abeyie, 1989, pp. 38–39). As Mann (1993) points out, skin tone may be of critical importance in understanding patterns of victimization and offending in intra-racial crimes.

In sum, official statistics on criminal behavior and criminal victimization use crude categories for classifying persons by race and ethnicity. The categories treat the American population as if it were divided into large, homogenous groups on the basis of skin coloration. Not only do the categories obscure important differences within racial and ethnic groups, they also may imply expectations about the propensity for criminal behavior and to criminal victimization for each group based on the group's social distance from the "normal," white state of being.

Sources of Data on Victimization

Before examining the data in detail, it is worthwhile to briefly consider its origins. The main sources of data on criminal victimization are the National Crime Victim Survey (NCVS) conducted by the Bureau of Justice Statistics and the Uniform Crime Reports collected by the Federal Bureau of Investigation. The FBI also disseminates the Supplemental Homicide Reports, which provide information on homicide victimization.

Data are collected in two ways. NCVS data are collected by sample survey interviews. The data provided by the FBI are collected on a voluntary basis by state and local law enforcement agencies. Each source of data has strengths and weaknesses, and nowhere is that more apparent than in attempts to compare persons on the basis of racial or ethnic identity.

The National Crime Victimization Survey

The NCVS is a large, complex, and ongoing sample survey of *households* in the United States. Housing units—apartments, single-family houses, rooming houses, and so on—are sampled, and every person over age 12 in a selected housing unit is interviewed. About 166,000 interviews in 84,000 housing units were conducted to estimate victimization for 1992 (U.S. Department of Justice, 1992; Zawitz, Klaus, Bachman, Bastian, Deberry, Rand, & Taylor, 1993).

The NCVS is one of the most sophisticated efforts to sample a population ever devised, but like all surveys, it has inherent limitations. The limitations may be summarized by saying that the NCVS *estimates* the *perceptions* of victimization by persons who reside in an identifiable housing unit.

Whether, and under what circumstances, a victimization has occurred is determined by the respondent, whose memory may be influenced by any number of factors. Not the least of these is the trauma engendered by the victimization itself. The reliability and validity of victim reports is thus subject to challenge. In particular, the accuracy of victim perceptions of the race, age, gender and state of intoxication of the offender may be questioned, and that is a matter of concern in describing victim-offender interactions (Mann, 1993).

Because the NCVS is a survey, it provides a sample estimate of victimization and is subject to sampling error. The smaller the subpopulation for which victimization rates are estimated, the greater the potential sampling error. For example, a greater likelihood of error is involved in estimating victimization rates for black women over the age of 65 than for all black women. Because households are surveyed, the NCVS does not speak to levels of victimization for persons who are not part of a household—the homeless.

The Uniform Crime Reports

The Federal Bureau of Investigation collects data from federal, state, and local law enforcement agencies on offenses "known to the police" and arrests, and uses this data as a basis for estimating a number of different crime rates. Of particular interest here is the detailed data collected for murder and nonnegligent manslaughter, for these offenses are not addressed in the NCVS.

Data on offenses known to the police is of little use for present purposes. The term refers to reports of criminal events that the police perceive to have merit. The identity of the offender is not known, and, until recently, no systematic effort has been made to collect data on the characteristics of the persons reporting the offenses. Arrest data is potentially more useful, but offenses for which arrests occur represent only a fraction of the victimizations that occur.

The major use of FBI data in describing patterns of victimization involves the study of homicides, especially murders and non-negligent manslaughters. Data on the characteristics of homicide victims is usually considered of high reliability.

Overall Patterns of Victimization

Before making comparisons among racial and ethnic groups, it will be helpful to have a feel for overall trends and patterns of criminal victimization as a basis for comparison. It is especially important to note that rates of criminal victimization are very high for *all* Americans, regardless of race or ethnic background, and that *overall rates of victimization are stable or declining for most offense categories.*

NCVS data for the past twenty years (1973–1992) reveals the following patterns of reported victimization (Zawitz, et al, 1993):

(1) One in four households in the United States is victimized each year. That is, a member of the household or the property of a household member is the target of a crime.

(2) Most victimization involves property crime.

(3) Overall rates of victimization have been stable or declining. But violent victimization has increased for teenagers and African-Americans.

(4) Persons who are male, or under 25, or single, or who reside in urban areas are more likely to suffer both crimes of violence and of theft.

(5) Handguns are used in about 10 percent of violent victimizations.

(6) The average dollar loss per crime (as estimated by victims) has increased substantially even when adjusting for inflation, from $142 in 1975 to $550 in 1991.

It is also useful to place official data for homicides in context. Messner and Rosenfeld (1993) compare U.S. homicide rates to those of 16 other developed nations, including Canada, Australia, Japan, France, Germany, and England, using World Health Organization data for 1988 (the most recent year for which comparative data were available). The United States had a homicide rate of 8.9 homicides per 100,000 residents. The developed nation with the next highest homicide rate was Finland, with a rate of 2.8 per 100,000 residents.

As this finding suggests, homicide (and, inferentially, other forms of victimization) is not a problem confined to urban residents and minorities. FBI data for 1988 indicate a homicide rate of 4.3 per 100,000 for white Americans and a rural homicide rate of 5.4 per 100,000 (Federal Bureau of Investigation, 1989). These rates may seem low when compared to the overall rate for the United States or to the homicide rate for large cities, but in each case they are considerably higher than the *total* homicide rates for other nations. Americans in *all* categories kill and are killed at alarming rates (Messner & Rosenfeld, 1993).

Messner and Rosenfeld (1993) also present data which make it clear that the American homicide problem is not a recent development. Although complete time-series data are not available, the data which does exist shows that the *average* levels of homicide in the United States during each decade of the twentieth century usually exceeded the *highest* levels of homicide for other developed nations for the same periods. There is reason to believe that American homicide rates were higher during the nineteenth century than the twentieth century.

The evidence suggests that the United States has always had very high levels of homicide, and the problem cannot be accounted for solely by reference to short-term changes such as increasing urbanization, patterns of internal migration such as Hispanic in-migration or African-American migration from southern rural areas to northern urban areas, or increases in the youthful population. The American crime problem seems to be a fundamental feature of its history. It is not a new problem, a youth problem, a black problem, an Hispanic problem, or an urban problem.

Variations in Victimization Rates by Race and Ethnicity

Two very general observations may be made on patterns of criminal victimization in the United States:

(1) African-Americans and Hispanic-Americans groups are more likely to suffer victimization;
(2) Persons are more likely to be victimized by members of their own ethnic or racial group than by members of another group.

The victimization surveys provide data on completed and attempted personal and household victimization. Personal victimizations are further divided into crimes of violence and crimes of theft. Within the category of crimes of violence, information is collected on rapes, robberies, aggravated assaults, and simple assaults. Personal crimes of theft include personal larcenies with contact, such as pocket picking and purse snatching, and personal larcenies without contact. These are thefts from any place other than the victim's home, such as the theft of cash from an automobile. Household victimization rates are calculated for burglary, household larceny, and motor vehicle theft.

The most recent NCVS data available is for the year 1992, and patterns of victimization in that year are similar to the patterns for earlier years. The 1992 data are summarized in Table 1. The table shows that blacks were much more likely to be victims of crime than whites or persons of other races.

Table 1. Victimization Rates Per 1,000 Persons Age 12 and Over, by Type of Crime, Race, and Ethnicity, 1992.

		Race		*Ethnicity*	
Offense Type	*White*	*Black*	*Other*	*Hisp.*	*Non-Hisp.*
Total Personal Crimes*	88.7	110.8	88.3	100.1	90.3
Robbery	4.7	15.6	5.1	10.6	5.4
Aggravated Assault	7.8	18.3	5.3	10.0	8.9
Simple Assault	16.8	15.2	13.3	16.8	16.4
Theft	58.8	60.4	64.6	61.9	58.9
Total Property Crimes	146.0	199.1	147.4	260.2	144.1
Burglary	46.4	68.4	44.3	69.9	47.3
Household Larceny	82.3	93.6	68.6	141.8	78.8
Motor Vehicle Theft	17.3	37.1	34.5	48.6	18.0

*Includes data on rape victimization not shown separately.
Source: Bastian, 1993, pp. 6–7.

As the Table 1 indicates, the degree of racial disparity in rates of victimization varied widely by type of offense. Blacks suffered from robbery victimization at a rate that was over three times the rate for whites. On the other hand, whites suffered a slightly higher rate of simple assault than blacks or other races.

When Hispanics are compared to non-Hispanics, a slightly different picture emerges. Hispanics are also more likely to suffer both personal and household victimization. Hispanics sustained robberies at about twice the rate of non-Hispanics, but suffered far higher rates of household victimization than non-Hispanics or blacks.

Racial differences in murder victimization in 1992 may be estimated from the Uniform Crime Reports (Federal Bureau of Investigation, 1993). The percent distribution of victims by race for earlier years are provided by the

Sourcebook of Criminal Justice Statistics, 1992 (Maguire, Pastore, & Flanagan, 1993). Table 2 shows 49.6 percent of the victims of murder in 1992 were categorized as black and 2.4 percent as other. The table also indicates that the percentage of murder victims who were black remained close to fifty percent for the last five years, although this represents an increase from the percentages observed from 1976 to 1986.

Within racial and ethnic categories, the risks of criminal victimization depend on a number of variables, and the variables differ for whites, blacks and Hispanics. In order to understand patterns of victimization, it is necessary to examine variations within groups.

Hispanic Victimization

NCVS Data: A 1990 study by the Bureau of Justice Statistics (Bastian, 1990) presents findings on the victimization of Hispanics between 1979 and 1986. For the entire period, Hispanics were more likely to be victims of personal crime and household crime than non-Hispanics. But the rates of violent victimization, victimization by theft, and household victimization show an overall decline during that period, and between 1979 and 1992.

There is a gradual but consistent drop in rates of personal theft from a high of 84 per 1,000 in 1979 to the 1992 rate of 61.9. Rates of household crimes show more fluctuation, but have declined from a high of 299 per 1,000 in 1979 to 260.1 in 1992. The 1992 rates of household victimization are higher than the rates observed in the mid-1980's. The same may be said for rates of violent personal victimization. Although rates dropped from 44 to 29 per 1,000 between 1979 and 1986, they increased to 38 per 1,000 in 1992.

In 1991, Hispanic females suffered rape victimization at a rate of 2.1 per 1,000 females compared to a rate of 1.4 for non-Hispanic females (U.S. Department of Justice, 1992). In 1992, the comparable rates were 0.7 per 1,000 Hispanic females and 0.8 per 1,000 non-Hispanic females (Bastian, 1993). The apparent decline in victimization rates may be an artifact of the sampling process: fewer than ten Hispanic women in the sample reported rape victimization in 1992. The Department of Justice does not regularly report trend data for Hispanics.

In the Bureau of Justice Statistics study, Bastian (1990) notes that the Hispanic population is more likely to have demographic characteristics associated with higher risk of victimization: "Compared to non-Hispanics, a larger percentage of Hispanics were younger and less likely to be over age 50; unmarried; less well educated; earning a low income; nonprofessional, with a higher unemployment rate; renters rather than owners; city dwellers instead of suburbanites or residents of nonmetropolitan areas" (Bastian 1990, p. 4).

When Bastian (1990) compared Hispanics to non-Hispanics with the same demographic characteristics, the differences in rates of victimization were somewhat reduced. But Hispanics were more likely than non-Hispanics to suffer robbery and aggravated assault even when other demographic characteristics were held constant. When victimized by violent crime, Hispanics were less likely to know the offender than whites or blacks in general. Hispanics were less likely than either blacks or whites to be victimized by an offender well known to them. Hispanics were no more likely than others to sustain injuries from violent crimes, or to receive medical attention for their injuries.

Hispanic victims of violent offenses, especially robbery and aggravated assault, were more likely than either blacks or whites to experience victimizations involving multiple offenders. Two or more offenders were involved in 61% of Hispanic robbery victimizations, compared to 45% of white robberies and 54% of black robberies. Bastian suggests that these figures may reflect the presence of youth gangs in urban Hispanic neighborhoods. Her suggestion is bolstered by the observation that Hispanic victims perceived the age of robbery offenders in multiple offender events to be under 21 in 44% of the cases (Bastian, 1990, p. 8).

Homicide Victimization: Although nationwide comparisons of Hispanic and non-Hispanic homicide rates are not available, several studies suggest that Hispanics suffer higher rates of homicide victimization than non-Hispanics. Smith, Mercy, and Rosenberg (1984) found that rates of Mexican and Mexican-American homicide victimization in the Southwest were 21.6 per 100,000 from 1976 through 1980, which was three times the national rate for whites in general.

A BJS study of murder cases adjudicated in 1988 in 33 of the nation's 75 largest counties also showed Hispanics sustaining high rates of murder victimization (Dawson & Boland, 1993). Although Hispanics comprised about ten percent of the population of these counties, they comprised 20 percent of the victims of murder. In 90 percent of these cases, the offender was also Hispanic.

African-American Victimization

NCVS Data: The 1992 rate of violent crime victimization for African-Americans—50.4 per 1,000 population—is the highest recorded in the twenty-year history of the NCVS. Victimization by personal theft has declined since 1973 for both whites and blacks, and the rates have been very similar since 1988. Blacks experienced household victimization at a higher rate than whites during the entire twenty-year period, but the rates of household victimization have declined fairly steadily since 1973 (Zawitz, et al, 1993).

As Table 1 shows, the greatest disparities in black and white victimization rates in 1992 occurred for robbery and aggravated assault. The ratios of black to white victimization are 3.3-to-1 for robbery and 2.3-to-1 for aggravated assault.

For 1991, the NCVS showed a rape victimization rate for black women of 1.0 per 1,000 women, compared to a rate of 1.5 for white women (U.S. Department of Justice, 1992). For 1992, the comparable figures are 1.6 per 1,000 for black women and 1.0 per 1,000 for white women (Bastian, 1993). The estimates for black women are based on 10 or fewer sample cases for both years. The 1991 figures are contrary to the trends for 1973 to 1990: in 15 of those 18 years, black women suffered higher rates of rape; the rates were the same for both races in 1977, 1982, and 1990 (U.S. Department of Justice, 1992a).

As was the case for Hispanic victims, the Bureau of Justice Statistics sponsored a study of black victimization between 1979 and 1986 (Whitaker, 1990). As with Hispanics, African-Americans are more likely than whites to fall into demographic groups that experience greater risk of criminal victimization. For example, 56 percent lived in central cities between 1979 and 1986, versus 24 percent of whites. Fifty-eight percent of whites were married compared to 37 percent of blacks. Black family income was less than fifteen thousand dollars for 56 percent compared to 32 percent of white families (Whitaker, 1990, p. 3).

When characteristics associated with victimization risk—sex, marital status, location of residence, and family income—were taken into account, rates of robbery and burglary remained consistently higher for blacks, but Whitaker did not find that to be the case for aggravated assault (1990, pp. 4–5). But when location of residence *and* other risk factors were controlled simultaneously, the differences between black and white victimization were often reduced, especially for residents of suburban and nonmetropolitan areas (Whitaker, 1990, pp. 5–6).

The combined effects of race, place of residence, and income are shown for robbery, aggravated assault, and burglary in Table 3. Compared to the overall effects of race alone shown in Table 1, the differences between races are considerably smaller. In four of the comparisons, white victimization rates are higher than black victimization rates.

NCVS data suggests that violent crimes committed against blacks are more serious than those against whites. Black victims were more likely to face an armed offender, be physically attacked, and when injured, to sustain serious injuries (Whitaker, 1990, pp. 7–8).

Homicide Victimization: As Table 2 indicates, African-Americans are, or have been nearly half of the victims of murder and nonnegligent manslaughter in recent years. When victimization rates are compared,

Table 2. Percent Distribution of Murders and Nonnegligent Manslaughters Known to the Police, by Race of Victim, 1970–1992.

Year	*Total Number of Murders & Nonnegligent Manslaughters*	*Percent White**	*Percent Black**	*Percent Other**
1970	13649	44	55	1
1971	16183	44	55	2
1972	15832	45	53	2
1973	17123	47	52	1
1974	18632	48	50	2
1975	18642	51	47	2
1976	16605	51	47	2
1977	18033	52	45	2
1978	18714	54	44	2
1979	20591	54	43	2
1980	21860	53	42	4
1981	20053	54	44	2
1982	19485	55	42	2
1983	18673	55	42	3
1984	16689	56	41	3
1985	17545	56	42	3
1986	19257	53	44	3
1987	17859	52	45	3
1988	18269	49	48	3
1989	18954	48	49	3
1990	20045	48	49	3
1991	21505	47	50	2
1992	22540	47	50	2

*Because of rounding, percentages may not total 100 percent.
Sources: Federal Bureau of Investigation, 1993, p. 16; Maguire, Pastore, and Flanagan, 1993, p. 390.

blacks are as much as seven times more likely than whites to be murdered. Black rates have increased from a low of 26.4 per 100,000 in 1984 to a rate of 34 per 100,000 in 1991. The 1991 rate is the highest since 1981: rates in

Table 3. Victimization Rates by Family Income, Race, and Location of Residence of Victim, 1979–1986.

Location of Residence & Income of Victim	*Type of Crime and Race of Victim*					
	Robbery		*Aggravated Assault*		*Burglary*	
	White	*Black*	*White*	*Black*	*White*	*Black*
Metropolitan Area						
Central City						
Less than $15,000	14.2	22.7	16.0	19.1	109.2	131.7
$15,000–24,999	8.1	13.8	13.2	11.9	88.1	106.3
$25,000 and more	6.8	12.4	9.0	11.1	83.4	128.0
Suburb						
Less than $15,000	7.2	8.9	12.1	15.1	77.8	116.7
$15,000–24,999	4.7	7.3	9.0	10.7	66.1	80.7
$25,000 and more	4.0	6.5	7.7	7.6	63.4	125.7
Nonmetropolitan Area						
Less than $15,000	3.4	4.0	10.0	11.1	70.9	80.7
$15,000–24,999	2.0	4.1	6.5	8.1	51.2	44.1
$25,000 and more	2.0	0.5*	5.5	1.2*	55.2	70.3

*Estimate is based on 10 or fewer sample cases.
Note: Robbery and aggravated assault rates are average annual rates per 1,000 persons. Burglary rates are average annual rates per 1,000 households. For burglary, personal characteristics are those of the head of the household.
Source: Whitaker, 1990, p. 6.

the seventies were also in the low to mid-thirties (Maguire, Pastore, & Flanagan, 1993).

Whitaker (1990) has calculated sex and age-specific rates for African-Americans for 1986 using Supplemental Homicide Reports from the FBI. Her calculations show adjusted (for missing data) rates as follows (Whitaker, 1990, p. 10):

	Adjusted Rate Per 100,000
Black Total	31.3
Male	52.3
Female	12.3
White Total	05.4
Male	07.9
Female	02.9

Note that homicide rates are more a function of race than sex. Specifically, black females have a higher rate than white males. This pattern was also found in an analysis of 1978 data by Reidel (1984), and data for 1976 to 1984 analyzed by O'Carroll and Mercy (1986).

When homicide rates are further classified by age categories, the same pattern of race and sex rankings emerges for each age group. For 1986, Whitaker (1990) found that the highest homicide rates for both sexes in both races were among persons age 20–24 and age 25–34. Black women in these age groups suffered victimization at rates exceeding 21 per 100,000 in 1986. Black men in these age groups suffered victimization at rates of 100 per 100,000 for ages 20-to-24 and 104.3 per 100,000 for ages 25-to-34 (Whitaker, 1990, p. 11). O'Carroll and Mercy (1986) found similar patterns for 1983.

Victim-Offender Relationships

The fear that European-Americans have of criminal victimization by African-Americans may be based on misperceptions. For the forms of victimization measured by the NCVS and for murder data, criminal offenses are predominantly *intra*racial. That is, black offenders are more likely to victimize blacks than whites, and white offenders are more likely to victimize whites than blacks.

This statement has been challenged by Wilbanks (1987), who focuses on the extent of interracial rape. Using 1981 victimization data, he calculates that over 55 percent of black offenders "choose" white victims. Wilbanks' conclusion is reached by simply noting the percentage of cases in which white rape victims perceive their assailant to be black.

O'Brien (1987) responds to such assertions by noting that the degree to which crimes are inter- or intraracial depends on the relative availability of white or black victims. To simplify his argument considerably, blacks composed about 11.7 percent of the population over age 12 (the age of those surveyed in the NCVS), and whites composed about 86 percent of that population. Assuming that black offenders select their victims without regard to race, 86 percent of their victims should be white. If it is the case that black offenders victimize a lower percentage of whites—and even Wilbanks data show this to be the case—then criminal victimization is more *intra*racial than expected. Using various, more refined assumptions about racial interaction, O'Brien finds victimization to be more intraracial than expected for homicide, rape, aggravated and simple assault, and robbery.

Rape: South and Felson (1990) address the problem of differential contact between blacks and whites. Using robbery incidents involving male offenders and female victims, they examine the percentage of incidents in which rapes occur and the racial identity of the parties involved. In these cases, the opportunities for rape are presumed to be equivalent regardless of the race of the victim, and thus the choices made by black offenders can be realistically examined. South and Felson (1990, p. 87) find that:

> To the extent that black offenders have a preference for the race of their victim, their choice is more likely a black victim than a white victim. Further, given equivalent opportunities, black rapists are no more likely to choose a white woman than white rapists are to choose a black woman. In fact, our evidence suggests that they may be somewhat less likely to do so.

Robbery: Robbery is the offense which most often involves interracial victimization (Hacker, 1992 p. 187), but even for robbery, the majority of offenses are intraracial. In Table 4, the distribution of victims and offender by race is presented for robberies, and all violent victimizations in 1992. As the table shows, whites were more likely to be victimized by blacks than the reverse. As was true of rape, robbery is more intraracial than one would expect based on the percentages of the population which are white and black. Based on data for 1979–1986, Whitaker (1990) reports that 80 percent of all violent victimizations involving single offenders and 66 percent of those involving multiple offenders were intraracial. For robbery, 63 percent of single-offender and 50 percent of multiple offender victimizations were intraracial (Whitaker, 1990, p. 9).

Murder: Murder was more likely to involve intraracial victimization than other violent offenses. FBI data for single victim/single offender murders in 1992 showed 92.4 percent of white victims to have been slain by white offenders and 86.1 percent of black victims to have been slain by black offenders (Federal Bureau of Investigation, 1993).

Another important aspect of victim-offender interaction concerns the degree to which the victim and offender are acquainted or intimate. Because this issue is especially relevant to the explanation of victimization, it will be discussed in the next section.

EXPLANATIONS OF VICTIMIZATION

The description of patterns of victimization above shows the greater likelihood that African-Americans and Hispanic-Americans will become victims of crime. It also demonstrates that black and Hispanic victimization cannot be explained by the distribution of African and Hispanic-Americans demographically. That is, variables such as income, gender, location of residence, marital status, or age distribution do not completely account for the differences in risk of victimization for whites and blacks or for Hispanics and non-Hispanics. We have also seen that violent victimization is mainly an intraracial phenomenon.

Table 4. Percent Distribution of Single-Offender Victimizations Based on Race of Victims, by Type of Crime and Perceived Race of Offender, 1991.

		Perceived Race of Offender			
Type of Crime and Race of Victims	*Number of Single-Offender Victimizations*	*Percent White*	*Percent Black*	*Percent Other*	*Percent Not Known*
Crimes of Violence					
White	3,634,310	74.5	17.1	7.1	1.3
Black	672,120	8.3	85.2	5.9	0.6*
Completed					
White	1,200,190	73.8	18.7	5.5	2.0*
Black	308,490	2.6*	92.3	4.4*	0.7*
Robbery					
White	378,430	39.5	44.4	11.3	4.8*
Black	173,180	4.0*	89.1	5.7*	1.2*
Completed					
White	229,560	40.5	47.6	5.7*	6.2*
Black	122,080	0.0*	92.3	6.0*	1.6*

*Estimate is based on about 10 or fewer sample cases.
Note: Percentages may not total 100 percent due to rounding.
Source: U.S. Department of Justice, 1992 (Bureau of Justice Statistics), p. 61.

These findings suggest that the racial or ethnic identity of crime victims may be of crucial importance in explaining patterns of victimization. And explanations of victimization are essential to developing policies to prevent victimization from occurring in the first place.

Approaches to the Study of Victimization

Criminal victimization may be studied at different levels. Broadly speaking, researchers have sought the determinants of variations in the risk of victimization among individuals and among geopolitical units, such as states, metropolitan areas, and cities.

Efforts to determine why some individuals are more likely than others to become crime victims have proven controversial. Early victimologists adopted what Karmen calls an "interpersonal interactionist perspective" which focused on instances in which victims shared responsibility for their victimization (Karmen, 1991, p. 396):

> They raised the possibility that the actions of the victim before, during, and after they were harmed can often be characterized as careless, risky, or downright inciting. They constructed typologies of victims, indicating that a sub-

> stantial proportion (depending on the crime) can be criticized or faulted for what they did or did not say or do. They anticipated that research studies of large numbers of incidents would reveal patterns of blameworthy behavior that contributed in some degree to their losses, injuries, and suffering.

Large-scale studies of victim "precipitation" of crimes such as rape (Amir, 1971), homicide (Wolfgang, 1958), and property crimes (Fooner, 1971) found evidence for this point of view, but also provoked a strong dissent. Critics of the "victim-blaming" approach noted that inquiries of this sort could always find some indicators that victims behaved irresponsibly in hindsight (Karmen, 1991, p. 397). The stance (critics argue) is similar to that of defense attorneys who put the victim on trial in rape cases by examining every aspect of her prior sexual conduct.

Victim-blaming approaches were also said to reinforce the rationalizations and neutralizing beliefs used by offenders to justify their actions, to undermine the higher purpose of alleviating suffering, and to reflect a simplistic belief in a "just world," in which victims deserve their victimization and the question is what victims have done "wrong" (Karmen, 1991, p. 398). Again, this attitude is often said to be present in cases of rape victimization.

In contrast to victim-blaming approaches, Karmen (1991) identifies "offender-blaming" and "institution- or system-blaming" perspectives on victimization. The offender-blaming perspective, which is very influential in criminal jurisprudence, holds offenders completely accountable for their offense and regards victims as innocent targets. The system-blaming perspective emphasizes "the social-political-economic relationships that generate both victims and victimizers" (Karmen, 1991, p. 299; Elias, 1986).

As the discussion so far implies, the blaming approaches carry a great deal of political and emotional baggage with them. Which approach seems best to policy advocates depends on their own interests and needs. For example, manufacturers of anti-theft devices for automobiles adopt a victim-blaming approach, urging car owners to purchase their products and warning them that they will be sorry if they do not. An offender-blaming approach to auto theft emphasizes the professionalism and technical skills of professional thieves. A system-blaming perspective shifts attention to automakers, insurance company executives, and law enforcement officials, who have not assigned priority to reducing the suitability of autos as targets of theft by improving vehicle security (Karmen, 1991).

The tension between the various blaming approaches is to some extent reflected in explanations for minority victimization. In a broad sense, most explanations may be regarded as "system-blaming," in that they locate the causes of variations in victimization in the context in which the victimization occurs. Most studies attempt to correlate victimization variables with such factors as poverty, income inequality, segregation, family disintegration, and so on. These studies address criminal victimization as caused by factors beyond the control of *either* the offender or the victim. The variables to be explained in this line of research are *rates* of victimization among geopolitical units. It is on these studies that this section is focused.

Theories of Victimization

Williams and Flewelling (1988) describe three general theoretical perspectives in the study of homicide rates that have also been applied to variations in other forms of victimization: "violent cultural orientation," "resource deprivation," and "social disintegration." These perspectives are used to explain offending and victimization in general, but have special relevance for the explanation of the victimization of racial and ethnic minorities. Other theorists (Peterson & Krivo, 1993) explain the victimization of African- and Hispanic-Americans as a function of their social isolation.

Subcultures of Violence

Theories based on violent cultural orientation—the idea of a subculture of violence—propose that conflict interactions are more accepted among members of some groups or among residents within some geographical regions, and that persons within such groups or regions are more willing than others to use force to settle quarrels or get their way (Peterson & Krivo, 1993). The high levels of intraracial violent victimization among blacks are often attributed to their membership in a violent subculture (Curtis, 1974; Messner, 1983; Sampson, 1985; Silberman, 1978).

A violent cultural orientation is understood in one of two ways by most criminologists. Most would probably align themselves with Cohen's (1955) understanding of a subculture as arising from " . . . the existence, in effective interaction with one another, of a number of actors with similar problems of adjustment" (p. 118). In Cohen's description, a subculture is a solution to a problem and will persist only so long as it serves the needs of its creators or those who succeed them. Cohen's idea of subculture portrays it as a relatively weak force in producing value systems, at least compared to the social structural features that give rise to the need for subcultural adaptations in the first place.

Another point of view describes subcultures as far more enduring, autonomous systems of value. Miller's (1958) description of a lower-class culture as " . . . a distinctive tradition many centuries old with an integrity of its own" is an example (p. 159). Wolfgang and Ferracuti's (1967) description of a subculture of violence, which does not attempt to account for the origins of subculture, implicitly endorses the strong view of subculture.

The strong view of subcultures defines a black "underclass" or a lower class culture in terms of values such as Miller's (1958) "focal concerns." The strong view may be categorized as belonging to the "cultural deviance" perspective on criminal etiology (Hirschi, 1969) exemplified by Sutherland's (1947) theory of differential association, which posits that a person becomes criminal because of a relative "excess of definitions favorable to violation of the law" learned in interaction with other persons, especially in intimate personal groups.

The problem with such theories is that they reject the idea that "general needs and values" can be causes of criminal victimization or criminal behavior, since noncriminal behavior is also caused by general needs and values (Sutherland, 1947, p. 58). Greed, then, cannot cause both aggressive sales techniques and petty theft. Unemployment cannot cause both inspired entrepreneurship and purse snatching. An artificially sharp distinction is drawn between criminality and non-criminality. But as Hawkins (1986) points out, "There are other plausible ways aside from the inculcation of values by which the economic, political, and social disadvantages of American blacks may produce high rates of homicide" (p. 113). The same may be said for other forms of criminal victimization.

Depending upon one's politics, strong subcultural theories have an additional weakness or strength: they may be used to rationalize a policy of viewing subcultural members as an intractable, threatening population—a "dangerous class"—whose criminality cannot be altered by changing economic or social conditions. This view is expressed by James Q. Wilson (1975, p. 54):

> If the lower class has focal concerns that make crime attractive or even inevitable, it is not clear how the government would supply "the lower class" with a new set of values consistent with law-abidingness. . . . One could supply the lower class with more money, of course, but if a class exists because of its values rather than its income, it is hard to see how . . . increasing the latter would improve the former.

From this perspective, *nothing* that government can do can affect subcultural crime, whether it is located in the lower class, a black underclass, or among white southerners. The only feasible stance toward criminal subcultures is to treat them as a threatening group and use the resources of the criminal justice system to contain and control them coercively.

Subcultural theories are in accord with victim-blaming strategies for explaining criminal victimization. Both offenders and victims are said to have values favorable to crime, and thus both can contribute to the production of a criminal event. For example, homicide may be described as the outcome of an altercation between two parties who share a violent orientation toward settling conflicts (Wolfgang, 1958).

To assess the relative importance of subcultural values in accounting for variations in victimization rates across geopolitical units, one might assume that the percentage of the population which is black indicates the relative strength of a black subculture of violence, and then employ percent black as a variable in a multivariate analysis (McKean, 1983). Sampson (1985) notes that, if there is a black subculture of violence, then an increase in the percentage of the population which is black should increase the opportunity for criminal contacts among members of a violent subculture as well as reinforcing the intensity and stability of the violent aspects of black culture.

Resource Deprivation

Researchers such as Blau and Blau (1982), Messner (1982, 1983), and Balkwell (1990) have hypothesized that variables such as unemployment, poverty, income inequality and income inequality between races or among ethnic groups will be associated with variations in crime and victimization rates. Williams and Flewelling (1988) point out that the reasons why such variables are associated with crime are not always spelled out by the researchers who employ them, a criticism that applies especially to Blau and Blau (1982).

Balkwell (1990) addresses this problem by developing an explicit statement of the role of ethnic inequality in producing diffuse anger. He proposes that large economic differences between ethnic groups leads members of the disadvantaged group to feel exploited. Whether or not exploitation is occurring, the belief that it is can produce resentment. Low incomes also imply low prestige and power, which make conflicts with members of more powerful groups futile and even dangerous. Thus disadvantaged group members learn to suffer indignities, but at the cost of venting their anger against less powerful and more accessible targets. *"Diffuse anger,"* then, leads to displaced aggression against family and friends (Balkwell, 1990, p. 56).

Harvey (1986) accounts for violence in black, inner-city neighborhoods in much the same way, referring to a "subculture of exasperation" (p. 155):

> The dearth of opportunities that are available to accrue reasonable incomes through socially sanctioned employment, to live in dignity and self-respect, and to realize the same pleasures and benefits as Whites, inevitably results in displays of discontent and outwardly directed aggression.

Although Balkwell and Harvey's accounts of the social psychological link make the connection between resource deprivation and crime more plausible, they also illustrate why Blau and Blau may have avoided delving into this area. Why *don't* some persons who experience resource deprivation relative to other groups commit crimes?

There are a number of plausible answers. "Weak" subcultural explanations, such as that used by Cohen (1955) to explain the formation of delinquent gangs, are one solution. To explain variations among cities or metropolitan areas in rates of victimization, a definitive solution to the problem is not required. One need only hypothesize that conditions of relative deprivation make high rates of victimization more likely.

Williams and Flewelling (1988) suggest another connection between resource deprivation and criminal victimization: resource deprivation may make social control less available, and thus increase the likelihood that persons will resort to violence. Following Gibbs (1981), they define social control as "... attempts by one person to change the behavior of another person through some form (real or perceived) of third party intervention" (Williams & Flewelling, 1988, p. 423). The third party may be a formal agent of control, such as the police or prosecutor, or an informal agent, such as a neighbor or friend.

Resource deprivation may reduce access to social control in two ways. First, it reduces one's ability to acquire the services of third parties, such as attorneys or counselors. Second, it may influence the responsiveness of formal social control agents, such as the police, to one's troubles (Williams & Flewelling, 1988).

Hawkins (1986) has proposed several ways in which African-Americans may have, or perceive themselves to have, less access to formal social control than other groups. He suggests that the racial identity of the victim and offender determines, and has historically determined, the severity of sentences imposed for homicides, with black victimization of whites punished most severely, followed by white victimization of whites, black victimization of blacks, and white victimization of blacks (Hawkins, 1986, pp. 117–119).

We shall examine the possibility that race influences the severity of sanctions for homicide in detail later in this chapter. Here we may summarize the evidence by saying that it usually supports the idea that the racial identity of the victim of homicide helps determine whether the death penalty is imposed. Hawkins argues that patterns of unfair administration of justice have led blacks "... to believe that the behavior of the law protects the lives of whites more than the lives of blacks" (1986, p. 119). This belief, says Hawkins, leads blacks to resort to violence as a means of social control more often than whites, and reduces the deterrent effects of criminal sanctions for murder. It also "devalues" black life compared to white life (Hawkins, 1986, pp. 119–120).

Hawkins (1986) further suggests that law enforcement authorities regard "prehomicide behavior," such as domestic disputes and assaults, as normal and inevitable for blacks, based on stereotypical views of blacks as "normal primitives" (Swigert & Ferrell 1977). Hawkins (1986) hypothesizes that: (1) African-Americans will be less likely to report offenses to the police; (2) When offenses are reported, that they will more often lead to homicide; (3) The police will be less responsive, available and cooperative in dealing with intraracial acts of criminal violence than in dealing with interracial acts; (4) The pattern of punishment for pre-homicide assault will agree with the pattern he describes for homicide, with assaults on whites punished more severely than assaults on blacks.

Social Disintegration

Williams and Flewelling (1988) include under this rubric the ideas of Durkheim and the Chicago School:

> As Shaw and McKay (1972) argued, a breakdown of community integration can weaken informal and institutional forms of social control, thus increasing the likelihood of criminal activity (Williams & Flewelling, 1988, p. 423).

Citing Crutchfield, Geerken, and Gove (1982), Williams and Flewelling say that community integration involves:

> (1) a high degree of consensus in norms, values, and goals; (2) a cohesiveness, or social solidarity; and (3) a sense of belonging or "we feeling" among persons living in the community in question.

Theorists who emphasize social disintegration, or disorganization, almost always link it strongly to resource deprivation. In explaining variations in rates of criminal victimization, it is often difficult to empirically distinguish the effects of deprivation from those of disintegration. The percentage of persons who are divorced or the divorce rate is often used to indicate the latter (Blau & Blau, 1982; Williams & Flewelling, 1988). Other variables which may more directly indicate a lack of consensus, cohesiveness, and sense of belonging include population size, overcrowded residences, educational levels, the percentage of vacant building units, and the percentage of the population who are recent migrants to the area (McKean 1983; Rose & McClain, 1990).

The variables listed above are implicated in making the formation of cohesive social units more difficult. For example, Gillis (1982) suggest that overcrowding impedes attempts at informal control while attracting attempts at formal control, which may produce high rates of officially measured crime. Overcrowding is associated with multi-unit dwellings where residents have less of a sense of control over their environment and a reduced ability to exercise surveillance over their living space (Newman, 1972).

Such variables may be understood as indicators of the capacity of social organizations, such as neighborhoods or cities, to regulate themselves, and "the capacity of constituent groups in a society to behave in terms of their acknowledged moral and collective goals" (Janowitz, 1975, p. 85). In areas with a large percentage of recent migrants, poorly educated persons, or troubled families, there are presumably fewer third parties able to serve as informal agents of social control in resolving disputes and enforcing community norms. For many, personal troubles may overwhelm the capacity to exercise control over much more than the very immediate physical and social environment.

Social Isolation

In addition to the causal mechanisms identified by Williams and Flewelling (1988), a factor of particular interest in explaining variations in criminal victimization for African-Americans, Hispanic-Americans and other racial or ethnic groups is the degree to which they are isolated from the rest of society. As we noted earlier, the ways in which persons are classified for the purpose of examining variations in victimization and criminality may reflect the social distance between dominant and subordinate groups in a society. Subordinate groups that are perceived as threatening are likely to be isolated from dominant groups both physically and socially.

Given a choice, dominant group members are likely to maintain social distance between themselves and such subordinate groups by making decisions that limit their interaction. To put it more plainly, European-Americans with the power to do so are likely to discriminate against African- and Hispanic-Americans in selecting friends, in hiring and promoting employees, in providing desirable governmental services, and in the rental or sale of housing.

In this context, "discriminate" is used literally to mean no more than to make choices which do not favor Blacks and Hispanics. The *motivation* for such choices is not addressed. Choices which maintain social isolation may be made due to prejudice, but they may also reflect no conscious bias or malicious intent.

Residential segregation, or "residential apartheid" as Hacker (1992) calls it, is one area in which discrimination is a well-documented phenomenon (Galster, 1987; Galster, Freiberg & Houk, 1987; Lake, 1981; Pearce, 1979; Schuman & Bobo, 1988; Turner, Stryk & Yinger, 1991; Wienk, Reid, Simonson, & Eggers, 1979). This form of social isolation is associated with a number of social problems such as unemployment, welfare dependency, unwed motherhood, and crime (Peterson & Krivo, 1993).

It is important to note here that discriminatory segregation is probably a cause of these problems. One might say that the social distance between whites and persons of color is physically manifested in residential segregation in a way that is clear to all members of society (Hacker, 1992, p. 38):

> If you are black, these [negative] white reactions [toward integrated housing] brand you as a carrier of contaminations. No matter what your talents or attainments, you are seen as infecting a neighborhood simply because of your race. It opens wounds that never really heal and leaves scars to remind you of how far you stand from full citizenship.

As Logan and Messner (1987) argue, segregation locates people in "networks of social opportunities—it influences prospects for employment, for public services, for educational advancement, for appreciation in home values, and more" (p. 510). One of the effects of this form of social isolation may be to contribute to the likelihood of criminal victimization for African and Hispanic Americans. Segregation is hypothesized to amplify the causal processes identified earlier:

(1) Residential segregation is a form of resource deprivation, which imposes a barrier to the achievement of "the American dream." As with income inequality, segregation should promote diffuse anger which should be reflected in higher rates of victimization by violent crime (Logan and Messner, 1987).

(2) Residential segregation may impede access to informal and formal social control, both as a form of resource deprivation, and as a factor in social disintegration (Peterson & Krivo, 1993, p. 1005):

> At a formal level, individuals in poor and predominantly black neighborhoods may be unable to obtain adequate police protection. At an informal level, segregated black communities may lack the internal resources to organize neighborhood structures to prevent crime. . . . These communities simply lack the monetary, social, and institutional resources to prevent crime.

From the point of view of social disintegration, segregation seems likely to amplify the personal troubles that sap the capacity for informal social control in a neighborhood. As a negative judgement of the worth of persons of color in American society, segregation is demoralizing. It tends to promote a sense of injustice and skepticism toward the legal system, as well as providing a neutralizing rationale (Sykes & Matza, 1957) for criminal behavior: those who condemn criminal behavior are the same as those who condemn on the basis of skin color.

(3) Segregation may also promote a subculture of violence, of either the strong or weak variety. Segregation provides precisely the sort of problem of adjustment that Cohen (1958) describes in his study of delinquent subcultures. A strong subcultural theory would seem likely to assign segregation a role as both cause and effect: segregation may help to originate an autonomous subculture, but the subculture itself would maintain its segregation once it was established.

Were this last hypothesis true, one would expect African-Americans to prefer a high level of residential segregation. Hacker reports that only about one in eight say they prefer a neighborhood which is mostly black. Around 85 percent would prefer an equal mixture of black and white neighbors (Hacker, 1992, p. 35).

(4) A fourth role that residential segregation may play in victimization concerns the effects that it has on opportunities for victimization. Messner and South (1986) suggest that segregation reduces opportunities for interracial contacts and increases opportunities for intraracial contacts. Segregation should therefore be positively associated with intraracial victimization rates and negatively associated with interracial victimization rates.

An Empirical Assessment of Victimization Theories

Earlier studies of variations in crime rates among cities and metropolitan areas typically used Uniform Crime Report data on offenses known to the police or arrests. The crime rates could not be or were not disaggregated by race or ethnicity (e.g., Blau & Blau, 1982; McKean 1983). More recent studies have remedied that problem for some offenses, and they provide the basis for the comments below.

Homicide

Most studies of criminal victimization concentrate on homicide—or more correctly, murder and nonnegligent manslaughter. Data on homicide victimization for American cities and metropolitan areas is readily available from the FBI in the form of the Supplemental Homicide Reports and the Comparative Homicide File developed by Williams and Flewelling (1988), which is based on the supplemental reports.

Sampson (1985) has used arrest rates for homicides in 1970 for the 55 largest cities in the United States to assess the relationship between the relative size of the black population and homicide. As noted above, if there is a strong black subculture of violence, one would expect a positive relationship between percent black and homicide even when indicators of deprivation, disintegration, and isolation are controlled for.

Sampson (1985) finds that percent black is an important variable in accounting for the *combined* homicide rates for whites and blacks. But it is not strongly related to *race-specific* homicide rates, that is, to white homicide rates or African-American homicide rates. The strong subcultural theory predicts a strong relationship—blacks should suffer higher homicide rates where the percentage of the population which is black is high. Although some of his results are surprising, they indicate that the strong subcultural theory does not account for black homicide victimization.

Peterson and Krivo (1993) present findings which most directly address the questions raised in our review of theories of victimization. Using homicide *victimization* data for 1979–1981 for 125 large cities with populations of at least 100,000 and black populations of at least 5,000, they directly assess the effects of several indicators of interest. Unlike Sampson's (1985) study, the percent black population was a statistically significant predictor of aggregate black homicide victimization, but the relationship was *negative.* Residential segregation was positively associated with overall homicide rates, and the percentage of the blacks employed in professional and managerial positions was negatively related to homicide. Of interest here are the variables which were *not* related to homicide in this study. They included income equality among blacks, black-white income inequality, poverty, the percentage of blacks who have graduated from high school, the percentage of black males aged 15–34, the divorce rate, the population, and the region of the country. The data undermines a number of stereotypes about the nature of urban crime.

Following Williams and Flewelling (1988), Peterson and Krivo (1993) further disaggregated black homicide rates on the basis of the victim-offender relationship into three categories: family homicide, acquaintance homicide, and stranger homicide. Family homicide was significantly related to percent graduating from high school, the percent professionally employed, and the region of the country in which the city was located (southern cities had higher rates of family homicide). Acquaintance homicide had statistically significant relationships to segregation, education, percent black (a negative relationship), and region. Stranger homicide was related to segregation, the percent professionally employed, the percentage of black males aged 15–34, and population size.

Peterson and Krivo (1993) interpret their results as contradicting the strong subcultural theories, although the findings do suggest a "southern cultural effect" for family and acquaintance killings. But the results also fail to support social disintegration and resource deprivation theories of victimization.

Noting that the effects of segregation exist only for homicides involving strangers and acquaintances, Peterson and Krivo suggest that it represents the effects of social isolation and lack of social control (Peterson & Krivo, 1993, p. 1020):

> First, if the pattern of segregation reflects resource deprivation, then we would expect the pattern of influence of this variable to be similar to that of the other inequality measures. . . . We do not find this to be the case. Second, acquaintance and stranger homicides can be distinguished from family killings in that they often occur in more public settings. Homicides that are more public may be escalated because of inadequate protection, i.e., "benign neglect" by law enforcement and other agencies, and the inability of neighborhoods to develop peacekeeping activities.

Based on these conclusions, Peterson and Krivo (1993) recommend that greater efforts be made to reduce residential segregation, although they recognize that patterns of housing discrimination are widespread and not easily altered. A more direct strategy for reducing homicide in black neighborhoods involves improving the response of police and emergency services, strengthening or reestablishing local social institutions such as churches, banks, schools, stores, and recreational facilities, and establishing community crime prevention programs.

Robbery

From 1972 until 1975, the National Crime Survey (the predecessor to the NCVS) measured victimization rates for twenty-six cities in the United States. Messner and South (1986) have used this data to examine the effects of the percentage black population, residential segregation, the percentage of whites with low income, the percentage of blacks with low income, and racial inequality in low income on inter- and intra-racial robbery victimization.

Messner and South (1986) find the percentage of residents who are black to be related to all four types of black-white intraracial and interracial victimization. The direction of the relationship varies: it is positive for the rates of black-on-black and black-on-white victimization and negative for the rates of white-on-white and white-on-black victimization. Residential segregation is negatively related to black-on-white robberies, but positively related to black-on-black robberies. The income variables do not play a large role in explaining any of the types of robbery victimization.

Messner and South (1986) suggest that their findings support the idea that inter- and intraracial patterns of offending are influenced by "macrostructural opportunity." A less provocative term might be macrostructural probability. Segregation should function to decrease interracial contact and increase intraracial contacts, and thus affect the probability of robbery victimization. Assuming that African-Americans and whites prefer intraracial contacts to interracial contacts, a larger black population enhances the probability of intraracial and interracial contacts for blacks, but decreases the probabilities of intraracial and interracial contacts for whites.

Robbery is the violent offense for which data is collected that most often involves victimization by a stranger. The U.S. Department of Justice (1992) reports that 84 percent of all robberies reported in 1991 were committed by strangers. The positive relationship between segregation and intraracial robbery found by Messner and South (1986), is thus in accord with the interpretation of the role of segregation in weakening social controls presented by Peterson and Krivo (1993) in their explanation of homicide rates.

The positive relationship that Messner and South (1986) find between percent black and intraracial robbery rates is in conflict with the small negative relationship that Peterson and Krivo (1993) find between the same variable and African-American homicide rates (homicide, as noted earlier, is the most intraracial of violent crimes). The discrepancy could be due to a number of factors, but a likely suspect is the small number of cases available to Messner and South (1986). In their study of homicide in 125 cities in 1980, Peterson and Krivo (1993) do not compare interracial and intraracial homicides. Future research should specifically apply the Messner and South hypotheses to homicide data, especially data for stranger homicides, which seem to be most like robberies in the way that victims and offenders interact. Williams and Flewelling (1988) report that stranger homicides are most likely to have originated in attempts to commit other crimes, such as rape or robbery.

The review of recent research on the correlates of personal victimization is hardly exhaustive or conclusive. Only a few studies disaggregate victimization rates in ways that allow African-American victimization to be examined separately from overall victimization, and appropriate data are simply not available to take a similar approach to Hispanic victimization. Although it is a truism that the correct specification of theoretically significant variables is more important to empirical analysis than the proportion of variance explained in any particular study, it is also worth noting that most of the models specified by the various researchers we have reviewed thus far do not account for the majority of variance in victimization rates.

The findings regarding the relationship of the percentage of the population which is black to victimization rates for blacks tend to cast doubt on the viability of strong subcultural explanations. A strong subculture of violence, involving a large proportion of urban African-Americans, would produce consistent positive relationships between percent black and violent victimization when other variables are controlled. The findings should be robust for various units of analysis at various times, if the subculture of violence has autonomy and tenacity in the face of varying historical and structural conditions. The statistically insignificant or negative relationships found between percent black and homicide arrests and victimizations by Sampson (1985) and Peterson and Krivo (1993) do not meet these expectations.

The results of studies of homicide and robbery allow the very tentative proposition that the social disintegration of *the capacity for social control,* especially as it is influenced by residential segregation, may be more likely to influence patterns of victimization for African-Americans than resource deprivation or a subculture of violence. That possibility may be further explored by examining how the social context in which victimization occurs influences the chances of victimization for individual households.

Household Victimization

Earlier in this chapter, we saw that the individual attributes of crime victims, such as income, gender, age, and location of residence, did not account for the greater likelihood of victimization for African-Americans or Hispanics. Similarly, research on the relationship between the percentage of the population which is African-American and victimization rates for cities was inconclusive. Depending on the units of analysis, the time, and the other variables in the analysis, percent black could have a positive, negative, or statistically insignificant relationship to black victimization rates. The findings cast some doubt on the strong subcultural explanation for African-American victimization, but do not allow definitive statements about the role of resource deprivation or social disintegration.

Smith and Jarjoura (1989) suggest that approaches which allow one to simultaneously examine the effects of individual and neighborhood characteristics might help to resolve these difficulties. In their research, they examine the relationship between individual household characteristics, neighborhood characteristics, and the risk of burglary victimization using data collected from 9,006 households in 57 residential neighborhoods in Rochester, New York; Tampa-St. Petersburg, Florida; and St. Louis, Missouri.

The results show a relationship between the race of household members and burglary victimization. But that relationship is due to neighborhood characteristics. African-American households are more likely to be victimized in areas with a high percentage of single parent households, *or* a high percentage of low income households, *or* a high percentage of youthful residents (Smith & Jarjoura, 1989, p. 632).

Smith and Jarjoura (1989) find that the overall risk of burglary victimization is influenced by racial heterogeneity, residential instability, and family disruption. All these variables have been implicated in social disintegration theories as indicative of a community's capacity for social control. Note that racial heterogeneity, the reverse of racial segregation, is positively related to overall burglary victimization. The findings are not directly comparable to those presented earlier regarding inter-city variations in African American victimization rates for violent crime, because Smith and Jarjoura do not present separate results for black households. The results are in accord with Messner and South's (1986) analysis of robbery victimization, in which segregation was negatively related to interracial robberies.

Segregation and African-American Victimization

The effect of segregation on the organization of cities and neighborhoods for social control is not clear, and is not resolved by the available research. Segregation may weaken controls by concentrating the black population in areas with other social problems (Peterson & Krivo, 1993). Segregation may simply reduce opportunities for interracial victimization, and not be directly implicated in the capacity for control (Messner & South, 1986). Low levels of segregation—high levels of heterogeneity—may also weaken controls by reducing community cohesiveness (Smith & Jarjoura, 1989).

It seems likely that the relationship between residential segregation and criminal victimization is complex. First, the relationship may not take a linear form. Second, the relationship seems especially likely to be sensitive to the way in which segregation is measured and the unit of analysis employed. Third, the relationship is probably historically and locale specific. That is, the effects of segregation may vary with time and place. For example, the almost complete apartheid that was the norm in American cities until the 1960's may have actually strengthened informal social controls in African-American neighborhoods, by reducing the degree of economic segregation possible and assuring close interaction between informal agents of social control and persons at risk of delinquent and criminal behavior.

Overall, the results are in accord with the suggestion made earlier that the relationship between social control and victimization is most often implicated by empirical analysis. This suggests that the ways in which agencies of control respond to African-American and Hispanic-American victims may have implications for understanding the risk of victimization. In particular the ways in which criminal justice agencies and victim assistance agencies deal with black and Hispanic victims are of interest (Hawkins, 1986).

VICTIMIZATION AND SOCIAL CONTROL

As described earlier, Hawkins (1986) hypothesizes that historical and current reactions to black victims by criminal justice agencies may shape patterns of homicide victimization. The higher rates of homicide suffered by African-Americans, he suggests, may be due in part to the belief that the law protects whites more than blacks, which leads to greater reliance on violence as a means of control, reduces the deterrent effect of punishment, and devalues the lives of black victims (Hawkins, 1986). Hawkins hypothesizes that patterns of punishment for homicide and "prehomicidal behavior" reveal that victimization of whites is punished more severely than victimization of African-Americans, that blacks are less likely to call the police than whites, and that the police are less responsive to black calls for help.

Before considering Hawkins's hypotheses and other ways in which formal agencies of social control influence patterns of victimization, it is important to examine the assumptions that underlie these issues. First, we are assuming that "there is a coherent criminal justice system operating in any particular social setting" (Duffee 1980; p. xv). Second, we are assuming that criminal justice agencies function as agencies of crime prevention. These assumptions are subject to debate (Duffee, 1980).

The ways in which criminal justice agencies define their goals may or may not reflect a consensus among the agencies which form a "system" of criminal justice. In the first place, there is considerable variation in the goals pursued by different types of agencies. For example, Wilson (1972) notes that police departments vary a great deal in their commitment to law enforcement as a primary goal.

Secondly, police departments, prosecutors, judges, and correctional agencies are not subject to common policy directives or centralized administration. In particular, the informal, unstated goals of the different agencies seem likely to conflict, if for no other reason than that they are all competing for the same scarce tax dollars. Portrayals of "the criminal justice system" as a monolithic protector—or oppressor—ascribe more consensus on policy to criminal justice agencies than can be observed to exist.

In addition to the question of how patterns of social control influence patterns of victimization, there is also the issue of whether criminal justice agencies particularly mistreat black and hispanic victims of crime. The general goal most often ascribed to criminal justice agencies is crime prevention through the detection, apprehension, prosecution, trial, and punishment of lawbreakers. Of interest here is the possibility that criminal justice agencies, especially the police, function instead to control minority groups which are perceived as threatening by a dominant majority (Chamlin & Liska 1992; Jackson, 1992; Lusane, 1991). For example, many African-Americans complain that the "war on drugs" is actually a war on young blacks (Bazemore & McKean, 1993; Hutchinson, 1990).

Of course, these goals are not necessarily in complete conflict with one another, but to the extent that the aim of criminal justice agencies is to protect whites from persons of color, then the victimization of persons of color seems unlikely to be a high priority.

The Criminal Justice Response to Crime Victims

This issue should be considered in the context of the evidence that criminal justice practitioners in some jurisdictions routinely mistreat *all* crime victims, or mistreat victims on the bases of criteria other than race or ethnicity, such as socio-economic status, gender, or the demeanor of the victim (Karmen, 1984). An even more basic consideration is how to determine if mistreatment has occurred. For example, although accusations of "blaming the victim" have taken on a negative connotation, the fact remains that some victims will seem more blameworthy to practitioners who operate in the framework of the adversary system, where the goal is to assign one hundred percent of the liability for harm and loss to one party.

The primary purpose of criminal justice agencies is usually thought to be the punishment of criminal offenders (Griffiths, 1970). The systems view of criminal justice typically depicts the agencies as contributing to a process which is designed to apprehend suspected offenders, sort out the guilty and the innocent, and appropriately sentence the guilty. Punishing criminal offenders is understood to contribute to the public good in several ways, but especially by the prevention of crime. It was Beccaria who provided the original argument that "The purpose [of punishment] can only be to prevent the criminal from inflicting new injuries on . . . citizens and to deter others from similar acts" (Beccaria, 1963 [1764], p. 42). Even those who wish the system to punish on the basis of just desert rather than prevention, or those who wish to rehabilitate, make the identification and disposition of offenders their priority.

Several observers have argued that criminal justice agencies make the punishment of offenders a priority to such an extent that they neglect the need to provide assistance to victims (Chu, 1991; Karmen, 1984; Wertheimer, 1991). Senator John Heinz, a sponsor of the Omnibus Victims Protection Act, says:

> One crime goes largely unnoticed. It is a crime against which there is no protection. It is committed daily across our nation. It is the painful, wrongful insensitivity of the criminal justice system toward those who are victims of crime. . . . The callousness with which the system again victimizes those who have already suffered at the hands of an assailant is tragic (quoted in Karmen, 1984, p. 125).

The double victimization of crime victims may take any number of forms. The police may not take a victim's report at face value. Once a report is accepted, the police may be unwilling or unable to effect an arrest or to recover property that has been stolen. Police and prosecutors may fail to inform victims of the status of their case. Prosecutors may drop cases, plea bargain, or unnecessarily withhold a victim's property when it is to be used as evidence. Police and prosecutors may fail to take measures to prevent intimidation of victims by offenders (Karmen, 1984). Perhaps the most unnecessary and galling complaint that victims have about criminal justice practitioners concerns the "second injury" inflicted upon the victims through impersonal, indifferent, or callous treatment by police officers and prosecutors (Karmen, 1984, p. 138).

Given that the punishment of offenders is the first priority of criminal justice agencies, some actions which will be perceived as mistreatment by victims may be unavoidable. But, as Wertheimer notes, appeals to the public good (versus the private interests of crime victims) cannot account for the "pattern of purposeless neglect" that characterizes the way in which the agencies treat victims (1991, p. 416). Instead, Wertheimer finds mistreatment of crime victims to be implicit in the state's assumption of the role of adversary of the offender (1991, p. 417):

> A systematic indifference to the crime victim's interests is an unintended outcome that needs only the natural tendencies of individuals operating a bureaucracy to become a virtual inevitability, resistible only by an aroused citizenry.... When those general dispositions operate within the peculiar structure and ethos of our criminal justice system, they become tendencies to treat the crime victim either as a mere resource for the system's aims or else as an unwelcome intruder with no legitimate stake in the institutional processes. Some officials, may, as individuals, sympathize with a victim's plight, but the internal logic of the system they work within provide few if any motives for respecting the victim's interests.

Criminal Justice and the Victimization of Persons of Color

If we accept the proposition that criminal justice agencies tend to mistreat all crime victims, we are still left with the question of whether persons of color are more likely to be mistreated than whites. Is there a pattern of "triple victimization" operating?

In his theory of the mobilization of law, Black (1976) proposes that "all else constant, lower ranks will have less law than higher ranks" (p. 17). In his view, the mobilization of the law is a resource which may be unevenly distributed in a society much as other resources are. Law—in the form of responses to complaints of victimization—may be more readily activated for persons of high status than persons of low status (Black, 1983, p. 39):

> Lower-status persons of all kinds—blacks and other minorities, the poor, the homeless—enjoy less legal protection, especially when they have complaints against their social superiors, but also when conflict erupts among themselves. To the police and other authorities the problems of these people seem less serious, their injuries less severe, their honor less important.

Mistreatment may take two forms: (1) an unwillingness to devote resources to the arrest, prosecution, and sentencing of offenders when the victim is a minority group member, as hypothesized by Black (1976) and Hawkins (1986); and (2) the provision of a lower quality or quantity of direct services to minority victims.

Supporters of the triple victimization hypothesis cite the familiar argument that the social distance between victims who are persons of color and criminal justice practitioners is responsible for differential treatment. Gross and Mauro (1989) cite research suggesting that "black victims may be seen as stronger and more threatening than equally passive white victims" (p. 113). They suggest that this effect is most likely to operate in capital cases (Gross & Mauro, 1989, p. 113):

> In a society which remains segregated socially if not legally, and in which the great majority of jurors are white, jurors are not likely to identify with black victims or to see them as family or friends. Thus jurors are more likely to be horrified by the killing of a white than of a black, and more likely to act against the killer of a white than the killer of a black. This reaction is not an expression of racial hostility but a natural product of interracial relations in our society. It is simply an emotional fact.

Gross and Mauro suggest that judges and attorneys are also subject to these effects. Even where a prosecutor is aware of and can overcome his personal bias, the prosecutor may make decisions based on predictions of how juries will respond to a case (Gross & Mauro, 1989, pp. 114–115).

Karmen suggests that such considerations influence decisions made in all sorts of cases (Karmen, 1984, p. 165):

> Apparently, the claims of victims from discriminated-against groups are not perceived as being entirely legitimate or compelling by the men at the helm of the criminal justice system. The credibility of calls for help from disadvantaged victims is eroded by a belief that these same people are offenders in other incidents. These stereotypical responses by the authorities poison relations between the two camps.

A related idea is that minority victims may be viewed as "legitimate victims." Williams (undated) argues that black women are seen as legitimate victims of sexual assault, based on myths about their sexual promiscuity. The myth provides the basis for denial of injury and blaming the victim, two "techniques of neutralization" (Sykes & Matza, 1957) that allow offenders to deny the seriousness of their crimes. Williams extends the idea of neutralization to the way in which some criminal justice practitioners view victims. Persons who are seen as legitimate victims are "neutralized," and their assailants are pursued, prosecuted, and punished with less zeal.

The implication, as noted by Karmen (1984), is that minority group victims are less likely to call upon the criminal justice system, turning to it "only under the most desperate circumstances" (1981, p. 166). As a result, Black (1983) predicts that the member of such group are more likely to resort to "self-help" in order to resolve disputes. That is, they are likely to take the law into their own hands. Crimes, then, may be committed as acts of control when legitimate methods of social control are not available (Black, 1983).

There are three empirical questions that must be addressed in order to evaluate this theory. First, is it in fact the case that the police and the courts are less responsive to the victimization of African-Americans and other minority group members? Second, are criminal justice agencies *perceived* as being less responsive? The perception may have the effect of increasing victimization even if the reality is different. Third, is there a link between the reality or perception of weakened social control (assuming that it exists) and rates of victimization? Below, we will review some of the recent research that bears on these questions.

Law Enforcement and Minority Victims

Attitudes toward Crime and Criminal Justice: Because perceptions may play an important role in the extent to which persons avail themselves of formal social control, the attitudes of blacks and Hispanics toward crime the police, and the courts are important. An examination of recent public opinion surveys reported in *The Sourcebook of Criminal Justice Statistics, 1992* (Maguire, Pastore, & Flanagan, 1993) suggests that African-Americans, and to a lesser extent Hispanic Americans, have an anxious outlook on crime and justice. On the one hand, they are in greater fear of crime. On the other, they have less faith in the ability of criminal justice agencies to deal effectively and fairly with crime. All the results reported below are from national opinion surveys reported in the *Sourcebook.*

When asked to list "real problems in *this* neighborhood," crime was listed by 49 percent of the black respondents and 27 percent of the white respondents, juvenile delinquency was listed by 32 percent of blacks and 20 percent of whites, and treatment by the police was listed by 18 percent of blacks and 7 percent of whites (Maguire, Pastore, & Flanagan, 1993, p. 163).

Black respondents were more likely than white respondents to indicate fear of crime. Forty-six percent of blacks surveyed reported a "sense of danger from gun violence" in 1993 compared to 34 percent of whites (Maguire, Pastore, & Flanagan, 1993, p. 186). In 1992, 58 percent of African-American respondents and 42 percent of white respondents reported that they were afraid to walk alone in some parts of their neighborhood at night (Maguire, Pastore, & Flanagan, 1993, p. 189). The percentage of blacks reporting this reached a high of 61 percent in 1982, declined to 45 percent in 1988, and has been increasing ever since (Maguire, Pastore, & Flanagan, 1993, pp. 190–191). Blacks and Hispanics were also more likely to report having modified their behavior due to crime by limiting the times and places when they shopped or worked, limiting the places they would go alone, purchasing a weapon, and installing a home security system (Maguire, Pastore, & Flanagan, 1993, p. 1992).

As Table 5 shows, Blacks and Hispanics are more likely than whites to rate their police poorly in a number of areas of performance. Recent research by Murty, Roebuck and Smith (1990) on the attitudes of black Atlanta residents toward the police replicates earlier studies which indicate that "Older, married, white-collar, highly educated, and employed respondents reported a more positive image of the police than did their counterparts—younger, single, blue-collar, low-educated, unemployed/underemployed respondents (Murty, Roebuck, & Smith, 1990, p. 255)." Those who had recent negative contacts with the police or were acquainted with someone who had recent negative contacts, and those who lived in high crime areas were more likely to report negative image of the police. Residence in high-crime census tracts was the single most important predictor of negative police image (Murty, Roebuck, & Smith, 1990, p. 256).

Table 5. Percentage Rating Police "Poor" in Selected Performance Areas,* by Race and Ethnicity, 1992.

	Race or Ethnicity		
Performance Area	*White*	*Black*	*Hispanic*
Solving Crime	8	17	9
Preventing Crime	11	18	19
Responding Quickly to Calls for Help and Assistance	7	16	9
Being Helpful and Friendly	5	12	11
Treating People Fairly	9	26	13
Not Using Excessive Force	7	16	23

Note: Respondents were asked, "How would you rate the police in your community on the following . . . " followed by the performance area. Response categories were "Excellent," "Pretty good," "Only fair," and "Poor."
Source: Maguire, Pastore, and Flanagan, 1993, pp. 169–172.

Like European-Americans, African-Americans are divided on the role of the courts: ten percent of black respondents think the courts deal too harshly with offenders, but 76 percent think that they are not harsh enough (Maguire, Pastore, & Flanagan, 1993, p. 197).

Only 26 percent of African-Americans surveyed support the death penalty for murder over life in prison without parole, compared to 56 percent of whites (Maguire, Pastore, & Flanagan, 1993, p. 205). More blacks than whites (73 percent versus 41 percent) thought that a black defendant would be likelier to get the death penalty than a white defendant for the same offense. Both blacks and whites thought that poor persons were more likely to get the death penalty than a person of average income (Maguire, Pastore & Flanagan, 1993, p. 208).

Reporting Crimes to the Police. If it is true that African-Americans are less confident in the fairness and effectiveness of police, it stands to reason that they would be less likely to report victimizations to the police as Hawkins (1986) and Black (1983) suggest. But an analysis of twenty years of data from the National Crime Victim Surveys indicates that there are no overall differences in reporting rates between black and white victims and between Hispanic and non-Hispanic victims. In 1991, 48.8 percent of white victims and 47.2 percent of black victims reported their victimizations to the police. For the same year, 50.1 percent of hispanic victims and 48.3 percent of non-Hispanic victims reported their victimizations (U.S. Department of Justice, 1992, pp. 104–105).

In a specific test of Black's (1976) hypothesis, Gottfredson and Hindelang (1979) found that the seriousness of the victimization event, not the social rank of the victim, was the best predictor of reporting. Gottfredson and Hindelang (1979) used income as an indicator of social rank, and did not specifically address racial or ethnic differences in reporting rates in their study.

How do these findings reflect upon the proposition that African-Americans are less likely than European-Americans to mobilize formal social control resources? The results are anomalous. If the seriousness of victimization events is a better predictor of the decision to call the police than race or ethnicity, then one would expect a *higher percentage* of minority group members to do so. As described above, blacks and Hispanics suffer more injurious victimizations (Harlow, 1989).

A more detailed examination of the 1991 data from the NCVS does not reveal consistent patterns when injury resulting from victimization is taken into account. In all cases, victims are more likely to report offenses in which an injury occurs (Maguire, Patore, & Flanagan, 1993, pp. 104–105). Table 6 shows reporting rates for violent victimizations resulting in injuries to the victim. African- and Hispanic-Americans are less likely than whites or non-Hispanics to report completed robberies with injuries, but more likely to report aggravated and simple assaults. Blacks, but not Hispanics, are more likely than their comparison group to report attempted robberies with injuries.

The percentages reported in Table 6 are probably not trustworthy due to the low number of respondents in each category, but they do cast some doubt on the assertion that the relationship between social status, crime seriousness and the decision to call the police is simply understood. A first step toward resolving the anomalous findings would be to examine NCVS data which has been aggregated for a multi-year period in order to address the problem of a low number of respondents falling into each category. Preliminary work by Whitaker (1990) on data for 1979–1986 shows that blacks are slightly more likely to report crimes of violence than whites. The

Table 6. Percentage of Violent Victimizations with Injury Reported to the Police, by Type of Crime and Race or Ethnicity of the Victim, 1991.

	Race		*Ethnicity*	
Type of Crime	*White*	*Black*	*Hispanic*	*Non-Hispanic*
Completed Robbery	75.4	65.0	65.8	74.5
Attempted Robbery	36.8	71.6*	28.1*	52.4
Aggravated Assault	60.4	80.3	83.0	62.1
Simple Assault	52.8	60.4	61.2	52.6

*Estimate is based on ten or fewer sample cases.
Source: U.S. Department of Justice, 1992, pp. 104–105.

seriousness of the offense is not taken into consideration. The differences in reporting are very small: zero percent for robbery, two percent for aggravated and simple assault, and six percent for rape (Whitaker, 1990, p. 8).

The results reported by Whitaker for rape victims are surprising from the point of view of the social status hypothesis. Black women are in some ways doubly marginalized, and therefore should be the least likely to call upon the police.

A survey by Wyatt (1992) of women in Los Angeles who had experienced sexual assault attempted to deal with some of the problems with the reporting of rape victimizations in surveys, including confusion over the definition of rape, self-blaming by victims, and anticipated lack of support for reporting (Russell, 1983; Williams & Holmes, 1981). Wyatt (1992) discovered that African-American women were far more likely not to have disclosed incidents of sexual assault to anyone until years after the event, and were less likely to have reported the incident to the police.

Are race and ethnicity related to the decision to report a crime to the police? The findings from the NCVS and other research do not yield a clear answer. There is a need for a multivariate analysis using a sufficient number of respondents to address the problem of too few cases in critical categories. Researchers may also need to be sensitive to whether especially traumatic forms of victimization are likely to be disclosed to researchers of a different race, ethnicity, or gender (Wyatt, 1992).

Police Response to Minority Victimization: Police officers may take the complaints of white victims and complainants more seriously than those of African-Americans. Smith, Visher, and Davidson (1984) addressed this question in a study of police-citizen encounters in sixty residential neighborhoods in St. Louis, Missouri; Rochester, New York; and Tampa-St. Petersburg, Florida. They discovered that:

> the police are more likely to arrest in situations involving white complainants, while denying black complainants in similar situations the protection of law. Differential responsiveness appears strongest with property crimes and encounters in which complainants want offenders arrested. In both situations, police are more responsive to white victims (Smith, Visher & Davidson, p. 248).

Bynum, Cordner, and Greene (1982) found that the police were more likely to follow up on and extensively investigate cases where the victim was white. In both this and the study by Smith, Visher, and Davidson (1984), the social distance between police officers and black victims is suggested as the reason for less responsiveness.

Prosecution and Minority Victims: A study by Myers and Hagan (1979) of defendants charged with a felony in Marion County (Indianapolis), Indiana, found that the decision to prosecute a case depended in part on the race of the victim (p. 446):

> Both black defendant-white victim and white intraracial events are more likely to be fully prosecuted than are black intraracial events. . . . Regardless of the offender's race, then, if the victim is white, the case is more likely to be prosecuted fully.

Myers and Hagan (1979) also found that prosecutors were more likely to try a case (rather than accept a guilty plea) if the victim was male, older, and employed, and if no serious victim misconduct was alleged. The researchers suggest that prosecutors "typify" the cases they consider on the basis of their prior experience with similar cases, with an eye to maximizing the likelihood of obtaining a conviction and a harsh sentence. The race, age, gender, employment, and criminal history of a victim all reflect upon the victim's credibility and therefore can influence the odds of conviction (Myers & Hagan, 1979).

Judicial Proceedings and Minority Victims

Sentencing for Homicides: The differential treatment of offenders on the basis of the racial or ethnic identity of the victim has been most thoroughly explored for capital cases. Studies of homicide cases in Florida (Radelet & Pierce, 1985), South Carolina (Paternoster, 1984), Georgia (Baldus, Pulaski, & Woodworth, 1983), and Kentucky (Keil & Vito, 1990) provide evidence that prosecutors are more likely to seek the death penalty for homicides involving white victims than black victims. Research by Klemm (1986) in Louisiana challenges this conclusion.

Gross and Mauro (1989) examined the effects of race of victim on death penalty sentencing for eight states: Georgia, Florida, Illinois, Oklahoma, North Carolina, Mississippi, Virginia, and Arkansas. In each case, they found that death sentences were more likely when the victim was white than when the victim was black, although the relationship was not always very strong. In general, the effect of the victim's race remained strong when other variables, such as the number of aggravating factors involved in the homicide and the relationship between the victim and the offender, were taken into account.

When the death penalty is applied, the probability that it will be executed is correlated strongly with the race of the victim. Bohm (1991) reports that between 1977 (when the Supreme Court declared the death penalty to be constitutional under some circumstances) and 1990, 140 persons were executed in the United States. Eighty-five percent of their victims were white. A white person has yet to be executed for killing a member of any minority group. Of the 55 black persons executed, only 29 percent were executed for killing a black person despite the intraracial character of most murders (Bohm, 1991, p. 78).

Trials and Sentencing for Other Offenses: The racial or ethnic identity of victims may have some effect on the outcomes of jury trials. Lafree (1989) studied 38 jury trials of sexual assault cases in Marion County (Indianapolis) Indiana and found that "Jurors were less likely to believe in a defendant's guilt when the victim was black (p. 219)." Interviews with jurors suggested that stereotypes regarding the sexual behavior of black women influenced some jurors. This is in accord with Williams' (undated) arguments, discussed earlier.

Lynch and Patterson (1990) have examined the relationship between the victim's race and sentencing for robbery and burglary cases in four jurisdictions: New Orleans, Louisiana; Tucson, Arizona; Norfolk, Virginia; and Seattle, Washington. In their analysis, they compare white to nonwhite victims. Lynch and Patterson (1990) find a relationship between race of victim and whether offenders are incarcerated:

> Relative to white defendants, and controlling for the effects of legally relevant criteria, type of crime, and jurisdiction, non-white defendants who victimize whites are significantly more likely to receive a prison term than white defendants, however, non-whites who victimize other non-whites are not significantly more likely to be incarcerated than whites who have victimized other whites (p. 55).

Lynch and Patterson (1990) do not find a relationship between the racial victim/offender relationship and the length of sentence received.

Under-Served Victims

Besides the question of how resources are allocated to prosecute offenders, there is also the issue of how direct services to victims are provided through victim/witness assistance programs and victim compensation programs. As was true in the examination of how cases are processed through criminal justice agencies, any discussion of whether minority victims are under-served must begin with the question of whether most or all victims are under-served or ineffectively served by such programs, regardless of minority/majority status. In this context, the *availability, utilization, underlying assumptions, and effectiveness* of victim programs are subject to scrutiny.

Victim-witness assistance programs are often justified as a means of improving the cooperation of victims and witnesses with prosecutors, thus enhancing the prosecutors' ability to win convictions. By removing barriers to cooperation, assistance programs seek to make cooperation with prosecutors less costly (Davis, 1983).

Some research by the Vera Institute (Davis, 1983) suggests that even well-run victim-witness assistance programs have little impact on the attendance of witnesses at hearings or the rates at which cases are dismissed. As suggested by the findings of Cannavale and Falcon (1976), Davis (1983) suggests that victim and witness cooperation is not essential to prosecutors in disposing of cases in the lower courts. In fact, actively "cooperative" victims and witnesses may actually be viewed as threatening because they threaten to disrupt relations between prosecutors and defense attorneys. Davis argues that the problem may be that victim/witness assistance programs are simply not in accord with the largely symbolic role that victims play in criminal proceedings.

A survey of victim-witness programs by Roberts (1990) provides some support for the analysis by Davis. Roberts finds that programs in large cities do not appear to serve the same proportion of victims as programs in smaller cities. The major complaints of program administrators in all locales (and regardless of whether the program is sponsored by the local prosecutor) is that they lack the funding, space, and staff to do an adequate job.

Direct evidence on the extent to which African-American or Hispanic-American victims are underserved was not found in the literature. A hypothesis which should be tested in future research involves referrals to victim-witness programs by police officers. Smith, Visher, and Davidson (1984) suggest that the social distance between police officers and African-American victims may influence the officers to be less responsive. If so, one would expect the same effect to operate in victim-witness program referrals.

A similar problem may exist with victim compensation programs. Such programs are infamous for red tape and delay, and strict eligibility requirements result in up to two-thirds of claimants receiving no compensation (Elias, 1983). Many states deny compensation to victims whose conduct is found to contribute to their victimization, and to victims who do not "cooperate" with law enforcement. Several states require victims of family violence to prosecute the offender to receive compensation (McGillis & Smith, 1983).

Given that blacks and Hispanics suffer disproportionately from violent victimization, one would expect persons from these groups to be overrepresented among the claimants and rewardees of victim compensation programs. Research by Elias (1983) indicates that this may not be the case. In a study of victims in New York and New Jersey, he found that race was not a factor in the decision to apply for compensation. When applicants were compared, Elias (1983) found that whites were slightly more likely than blacks to be awarded compensation.

Another aspect of the treatment of minority victims by criminal justice practitioners is the extent to which practitioners possess awareness of and sensitivity to cultural differences among victims. Cook, Smith, and Harrell (1987) suggest that "psychological distress is the central, dominant reaction of crime victims" and that "prior life stress" further aggravates their pain (p. 15). If so, sensitivity to psychological suffering would seem to be essential to informal and formal attempts to serve all victims of crime by all practitioners who come into contact with victims. Beyond a general sensitivity to psychological stress, practitioners need to understand " . . . the psychological impact of victimization in different minority groups and premises and essential components of culturally sensitive victim treatment" (Ogawa, 1990).

Improving Services to Minority Victims

As the issues presented above suggest, improving services to minority victims must be addressed in the context of improving services to all crime victims, as well as improving sensitivity to minority cultures. As this implies, improving services may have to do with questions about the nature and purposes of criminal justice as it relates to the victims of crime. These questions go beyond such recommendations as improving training, reallocating resources, or streamlining service delivery.

At a minimum, two widely-held assumptions about criminal justice must be questioned: (1) the assumption that criminal justice has mainly to do with the efficient processing and punishment of the maximum number of criminal offenders, and (2) the corollary assumption that criminal justice is a matter of developing and implementing sophisticated technologies for behavioral control of the population. As DiIulio (1992) argues, a "democratic vision" of criminal justice requires that " . . . all citizens have the right and responsibility to participate in the system. Citizens are co-producers of justice" (p. 8).

DiIulio (1992) identifies four purposes for criminal justice (p. 10):

(1) Doing justice,
(2) Promoting secure communities,
(3) Restoring crime victims, and
(4) Promoting noncriminal options.

In particular, criminal justice best serves victims when it *prevents crimes from occurring* and aims overtly and directly at *healing the harm suffered by victims.* The prevention of crime has the benefit of reducing levels of victimization.

Efforts to heal the harm suffered by victims may require practitioners to place less emphasis on imposing penal sanctions on offenders. For example, in deciding whether to incarcerate an offender, the inability of imprisoned offenders to make financial restitution to their victims should be at least as important a consideration as the dubious gains to be realized by "making an example" of the offender by imposing a lengthy term of imprisonment. The second alternative is a good example of decision-making in service of a theory, rather than in service of people.

Alternative methods of resolving disputes, using mediation mechanisms rather than adversary decision-making, may provide one basis for moving toward the goal of helping victims to recover from crime (McGillis, 1986). Programs employing alternative mechanisms may have their own problems, such as providing a less satisfying level of justice to clients (Auerbach, 1984), and extending social control over clients without the benefit of due process of law (Tomasic & Feeley, 1982). The question is especially relevant to minority victims, who may perceive alternative methods of dealing with crime as second-best.

CONCLUSION

In this chapter we have explored patterns of criminal victimization, explanations for those patterns, and the treatment or mistreatment of African-Americans and Hispanic-Americans by criminal justice agencies.

The analysis has left open the question of how criminal justice practice may contribute to the victimization of Americans in general and especially Black and Hispanic Americans. Although the capacity for social control has been implicated as a causal factor, the role of criminal justice as an agency of social control is not clear.

The goals which the author suggests—preventing crime and healing victims—may not be the primary goals of criminal justice agencies. Both goals would seem to require criminal justice practitioners to be especially sensitive to the problems of poor, black, and Hispanic crime victims, but nothing in our review of the literature suggests that this is the case. Instead, the research reviewed here supports the position that criminal justice agencies function to control minority populations which seem threatening to the white majority in the United States.

The situation is not necessarily dichotomous. *Both* crime prevention and the control of threatening populations may be goals of criminal justice. As noted earlier, high rates of violent crime have afflicted the United States throughout this century and affect every segment of the population. But if one goes strictly by the "outcomes" of criminal justice work, it is of interest to recall that overall rates of victimization have remained stable or declined in the past twenty years even as rates of African-American and Hispanic-American victimization have increased. At the same time, rates of correctional supervision for black and Hispanic men have reached all-time highs. Nationally, nearly one in four black men and one in ten Hispanic men between the ages of 20 and 29 are behind bars, on probation, or on parole (Currie, 1993).

These remarks should not be read to support any notion of a conspiracy to control the black population (Hutchinson, 1990; Lusane, 1991) or even to suggest that there is a great deal of overt prejudice toward African-Americans or Hispanic-Americans. Much of the variation in victimization levels we have documented seems to be due to factors such as segregation and social disorganization, which are not directly under the control of criminal justice agencies. Further, criminal justice agencies seem to routinely abuse and neglect all victims of crime.

This suggests that crime victims in general, but especially minority victims, are perceived by criminal justice practitioners as "them"—as socially distant groups with whom it is difficult to identify and who may threaten the established routines of the criminal justice process. This perception *is* something that criminal justice agencies can and should address.

REFERENCES

Amir, M. (1971). *Patterns in forcible rape.* Chicago: University of Chicago Press.

Auerbach, J. (1984). *Justice without law.* New York: Oxford University Press.

Bailey, F. Y. (1991). Law, justice, and "Americans": An historical overview. In M. J. Lynch & E. B. Patterson (Eds.), *Race and criminal justice,* pp. 10–21. Albany, NY: Harrow and Heston.

Baldus, D. C., Pulaski, C. A., & Woodworth, G. (1983). Comparative review of death sentences: An empirical study of the Georgia experience. *Journal of Criminal Law and Criminology, 74,* 661–753.

Balkwell, J. W. (1990). Ethnic inequality and the rate of homicide. *Social Forces, 69*(1), 53–70.

Bastian, L. D. (1990). *Hispanic victims.* Washington, DC: U.S. Department of Justice, Bureau of Justice Statistics.

Bastian, L. D. (1993). *Criminal victimization 1992.* Washington, D.C.: U.S. Department of Justice, Bureau of Justice Statistics.

Bazemore, G., & McKean, J. (1993). Minority Overrepresentation. In L. S. Thompson & J. A. Farrow (Eds.), *Hard time, healing hands: Developing primary health care services for incarcerated youth,* pp. 99–119. Arlington, VA: National Center for Education in Maternal and Child Health.

Beccaria, C. (1963 [1764]). *On crimes and punishments* (H. Paolucci, Trans.). Indianapolis, IN: Bobbs-Merrill.

Black, D. (1976). *The behavior of law.* New York: Academic Press.

Black, D. (1983). Crime as social control. *American Sociological Review, 48,* 34–45.

Blau, J. R., & Blau, P. M. (1982). Metropolitan structure and violent crime. *American Sociological Review, 47,* 114–128.

Bohm, R. (1991). Race and the death penalty in the United States. In M. J. Lynch & E. B. Patterson (Eds.), *Race and Criminal Justice,* pp. 71–85. Albany, NY: Harrow and Heston.

Bynum, T. S., Cordner, G. W., & Greene, J. R. (1982). Victim and offense characteristics: Impact on police investigative decision-making. *Criminology, 20,* 301–318.

Cannavale, F., & Falcon, W. (1976). *Witness cooperation.* Lexington, MA: D.C. Heath.

Chamlin, A., & Liska, A. (1992). Social structure and crime control revisited: The declining significance of intergroup threat. In A. E. Liska (Ed.), *Social Threat and Social Control,* pp. 23–44. Albany, NY: State University of New York Press.

Chu, J. T. (1991). A systems science approach to crime, criminal justice, and victim justice. In D. Sank & D. I. Caplan (Eds.), *To be a victim: Encounters with crime and injustice,* pp. 117–140. New York: Plenum Press.

Cohen, A. K. (1955). *Delinquent Boys: The culture of the gang.* New York: Free Press.

Cook, R. F., Smith, B. E., & Harrell, A. V. (1987). *Helping crime victims: Levels of trauma and effectiveness of services.* Washington, DC: U.S. Department of Justice, National Institute of Justice.

Crutchfield, R. D., Geerken, & Gove, W. R. (1982). Crime rate and social integration. *Criminology, 20,* 467–78.

Currie, E. (1993). *Reckoning: Drugs, the cities, and the American future.* New York: Hill and Wang.

Curtis, L. A. (1974). *Criminal violence.* Lexington, MA: Lexington Books.

Davis, R. (1983). Victim/witness noncooperation: A second look at a persistent phenomenon. *Journal of Criminal Justice, 11,* 287–299.

Dawson, J. M., & Boland, B. (1993). *Murder in large urban counties, 1988.* Washington, DC: U.S. Department of Justice, Bureau of Justice Statistics.

DiIulio, J. J. (1992). *Rethinking the criminal justice system: Toward a new paradigm.* Washington, DC: Bureau of Justice Statistics, U.S. Department of Justice.

Duffee, D. E. (1980). *Explaining criminal justice: Community theory and criminal justice reform.* Cambridge, MA: Oelgeschlager, Gunn, and Hain.

Elias, R. (1983). *Victims of the system: Crime victims and compensation in American politics and criminal justice.* New Brunswick, NJ: Transaction Books.

Elias, R. (1986). *The politics of victimization.* New York: Oxford University Press.

Federal Bureau of Investigation. (1993). *Crime in the United States, 1992.* Washington, DC: U.S. Department of Justice, Federal Bureau of Investigation.

Federal Bureau of Investigation. (1989). *Crime in the United States, 1988.* Washington, DC: U.S. Department of Justice, Federal Bureau of Investigation.

Fooner, M. (1971). Money and economic factors in crime and delinquency. *Criminology, 8,* 311-320.

Galster, G. C. (1987). Residential segregation and interracial economic disparities: A simultaneous equations approach. *Journal of Urban Economics, 21,* 22–44.

Galster, G. C., Freiberg, F., & Houk, D. L. (1987). Racial differentials in real estate advertising: An exploratory case study. *Journal of Urban Affairs, 9,* 199–215.

Georges-Abeyie, D. E. (1989). Race, ethnicity, and the spatial dynamic: Toward a realistic study of black crime, crime victimization, and criminal justice processing of blacks. *Social Justice, 16*(4), 35–54.

Gibbs, J. P. (1981). *Norms, deviance and social control.* New York: Elsevier.

Gillis, A. R. (1974). Population density and social pathology: the case of building type, social allowance and juvenile delinquency. *Social Forces, 16,* 306–314.

Gottfredson, M. R., & Hindelang, M. J. (1979). A study of The Behavior of Law. *American Sociological Review, 44,* 3–18.

Griffiths, J. (1970). Ideology in criminal procedure, or a third "model" of the criminal process. *Yale Law Journal, 79,* 359–371.

Gross, S. R., & Mauro, R. (1989). *Death and discrimination: Racial disparities and capital sentencing.* Boston: Northeastern University Press.

Hacker, A. (1992). *Two nations: Black and white, separate, hostile, and unequal.* New York: Charles Scribner's Sons.

Harlow, C. W. (1989). *Injuries from crime.* Washington, DC: U.S. Department of Justice, Bureau of Justice Statistics.

Harvey, W. B. (1986). Homicide among young black adults: Life in a subculture of exasperation. In D. F. Hawkins (Ed.), *Homicide among black Americans,* pp. 153–171. Lanham, MD: University Press of America.

Hawkins, D. F. (1986). Black and white homicide differentials: Alternatives to an inadequate theory. In D. F. Hawkins (Ed.), *Homicide among black Americans,* pp. 109–135. Lanham, MD: University Press of America.

Hirschi, T. (1969). *Causes of delinquency.* Berkeley, CA: University of California Press.

Hutchinson, E. O. (1990). *The mugging of black America.* Chicago, IL: African American Images.

Jackson, P. I. (1992). Minority group threat, social context, and policing. In A. E. Liska (Ed.), *Social Threat and Social Control,* pp. 46–57. Albany, NY: State University of New York Press.

Janowitz, M. (1975). Sociological theory and social control. *American Journal of Sociology, 81,* 82–108.

Karmen, A. (1984). *Crime victims: An introduction to victimology.* Monterey, CA: Brooks/Cole.

Karmen, A. (1991). The controversy over shared responsibility: Is victim-blaming ever justified? In D. Dank & D. I. Caplan (Eds.), *To be a victim: Encounters with crime and justice,* pp. 395–408. New York: Plenum Press.

Keil, T., & Vito, G. (1990). Race and the death penalty in Kentucky murder trials: An analysis of post-Gregg outcomes. *Justice Quarterly, 7,* 189–207.

Klemm, M. (1986). *The determinants of capital sentencing in Louisiana, 1979–1984* [doctoral dissertation]. New Orleans, LA: University of New Orleans (cited in David W. Neubauer (1992), *America's Courts and the Criminal Justice System,* 4th edition. Belmont, CA: Wadsworth).

Koppel, H. (1987). *Lifetime likelihood of victimization.* Washington, DC: U.S. Department of Justice, Bureau of Justice Statistics.

LaFree, G. D. (1989). *Rape and criminal justice: The social construction of sexual assault.* Belmont, CA: Wadsworth.

Lake, R. W. (1981). *The new suburbanites: Race and housing in the suburbs.* Newark, NJ: Center for Urban Policy Research, Rutgers University.

Logan, J. R., & Messner, S. F. (1987). Racial residential segregation and suburban violent crime. *Social Science Quarterly, 68,* 510–527.

Lusane, C. (1991). *Pipe dream blues: Racism and the war on drugs.* Boston, MA: South End Press.

Lynch, M. J., & Patterson, E. B. (1990). Racial discrimination in the criminal justice system: Evidence from four jurisdictions. In B. D. MacLean & D. Milovanovic (Eds.), *Racism, Empiricism, and Criminal Justice,* pp. 51–59. Vancouver, Canada: Collective Press.

Lynch, M. J., & Patterson, E. B. (1991). *Race and criminal justice.* New York: Harrow and Heston.

Maguire, K., Pastore, A. L., & Flanagan, T. J. (eds). (1993). *Sourcebook of criminal justice statistics—1992.* Washington, D.C.: U.S. Department of Justice, Bureau of Justice Statistics.

Mann, C. R. (1993). *Unequal justice: A question of color.* Bloomington, IN: Indiana University Press.

McGillis, D. & Smith, P. (1983). *Compensating victims of crime: An analysis of American Programs.* U.S. Department of Justice, National Institute of Justice.

McGillis, D. (1986). *Community dispute resolution and public policy.* Washington, DC: U.S. Department of Justice, National Institute of Justice.

McKean, J. B. (1983) *Sources of crime among metropolitan areas* [doctoral dissertation]. Tallahassee, FL: Florida State University.

Messner, S. F. (1982). Poverty, inequality, and the urban crime rate. *Criminology, 20,* 103–114.

Messner, S. F. (1983). Regional and racial effects on the urban homicide rate: The subculture of violence revisited. *American Journal of Sociology, 88,* 997–1007.

Messner, S. F., & Rosenfeld, R. (1993). *Crime and the American dream.* Belmont, California: Wadsworth.

Messner, S. F., & South, S. J. (1986). Economic deprivation, opportunity structure, and robbery victimization: Intra- and interracial patterns. *Social Forces, 64*(4), 975–991.

Miller, W. B. (1958). Lower class culture as a generating milieu of gang delinquency. *Journal of Social Issues, 14,* 5–19.

Murty, K. S., Roebuck, J. B., & Smith, J. D. (1990). The image of the police in black Atlanta communities. *Journal of Police Science and Administration, 17*(4), 250–257.

Myers, M., & Hagan, J. (1979). Private and public trouble: Prosecutors and the allocation of court resources. *Social Problems, 26,* 439–451.

Myrdal, G. (1944). *An American dilemma: The negro problem and modern democracy.* New York: Harper and Row.

Newman, O. (1972). *Defensible Space: Crime prevention through urban design.* New York: Collier.

O'Brien, R. M. (1987). The interracial nature of violent crimes: A reexamination. *American Journal of Sociology, 92*(4), 817–835.

O'Carroll, P. W., & Mercy, J. A. (1986). Patterns and recent trends in black homicide. In Darnell F. Hawkins (Ed.), *Homicide among black Americans,* pp. 29–42. Lanham, MD: University Press of America.

Ogawa, B. (1990). *Color of justice: Culturally sensitive treatment of minority crime victims.* Sacramento, CA: California Office of Criminal Justice Planning.

Parrillo, V. (1985). *Strangers to these shores.* New York: John Wiley and Sons.

Paternoster, R. (1984). Prosecutorial discretion in requesting the death penalty: A case of victim-based racial discrimination. *Law and Society Review, 18,* 437–478.

Pearce, D. M. (1979). Gatekeepers and homeseekers: Institutional patterns in racial steering. *Social Problems, 26,* 325–342.

Peterson, R. D., & Krivo, L. J. (1993). Racial segregation and black urban homicide. *Social Forces, 71,* 1001–1026.

Radelet, M., & Pierce, G. (1985). Race and prosecutorial discretion in homicide cases. *Law and Society Review, 17,* 587–621.

Riedel, M. (1984). Blacks and homicide. In D. Georges-Abeyie (Ed.), *The criminal justice system and blacks,* pp. 51–60. New York: Clark, Boardman.

Roberts, A. R. (1990). *Helping crime victims: Research, policy, and practice.* Newbury Park, CA: Sage.

Rose, H. M., & McClain, P. D. (1990). *Race, place, and risk: Black homicide in urban America.* Albany, NY: State University of New York Press.

Russell, D. (1983). The prevalence and incidence of forcible rape in females. *Victimology, 7,* 81–93.

Sampson, R. J. (1985). Race and criminal violence: A demographically disaggregated analysis of urban homicide. *Crime and Delinquency, 31,* 47–82.

Schuman, H., & Bobo, L. (1988). Survey-based experiments on white racial attitudes toward racial integration. *American Journal of Sociology, 94,* 273–99.

Shaw, C. R., & McKay, H. D. (1972). *Juvenile delinquency and urban areas.* Chicago: University of Chicago Press.

Silberman, C. E. (1978). *Criminal violence, criminal justice.* New York: Random House.

Smith, D. A., Visher, C. A., & Davidson, L. A. (1984). Equity and discretionary justice: The influence of race on police arrest decisions. *Journal of Criminal Law and Criminology, 75,* 234–249.

Smith, J. C., Mercy, J. A., & Rosenberg, M. L. (1984). *Comparison of homicides among*

Anglos and Hispanics in five southwestern states. Atlanta, GA: Center for Disease Control.

Smith, D. A., & Jarjoura, G. Roger. (1989). Household characteristics, neighborhood composition, and victimization risk. *Social Forces, 68,* 621–640.

South, S. J., & Felson, R. B. (1990). The racial patterning of rape. *Social Forces,* pp. 71–93.

Sutherland, E. H. (1947). *Principles of Criminology.* Philadelphia: J.B. Lippincott.

Swigert, V. L. & Ferrell, R. A. (1977). Normal homicides and the law. *American Sociological Review, 42,* pp. 16–32.

Sykes, G. M., & Matza, D. (1957). Techniques of neutralization: A theory of delinquency. *American Sociological Review, 22,* 664–670.

Tomasic, R., & Feeley, M. (eds). (1982). *Neighborhood justice: Assessment of an emerging idea.* New York, NY: Longman.

Turner, M. A., Struyk, R. J., & Yinger, J. (1991). *Housing discrimination study: A synthesis.* Washington, DC: U.S. Department of Housing and Urban Development, Office of Policy Development and Research.

U.S. Department of Justice. (1992). *Criminal victimization in the United States, 1991.* Washington, DC: U.S. Department of Justice, Bureau of Justice Statistics.

U.S. Department of Justice. (1992a). *Criminal victimization in the United States: 1973-1990 trends.* Washington, DC: U.S. Department of Justice, Bureau of Justice Statistics.

Werthhiemer, R. (1991). Preferring punishment of criminals over providing for victims. In D. Sank & D. I. Caplan (Eds.), *To be a victim: Encounters with crime and justice,* pp. 409–421. New York: Plenum Press.

Whitaker, C. J. (1990). *Black victims.* Washington, DC: U.S. Department of Justice, Bureau of Justice Statistics.

Wienk, R. E., Reid, C. W., Simonson, J. C., & Eggers, F. J. (1979). *Measuring racial discrimination in American housing markets: The housing market practices survey.* Washington, DC: U.S. Department of Housing and Urban Development.

Wilbanks, W. (1985). *The myth of a racist criminal justice system.* Belmont, CA: Brooks/Cole.

Williams, J., & Holmes, K. (1981). *The second assault: Rape and public attitudes.* Westport, CT: Greenwood.

Williams, K. R., & Flewelling, R. L. (1988). The social production of criminal homicide: A comparative study of disaggregated rates in American cities. *American Sociological Review, 53,* 421–431.

Williams, L. M. (Unknown). *Race and rape: The black woman as legitimate victim.* Rockville, MD: U.S. Department of Health and Human Services, National Institute of Mental Health.

Wilson, J. Q. (1972). *Varieties of police behavior: The management of law and order in eight communities.* New York: Atheneum.

Wilson, J. Q. (1975). *Thinking about crime.* New York: Vintage.

Wolfgang, M. (1958). *Patterns in Criminal Homicide.* Philadelphia: University of Pennsylvania Press.

Wolfgang, M., & Ferracuti, F. (1967). *The subculture of violence: Towards an integrated theory in criminology.* London: Tavistock.

Work, M. N. (1913). Negro criminality in the South. *Annals of the American Academy of Political and Social Sciences, 49,* 74–80.

Wyatt, G. E. (1992). The sociocultural context of African American and white American women's rape. *Journal of Social Issues, 48,* 77–91.

Zawitz, M. W., Klaus, P. A., Bachman, R., Bastian, L. D., DeBerry, M. M., Rand, M. R., & Taylor, B. M. (1993). *Highlights from twenty years of surveying crime victims: The National Crime Victimization Survey, 1973-1992.* Washington, DC: U.S. Department of Justice, Bureau of Justice Statistics.

CHAPTER FOUR

NATIVE AMERICANS IN CRIMINAL JUSTICE

Kurt Siedschlaw and James N. Gilbert

INTRODUCTION

Although long ignored by traditional critical examination of criminal justice within the United States, Native American justice systems are no less significant than our larger, more familiar systems of justice. Although in many cases predating white legal systems, Indian justice has until relatively recently been one of the forgotten stepchildren of bureaucratic, historical, and cultural study.

Many factors contributed to this neglect such as the diversity of tribes, public and governmental disinterest, and geographic remoteness. Yet, the historical reality of the American Indian as a beaten and ignored enemy is quite possibly the single most significant causal element. Until the late 1960s, Indian justice was rarely mentioned in the literature of American criminal justice. As the general public gradually became aware of the horrendous level of crime common place on many reservations, attention once again turned toward Indian populations. In addition to intolerable rates of reservation crime, the emergence of the politically active Indian civil rights movement during the 1970s resulted in increased attention. Finally, the early 1990s has produced a new wave of interest in Indian affairs as expressed in an outpouring of popular fiction and cinema. While popular recent interest has been centered upon Native American history, art and culture, Indian crime and justice continues to be studied by justice researchers and students alike.

This chapter details the past and present involvement of Native Americans within the American criminal justice system. The historical origins of Indian justice will be discussed as will topics of contemporary importance. Through a relatively complex historical and social process, the status of Indians as justice practitioners, victims, offenders, and citizens, is unique within our society. Initially, the chapter will trace the historical development of organized Indian systems of policing. The development of Indian policing quite accurately mirrors many of the related central issues of current concern to Indian populations. Accordingly, the distinct developmental factors which created an Indian police and connecting criminal justice subsystems will be detailed. The chapter will then discuss contemporary Indian justice issues, many of which are directly linked in a causative fashion to past developments. This latter portion of the chapter will particularly detail the definition and concept of Indian multiculturalism, the linkage of Indian spirituality to justice concepts, and opposing values which often cause confusion and conflict between Indian and white populations.

THE DEVELOPMENT OF INDIAN JUSTICE

In a similar fashion to any organized social community, Indian reservations have instituted various systems of legal control. The Bureau of Indian Affairs currently reports 287 Indian reservations within the confines of the United States; each having some form of organized criminal justice. The evolution of the current state of Indian policing can be traced to at least the 17th century. Fearing their Indian neighbors, British colonial governors urged some type of police presence among local villages. However, early Native American accounts clearly indicate that many tribes had formed well-established self-policing elements long before the advent of European colonization. As French (1982) observes, early plains-dwelling Sioux possessed their own tribal police, called the Akicitas. Exhibiting an early form of consolidated government, the Akicitas possessed a connected judicial system and various forms of redress for wrongdoing. Such early tribal "police societies" as detailed by Hagan (1966) were "not a law unto themselves but, rather, carried out the will of the tribe . . . members of the society selected to act as police enforced the rules" (p. 13). While membership requirements differed from tribe to tribe, only the most proven of warriors were generally selected to perform policing duties. The duties of the early Indian police varied, yet in most tribes their value was greater in external warfare than in domestic in-village needs. For example, prior to and during an attack upon enemy tribal forces, the Akicitas Sioux "police" were primarily responsible for keeping younger warriors under control to preserve the element of surprise.

With the ever increasing number of whites settling near or on traditional Indian land, some tribes sought to emulate the new, more powerful culture. In particular, the Cherokee and Choctaw Indians are cited as tribes which most rapidly acculturated white norms; including the adoption of European-based criminal justice (Hagan, 1966; Kidwell & Roberts, 1980). The Cherokee nation developed a relatively sophisticated legal code in 1808, and organized a police group termed the "lighthorse" to enforce their laws. As McKee and Schlenker (1980) note, this practice was soon diffused to other tribes, as demonstrated by the Choctaws which established a mounted tribal police force in 1812 known as the "Light Horsemen."

Yet, the period of 1830 to 1870 proved to be the single most crucial to the development of Indian police, as the pattern of federal control still evident in the 1990s was firmly established. This period is noted for a relentless government policy of Indian relocation. Tribe after tribe of Native Americans were removed from their traditional homelands, often in the East, and isolated in "enclaves where missionaries and government officers could pursue their goal of civilizing the Indian" (Rosen, 1976, p. 2). Accordingly, federal Indian policy became explicitly designed to assimilate the Indian into white culture by initial containment followed by indoctrination and imitation. This concept permeated literally every area of established Indian culture including religion, education, and criminal justice.

The federal government, through its formal representative upon the reservation, sought to demonstrate the superiority of the ways of white culture in comparison to Native American practices. Accordingly, reservation agents routinely ignored or rapidly disbanded tribal justice traditions and village warrior societies. Urged or forced in their place was the creation of a government-controlled Indian police. Thus the origins of the first federally sponsored Indian police is thought to be Thomas Lightfoot's efforts concerning two Nebraskan tribes. Lightfoot informed Washington in 1869 that "I have appointed a police, whose duty it is to report to me if they know of anything wrong" (Etheridge, 1977, p. 74). Such early attempts to establish tribal police were generally successful, for as a beaten enemy most tribes were totally dependent upon the government for their survival. Compared to policing units, judicial and correctional tribal organizations were generally formed during latter periods, as their need was not as crucially perceived by reservation agents.

Native American Justice and the Bureau of Indian Affairs

In the 19th century, as now, the federally authorized Bureau of Indian Affairs (BIA) was a major force in the continuing development of Indian criminal justice. A division of the United States Department of the Interior, the BIA responded cautiously to the request of early reservation agents such as—Thomas Lightfoot (Sac-Fox), John Clum (Apache), and William Arny (Navajo). Such caution was naturally based upon a hesitancy to sanction and arm a former powerful enemy. Yet, white reservation officials were quite eager to establish Indian police units for two central reasons; crime control among their own people, and to wrestle control of the reservation from military domination.

As the newly formed Indian police demonstrated their tenacity and worth, the Commissioner of Indian Affairs, John Q. Smith, began to actively support their continued existence. Believing a system of law and order would hasten the civilizing of the Indians, Smith requested Congressional funding in 1876. As the Indian police concept gained support, the former practice of using military units to police the various reservations gradually dissipated. In 1879, Congress accepted the logic of using Indians to police fellow Indians, appropriating thirty thousand dollars for their continued funding (Wachtel, 1982).

Although the early BIA controlled Native American police units were patterned after white justice concepts, they did offer a positive element to Indian people. While Indian social and traditional systems were rapidly undergoing change, the police offered a point of contact between the reality of the present demands of the white and what remained of their old system of Indian to Indian "law and order" (Vantine, 1978). Yet, many Indians deeply resented any official attempt to alter their traditional methods, including the development of police elements patterned after the white methods of organization and control. Indian police officers were often viewed as simple repressive tools of the oppressors, a pattern which would repeat itself during the 1970s.

Traditionalist suspicions were confirmed as a number of major Indian leaders were killed during encounters with Native police officers, including the nationally reported killing of Chief Sitting Bull in 1890. Indeed, as Russel (1960) suggested, the killing of traditional leaders may have been motivated by reasons more sinister than the necessary discharge of duty. Concluding that the Indian police were a device for civilizing the Indian, some believed that the Native police were purposely manipulated against the traditionalists by depriving them of tribal influence and political power. However, agency controlled police grew quickly into a standard, unique reservation feature. By 1881, 49 of the 68 Indian reservations had developed some form of policing (Indian Law Enforcement History, 1975). As reservation police continued to expand, judicial and correctional duties continued to remain off the reservation. When Indian defendants were to be tried within criminal court, they generally were dealt with in State or territorial courts. In a similar fashion, convicted Indians would normally serve their prison or county jail sentences within established white institutions.

While the Department of the Interior through the supervision of the Bureau of Indian Affairs regulated reservation justice from afar, most Indian police forces were operating as separate bureaucratic organizations. As crime increased and the departments grew, many jurisdictional questions naturally arose. It became obvious that new federal legislation would be required if the Indian police were to continue to operate in a "legal" fashion. Accordingly, in 1885, the United States Supreme Court held in *Ex Parte Crow Dog* (109 US 556) that federal courts did not have jurisdiction to handle cases where both the victim and offender were Indians and the crime occurred on an Indian reservation (Wachtel, 1982). The written decision strongly suggested that Congress enact a legislative remedy, which resulted in passage of the Major Crimes Act of 1885. This Act remains the guiding legal authority of Indian justice today which gave federal courts and the police jurisdiction over specified crimes involving Indian suspects and victims on reservation lands. The practical results of the Act not only cleared the way for federal judicial prosecution, but firmly established the control and legitimacy of a BIA controlled Indian police throughout the United States.

With the legal authority of the United States government firmly established under the Major Crimes Act, the federally sponsored BIA Indian police remained the sole reservation law enforcement presence for many decades. This status, however, was to be dramatically altered in 1975 when Congress passed the Indian Self Determination and Education Assistance Act. This Act specifically authorized each tribe the clear option of utilizing the existing BIA police or creating an independent, tribally controlled and supervised option.

CONTEMPORARY INDIAN JUSTICE OPERATIONS

Nearly 1,400,000 Native Americans currently reside in the United States. Approximately one-half of this population is found within 287 federal and state land holdings designated as Indian reservations scattered throughout the country (Lorentino, 1989). The United States Department of the Interior has determined that the Major Crimes Act applies to approximately 72 percent of all reservations, with the remaining reservations utilizing law enforcement programs which are provided by, or contracted with, non-Indian state or county authorities (Department of Interior Memorandum, 1993). Thus, the traditional BIA supervised or tribally controlled Indian police still predominate. Federally controlled BIA police are present on 37 percent of the reservations, and operate through the direction of the Secretary of the Interior. Roughly one out of three Indian police officers are BIA rather than tribal, totaling nearly 450 men and women throughout the nation's reservation system. BIA police are, in a technical sense, officers of the tribal courts, but in practice answer directly only to BIA officials in Washington, D.C. Unique from any other federal enforcement agency such as the Park Police or Border Patrol, BIA Indian police provide law enforcement to permanent resident communities within specific geographic areas. Governed by the same general policies accorded to non-police employed by the BIA, criminal justice personnel are covered by the rules of the United States Civil Service.

In response to the Indian Self Determination Act numerous tribes have exercised their option to create independent police, and to a more limited degree, courts and correctional operations. By the mid-1990s, nearly 60 percent of all Indian reservations covered by the Major Crimes Act had opted for more tribal control, thus breaking from the 19th century precedent of total BIA domination. The nearly 100 tribes within this status continue to receive funding and limited supervision from the Bureau of Indian Affairs. However, the tribal governments exercise near total control over the hiring, training standards, and enforcement policies of their reservation police. Thus, tribally controlled Indian police units are believed by some to be more responsive and sensitive to their policed populations than BIA Indian police operating under nationwide federal standards and practices. The BIA model does ensure a uniform and often higher level of training and professionalism which is not always inherent in tribal departments policing within the often super-charged political atmosphere of reservation government.

A relatively small number of Indian reservations have reflected both the BIA and tribal options of justice administration. Electing to contract with local non-Indian police or sheriff's departments, nearly 30 percent of all reservations have no Indian dominated justice system. Typically, this type of reservation is much smaller than other Indian reservations and selects an "off reservation" justice system due to practical fiscal considerations.

Contemporary Indian criminal justice operations are severely challenged in the 1990s in a similar fashion to the crime crisis in non-Indian communities. In addition to natural crime increases based upon increased population, drugs, or other socially induced factors, reservation crime is impacted by historical elements unique to the American Indian. Unemployment, assaultive crime, substance and child abuse all occur within Indian reservations far out of proportion to non-Indian populations. In particular, the rise in juvenile crime has been noted in the past decade; a problem which traditionally has not been as longstanding in nature as adult Indian criminality. There are currently 67 correctional detentional facilities on reservations throughout the United States serving both adult and juvenile offenders. Of the total, only six (having a true bed capacity of just 87 beds) are exclusively reserved for juveniles. Most tribes are experiencing an unprecedented rise in juvenile crime which now far exceeds the existing detention capacities. The Nez Perce, for example, filed 43 juvenile cases within their tribal court in 1991 and 70 cases in 1993; an increase of 67 percent within two years (Indian Country Today, 1993). Such increases are unfortunately typical of the current state of Indian delinquency within many reservations.

Other contemporary concerns continue to focus upon the efficiency and professional conduct of the BIA police model. As detailed above, the relationship between BIA personnel and traditionalist Indians has been historically strained. An unfortunate legacy of suspicion continues to exist within some reservations, as typified by a recent Associated Press investigation. The independent six-month investigation found that BIA officers were accused of 17 cases of excessive force on six reservations within a recent three year period. The Associated Press concluded that none of the accused officers were disciplined or punished; not even when medical evidence demonstrated injury through choking, beatings, or kickings (Indian Country Today, 1993).

In their defense, BIA police officials have stated that force is often inevitable in the course of making violent arrests. Yet, much of the suspicion continues aided by the lack of civilian complaint boards and the perception that BIA police officers are answerable only to distant Washington supervisors.

Regardless of whether a reservation justice system is federal or tribal in nature, policing, judicial processing and corrections are often complex and difficult tasks. In addition to high levels of crime, Indian criminal justice practitioners are typically overworked, underpaid, and inadequately trained. Many reservations are vast with populations sparsely dispersed. The Rosebud reservation is typical, with only eleven police officers policing a population of 18,000 within an area the size of Connecticut. Yet, officers routinely make arrests out of proportion to their numbers, straining the limited resources of tribal courts and jails.

However difficult criminal justice is within Native American reservations, its practice is vastly confounded by the complexities of culture. Misunderstandings, mistakes, tragedies, exploitation, and disasters have occurred in the past due to Euro-Americans claiming to speak for Native American people. It is suggested that if one expects to consider the impact of culture on a group of people and the relationship between groups one should understand their own cultural base. Informal surveys taken by the authors of white, middle class, college students at a small university has resulted in the fact that very few even acknowledged that they had a cultural basis of their own that influenced their view of life. The Euro-American majority culture tends to view itself as "the" culture. Often this view is taken without understanding what that culture is.

If one is to begin to understand Native American cultures, one must dedicate oneself to talking with, listening to, observing and interacting with Native American people. Even having done these things, there are limits to understanding. The Euro-American approach to life, and most issues stresses the "scientific" approach. This perspective maintains that one can break any factor of life into its smallest divisible part, analyze the relationships between the parts, put it back together again and you will "understand" that factor of life. Other cultures, especially the Native American cultures, defy scientific method. To dissect a culture is to diminish or destroy the reality and potential of the whole. As a result, any effort to consider how Native

Americans and the criminal justice system interact will diverge from scientific methods in part. The effort to explain aspects of Native American culture and spirituality automatically diminishes the experience of personal understanding and awareness.

If multiculturalism is a process created to provide an understanding of a culture by examining, comparing and contrasting one culture to another, does it automatically presume that one culture is dominant and thus right, and other cultures must be compared, good or bad, to the dominant culture? Euro-Americans have progressed from the eastern shores to the Pacific coast with the idea that they, as the enlightened species, were right because of divine right or by right of conquest. It is time to set aside the conquest and "manifest destiny" ideology and begin to understand the Indian cultures that so much effort has gone into destroying.

EURO-AMERICAN MULTICULTURALISM

In order to examine multiculturalism, what it is and how the concept affects or is affected by Native Americans and the criminal justice system, one must begin to understand that cultures are defined by Euro-American perspectives. Wendy Rose (1992) puts the issue of understanding culture into perspective:

> The "core" of information constituting the essential canon of every discipline in academe—from philosophy to literature, from history to physical science, from art to mathematics—is explicitly derived from thought embodied in the European tradition. This is construed as encapsulating all that is fundamentally meaningful within the "universal attainment of human intellect." The achievements and contributions of all other cultures are considered, when they are considered at all, only in terms of appendage (filtered through the lens of Eurocentric interpretation), adornment (to prove that other traditions, unlike those derived from Europe, are narrowed and provincial rather than broad and universal) (p. 407).

Interviews by the authors with Native American inmates in a state prison system might be summarized in a statement that multiculturalism may be the study of a culture that examines and appreciates another culture without demeaning, damaging or destroying that culture. A Native American inmate observed that the boundary between recognizing differences but not stealing from, or damaging a culture is, in its positive sense, multiculturalism. Can Euro-American, or Hispanic or Afro-American criminal justice professionals allow themselves to examine Native American cultures, strive to understand Native American cultures without judging, attacking, demeaning or stealing from that culture? We Euro-Americans view ourselves as the most important aspect of life; and in order to insure that non-conformist perspective, we identify differences to reinforce our nonconformity. These people are different from those people. This set of ideas is different, separate and unique from that set of ideas.

To begin an understanding of Native Americans, multiculturalism, and the criminal justice system, a person must step away from what has tended to be a judgmental, conquest-makes-right, governing, and controlling approach to life and consider the alternative. Much of what may be presented as multicultural training and education can be categorized as a distraction or placebo. Take this, learn and understand. Agencies that might provide a training component for several hours of lecture, pictures, slides and/or movies meant to highlight aspects of a culture may be fooling the presenters and those receiving the training into a belief they are now "multicultural." Whatever the intent of such multicultural training, it may dissipate and fail because it does not begin to address what a culture is. If one is to understand the Native American, one must determine what Native American you are talking about. Is the training meant to help understand behavior, reactions, perception of life, customs, values, etc.? If it is, prepare yourself for a lifetime learning experience. Each Native American by lineage, blood, custom and his/her own understanding has a culture. The rural Native American's culture has been modified and shaped by those surroundings. The urban Native American has had his/her ancestral culture shaped and affected by that environment. The Ute, Winnebago, Santee, Omaha, Lakota, Dakota, Brule, Comanche, Apache, Hopi, Navajo and hundreds of other clans and tribes, both recognized and not recognized by the United States government, each represent a separate and distinct culture.

Tribal diversity creates an insurmountable task if there is to be an attempt to understand the cultures of Native American people. It is this reality of the complexity of Native American cultures that leads to a presentation of an aspect of Native American culture that a number of Euro-Americans have noted and begun to appreciate. That aspect is Native American spirituality.

NATIVE AMERICAN SPIRITUALITY

Cultural Foundation in Spirituality

One aspect of the Native American culture, that may be most significant in the development of an understanding that is implied within a multicultural ideal, is that of Native American spirituality. Spirituality is an aspect of Native American culture that Euro-Americans thought they had packaged in something called religion. Since Euro-Americans were "successful" at the conquest and are the carriers of the religious banner of Christianity and

Judaism, then Euro-Americans tend to know and control the understanding and definition of spirituality. A strange, but understandable, phenomena has been taking place in the United States. Native Americans have been beset with non-indigenous people wanting to experience Native American life. New religions have developed based on Native American traditions and ceremonies (Rose, 1992, p. 414). From the onset it needs to be understood that Native American life and Native American spirituality is not something to be experienced but rather something to be lived. The exploration of Native American spirituality has, at times, taken on a "cultural imperialism" that parallels the relationships between the dominant culture and Native American people (Rose, 1992, p. 404). The Euro-American tends to want to take and possess what they observe and admire. One can not take and possess spirituality no more than one can take and possess Native American identity.

Part of Native American identity and spirituality is being a conformist. Euro-Americans tend to be non-conformists. They prefer to identify distinctions. They tend to make distinctions, separate, and divide. Native American spirituality defies distinction, dissection and analysis. The great obstacle in describing Native American spirituality is the simple effort to separate it into component ideas or concepts and put it into writing. Native Americans have primarily an oral history. Being a story teller is an honored and prestigious calling. The story teller, in using native language, paints pictures through spoken word, intonation, and expression; much more than words are communicated. In the effort to conform to Euro-American methods these stories have been recorded, translated, and put into writing. Does the story then maintain the same meaning as the story teller gave? The words are there but the meaning is in the telling. The same phenomena exists when considering an attempt to explain Native American spirituality.

An immediate detriment to putting Native American spirituality into writing is that the meaning is either diminished or lost entirely. Spirituality, among Native American people, is demeaned by sharing it for other than spiritual enhancement purposes. Allow us to provide an example. An interview with a Native American inmate serving a long sentence revealed that this inmate was gaining insight, inspiration and understanding and developing coping skills through activities and communication with a Holy Man of his tribe. The interviewer, being a former parole officer, immediately saw benefit in packaging the involvement with the Holy Man into a parole plan and selling it to the parole board. This could be a potential benefit if explained properly and enhance the inmate's parole possibilities. The inmate immediately pointed out to the former parole officer the interviewer's lack of understanding. To use the insight achieved through activity with the Holy Man, meant to gain spiritual insight. Such insight could never be used for personal gain, as the spiritual value of the communications would be destroyed. Thus, the inmate would not use his learning and contact with a Holy Man in seeking consideration for parole.

THE NATIVE AMERICAN AS A CONFORMIST

The Native American is a conformist. The historical, cultural, basis for Native American existence is to give up individuality to the values of the group or the greater whole. One's personal life values are secondary to the group and the family, with the whole more important than the individual. The true whole is the cosmos, all things and everything. Nature, the Earth, Sky, Wind, Sun, all creatures are the whole. Native Americans are not accidentally identified by tribal affiliation. The tribe or clan is the basis for survival. Each member of the tribe has his/her role, as does each member of the universe. Even the historical method of naming people reflects a difference between the Native American and the Euro-American. Native Americans, traditionally, tend to name people after aspects of nature or what attribute another may see in them, Yellowtail or Black Elk, Crow Dog or Spotted Tail. A connection is directly made with the natural rather than encouraging an individual as an isolated entity unto ones self through a name devoid of nature like John Smith. The Indian name could come from a physical characteristic, a natural event, a creature or item of nature, while Euro-Americans name children as separate, individual entities rather than as part of a natural sphere.

Native American values tend to emphasize community, family and then the individual. It would appear that Euro-American values favor individuality, and then consider family and community. To be banished from the tribe was the worst punishment within the tribe. To be assigned responsibility and acknowledged by the group as having made a useful contribution (to the community) is the highest accolade (Rose, 1992, p. 411). Euro-Americans prize the individual, reinforce and praise the one that makes it on their own. Native American children, taught in traditional settings, were taught by story telling, the sharing of philosophies, examples, and an awareness of and respect for the supernatural (Gilliland & Reyhner, 1988, pp. 21–32, 129). All of these aspects require a trust and faith in the selection of the teacher and the method of teaching and sharing. It appears that Native American children learn to accept phenomena because of the person from whom they are learning. They proceed based on a faith in the value system and the people around them. Euro-American children appear to be encouraged to learn by analysis, breaking down the problem into component parts to see how and why it works and trying to reconstruct it. A Native American, taught in a traditional setting, would accept, by faith, the teaching of an elder, the Euro-American would question, doubt and challenge what they perceive.

OPPOSING VALUE CONCEPTS

Examples of possible diametrically opposing concepts.between the Native American culture and the Euro-American culture might be illustrated by what one would encourage, value, and give priority to. Interviews with Native American people tend to suggest the following representation, with the value on the left being of greater importance, followed by the other values.

	COMMUNITY		
Native American	community	family	self
Euro-American	self	family	community
	LEARNING		
Native American	super natural	philosophy values knowledge and technology	wisdom
Euro-American	technology	knowledge values wisdom and super natural	philosophy
	PHILOSOPHY		
Native American	faith	reason	logic
Euro-American	logic	reasone	faith
	WEALTH		
Native American	family	happiness	assets
Euro-American	assets	happiness	family

FREEDOM

The Euro-American strives to be "free," independent of all others, unbound. The Native American adds meaning to life through obligations and responsibilities at home (Rose, 1992, p. 411).

POWER

It has been suggested that the meaning of the term power to a Native American will first be associated with the concept of healing while the

Euro-American will think first in the terms of influence of use of energy or other resources in order to control nature or others.

EURO-AMERICAN COMPARTMENTALIZATIONS: RIGHT AND WRONG

Euro-Americans have compartmentalized all aspects of life. Power, religion, knowledge, freedom, learning, wealth, and community. Each exists as an individual concept that is separate and distinct, one from the other (Deloria, 1985, p. 9). In an effort to understand the world, each value, belief, norm, or ideal is explained and packaged by Euro-American analytic, scholarly examination. The dominant culture that controls and organizes our government, education, community and daily life does so with the pattern of action that demonstrates that Euro-Americans consider themselves to be uniquely qualified to explain the rest of the world and how it should function (French, 1982, p. 181; Rose, 1992, p. 4060). An identifiable aspect of the Euro-American ideal of how life should function exists within the ritualistic form of governing that is called the criminal justice system.

The Euro-American way is one of non-conformist, individualistic right and wrong. The method prescribed for determination of right and wrong is adversarial. The rules for the functioning of this system are presented in separate legal concepts that have been written down and are embodied in the United States Constitution and the Bill of Rights. Each individual right identified within the Constitution is supported by stare decisis or legal precedent. Actions of the individual are controlled by defined acts of commission or omission, and each has a prescribed penalty for a violation of "the law." The system functions under prescribed rules of procedure. Those who maintain the system must develop, to greater or lesser extent, an understanding of the interrelationship of the laws and how those laws might apply to an individual set of circumstances.

Individual police officers, correctional officers, lawyers, judges, administrators, educators, and politicians have, for the most part, been bathed in the Euro-American view of life and how that life should be organized and how it should function. The student of criminal justice in the United States begins with the premise that this is the appropriate way. There is no other acceptable method of dealing with life and controlling the world and those within the world. One must control the world around them. One side wins the other loses and the loser must be punished. It is a "zero-sum" game. The objective examination of other cultures can contribute to an understanding of what might be "just" or "fair." The criminal justice system is fashioned in such a way as to label the winner of a courtroom conflict as being "right." The adversarial system assures that one party or the other will be the loser.

Whichever side wins through the use of the laws and the rules of procedure has accomplished "justice." The dominate ideal of the Euro-American method of justice is that the "winner" is right, the loser is wrong and that is fair.

Interviews with prosecuting attorneys, defense attorneys, Native American leaders and Native American inmates suggests that the Native American defendant does not adopt or use the adversarial system (Nebraska Commission, 1993, p. 39). The Native American defendant, although interested in his/her rights, does not "fight" the system as other defendants. Culturally, Native American values look first to what is right for the community, then the family and then to the self. When facing criminal charges the Native American tends to consider what he had done to "my" community. The possessive "my" is used because the Native American does consider what the effect of his/her action has had or is having on the Native American within their community. Native American culture considers values and the impact of ones actions on life, regardless of judgements of right and wrong. In the consideration of important reference points, the Native American will ask what impact his actions have, or will have upon his family. Here again, the family for the Native American involves much more than biological parents and biological siblings. The Native American culture considers uncles as fathers, aunts as mothers and cousins as brothers and sisters. Within Native American culture the family really is an "extended" family. Uncles are to be respected and listened to as one would a biological father. The same for aunt-mothers. Elders are given much more respect among Native American families. A small, frail eighty year old grandmother can gain immediate compliance of a rowdy twenty year old far easier than a fully equipped squad of riot police.

Of the Native American prison inmates interviewed by the authors none denied having committed the acts as alleged. This is a bit unexpected as most white inmates continue to protest their convictions throughout their imprisonment. It is not suggested that all Native American defendants do not use the legal recourse available to them, but it appears that they tend to have accepted responsibility for their act. Prosecuting attorneys and defense attorneys alike indicated that Native American defendants tend not to fight the system. The question is raised as to whether, due to their cultural perspective, Native American defendants accept plea bargain offers much more easily than non-Native American defendants. At least two Native American inmates stated directly, "I just wanted to get my time done and get back home." The Native American defendant may not fair well in court litigation because their cultural concept of "right" and "justice" encompasses elements of nature and spirituality that confuses and frustrates the Euro-American mind. Euro-Americans thus reject the concept of justice being interrelated with the earth, animals, plants, wind, sun and all of nature. The

Euro-American approach is much less universal and complex. The Euro-American can understand the law, winning and losing on a legal technicality, but has great difficulty understanding the combined concepts of spirituality, nature and justice. The Euro-American lawyer operates in an environment where the tools of a legal system, designed to assist in the representation of individuals against one another or against the State, often comes in conflict with what the system is attempting to accomplish (Price, 1969, p. 191).

Even if the Native American is not culturally attuned to using the criminal justice system and its adversarial approach to resolution of conflict, it should not be assumed that the Native American is dependent or passive. An Eskimo grandmother observed, "The white man never listens to anyone, but he expects everyone to listen to him. So, we listen! The wind isn't a good listener! The wind wants to speak, and we know how to listen. We have survived here because we know how to listen. The white people are like the wind; they sweep over everything" (Nabokov, 1991, p. 431). Aggressive competitiveness and individuality stand in stark contrast to most American Indian cultures and teach that the norm of behavior is to submerge the individual within the group (Trafzer, 1986, p. 50).

NATIVE AMERICANS "DO TIME BETTER"

A study completed in the fall of 1993 examined Native Americans in the Nebraska criminal justice system and showed that it is a common perception among legal practitioners of the system, Native American defendants, law enforcement personnel, and correctional personnel alike, that "Indians do time better" (Nebraska Commission, 1993). When this statement was first discovered in interviews with non-Native American law enforcement personnel, prosecutors, judges and defense counsel it was viewed as a prejudicial statement that reflected a deep seeded racially prejudiced attitude. Native American law enforcement officers and Native American inmates later supported the statement. Native Americans are found in the Nebraska prison system at a rate that is at least six times greater than the presence of Native Americans in the general population. Minority over-representation, is also supported when examining other minority representations elsewhere. A factor that does appear to develop when Native Americans are sent to prison is that for the years from 1982 thru 1991, Native American inmates spent less average time in prison in all the offense categories examined except for drug offenses.

Native American inmates in Nebraska between 1982 and 1991, average less time served per offense category than either Black or White inmates. The exception involved drug offenses. In the category of drug offenses there were only two Native Americans sent to prison from 1982 thru 1987. From

1988 thru 1990, nineteen Native Americans were sent to prison on drug charges and served an average of 1.76 years. For the three years from 1988 thru 1990, Black inmates served an average of 1.50 years and white inmates serving time on drug charges served six more months than either Black or White drug offenders. Native Americans imprisoned on drug charges do not do easier time or less time.

The point that is to be made is that, except for Native American drug offenders, there is support for the idea that Native American offenders either perceive the system differently or are perceived by the system differently than non-Native American offenders. That difference, when dealing with the criminal justice system, is represented here as a cultural perspective held by Native Americans that does not compartmentalize aspects of life and existence into right and wrong and good or bad. The cultural spirituality that exists among Native American people runs contrary to Euro-American adversarial system and the win or lose results of that system.

SUMMARY AND CONCLUSION

A presentation or discussion of Indian multiculturalism must engrain a realization of Euro-American ethnocentrism. The complex material achievements of the type we as Americans possess, or rather by which we are often possessed, are usually obtained at the expense of human and spiritual values (Brown, 1991, p. 32). Euro-Americans proceed through life supported by such concepts as "progress," "Manifest Destiny," or the inevitability of our own way over all other life patterns. Native American people live by different life patterns. Many of these alternative life patterns have brought fulfillment, beauty, and dignity in a measure we, in the dominant society, cannot know so long as we continue in our present direction (Brown, 1991, p. 29).

Time and place do not mean the same to Native Americans as they do to Euro-Americans. Euro-Americans are progress oriented. We function, exist, and our reality is in linear time (Brown, 1991, p. 49). Accordingly, in the process of serving time in prison, each day is as meaningless as the day before. Each activity is partaken of in order to pass time. Progress is counted in minutes, hours, weeks and months of time served.

In contrast, Native American languages lack past and future tense; reflecting a perennial reality of the now. It is impossible in Native American thought to conceive of progress in the non-Indian linear sense—that quantitatively interpreted cumulative process in which time is served. For the Euro-American the more and the new are quickly and automatically identified with the better. For the Native American the "now" is what is important (Brown, 1991, pp. 49–50).

Native American beliefs affirm the interrelated sacredness of time and place. Natural events in the lives of Native American people make the place and time that they are experiencing sacred and part of the whole of life. Events of animal beings, which are communicated through oral traditions of myths or folklore, serve to grace, sanctify, explain, and interpret each detail of the place and time being experienced (Brown, 1991, p. 51). The presence of a hawk on its daily flight over a prison gave to a Native American inmate a connection with Wakan-Tanka, the Great Mysterious. The life and flight of the hawk might go unnoticed by the non-Native American perception. The presence and/or absence of the hawk gave to the Native American inmate a sacred connection at that time and in that place, to his understanding of life and his current experience. The Native American, who has been able to maintain aspects of his/her cultural heritage and spirituality may be able to "do time" better due to a cultural value that combines time, place and what is being experienced into an understanding of spirituality that constantly absorbs every experience into an understanding of life. Such affirmations and experience (such as communing with a hawk overhead in a prison yard), of sacred time and sacred place . . . , tend to free humanity from the oppressing limits of profane time and profane place. Attempts by contemporary humans to "conquer" time and space, even to "conquer" specific places, are incomprehensible to the Native American (Brown, 1991, p. 52). Native Americans are more tolerant, accept their way of life and seem passive in general, whereas white Americans continually change their lifestyle and appear impatient (Trafzer, 1986, p. 8).

To recognize and consider the value, quality and spirituality of other cultures is inherent in the positive aspects of multiculturalism. The Native American provides a truly American heritage that can be found nowhere else in the world, and that can provide values sorely needed in a culture seeking purpose and direction (Brown, 1991, p. 30). If we can understand, not adopt or attempt to steal, the truths that are important to the Native American and which they find in their relationships to nature, then we may become enriched, our understanding will deepen, and we shall be able to give to the American Indian heritage its rightful place among the great spiritual traditions of humankind (Brown, 1991, p. 46). If we listen to each other, we will not necessarily erase differences, but perhaps use it to our mutual advantage (Pommersteim, 1993, p. 358). As Brown writes:

> Can it not be affirmed that all peoples, regardless of skin color, ethnic background, or religious affiliation, are rightful members of one family of humankind? Should not differences of appearance, culture, or religion be affirmed as valid and even necessary expressions of a greater reality, so that they may contribute to a richer world? Any alternative cannot but lead to drab mediocrity and ultimate chaos (Brown, 1991, p. 68).

REFERENCES

Brown, J. E. (1991). *The Spiritual Legacy of the American Indian.* New York: Crossroads.

Department of the Interior Memorandum. (1993, September 7). Washington, D.C.: Bureau of Indian Affairs.

Etheridge, D. (1977). Law Enforcement of Indian Reservations. *The Police Chief,* 44, 74–77.

French, L. (1982). *Indians and Criminal Justice.* Totowa, NJ: Allanheld-Osmun.

Gilliland, H., and Reyhner, J. (1988). *Teaching the Native American.* Dubuque, Iowa: Kendall Hunt Publishing.

Hagan, W. T. (1966). Indian Police and Judges: *Experiments in Acculturation and Control.* New Haven, CT: Yale University Press.

Indian Country Today. (1993, November 10).

Indian Law Enforcement History. (1975). BIA, Division of Law Enforcement Services, Washington, D.C.

Kidwell, C. S., and Roberts, C. (1980). *The Choctaws: A Critical Bibliography.* Bloomington, IN: Indiana University Press.

Lorentino, Q. (1989). Interview with Q. Lorentino, Bureau of Indian Affairs, Washington, D.C.

McKee, J., and Schlender, J. (1980). *The Choctaws.* Jackson, MS: University of Mississippi Press.

Nabokov, P. (Ed.). (1991). Native American Testimony. New York: Penguin.

Pommersteim, F. (1993). Making All the Difference: Native American Testimony and the Black Hills. *North Dakota Law Review, 69*(2).

Price, M. E. (1970). Lawyers on the Reservation: Some Implications for the Legal Profession. *Arizona State Law Journal, 161.* Arizona State University.

Rosen, L. (Ed.). (1976). *Law and Contemporary Problems: The American Indian and the Law.*

Trafzer, C. E. (1986). *American Indian Identity, Today's Changing Perspectives.* Sacramento, CA: Sierra Oaks.

Wachtel, D. (1982). Indian Law Enforcement. In L. French (Ed.). *Indians and Criminal Justice.* Totowa, NJ: Allanheld-Osmun.

Vantine, J. L. (1978). The Metal Breasts. *North Dakota History, 45.*

Video References

(Available through the Native American Public Broadcasting Consortium, P.O. Box 83111, Lincoln, NE 68501).

Aboriginal Rights, I Can Get It for You Wholesale. (1976). Length: 60:60. Produced by: TV Ontario.

Great Spirit Within the Hole. Produced by Chris Spotted Eagle.

In the White Man's Image. (1991). Length: 51:22. Produced by: Native American Public Broadcasting Consortium and Nebraska Educational Television.

Live and Remember. Length: 28:54. Henry Smith, Solaris/Lakota Project.

Nations Within A Nation. Length: 58:30. Produced by: Department of Sociology—Oklahoma State University.

The Probable Passing of Elk Creek. (1984). Length: 60:60. Produced by: WGBY-TV.
Red Road: Toward the Techno-Tribal. (1984). Length: 26:52. Produced by: KBDI-TV.
Return of the Raven, The Edison Chiloquin Story. (1985). Length: 47:00. Produced by: Barry Hood Films.

CHAPTER FIVE

LATINOS: THE CONCEPTUALIZATION OF RACE

LAURA B. MYERS, MYRNA CINTRON, AND KATHRYN E. SCARBOROUGH

INTRODUCTION

This chapter explores the social construction of knowledge as it applies to the conceptualization and operationalization of race in criminal justice, using Latinos as a specific example of the problems associated with development of this knowledge. The social construction of knowledge applies to the perceptions of researchers as they conceptualize and operationalize key variables. The current state of race research is to emphasize African Americans as a minority, while ignoring or misrepresenting other groups. This creates three problems for criminal justice research. First, numerous groups are neglected in the measurement of race. Second, if these groups are included, they are collapsed into the categories of non-white or other. Third, when any race is included in the race variable, African Americans or otherwise, the diversity within the group is not taken into account.

The consequences of these errors are numerous. First, if race research neglects other groups, public policy actions will be misguided and might fail. In addition, when these groups are combined into a single category such as non-white or other, researchers often incorrectly analyze the behavior of such groups using the same assumptions used to study African American behavior. Finally, if various races are assumed to be homogeneous and their diversity is not taken into account, then our knowledge concerning the race-crime relationship will be incorrect and public policy action is once again misguided.

In this chapter, a justification will be provided for the inclusion of all groups when studying race and the need to account for the diversity of all races. Using Latinos as an example, data and literature will be used to demonstrate the importance of including Latinos in the race variable. This justification strategy should be used for the inclusion of all races and ethnicities. The chapter will present the need to include the Latino perspective in future/contemporary criminal justice research.

THE CURRENT CONCEPTUALIZATION OF RACE

The Lack of Consensus on the Definition of Race

The emphasis on African Americans and crime in criminal justice research has meant that numerous groups have been neglected in the measurement of race. When other groups have been included, they have been collapsed into the categories of "non-white" or "other" with the consequence that their diversity has not been taken into account.

In essence, the way race has been defined in race and crime research is different from the way the various minority groups would have it defined because it ignores the minority perspective (LaFree & Russell, 1993). The current definition is derived from use of official measures of race. These measures fail to account for the diversity of race and ethnicity inherent in the race concept.

Official measures such as the United States Census, the National Crime Victimization Survey, and the Uniform Crime Report do not mandate a standard criteria for the definition of one's race nor do they attempt to externally verify the information. The result is a conglomeration of various people's perceptions concerning race that may or may not be accurate. In addition, the tendency of these official measures to subsume other races, such as Latinos, into the category of "white," "non-white," or "other" destroys any knowledge of their racial diversity (LaFree & Russell, 1993).

The failure to account for ethnicity in the proper definition of race is also problematic. When Latinos and Asians are separated into single categories, the diversity within each race, or ethnicity, is lost. Latinos, for example, are comprised of many ethnic groups, each with unique cultural characteristics. Puerto Ricans, Mexicans, and Cubans are three of the major Latino ethnic groups that have migrated to the United States in large numbers.

The neglect of entire groups of racial minorities in the proper conceptualization of race or the assumption that the commonalities of these groups is sufficient reason to collapse them together under the headings "Latino" or "Asian" has and will result in invalid conclusions regarding each group. According to LaFree and Russell (1993), "the classification practices of official data gatherers, combined with historical definitions of race, have had a direct impact on the study of crime" (p. 282). What is known about the relationship between race and crime will be damaged unless efforts are made to properly conceptualize race. The impact of such misconceptualization on social policy would be devastating as researchers "continue to pursue the wrong or incomplete questions about important issues" (Stanfield, 1993a, p. 14).

The Influence of Perceptions on Proper Conceptualization

Continued reliance on official measures of race in race and crime research only compounds efforts to fully understand the race-crime relationship. The use of official data and the language used to interpret the data are regarded as objective methods for analyzing race which fail to depict the true nature of race. The claim of objectivity disguises the critical biases that may be hidden in the use of methods based on such data (Stanfield, 1993a). Official data can only reveal the relationships between variables. The data simply cannot show why those variables are related (Pope, 1982).

The Uniform Crime Report, for example, suggests that minorities are overrepresented in the criminal justice system. However, the same numbers do not reveal the reason. The task of race and crime researchers has been to demonstrate the reasons for those numbers. At the same time, stereotypes and myths regarding minorities have become entrenched in American culture due to the continued reliance on official data (Pope, 1982). Studies based on such data continue to serve as examples of political and cultural bias regarding race (Stanfield, 1993a). The consequence of relying on these studies has meant that "confirmations based on folk wisdom have taken precedence over the pursuit of truth" (Stanfield, 1993a, p. 6).

Myths

The myths regarding race and crime have become well known (Napper, 1977; Pope, 1982; Stanfield, 1993a). The unquestioned reliance on official data in research has meant that many published studies continue to support the issue of the overrepresentation of African Americans without exploring the reasons for this phenomena.

Researchers also continue to make strong statements regarding race and crime derived from this data. The idea that blackness and criminality are synonymous is derived from studies which indicate that Blacks are more likely than people of other races to be arrested and convicted.

This stereotype is further exacerbated when the results of this research are used by the media and the political infrastructure to sell the news and to win elections. Often in an attempt to make information newsworthy, the media engage in both selection and presentation bias. Selection bias involves selecting only the crime news thought to be of interest to the consumer. Selection bias studies have compared reported topics with objective measures, such as police reports, and found a large difference between what is reported and what actually occurs. Presentation bias means that once a story is selected, certain characteristics of the story are highlighted to make the story even more interesting. Presentation bias studies have revealed that the race of the offender is noted more often when the offender is a minority than when the offender is white. Most reported items support what consumers believe to be the most problematic, that Blacks are committing a majority of the crime and that most crime is violent (Etten & Myers, 1991).

Finally, the use of this data continues to cause a division between the races in the United States. The use of official data by researchers, educators, politicians, and the media only serve to invigorate already ill-conceived perceptions regarding race. As a result of these misperceptions, the attempt to alleviate racism will continue to be difficult.

A review of the criticism of news coverage on race and crime demonstrates the potential effect these myths can have. When the media perpetuate these stereotypes there is a potential to create a fictitious crime wave in the minds of the public (Fishman, 1981). The public can be induced to panic unnecessarily over crime issues (Voumvakis & Ericson, 1984; Young, 1981b). The media also may become "protectors of the status quo",as they continually bombard the public with crime myths (Chibnall, 1981; Humphries, 1981; Knight & Dean, 1982; Lichter, Rothman, & Lichter, 1986; Marsh, 1988; Quinney, 1979; Young, 1981a). In reaction, certain members of the public begin to fear their environment unnecessarily and begin to alter their lifestyles (Jaehnig, Weaver, & Fico, 1981; Skogan & Maxfield, 1981; van Dijk, 1978). So from a policy perspective, criminal justice decision makers may have to alter their practices to meet these perceptions rather than the reality of the situation (Pritchard, 1986; Smith & Pollack, 1989).

A current example of the media's perpetuation of these stereotypes is the Rodney King situation and the riots in Los Angeles. Media coverage made it seem that most of the rioters were black and were rioting in response to the verdict (Stanfield, 1993b). This image was perpetuated because the media neglected its ethical responsibility to portray the story accurately and objectively.

Consequently, the perpetuation of race and crime myths mean that rational and accurate crime control policies will be an impossibility (Braithwaite, 1987) until the conceptualization of race is properly understood. It is vital that race research receive serious attention so that the necessary epistemological and theoretical efforts can be made (Stanfield, 1993a).

> The dramatically changing world in which we live demands that we cease to allow well-worn dogma to keep us from designing research projects that will provide the data necessary for the formulation of adequate explanations for the racial and ethnic dimensions of human life. If we do not do so, the social sciences in the United States and abroad will become increasingly marginal as ethnicity and race become increasingly dominant in the problems faced by United States society and the world in general (Stanfield, 1993a, pp. 6–7).

RACE AS A SOCIAL CONSTRUCTION

To properly conceptualize and operationalize a variable may seem a simple task for a researcher, but the importance of the process is critical when one remembers the relationship between that process and demonstrating causality. In demonstrating causality, it is assumed that all observable phenomena can be classified and quantified (Hagan, 1989). Until recently, the operationalization of race in most studies has seemed to be the product of this assumption in that few have questioned its traditional definition (Moore, 1973; Stanfield, 1993a).

The concept of race is one of the more complex variables that researchers have attempted to define, but unfortunately it has suffered from incomplete and simplistic efforts. When one subjects the race variable to a test of construct validity, it becomes clear that only face validity has been sufficient for the proper understanding of the concept. The common terms of "white" and "Black" "actually have little empirical meaning, except in the most stereotypical ways" (Stanfield, 1993b, p. 17). Categorizing race in a simplistic and invalid way has been common for so long that the necessary "epistemological and theoretical questioning regarding the nature of identity and consciousness in race-centered societies" (Stanfield, 1993b, p. 18) has yet to take place in a meaningful way.

How can race as a concept fail to include all race groups in the proper specification of the variable? To view crime as an African American problem in research has been the conventional method for exploring the race-crime relationship. Consequently, the race variable has been defined as African Americans versus whites or African Americans versus others.

Takagi (1981) notes that even this process is a relatively new event in sociological research. Prior to the 1970s many researchers failed to include a minority perspective in the conceptualization of race as applied to African Americans. It is only in the last few decades that efforts have been made to include the minority voice (Moore, 1973) in the proper conceptualization and interpretation of race.

But to study the race-crime relationship from only the African American experience distorts the true nature of the relationship. While African Americans are disproportionately represented in criminal justice statistics, this is not a sufficient reason to exclude other races from the study of the race-crime relationship. Indicators are now showing that other races are over-represented in the criminal justice system as well. While the crisis for these other groups may not be of the same magnitude as that of African Americans, it seems that understanding the race-crime relationship earlier in the process rather than after mistakes have been made might serve criminal justice policy and the people of these races in a more informed way.

A related problem in the proper conceptualization of race involves collapsing these other groups into one category. Because their representation is less than that of African Americans, members of other groups are often merged into a single category. The result is a lack of understanding of the relationship between race and crime for these separate groups.

Finally, how can a proper conceptualization of race fail to account for the diversity within any race, African American or otherwise? Latinos and Asians are often assumed to be a homogenous group without regard for their cultural differences. Stanfield (1993b) refers to this phenomenon as the "fallacy of homogeneity" (pp. 19–21). Because of the tradition of work focusing on African Americans, researchers have tended to assume that all members of a race are the same without acknowledging differences within the group. This has meant that Latinos, Asians, Indians, and others have been studied under the assumption of internal consistency resulting in less valid outcomes. Latinos can include Mexican Americans, Puerto Ricans, Cubans, and others, each with their own cultural heritages. Asians can be Chinese, Taiwanese, Filipino, or Vietnamese, just to name a few. This fallacy also has meant that studies of "Blacks" have primarily been conducted using the African American model which fails to acknowledge that "Blacks" are made up of people not only with African and/or slave heritage, but many other backgrounds. Even when a person identifies racial identity as African American there is still great diversity regarding past tribal affiliation and tribal status, African region, and American region (Stanfield, 1993b).

The argument for the application of the minority perspective to the study of race, crime, and social policy reveals the importance of not only including all groups, but properly specifying the nature of those groups. Minorities as a whole are overrepresented in the criminal justice system, not just African Americans. Because of the civil rights movement and the social history of the United States, however, the primary focus of criminal justice race research has been on the African American. Other groups have been neglected for the same reason that African Americans were neglected for so long. Because of the power differential, African Americans either were not aware of their situation or were powerless to address it (Moore, 1973). Today other minority groups find themselves in the same position that African Americans did prior to the Civil Rights Movement.

While it is argued that other minority groups must be included in the proper conceptualization of race, a rigid approach to the study of race and crime which relies only on observable data is insufficient for a proper understanding of the relationship. The interpretation of the data must be informed by the thoughts and experiences of each minority group as well as subgroups within each group (Collins, 1990; Moore, 1973; Pope, 1982; Takagi, 1981). Complementing objective data with a qualitative knowledge base for each minority group "seeks to penetrate—and emancipate—the consciousness of persons described by such data" (Takagi, 1981, p. 50). Any research effort that fails to include a minority perspective is omitting significant variables in the relationship (Moore, 1973).

UNDERSTANDING RACE: AN INTERACTIVE MODEL

A solution for the misconceptualization of race is to utilize a suitable framework that would take into account all minority groups and the diversity within each group. Of course, this cannot be a simple model. The model must be interactive so as to include all relevant aspects of the conceptualization of race. One model suggested in the literature fits the argument outlined above. This model includes the interaction of structure, culture, and biography in the proper conceptualization of race (Takagi, 1981). The interactive race model is as follows: Structure × Culture × Biography.

Using the framework of structure, culture and biography is critical in the reconceptualization of race. Past formulations of the concept have been based on the assumption of assimilation and homogeneity. This means that methodologies constructed to examine the race-crime relationship have assumed that races and cultures were more alike than different because subordinant races should have been in the process of assimilating to the dominant culture (Stanfield, 1993b). This framework corrects that assumption and allows for the understanding of racial and ethnic differences.

The tendency of race research to dichotomize the race variable into categories of "white" and "Black" demonstrates a lack of sensitivity to those differences. The "fallacy of monolithic identity" underlies this dichotomy with the assumption that people of mixed race and culture "are either marginal persons or in pathological identity crisis" (Stanfield, 1993b, p. 21). The categories of "white", "Black" or "Latino" have no real meaning because no race is racially or culturally pure. It is in fact the process of assimilation, accompanied by reciprocal acculturation and miscegenation, that have resulted in diverse European Americans and Black Americans, to name only a few (Stanfield, 1993b).

Structure

With the knowledge that no race is racially or culturally pure as our socialization and myths would have us to believe (Stanfield, 1993b), researchers must explore that diversity to understand the response of individuals to the social structure. Structure refers to the structural factors in society over which the individual has no control. For the purpose of this model, the primary structural factor would be racial identity. Other factors include common occupations, the income structure, and the housing, religious, legal, political and education systems. Using structure to understand race means that racial identity cannot be understood in isolation, but must be seen in relation to other structural factors in the community that lead to particular outcomes for individuals, in this case, discrimination. Collins (1990) refers to this structural relationship as an understanding of the sociohistorical context of which the race of the individual is a factor.

Including structure in the proper conceptualization of race means accounting for the history of the relationship between race or racial identity and the other structural components of class, gender, religion, age, region, and language which affect all members of the community. Race research methodology must account for the interaction of the past, present, and future of a particular race (Pope, 1982). One cannot properly understand the minority experience without knowledge of a particular race's experiences in the past, present, and what may yet surface in the future.

More importantly, an understanding of structural relationships imbedded in history involves recognition of the relationship of all races to the dominant culture under analysis. In the United States, the dominant culture is European American whose members have been socialized to assume that they are culturally pure. To properly conceptualize race means acknowledging how this dominant culture evolved, how it has perpetuated fallacies of racial purity, and how it has oppressed other races within its domain (Stanfield, 1993b).

Culture

The cultural component of the model involves an understanding that even when the structural constraints of a community are identified, the people of that community will still relate to that structure in culturally distinctive ways. With knowledge of a group's cultural identity, the response of different cultures to the structural system becomes clearer. In this way, the options available to the individual will be understood, especially when those options are contradictory to those of the majority culture (Takagi, 1981). A valid conceptualization of race cannot measure the response of those of another culture against a white middle-class standard.

Biography

The final component of this model allows for individual differences. Since race is a structural factor that interacts with other factors and the culture of the individual defines the options that the individual may possess in relation to that structure, this does not mean that all individuals of a given race will act in the same manner. Biography refers to the fact that individuals within a race still have a chance to affect their own futures. It cannot be assumed that all individuals within a culture react to situations in the same way. A proper understanding of race means realizing that everyone is in the process of acting either in a positive or negative way to form their futures. Some people are enhancing their chances of success by getting an education, working hard, and becoming involved in efforts that will give them and perhaps other members of their race more power, while others make choices that propel them toward failure, i.e. committing crime (Takagi, 1981).

Biography becomes an important component of the model when it is realized that many theoretical models on race and crime perpetuate the myth that all members of a culture act in a consistent manner. It would be a tragedy to assume that all members of a race are lazy, on welfare, or involved in deviant activities. Individual differences must be acknowledged or stereotypical myths will only be strengthened. This component alone demonstrates why the conceptualization of race is a complex process.

APPLICATION OF THE MODEL

Conceptualizing race using this framework involves analyzing the critical components necessary in a proper and valid understanding of race. This model should be used to not only engage in valid race research, but it also should be used to critically evaluate the race research literature.

Once this interactive model has been fully explored for the multiple races to be analyzed, the researcher will be able to appropriately conceptualize the race variable, construct a suitable methodology for study (including all other relevant variables), and accurately interpret the results. To use the model correctly, the researcher must explore each component of the model early in the research process. Otherwise, the errors will only build on one another and invalid outcomes will likely be the result.

Structure

Accounting for the structural aspects of race means understanding how race as a structural factor relates to the sociohistorical context. It is critical that the relationship between race, the economy, historical precedent, the religious system, the legal system, the governmental apparatus, and other structural components be understood. Knowledge of these structural components will mean that the researcher is fully aware of all races and the relationship of those races to the structure of the community. At this stage, the researcher should collect and/or engage in historical and comparative research to acquire the knowledge of the relationship of various races to the social structure (Stanfield, 1993a).

LaFree and Russell (1993) illustrate the importance of structural factors in their recommendation that a knowledge of the legal system to aid in the understanding of race is imperative. They state that researchers must understand "the historical and legal context in which the American criminal justice system has developed" (p. 283). It is important to know how the law has been used as a mechanism of social control to racially discriminate against its citizens, and it is necessary to understand the context in which legal decisions are made. The biases of the legal system must be acknowledged (Stanfield, 1993a) prior to engaging in research.

Culture

Learning about the cultures of various individuals is important to the proper conceptualization of race, because it produces the knowledge of how various cultures adapt and react to the structure of the community. The assumption of homogeneous response neglects this issue. It is critical to have a thorough knowledge of cultural response for all groups. Acquiring this knowledge has often been thought to be too difficult and that which should only be undertaken by those of each culture.

However, Takagi (1981) and others recommend that strong efforts be made to acquire this knowledge. It is critical to learn about community structure and cultural differences from members of each group. This can be accomplished by gathering and using research on the community and the various cultures. Such research has more fully explored these groups and will provide valuable assistance to the researcher. It also means including members of those groups in the research process. To have a thorough understanding of the culture also means validating current knowledge with members of that culture.

The issue of minority research conducted only by minorities might seem to be a solution. It is vital that barriers which have inhibited minorities from publication be eliminated so that minority-informed research can be heard. But the minority researcher also may have trouble understanding the reality of the subjects under study. While they may be of the same race, a social scientist is likely to face class differences with subjects, which means that the minority researcher must make extra efforts to learn and understand minority subjects and to acquire their trust.

Gertz and Myers (1992) make this suggestion in their exploration of the validity of cross-cultural criminal justice research. When an American researcher attempts to study criminal justice and criminology in another country, the same problems emerge. The researcher must have an understanding of the sociohistorical structure of the setting being researched and a knowledge of cultural response. If one cannot visit the country for a long period of time, it often helps to acquire the assistance of natives who are willing to teach their cultural perspective to the researcher.

This suggestion should be mandatory in race research. The designing, implementation, and interpretation of race and crime research should include members of the minority groups involved (Pope, 1982). So while the criminal justice discipline is doing more race and crime research, the question of whether it is properly informed minority research can be answered with an accurate understanding of cultural differences (Moore, 1973).

The Question of Ethnicity

The interactive model suggested here does something that many race studies fail to do. Those studies make the concepts of race and ethnicity appear equivalent (LaFree & Russell, 1993). Race and ethnicity must be separated for a valid understanding of race. LaFree and Russell (1993) note definitions of ethnicity by Mann (1993) and Georges-Abeyie (1984) that help to inform the researcher of the difference between the two concepts. Mann refers to ethnicity as a groups' association with a particular culture or cultures (p. 3) and Georges-Abeyie sees ethnicity as the "intersection of race, culture, and place of origin" (p. 11). Without this distinction, researchers may stop at the inclusion of race categories, and fail to include ethnic differences within those race groups. Making that distinction clear would allow for the use of culture in race research.

Biography

Finally, the biography of the individuals that make up a cultural group must be acknowledged by the researcher. Once the structural components and the cultural reaction/adaptation is accounted for, so too must the individual responses of the various cultural members. This means being cautious enough not to assume or allude to the idea that all members of a cultural group will react in the same way.

RECONCEPTUALIZING RACE

The need to reconceptualize race in race and crime research is evident. Claims have been made for the last twenty-five years that the minority perspective should be included in the proper conceptualization (Pope, 1982). Suggestions have been made that past studies have been the product of grants awarded to proposals that were "traditional, conventional, and did not challenge prevailing conceptions" (Pope, 1982, p. 248).

While the criminal justice discipline has heeded that warning and increased research on the African American experience, Moore's (1973) point made two decades ago that "questions within the profession about the validity and fruitfulness of our conceptual and analytical frameworks have been rare" (p. 66) is still applicable and must be acknowledged today.

The proper study of the relationship between race and crime is complex. It is not simply a matter of exploring the strict relationship between race and crime, but it is an interactive relationship that must be explored through many facets. The relationship between race and all other relevant factors must be understood in relation to crime.

The interactive model of structure, culture, and biography is aimed at understanding the relevant factors in the accurate conceptualization of race. If used correctly, the conceptualization of race should encompass all races included in the geographic region under study and will account for the diversity within races.

To further illustrate the importance of this reconceptualization, data and literature on Latinos will be discussed as an argument for the inclusion of Latinos in the race variable while accounting for diversity within this group.

THE LATINO EXPERIENCE

The following is a justification for the inclusion of Latinos in the conceptualization of race. The justification also involves exploring the diversity of Latinos and demonstrating the importance of this information in the conceptualization of race. All arguments are based on the interactive model of Structure × Culture × Biography.

Crime Perceived as a Minority Problem

Exploring **social structure** and race means acknowledging that not all Blacks are African Americans, not all African Americans are the same, and more importantly that the traditional African American model cannot be applied to other races. Theory and research in criminal justice has uncritically portrayed the problem of crime in the United States as a minority problem (Flowers, 1988; Georges-Abeyie, 1984; Mann, 1993). The knowledge so gained has been extended to all minority groups. With little critical examination, researchers explain crime in the Latino communities with the concepts, methods and theories, and programs developed for African Americans.

At first glance this approach might seem appropriate. After all the problem of crime is a urban underclass problem and Latinos, like African Americans, share a minority status, have low income, live in urban centers, have low levels of educational achievement, are clustered in low paying, low skilled occupations, and are overrepresented in national crime statistics and in the prison population. Using the model described in this chapter, it is clear that the current African American model is inappropriate for Latinos. The meaning of the Latino perspective for criminal justice research must be clarified.

Only recently has crime in the Latino population surfaced as a legitimate research topic in criminal justice. Crime as a minority population problem has traditionally emphasized the African American population. Thus our concepts, theoretical models and policy decisions have been developed with African Americans in mind. But African Americans and Latinos differ in many respects. This section examines several of our concepts and theoretical models to highlight the differences among these two groups.

The terms Black or Latino/Hispanic while being ascribed social statuses are categories that denote significant differences. The concept "Black" in social science research commonly refers to "African Americans." "Latino," "Hispanic," "Chicano," "La Raza," "Mexican American," "Puerto Rican," "Boricua," "Spanish American," "Latin American," "Spanish origin," "White person of Spanish surname," on the other hand, refers to a national origin category for Latinos (Garcia, 1981; Hayes-Bautista, 1980). All such individuals, when asked, would trace their origins to one of the spanish speaking countries in the New World colonized by Spain.

What researchers do not account for is that the use and the meanings denoted by these two concepts, Latinos and African Americans, vary (Georges-Abeyie, 1986). To say that someone is African American denotes a social category consisting of a distinctive history of slavery, racial subordination, and political activism against social inequalities (racism, discrimination, segregation, fair housing, etc.). This denotes the common experiences of this group in the United States, a society where one is legally classified as either white or Black.

The Latino/Hispanic concept, on the other hand, represents diverse national origin groups. Diverse not just in their timing and reasons for coming to the United States, but also in social class, education, generations in the United States and race. Latinos are a racially mixed group. For many Latinos race is not a dichotomy, it is a matter of degree, of shades of color and diverse physical appearance (the Spanish language contains many words to describe the different racial mixtures between Amerindians, Spanish, Africans, and other groups). While racial prejudice does exist among Latinos, it does not follow the strict color lines used in the United States. As a result, the racial experiences (discrimination, prejudice, racism, segregation, etc.) of the Latino groups in the United States will vary (Chapa, 1990; Stolzenberg, 1990).

Immigration Patterns

Two other problems that arise when using the African American model are theoretical in nature. Current theoretical explanations do not account for the degree to which criminal behavior is affected by immigration status. This means acknowledging **cultural differences and structural factors.** While the work of Shaw and McKay (1942) and Park (1936) accounted for the percentage of foreign born population in their work on the concentric zone theory of crime, these theorists emphasized the idea that crimes committed by minority groups would decrease as these groups moved away from the transition zone and assimilated into the American culture.

Why have researchers ignored migration in their theoretical explanations in general and in minority crime in particular? Traditional explanations assume that immigration plays no significant role in criminal behavior because African Americans are native born and consequently should be assimilated to the dominant culture. Such explanations fail to acknowledge cultural heritage. As a result, theoretical explanations of African American crime do not account for migration patterns. Immigration is of even more importance in the Latino population. Latinos can be found in a variety of legal statuses, for example, new immigrant, undocumented, fifth generation, to new citizens. Some have education but due to their recent migration lack the language skills necessary to earn a decent wage; other groups may have a long history of discrimination and segregation. Some Latinos are just learning to recognize instances of discrimination or racism, while many others are just learning about freedom of expression. While many Latinos have assimilated to a degree and claim that this is the land of opportunities, there are still many others for whom opportunities are minimal, and there are many more who will always be reminded of their national origin (Portes, Parker, & Cobas, 1980).

Any description of the group, whether it is economic, social, political, or cultural, must account for migration patterns (Moore & Pinderhughes, 1993). Criminal justice models are no exception. Any description of crime in this population subgroup requires the inclusion of the immigration variable. Immigration patterns for any race would be a **structural and cultural factor** that should be obtained for an **historical analysis** of the race. Immigration status might affect criminal rates and victimization patterns; it can also help explain fear of crime and criminal incident reports; and it can affect perception of police work and trust in the criminal justice system (Carter, 1985, 1986; Lampe, 1984; Mirande, 1980; Shai & Rosenwaike, 1988; Starrett, Connolly, Decker, & Araujo, 1988).

Culture

The second theoretical problem deals with the assumptions made about the causes of criminal behavior, for example, the conceptualization of culture and the cultural forces that are thought to cause some people to commit crime. Strain, cultural deviance and subcultural theories assume some relationship between cultural values and crime.

Strain theories (structural-functionalist perspective, anomie, goals and means disparity) claim that culture is uniformly learned and all members of society subscribe to one set of general cultural values (the middle class values and its emphasis on economic success). Cultural deviance theory (social disorganization, differential association, culture conflict, formation of subcultures) on the other hand, assumes a culturally diverse society, where different social classes exhibit different cultural values and where the values of one class conflict with those of another (Adler, Mueller & Laufer, 1991).

According to strain theory, those who do not have the legitimate means available to them (minorities, lower class people) turn to illegitimate means to reach the culturally prescribed goal of economic success. In contrast, cultural deviance theory claims that when lower class people conform to their own value system, they may be violating conventional norms.

Criminological theory appears to take culture for granted. Under this assumption, there is either one, monolithic culture to follow or there are different cultures in conflict. The general assumption is that all members of society have assimilated to one or another cultural group. Cultural standards are learned, norms of behavior observed, while customs and traditions are practiced and protected as they are passed down from one generation to another.

It is possible then that our actions and behaviors (deviant, criminal or law abiding) demonstrate the extent to which we conform to the demands of the culture we have assimilated into (Portes, et al., 1980). Many sociologists have addressed the process of adaptation and assimilation of immigrant groups as they learn the new cultural values and norms of the American culture (Thomas and Znaniecki's (1958) *The Polish Peasant in Europe and America;* Whyte's (1981) *Street Corner Society: The Social Structure of an Italian Slum;* and Moore's (1978) *Homeboys, Gangs, Drugs, and Prison in the Barrios of Los Angeles).*

But what if in a diverse society, such as the United States today, all cultural groups are having difficulties in defining, learning and teaching what is considered appropriate or normal behavior? If all cultural groups are having difficulties, is it possible that there are **group differences** in the degree, amount and/or type of difficulty? And if there is variation, could it be possible that some groups are not assimilating the culturally prescribed norms of any group?

These are questions left unanswered by criminal justice theories. Since Latinos are found in a variety of legal migration statuses (new immigrants, first generation, citizens, fifth generation American, etc.), and because of their diverse timing in coming to the United States, researchers must take into account the role that **culture** (multiple cultures) and **assimilation** (different levels of assimilation) play in criminal behavior (Dashefsky, 1975; Padilla, 1986; Portes, et al., 1980). The strong cultural presence of the Latino population warrants and provides a unique opportunity for analysis that extends the current cultural approaches. This new approach would provide insight into how members of large ethnic groups function in multicultural worlds. (For a critique of the traditional social science model and its applicability to the Latino groups see Blea, 1988; Marín & Marín, 1991; Mirande, 1985).

ACKNOWLEDGING LATINOS WITHIN THE SOCIAL STRUCTURE

The determination of which races to study means including all races within the **social structure**. Consequently, including Latinos means asking why Latinos should be included in the race variable? The answer to this question, while long and complex, means gaining an understanding of the sociohistorical context for Latinos.

From 1970 to 1980 the Latino population changed from 9.1 to 14.6 million, an increase of 60 percent. By 1990 it had increased by another 47 percent, to 21.4 million. A further breakdown indicates that Mexican Americans constituted 64% of all Latinos, Puerto Ricans accounted for 11% and Cuban Americans made up 5% of the Latino population subgroup. Together, these three groups account for almost 80% of the nation's Latinos (de la Garza, DeSepio, Garcia, Garcia & Falcon, 1992). This increase has also been accompanied by geographical dispersion and changes in the national origins of the groups. For example, immigrants' first stops are no longer the large metropolitan centers but suburbia (Mahler, 1992), however, large clusters of "new" immigrants from Central and South America can be found in Miami, New York and California.

Reasons for the increase include a higher birth rate and heavy immigration from Central and South America in addition to recent Cuban exiles and a constant flow of Mexican immigrants. Sassen (1992) offers another perspective for the migration of groups to the United States that helps understand the change in the demographic profile of the United States:

> The central role played by the United States in the emergence of a global economy over the past 30 years lies at the core of why people migrate here in

ever-increasing numbers. U.S. efforts to open its own and other countries' economies to the flow of capital, goods, services and information created conditions that mobilized people for migration, and formed linkages between the United States and other countries which subsequently served as bridges for migration. Furthermore, the relatively open nature of the U.S. labor market, epitomized by the notion that government should stay out of the marketplace, provides a necessary condition for immigration to occur (pp. 14–15).

ACCOUNTING FOR LATINO DIVERSITY

Marín and Marín (1991) urge social researchers to become familiar with the basic **cultural values** held by the communities they study. Allocentrism (cooperation), simpatia, familialism, power distance, personal space, time orientation, and gender roles are some cultural values identified among Latinos in the United States (Marín & Marín, 1991). However, "there is a certain level of disagreement among researchers as to the meaning and implications of some of these values" (1991, p. 11). That is, there are important differences among all the Latino national origin groups. The different meanings and implications of these values could be based on such characteristics as individual preferences, religious affiliation, generational differences, linguistic preferences, age, gender, etc.

Marín and Marín also report "that care needs to be taken when analyzing and interpreting Hispanic data because of concerns that Hispanics may often provide inaccurate and socially desirable responses, may produce large portions of missing data, may prefer extreme and acquiescent responses, and may show low self-disclosure to strangers" (1991, p. 101). It is not that subjects are purposely biasing the responses. It is most likely that cultural values i.e., gender roles, simpatia, familialism, affect the Latino subjects' responses and response rate.

It is also useful to understand the relationship between **group identity and behavior** (ethnicity, cultural traditions, attitudes toward the criminal justice system, etc.). In the criminal justice literature, various studies have linked violent offenses to cultural and subcultural elements. Wolfgang and Ferracuti (1967), for example, discuss aggression as a common conflict-solving norm, while the culture of poverty has been identified as another source of violent behavior (Lewis, 1966) among minority group members. Low academic achievement among Latinos has been linked to the cultural characteristics of the group; while lack of organizational skills (political and social) is at the heart of many of the social problems confronted by the group which prevents upward mobility and accommodation (Blea, 1988).

Moore and Pinderhughes (1993) have identified the features that distinguish the early literature on two Latino groups. Mexican Americans have fascinated and intrigued anthropologists and popular writers because of their cultural tenacity to confront the conditions of poverty they lived in. Other studies reinforced cultural stereotypes such as fatalism and familistic values (1993:xx–xxi). By contrast, studies of Puerto Ricans emphasize the different waves of migrant workers and their demographic characteristics, class composition and settlement patterns in New York City. While popular stereotypes characterized the first wave of Puerto Rican workers as unskilled and illiterate, many were prepared to enter the urban work force. Later waves were poorly prepared for urban work, another included a large number of females, while another included larger numbers of males. Passivity, welfare mentality and political dependence are topics that run throughout this literature (1993:xxi–xxii).

Researchers working with Latino subjects must understand not only the demographic characteristics of the group but also their cultural values and norms (Marín & Marín, 1991, p. 17) to eliminate the influence of these stereotypes. There is not only a need to learn about the cultural identities of Latinos, but there is also a need to engage in research that would positively portray that culture.

> Very few studies have been done on Chicano group behavior. Most of what has been done has been assessed deviant. Most attention to Chicano group behavior has gone to gangs . . . and frequently feeds racist academic tendencies and stereotypes. There is a need for studies focusing on what supports Chicano culture (Blea, 1988, p. 92).

Despite the census data mentioned above, there continues to be little in-depth knowledge of Latino attitudes and behaviors. According to de la Garza (1993) this is due in part to "the fact that survey researchers have shown little interest in collecting such data" (1993, p. B1).

A Heterogeneous Population Group

Researchers interested in the study of the Latino population should be aware of the within group differences that exist in this population. While we are more likely to accept the notion that not all Latinos are poor, we are least likely to be aware of the fact that Latinos are not a homogenous population group. Latino subpopulation groups represent a diverse representation of national origin groups (the Caribbean as well as North, South, and Central America) which are fragmented by country of origin, social class, generation, and historical differences before and after coming to the United States.

The term Latino or Hispanic has no independent life of its own and no real existence (Padilla, 1986) apart from the category created by the federal government to provide data on people of Mexican, Cuban, Puerto Rican, and other Latino origins in the United States. There is no precise, universally accepted definition of group membership (Latino or Hispanic), and Latinos do not agree on the appropriate group label (de la Garza, et al., 1992; Marín & Marín, 1991). Latino researchers have made the observation that confusion in identifying Latino research populations has both research and legal consequences (Hayes-Bautista & Chapa, 1987; Hayes-Bautista, 1980; Treviño, 1987).

Further the Latino subpopulation groups have been misrepresented in the literature. The traditional assumption has been that there is a distinctly "hispanic market" and a homogeneous population. Latinos are unified by language and cultural styles, sharing political and economic interests (Caplan, 1987; de la Garza, et al., 1992). That the Latino national origin groups are distinctive is a more recent assumption (Bean & Tienda, 1987, p. 2).

The largest and most significant Latino national origin groups are the Mexican Americans, Puerto Ricans, and Cuban-Americans. These groups have historically concentrated in nine states and over two thirds live in California, New York, and Texas alone (de la Puente, 1992). However, their reasons for coming to the United States, history in the United States, and politics and contributions to the United States are very diverse.

Mexican Americans

Mexicans were here before California and Texas were part of the United States, and became "Americans" after the territory was annexed into the United States. In addition, the United States' historical economic dependence on cheap labor has allowed many Mexicans to cross the border into the United States. Despite increasing restrictive migration legislation, thousands continue to cross the border to work. High migration rates and fertility levels mean that the Mexican population is quite young. On the average, Mexican Americans are 9.5 years younger than nonLatinos and the typical household is made up of 3.8 persons, compared with 2.6 persons in non-Latino households (U.S. Census Bureau, 1991). The following factors create cause for concern: high drop out rates among students; the relative earnings of blue-collar workers; class distribution and associated life chances of Mexican workers are worse now than they were in the 1970s (Chapa, 1990). According to Chapa (1990),

> rather than splitting into a middle class and an underclass, as Wilson argues is happening to the Black class structure, it appears that Mexican Americans can be divided into two groups. One group composed of middle class and white collar workers is analogous with William Wilson's middle class. The other consisting of blue collar and lower class workers has many of the characteristics of this lower class group (p. 17).

Continuous migration, industrial changes in the Southwest, and problems in schooling combine to constrain advancement (Moore & Pinderhughes, 1993). However, most research continues to focus on the foreign-born Mexicans immigrants, largely ignoring the United States born Mexican Americans.

Puerto Ricans

The United States took possession of Puerto Rico at the end of the Spanish American War in 1898. Puerto Ricans were granted American citizenship in 1917, months before the United States entered World War I. The colonial relationship between the island and the mainland has encouraged migration. The search for better economic conditions, labor recruitment, having relatives on the mainland, low air fares, and easy movement between the two countries makes migration a likely event among Puerto Ricans. Puerto Rican families are the most economically disadvantaged Latino group (38 percent of all Puerto Rican families fell below the poverty line).

> A growing portion of these families were concentrated in poor urban neighborhoods located in declining industrial centers in the Northeast and Midwest, which experienced massive economic restructuring and diminished employment opportunities for those with less education and weaker skills (Moore & Pinderhughes, 1993, p. xix).

The concentration of employed in low-wage manufacturing and service jobs and the displacement of many others from labor force participation have been the primary generating forces of widespread poverty among the Puerto Ricans (Sullivan, 1993).

Cubans

Cubans began arriving in the United States between 1960 and 1980 after the Castro revolution. Massive federal and state assistance contributed to the growth and strength of the Cuban community in Miami. Unlike other Latino migrants, early Cuban refugees were educated, middle- and upper-class professionals and this group is still welcomed as political refugees. The last wave of Cuban refugees, popularly known as the Marielitos, have not fared as well as previous refugees. A combination of factors help understand their current condition: the circumstances under which they left Cuba, many spent time in detention centers after arriving in the United States, the "deviant" group label, depiction of criminal and mentally ill by the popular press, and the negative reception of many by the established Cuban community.

As a group, Cubans represent the economic success story among all the Latino groups. Cubans have higher income levels (individual and family), own more businesses, and have higher levels of education and political power than any other Latino groups. Stepick & Grenier (1993) make two interesting points. First, while not all Cubans are economically successful, even those that are poor have continued to play an important role within the Cuban community in Miami. Second, while Cubans have received probably more welfare assistance than other Latino groups, they have used it to establish an entrepreneurial enclave. It appears that human potential along with the social, economic and political circumstances merged to produce the success that keeps regenerating the Cuban community in the Miami-Dade area (p. 79).

Other Latinos

In recent years many other groups have begun migrating to the United States, but few have been recognized as political refugees. Many stay as undocumented workers. The diversity among the Latino groups is more significant as "new" Latino immigrant groups become more visible in every major city in the country. The new Latino groups include large clusters from the Caribbean (Dominicans); from Central America (Salvadoreans, Guatemalans, Nicaraguans); and from South America (Peruvians, Colombians). (See Chinchilla, Hamilton & Loucky (1993) and Rodriguez (1993) for a description of Central American immigrants)

Legal Status

The Latino population is diverse in yet another area. The population represents different legal statuses in the United States. Not all Latinos are immigrants, for many were born citizens of the United States (Puerto Ricans), or are second or fifth generation Americans (Mexican Americans). Others are recent immigrants (Nicaraguans, Salvadoreans, Peruvians, etc.), while many recent immigrants have joined communities whose roots go back to their countries of origin (Texas, California). If these status differences are not recognized within a given race, then the assumption of homogeneity will continue.

CAUTIONS IN RACE CONCEPTUALIZATION

Even when Latinos are acknowledged as a viable race and their diversity is taken into account, the job of the researcher is not yet complete. The researcher must be sensitive to stereotypes that continue to be perpetuated and to mistakes which are made persistently in the study of Latinos.

Recognition of Stereotypes

Compared to Jews, African Americans, Asians, and Southern whites, Americans perceive Latinos as second only to African-Americans in terms of being lazy rather than hard working, and living off welfare rather than being self-supporting (Smith, 1990). Smith's (1990) survey also found that Latinos are seen as the nation's least patriotic group, while in Fuchs's (1990) survey, it is reported that Latinos threaten the physical and political integrity of the nation (p. 255–256). These ideas or stereotypes are voiced occasionally, as recently as the North American Free Trade Agreement discussions and often when the issue of undocumented workers is discussed.

It is generally accepted that all Latinos are very religious, and that most do not speak the English language. These two ideas must be taken with caution. Not all Latinos are devout Catholics. As a matter of fact, the protestant groups are the fastest growing denomination in Latin America and in Latino communities in the United States. And while it is true that some older Latinos do not speak the English language, it is also true that many third and fourth generation Latinos in the United States do not speak Spanish (Baca-Zinn, 1980).

Persistent Mistakes Made in the Study of Latinos

Independent national surveys and public opinion polls have systematically undersampled Latinos. The population that is more frequently sampled is the one that resides in urban centers (barrio), while other Latinos are undersampled (mobile, educated, living in the suburbs, etc.). It is seldom indicated if respondents to surveys are native born or foreign born; if they are native born, are they second, third or fourth generation?

When Latinos are included in national surveys and opinion polls, the several subgroups are not identified separately so as to know whether the views presented are those of Mexican-Americans, first generation Mexican American, Cuban American, Puerto Rican, or others. On many important issues, such as political affiliation and participation, socioeconomic status, and education, there are key differences among these groups and therefore it is necessary to identify which groups' views and opinions are being reported. Not identifying various groups only hinders research efforts that attempt to identify Latino voter attitudes, fear of crime, criminal victimization, or social concerns.

It is generally assumed that what unites all Latinos is their language and cultural practices, but respondents' language abilities are seldom measured, either objectively or subjectively. Research efforts must account for the ability to speak Spanish and for the various dialects spoken within the Latino population.

Virtually all surveys equate national origin with ethnic identity, and it is assumed that Latinos of varying national origins identify themselves as Latinos/Hispanics, rather than with their national origin. National origin, ethnicity and race vary among the population subgroups.

Research claims about Latinos (behaviors, attitudes, etc.) must be taken with caution. According to de la Garza, et al. (1992), it is impossible to document Latino community concerns in the same way that the concerns of other Americans are documented. This lack of documentation leads de la Garza, et al. (1992) to suspect data of both national political parties and would lead to criticism of policy based on that data.

POLICY IMPLICATIONS

The model for conceptualizing the race variable presented in this chapter is designed to not only improve the validity of the race concept, but also to improve social policy decisions and implementation. The relationship between theory, research, and policy is critical in the social sciences. Without well-informed theory, research is inadequate and policy generated from the research may then be faulty. Therefore, relevant social policy begins with valid research. If initial assumptions concerning the conceptualization of race are in error, then research results and subsequent policy decisions based on that research are incorrect.

The model presented in this chapter, which integrates structure, culture, and biography, is essential for an appropriate conceptualization of race in criminal justice research. The first step in the correct conceptualization of race is to educate researchers in the utility of the model, and then to inform policy makers as well as the public.

This chapter demonstrates how current conceptualizations of race may neglect minority groups other than African Americans and may ignore diversity of the groups when they are included. The implications for public policy are immense. If policy choices are based on incorrect assumptions about minority groups, or even worse, if minority groups are ignored, the long term consequences could be damaging. At best, no damage would occur, but then no positive change would occur either. The policy would be simply ineffective and a waste of money.

Once race and crime researchers become aware of the potential damage that could result from the misconceptualization of race, it is then the researcher's obligation to attempt to correct the errors of the past. With a more valid conceptualization based on the interactive model, criminology, as a discipline, will have better informed answers about why certain race and ethnic groups are disproportionately represented in the criminal justice system. Additionally, criminologists may be able to suggest ways in which the system itself could be modified to remedy those problems.

While this is a good beginning, it is not enough. To insure that criminal justice policy benefits from the accurate conceptualization of race, both policy makers and the public must be educated about the implications the conceptualization of race. The contemporary conceptualizations of race perpetuate myths and stereotypes that may lead to incorrect assumptions among the public. These perceptions are perhaps responsible for the heightened sense of fear that many people have regarding race and crime. Even though this sense of fear may not be based on fact, it still is strong enough to influence policy makers and consequently the policy they produce.

Consequently, politicians must react and develop policy based on the claims of the public if they intend to accomplish their goals. There is little time to determine the accuracy of public perceptions because political decisions must often be made quickly. Policy makers must act in limited time or perhaps risk losing at the next election.

The example of Latinos highlighted in this chapter illustrates the need for educating researchers, policy makers and the public. Despite the growing impact of Latinos in this country, there is little discussion among criminal justice experts about theoretical, research, and practical issues that are salient in the study of the Latino population. Criminal justice concepts, theories, research and policy decisions continue to focus on crime as a minority population problem. This approach, however, has traditionally emphasized the African American population and ignored other minorities.

It is clear that the terms "Black" or "Latino," while being ascribed social statuses, are categories that denote significant differences. Latinos are a racially mixed group, but in criminal justice this group has inconsistently been categorized as "white," "Black," or Hispanic, but often Latinos are relegated to the "all others" category. More frequently however, Latinos have been ignored altogether. This inconsistency has led to a serious gap in knowledge in which detailed and specific information about the racial/ethnic composition of the Latino population is lacking.

The chapter also critiqued criminal justice theoretical models. The argument was made that migration and culture are salient theoretical issues in the study of the Latino population. Since Latinos are found in a variety of migration statuses, criminal behavior and victimization rates may be affected. Migration status can also help explain fear of crime and the reporting of criminal activities to authorities. Ultimately, migration status can affect the trust and confidence Latinos have about criminal justice representatives as well as the perceptions Latinos have about the American criminal justice system.

The strong cultural presence of the Latinos warrants and provides a unique opportunity for the reanalysis of traditional cultural explanations offered in criminal justice models. Most criminal justice models are based on the assumptions that there is only one culture to follow, or diverse cultures are in conflict. Many Latinos function in two cultural worlds, however. Since Latinos are found in a variety of migration statuses, with diverse timing and reasons for coming to the United States, criminal justice models must take into account the role these statuses might play in deviant/criminal behavior.

The discussion of Latinos also described the diversity that exists within this population. The Latino population, however, continues to be misrepresented as a homogeneous group. They are described as one cultural group, unified by language, religion, and values, who share identical political and economic interests. Researchers working with Latino subjects should be aware of the within-group differences found in this population.

Until a more valid conceptualization of race is complete, criminal justice will have little accurate knowledge regarding the causes of crime, how the criminal justice system operates, and pertinent issues regarding offenders, victims, and practitioners in relation to race. More importantly, minority groups other than African Americans, such as Latinos, Asians, and American Indians, will continue to be either neglected or misrepresented in criminal justice policy decisions.

The impact of the neglect of African Americans is what caused the debate surrounding the conceptualization of race over twenty years ago. At that time, the need to include the minority perspective in the proper conceptualization of race was recognized and addressed. Now it is time to apply that knowledge in a more comprehensive manner to depict the reality of all races and ethnicities in criminal justice research and policy making.

CONCLUSION

Race and crime research in criminal justice has tended to emphasize African Americans in the study of the minority crime problem in this country. This tendency has meant that other races and ethnicities have either been ignored or misrepresented in this research. The result has been an invalid depiction of the race-crime relationship because not all races are included and the diversity within all races has not been taken into account.

The consequence of this neglect is that we have little valid knowledge regarding the causes of crime, how the criminal justice system operates, and the issues of offender, victim, and practitioner in relation to the correlate of race.

The solution is a reconceptualization of the race variable in race and crime research. Traditional conceptions have long relied on official measures, the assumption of assimilation, and the African American model. The time has come to accurately conceptualize race so that all races will be included in the study of crime and criminality and valid conclusions can be drawn from results because they are derived from a knowledge of the diversity of those races.

The model proposed in this chapter, Structure X Culture X Biography, provides the criminal justice researcher with the tools necessary to accurately depict the race-crime relationship. Knowledge of social structure would give the researcher the information necessary to understand the relationship of all racial identities to the social structure under analysis. An appreciation for cultural differences breaks the traditional assumption of assimilation and allows the researcher to explore the nature of cultural adaptation and response. Finally, the acknowledgement of biography means that the researcher is further cautioned to realize and substantiate that results are not generalizable to all members of a race or culture because individuals have the ability to effect their futures.

The Latino example described in this chapter illustrates how a race should be explored in the proper conceptualization of race. In the description, the relationship of Latinos to the social structure and their cultural uniqueness were briefly discussed. To further highlight their within-group diversity, the three major Latino ethnicities were discussed, as were less known Latino groups, and differences in legal status. Finally, several cautions associated with a proper understanding of Latinos were discussed.

The Latino example illustrates how all races should be analyzed in a proper conceptualization of race. The significance of race and criminal justice makes it imperative that researchers make a concerted effort in the reconceptualization of race. If not, what is known about crime causation, the criminal justice system, and the issues of offenders, victims, and practitioners will continue to suffer. Even worse, what is known will continue to be in error and will serve as myths and stereotypes that will continue to hinder the criminal justice process.

The impact of these myths and stereotypes on criminal justice policy is and will continue to be tremendous if a reconceptualization of race does not occur. The legal system and its crime control policies appear to assume that individuals have complete control over societal structure and their own cultural identity. The system itself even makes judgements about these individuals without regard for the diversity of their cultures (Takagi, 1981).

A better informed public policy would be one that accounted for the relationship between structure and culture. The responses of individuals could be understood in relation to their values and ideals, rather that in relation to those of the majority culture. Then we might not only understand more about why certain cultures are disproportionately represented in the criminal justice system as offenders, victims, and practitioners, but the system itself could be modified to remedy those problems.

REFERENCES

Adler, F., Mueller, G. O. & Laufer, W. S. (1991). *Criminology.* New York: McGraw Hill Inc.

Baca-Zinn, M. (1980). Gender and ethnicity changes among Chicanos. *Frontiers. 5*(2), 18–24.

Bean, F. & Tienda, M. (1987). *The Hispanic population of the United States.* Sage Publications.

Blea, I. I. (1988). *Toward a Chicano social science.* New York: Praeger.

Braithwaite, J. (1987). From bodigies and widgies to J. R. Ewing: Beyond folk devils in media depiction of crime. *Proceedings of the Institute of Criminology, Media Effects on Attitudes to Crime, 72,* 55–59.

Caplan, B. (1987). Linking cultural characteristics to political opinion. In R. de la Garza (Ed.)., *Ignored voices: Public opinion polls and the Latino community.* Austin, TX: University of Texas Press. pp. 158–169.

Carter, D. L. (1985). Hispanic perception of police performance: An empirical assessment. *Journal of Criminal Justice, 13*(6), 487–500.

Carter, D. L. (1986). Hispanic police officer's perception of discrimination. *Police Studies, 9*(4), 204–210.

Chapa, J. (190, May). The myth of hispanic progress: Trends in educational and economic attainment of Mexican Americans. *Harvard Journal of Hispanic Policy, 9,* 3–18.

Chibnall, S. (1981). The production of knowledge by crime reporters. In S. Cohen & J. Young (Eds.)., *The manufacture of news. Deviance, social problems & the mass media.* (2nd edition). Beverly Hills: Sage. pp. 75–97.

Chinchilla, N., Hamilton, N. & Loucky, J. (1993). Central Americans in Los Angeles: An immigrant community in transition. In J. Moore & R. Pinderhughes (Eds.) *In the barrios: Latinos and the underclass debate.* New York: Russell Sage Foundation. pp. 51–78.

Collins, P. H. (1990). *Black feminist thought: Knowledge, consciousness, and the politics of empowerment.* Boston, Mass: Unwin Hyman.

Dashefsky, A. (1975). Theoretical frameworks in the study of ethnic identity: Toward a social psychology of ethnicity. *Ethnicity, 2,* 10–18.

de la Garza, R. (1993). Researchers must heed new realities when they study Latinos in the U.S. *Chronicle of Higher Education, June 2,* B1–B2.

de la Garza, R., DeSepio, L., Garcia, F.C., Garcia, J., & Falcón, A. (1992). *Latino voices: Mexican, Puerto Rican and Cuban perspectives on American politics.* Boulder: Westview.

de la Puente, M. (1992 January). The census undercount of the Hispanic population. *Latino Studies Journal, 3,* 67–81.

Etten, T.J. & Myers, L.B. (1991). The subjectivity of objectivity: a critical review of research on biased newspaper crime coverage. Paper presented to the American Society of Criminology, November 20–23, 1991 San Francisco, California.

Fishman, M. (1981). Crime waves as ideology. In S. Cohen & J. Young (Eds.), *The manufacture of news. Deviance, social problems & the mass media* (2nd ed., pp. 98–117). Beverly Hills: Sage.

Flowers, R.B. (1988). *Minorities and criminality.* New York: Greenwood Press.

Fuchs, L. (1990). *The American kaleidoscope: Race, ethnicity and the civic culture.* Hanover: Wesleyan University Press.

Garcia, J. (1981). Yo soy mexicano . . . : Self Identity and sociodemographic correlates. *Social Science Quarterly, 62*(1), 88–98.

Georges-Abeyei, D.E. (1986). Race, ethnicity, and the spatial dynamic: Toward a realistic study of black crime, victimization, and criminal justice processing of blacks. *Social Justice, 16*(4), 35–54.

Georges-Abeyie, D.E. (1984). Definitional issues: race, ethnicity, and official crime/victimization statistics. In D. Georges-Abeyie (Ed.), *The criminal justice system and blacks* (pp. 5–19). New York: Clark Boardman.

Gertz, M.G. & Myers, L.B. (1992). Impediments to cross-national research: Problems of reliability and validity. *International Journal of Comparative and Applied Criminal Justice, 16,* 57–65.

Hagan, F.E. (1989). *Research methods in criminal justice and criminology* (2nd ed.). New York: Macmillan.

Hayes-Bautista, D. (1980). Identifying "Hispanic" populations: The influence of research methodology upon public policy. *American Journal of Public Health, 70*(4), 353–356.

Hayes-Bautista, D. & Chapa, J. (1987). Latino terminology: Conceptual bases for standardized terminology. *American Journal of Public Health, 77*(1), 61–68.

Humphries, D. (1981). Serious crime, news coverage, and ideology: a content analysis of crime coverage in a metropolitan paper. *Crime and Delinquency, 27,* 191–205.

Jaehnig, W. B., Weaver, D. H., & Fico, F. (1981). Reporting crime and fearing crime in three communities. *Journal of Communication, 33,* 88–96.

Knight, G. & Dean, T. (1982). Myth and the structure of news. *Journal of Communication, 32,* 144–162.

LaFree, G. & Russell, K. K. (1993). The arguement for studying race and crime. *Journal of Criminal Justice Education, 4,* 273–288.

Lampe, P. E. (1984). Ethnicity and crime: perceptual differences among Blacks, Mexican Americans and Anglos. *International Journal of Intercultural Relations, 8*(4), 357–372.

Lewis, O. (1966). *La vida: A Puerto Rican family in the culture of poverty.* New York: Random House.

Lichter, S. R., Rothman, S., & Lichter, L. S. (1986). *The media elite.* Bethesda, Maryland: Adler and Adler.

Mahler, S. J. (1992, July 20–24). First stop: Suburbia. Report on the Americas, *North American Congress on Latin America, 26*(1).

Mann, C. R. (1993). *Unequal justice.* Bloomington, Indiana: University Press.

Marin, G. & Marin, B. V. (1991). *Research with Hispanic populations.* Newbury Park: Sage Publications.
Marsh, H. L. (1988). *Crime and the press: does newspaper crime coverage support myths about crime and law enforcement?* Unpublished doctoral dissertation, Sam Houston State University, Huntsville, Texas.
Mirande, A. (1980). Fear of crime and fear of police in a Chicago community. *Sociology and Social Research, 64*(4), 528–541.
Mirande, A. (1985). *The Chicano experience.* South Bend, IN: University of Notre Dame Press.
Moore, J. W. (1972). Social constraints on sociological knowledge: academics and research concerning minorities. *Social Problems, 21,* 65–77.
Moore, J. W. (1978). *Homeboys, gangs, drugs and prison in the barrios of Los Angeles.* Philadelphia: Temple University Press.
Moore, J. W. & Pinderhughes, R. (1993). *In the barrios: Latinos and the underclass debate.* New York: Russel Sage Foundation.
Napper, G. (1977). Perceptions of crime: problems and implications. In R. L. Woodson (Ed.)., *Black perspectives on crime and the criminal justice system.* Boston, Mass.: G. K. Hall.
Padilla, F. (1986). On the nature of Latino ethnicity. *Social Science Quarterly, 65,* 651–664.
Park, R. E. (1936). Human ecology. *American Journal of Sociology, 42,* 1–15.
Pope, C. E. (1982). Race, crime and criminological research: some unintended consequences. *Humanity and Society, 6,* 243–256.
Portes, A., Parker, R. N., & Cobas, J. A. (1980). Assimilation or consciousness: Perceptions of the U.S. society among Latin American immigrants. *Social Forces, 50*(1), 200–224.
Pritchard, D. (1986). Homicide and bargained justice: The agenda setting effect of crime news on prosecutors. *Public Opinion Quarterly, 50,* 143–159.
Quinney, R. (1979). *Criminology* (2nd ed.). Boston: Little, Brown.
Rodriguez, N. P. (1993). Economic restructuring and Latino growth in Houston. In J. Moore & R. Pinderhughes (Eds.)., *In the barrios: Latinos and the underclass debate* (pp. 101–128). New York: Russell Sage Foundation.
Sassen, S. (1992, July 14–19). Why migration?. Report on the Americas, *North American Congress on Latin America, 26*(1).
Skogan, W. G. & Maxfield, M. G. (1981). *Coping with crime: Individual and neighborhood reactions.* Beverly Hills: Sage.
Shai, D. & Rosenwaike, I. (1988). Violent deaths among Mexican-, Puerto Rican- and Cuban-born migrants in the United States. *Social Science and Medicine, 26*(2), 269–276.
Shaw, C.R. & McKay, H.D. (1942). *Juvenile delinquency and urban areas.* Chicago: University of Chicago Press.
Smith, A. B. & Pollack, H. (1989). To what extent should prosecutors intrude in the sentencing process? *The Justice Professional, 4,* 157–171.
Smith, T. (1990). Ethnic survey. *National Opinion Research Center,* Report No. 19. Chicago: University of Chicago.

Stanfield, J.H. (1993a). Methodological reflections: An introduction. In J.H. Stanfield II & R.M. Dennis (Eds.), *Race and ethnicity in research methods,* (pp. 3–15). Newbury Park, CA: Sage Publications.

Stanfield, J.H. (1993b). Epistemological considerations. In J.H. Stanfield II & R.M. Dennis (Eds.), *Race and ethnicity in research methods,* (pp. 16–36). Newbury Park, CA: Sage Publications.

Starrett, R.A., Connolly, M.P., Decker, J.T., & Araujo, A. (1988). The crime reporting behavior of Hispanic older persons: A causal model. *Journal of Criminal Justice, 16*(5), 413–423.

Stepick, A. III & Grenier, G. (1993). Cubans in Miami. In J. Moore & R. Pinderhughes (Eds.), *In the barrios: Latinos and the underclass debate,* (pp. 79–100). New York: Russell Sage Foundation.

Stolzenberg, R. (1990, February). Ethnicity, geography and occupational achievement of Hispanic men in the United States. *American Sociological Review, 55,* pp. 143–154.

Sullivan, M.L. (1993). Puerto Ricans in Sunset Park, Brooklyn: Poverty amidst ethnic and economic diversity. In J. Moore & R. Pinderhughes (Eds.), *In the barrios: Latinos and the underclass debate,* (pp. 1–25). New York: Russell Sage Foundation.

Takagi, P. (1981). Race, crime, and social policy: A minority perspective. *Crime and Delinquency, 27*(1), 48–63.

Thomas, W.I. & Znaniecki, F. (1958). *The Polish peasant in Europe and America.* New York: Dover Publications.

Treviño, F. (1987). Standardized terminology for Hispanic populations. *American Journal of Public Health, 77*(1), 69–72.

U.S. Bureau of the Census (1991). The hispanic population in the United States: March 1990. Current Population Reports, series p-20 no.455. Washington, D.C.: U.S. Dept. of Commerce.

van Dijk, J.J.M. (1978). Public attitudes toward crime in the Netherlands. *Victimology, 3,* 265–273.

Voumvakis, S. E. & Ericson, R. V. (1984). *News accounts of attacks on women: A comparison of three Toronto newspapers.* Toronto: University of Toronto, Centre of Criminology.

Whyte, W. F. (1981). *Street corner society: The social structure of an Italian slum.* Chicago: University of Chicago Press.

Wolfgang, M.E. & Ferracuti, F. (1967). *The subculture of violence: Towards an integrated theory in Criminology.* Beverly Hill: Sage Publications.

Young, J. (1981a). Beyond the consensual paradigm: A critique of left functionalism in media theory. In S. Cohen & J. Young (Eds.), *The manufacture of news. Deviance, social problems & the mass media* (2nd ed, pp. 393–421). Beverly Hills: Sage.

Young, J. (1981b). The myth of drug takers in the mass media. In S. Cohen & J. Young (Eds.), *The manufacture of news. Deviance, social problems & the mass media* (2nd ed, pp. 326–334). Beverly Hills: Sage.

CHAPTER SIX

RACE IN CRIME STORIES

DENNIS M. ROME AND STEVEN M. CHERMAK

INTRODUCTION

Crime is one of the most celebrated topics that news organizations use to sell its product. Of the large number of crimes available each day, the news media selectively choose those they think are worthy of presentation. Researchers have increasingly acknowledged the importance of studying what gets presented in the news about crime. A large body of research examining crime in the news media has resulted from this scholarly interest. The existing research has documented the types of crime that get presented, the sources used for story information, and the process used to generate stories. Although the amount of research on the overall presentation of crime in the news media has increased dramatically, specific issues have been ignored. For example, portrayal of the race of victim and the race of defendant has been neglected. This chapter fills this gap by examining the newsworthiness of race and how it affects the production of news about crime.

The presentation of African Americans and Hispanics in the news media is an important topic to examine. Media coverage of racial issues has serious consequences for news consumers because what a person "knows" is a function of his or her life experiences. Individuals socially construct their reality when interpreting events which is shaped by personal experiences, interactions with groups, and exposure to different institutions. Media are another important source of influence on how the public makes decisions and forms opinions (Altheide, 1984; Quinney, 1970; Turner, 1990). The news media provide the public with images from which they construct reality. Since most people have limited daily exposure to crime, the news media are an important surrogate information source, shaping how the public thinks.

This chapter begins by highlighting previous research on the presentation of race and crime in the news. We then present a discussion of the news production process because an understanding of the social construction of news is important before dissecting how race influences the decision-making of reporters and editors. The final section discusses how racial issues are presented in the news and their effect on the news production process. We conclude by offering suggestions for improving the depiction of African Americans in crime news.

THE MASS MEDIA, RACE, AND CRIME

> A specific kind of crime coverage in the media provides the source for building criminal conceptions. A conception of crime is presented in the mass media. That conception, diffused throughout the society, becomes the basis for the public's view of reality. Not only is a symbolic environment created within society, but personal actions take their reference from that environment. Indeed, the construction of a conceptual reality is also the creation of a social reality of actions and events (Quinney, 1970, p. 285).

The public relies heavily on the mass media for information about crime, law, and criminal justice (Graber, 1980, Quinney, 1970). Crime is a prevalent topic in virtually every type of media source, including television, radio, newspapers, books, music, comics, and movies. Research indicates that public perceptions of crime are formed on the basis of information appearing in various forms of media. For example, Chaffee and Choe (1981), Dominick (1978), and Graber (1980) found that ninety-five percent of those polled cited the mass media as their primary source of information about crime. The public is fascinated by crime and attend closely to what is presented. Research indicates that crime is among the most frequently read newspaper categories (Graber, 1980; Skogan and Maxfield, 1981; Swanson, 1955), providing details about crime which enable consumers to discuss the causes and solutions to the crime problem (Ryan and Owen, 1976).

The news media is one of the more important source formats that display images of crime. Even a casual viewer of the evening news (local or national) observes that crime stories are a staple of the news diet. Crime is routinely covered in the news because it occurs frequently and is "newsworthy" due to its inherent human-interest quality. Cohen (1975) maintains that crime, in comparison with other topics, is well-covered and prominently displayed. A fair share of crime news appears on the front page accompanied by banner headlines.

Another reason for the frequent presentation of crime is the practice of using crime news as filler (Gordon and Heath, 1981; Graber, 1980). Crime news is seldom in short supply, so that, on a "slow news day," column space or air time may be filled in with crime stories. If crime news is routinely employed in this way, then the amount of time or space devoted to crime will not accurately reflect the actual number of crimes. Crime news may also be increased in an effort to raise circulation or viewership, or be heavily featured in order to appeal to a certain segment of the audience (Dominick, 1978; Gordon and Heath, 1981).

Editors, newsroom staff, and broadcasters play an important role in shaping political reality and perceptions of criminal reality because they select, produce, and display news (McCombs and Shaw, 1972). Consumers evaluate the significance of a particular crime from the amount of information and space given to a crime story. Smith (1984), Ditton and Duffy (1983), and Sheley and Ashkins (1981) suggest that bias in newspaper reporting might create and define a broad public awareness of crime that is substantially different from any "reality" contained in the official statistics. In fact, Gormley (1975) maintains that the press may not be successful much of the time in telling people what to think, but it is stunningly successful in telling its readers what to think about.

Existing research examining news coverage of the African American community reveals disturbing biases and patterns of blatant distortion at the hands of the nation's largest and most respected print and broadcast media. Indeed, some analysts warn that the power that once toppled a president now works the equivalent on the African American community, thwarting African American social advancement by conveying the illusion of impartial reporting while applying vastly different standards to news coverage of whites and African Americans. Young people, both African American and white, may be at particular risk of internalizing these misperceptions because their experience leaves them ill-equipped to challenge news reports (Johnson, 1991). According to Raspberry (1971):

> The press is also charged with paying too much attention to the newly-organized poor and the black militants and thereby distorting its coverage of black people generally. Now that is a fairly serious charge and it may be justified. It at least warrants some exploration. Newspapers, and now television stations and radio stations, are wrestling with this very question. It comes about partly because of the nature of news. If news is the unusual occurrence, the extraordinary event, then it does tend to distort unless the reader knows something about the ordinary people involved. For example, a story about a suburban housewife who goes berserk and does something weird—murders her family or whatever—is news. Obviously when she does this she becomes news. But the readers already know lots and lots of ordinary suburban housewives, so they are able to fit the eccentric one into some sort of context.
>
> If we apply the same guidelines to a coverage of the [black] community and write about the ones who do something extraordinarily good or extraordinarily bad and you don't know anything about ordinary black people, you don't have the context in which to fit the extraordinary ones. The result, of course, is distortion. (p. 125)

Biased reporting could easily be used by the average reader to develop an inaccurate description of African Americans and Hispanics. For example, a 1990 survey of 3,125 news stories collected at random over a one-month period in Boston revealed striking differences in news coverage from white and African American owned media outlets. In the white media, 85% of the news about Boston's predominantly African American neighborhoods reinforced negative stereotypes of African Americans as prone to violence and crime, and unable to maintain cohesive families. In contrast, news from the African American media—comprising stories from the same neighborhoods and collected over the same 30-day period—depicted the African American community with more balance, reporting entrepreneurial breakthroughs, drug arrests, high academic achievement, classroom problems, and successful campaigns to remedy poor living conditions, and community malaise. The positive stories rarely appeared in the white owned media.

In a region whose African American community totals 15% of the population (with a 22% African American population in Boston proper), the study also found a persistent tendency for white reporters to seek out white experts for comments, even on such issues of vital concern to the African American community as unemployment. Boston's white-owned media outlets displayed reluctance to cite racism as an underlying factor in news events ranging from white-on-African American harassment to educational disparities to employment discrimination. The study concluded that while the white media portray themselves through their charitable work and public service announcements as advocating racial harmony, their news coverage perpetuates racism by reinforcing common negative assumptions about African Americans, failing to show positive African American role models, and neglecting to discuss racism as an important social force (Johnson, 1990; Reed, 1990; Turner, 1990).

Patricia Raybon, a former editor of *The Denver Post's Sunday Contemporary Magazine* argues that the media is guilty of a severe bias against African Americans and that it is inaccurate journalism. She says (1989):

> This is who I am not. I am not a crack addict. I am not a welfare mother. I am not illiterate. I am not a prostitute. I have never been in jail. My children are not in gangs. My husband doesn't beat me. My home is not a tenement. None of these things defines who I am, nor do they describe the other black people I've known and worked with and loved and friended over these 40 years of my life. Nor does it describe most of black America, period. Yet in the eyes of the American news media, this is what black America is: poor, criminal, addicted and dysfunctional. (p. 11)

Raybon further argues that the media coverage of African America is so one-sided and so imbalanced that the most victimized and hurting segment of the African American community, a small segment at best, is presented not as the exception but as the norm. She maintains that it is an "insidious" practice and all the uglier for its blatancy. Raybon continues (1989):

> I have observed a steady offering of media reports on crack babies, gang warfare, violent youth, poverty and homelessness—and in most cases, the people featured in the photos and stories were black. At the same time, articles that discuss other aspects of American life—from home buying to medicine to technology to nutrition—rarely, if ever, show blacks playing a positive role, or for that matter, any role at all. (p. 11)

The daily message transmitted is that African Americans are dysfunctional and un-whole. America never learns the truth about what is actually a wonderful, vibrant, creative community of people. Raybon further maintains that (1989):

> Most black Americans are not poor. Most black teenagers are not crack addicts. Most black mothers are not on welfare. Indeed, in sheer numbers, more white Americans are poor and on welfare than are black. Yet one never would deduce that by watching television or reading American newspapers and magazines.
>
> Why does the American media insist on playing this myopic, inaccurate picture game? In this game, white America is always whole and lovely and healthy while black America is usually sick and pathetic and deficient. Rarely, indeed, is black America ever depicted in the media as functional and self-sufficient. The free press, indeed, as the main interpreter of American culture and American experience, holds the mirror on American reality—so much so that what the media says it is, even if it's not that way at all. The media is guilty of a severe bias and the problem screams out for correction. It is worse than simply lazy journalism, which is bad enough; it is inaccurate journalism. (p. 11)

Raybon believes that the best way to understand how and why American news media deal with the reporting of intergroup relations is to watch them in action. For many social scientists, this means critically scrutinizing what gets written in newspapers or what gets displayed on television (Chaffee and Choe, 1983; Ditton and Duffy, 1983; Smith, 1984). Perhaps the picture that Raybon painted for African Americans is in fact due to biased reporting.

Research has documented the news media's limited coverage of race in poverty, protest, and crime stories. For example, Ginsburg (1989) suggests that the corporate media's coverage of African American poverty is from the perspective of pathology rather than in the context of economic crisis, corporate policies, or management agendas that promote the very conditions affecting African Americans, perpetuating their distress. It is Ginsburg's (1989) contention that the media presentation of black poverty should take place within an economic context (p. 35). For example, the press should note that it is the "inner working of a profit-driven system that has maintained black poverty above 30 percent for more than a generation" rather than black family structure. Ginsburg (1989) argues further:

> There is no "tangle of pathology" in the poor black community. Rather, there are those—like the corporate media . . . for whom that empty construct is so very convenient, and so very destructive to this nation's blacks. (p. 53)

In fact, historically, organized protests arranged and attended by African Americans are presented by newspapers as militant gatherings. Note the following examples identified in two major metropolitan dailies: the *New York Times (NYT)* and *The Atlanta Constitution (AC):*

1). In an article entitled "Negroes and Police Scuffle in Atlanta," (*NYT,* August 19, 1966), which described a protest by the Student Nonviolent Coordinating Committee, the newspaper described that the " . . . negro pickets shouted 'Black Power!' " and the protesting group was referred to as "a militant civil rights group." This type of reporting explicitly suggests to the reader that the Student Nonviolent Coordinating Committee was a wrongful, unlawful, and illegal group that threatened the white establishment.

2). An article entitled "Le Roi Jones Jailed in Manacles After Outburst in Jersey Court" (*NYT,* October 10, 1967), is accompanied by a photograph of Jones and not only is Jones described as a "militant negro" by the newspaper, but the crowd of African Americans that gathered outside of the court were also labeled as "militant negroes."

3). In an article entitled "12 Negroes Jailed After Picket Fight" (*AC,* August 19, 1966), the Student Nonviolent Coordinating Committee (SNCC) was referred to as a "militant group." The newspaper reported that the group had began to "shout black power slogans."

4). In an article entitled "7 Whites Arrested in NY; Negroes Attack Newsman" (*AC,* July 24, 1964), the Congress of Racial Equality (CORE) was referred to as a "gang of militant negro youths." The newspaper went further to describe the African American community: "As darkness fell on the dingy, tenement streets, steel-helmeted police braced for a possible renewal of rioting—patrolled the area on foot."

5). Note the depiction of the Black Liberation Army and the Black Panther Party in the article: "Slaying of One of the Last Black Liberation Army Leaders Still at Large Ended a 7-month Manhunt" (*NYT,* November 16, 1973). In this article the newspaper described the Black Liberation Army as " . . . a loosely knit amalgam of terrorists that arose out of a Black Panther faction, and described as linked to the assassinations of at least five police officers and the wounding of a dozen others."

Similar instances of a distortion of African Americans have been identified in media coverage of crime events. For example, a news story entitled "500 Hunt 'Drifter' in Girl's Slaying: Fingerprints Help Identify Suspect—Massachusetts Police Join In Search" (*NYT,* February 28, 1961) was accompanied by a three-and-a-half by one-and-a-half inch photograph of an African

American man, and the newspaper went further to report that the suspect was "toothless and a heavy drinker partial to beer!" A more recent case is the media portrayal of the crimes of Willie Horton. Lee Atwater, former Chair of the Republican Party, used photographs of an African American escaped convict to convince voters that Mike Dukakis approved an early release program for dangerous prisoners—the implication here that African Americans (Willie Horton) might just show up at your door!

Rhodes (1987) argued that the Emmett Till murder case in 1955 marked the turning point in the coverage of African Americans by the white American press. The Till case gave America a harsh, inescapable glimpse of racial violence and injustice. Till, an African American teenager from Chicago, was murdered in 1955 while visiting relatives in Mississippi. The Till murder was covered extensively in the press, since the two white men charged with killing him were acquitted by an all white, all male jury on murder charges and later that year were found innocent by a twenty man all white grand jury on kidnapping charges. Rhodes (1987) reports that most Southern papers denounced Till's murder, but as the Northern white and African American presses began investigating the case, anti-African American backlash erupted in Southern publications. Vehement criticism of the South came from *The Crisis,* published by the National Association for the Advancement of Colored People (NAACP), and other African American publications followed suit. Editorials appearing in *Life* magazine and the *New York Times* wounded Southern pride, and the Southern press retaliated. This media "civil war" continued for about a year after the Till case, raising the question of how to handle race related news in the media.

By 1960, according to Rhodes (1987), observers and the press itself agreed that coverage of African Americans had improved in both the Northern and Southern press. Although one still wonders if this is the case considering more recent coverage of celebrated crime stories. For example, when a 28-year-old jogger was attacked and gang-raped several years ago in New York City's Central Park by a group of youths, her struggle for survival was chronicled in spectacular media coverage that mirrored the city's sense of outrage. Yet, when a similar incident occurred several weeks before, the media were silent. In this instance, a 29-year-old woman was attacked on the roof of a 21-story building by two armed men. The pair raped the woman, then forced her to jump from the roof. Miraculously, the naked woman managed to grab a television cable that broke her fall long enough for her screams to alert neighbors, who saved her life (Cose, 1989).

The jogger, a resident of New York's affluent Upper East Side, was white. Her attackers were African American and Hispanic. The second woman was a resident of Harlem. She and her attackers were persons of color. Cose (1989) suggests that while the particulars of the two cases differed in important ways, the differential news coverage given the two crimes reflects unspoken judgments of newsworthiness by the affluent managers of New York's predominantly white-owned media. That the assailants of the Central Park jogger were African American and Hispanic confirmed a stereotype and heightened the news value of the story; that the victim was a successful investment banker made the story so urgent that it would have received widespread media coverage even if her attackers had been white. Conversely, while an African American or Hispanic woman may have received the same brutal treatment from the Central Park attackers, her plight would not have received broad news coverage unless she was prominent in the community or possessed at least one other of the attributes the media historically take great interest in covering (Cose, 1989).

Meg Greenfield, a national syndicated columnist argues that such reporting is blatantly biased. She writes (1989):

> Every time we say that the vicious acts of some ghetto criminal were only to be expected and extenuate them by suggesting that they are probably the norm in that put-upon world, we are doing a disservice to the very people we should be most trying to help and whom we have the greatest reason to admire. The real stories of guts and virtue are the stories of those millions of people trapped in the poverty swamp who are resisting the temptations all around them and who are struggling mightily and honorably to do right and do well with little available to them.
>
> I know that in saying this I enter a journalistically suspect and politically unrespectable realm. But I am not just succumbing here to the cheerful-news syndrome, the look-how-many-planes-didn't-crash-today school of reporting. I think our reflexive habit of projecting the crimes and defaults of the few onto the many, of universalizing and even, in some cases, romanticizing the worst elements of the ghetto pathology is self-indulgent, cruel and, yes, racist. (p. 86)

Although a significant amount of research exists that concludes that various topics are narrowly presented in the news along racial lines, a number of gaps in our knowledge continue to exist. For example, there are few studies that consider how the race of defendants and victims affect the production of news and when race is included and excluded within a crime story. The remainder of this chapter fills this gap. First, however, it is necessary that we discuss the news production process and traditional explanations regarding the newsworthiness of various events.

THE SOCIAL CONSTRUCTION OF NEWS

Only a small portion of the large number of crimes that occur can be presented as news because of space constraints. News personnel and criminal justice sources struggle among themselves to control what is presented about crime, making a series of discretionary decisions during progressive steps of the news production process. The first step is controlled primarily by source organizations who determine the level of access reporters have to the crimes known to the police. The second step is where news personnel select a range of potential stories from the large number made available from the source organization. As with any other kind of potential news material, the central criterion for choosing crime stories is "newsworthiness." Third, news and source organizations struggle to determine what information is included in a selected story during the production stage of the news process. Finally, the constructed crime story competes with other potential stories for news space when determining what is presented to the public.

Gaining Access to the Crimes Reported to the Police

The police are a primary news filter, deciding which crimes are offered to a reporter for potential news selection. The news media immediately rely on a picture of crime that is limited because the majority of crimes are never reported to the police (U.S. Department of Justice, 1992). The news media's heavy reliance on the police for story suggestions results from concerns about their own organizational needs. Organizational resources to cover crime news, such as the number of personnel and news space allowed per topic, are limited. Relying on the crimes that are known to the police allows them to satisfy the news demand for stories on crime with minimal amounts of organizational costs and time-consuming complications.

News organizations are physically structured to meet crime story demands. Most crime stories are produced by reporters assigned to cover the "police beat." Beat reporters develop news stories from a decentralized location removed from their editors and management. Police beat reporters have a considerable amount of discretion to produce crimes that they deem newsworthy, because of the limited amount of direct supervision. Typically, news media will have an office for reporters located at police headquarters. This location gives reporters the opportunity to interact and develop ongoing relationships with police sources. In addition, the physical location of the police beat allows reporters to gain access to police documents, such as police blotter reports, arrest documents, and official memorandum, which contributes to their efficient production of crime stories.

The news media also benefit from their reliance on these sources because the police are publicly accepted as an authoritative voice on crime and criminal justice issues. The cultural acceptance of the police as an important source of news helps to legitimize the news organization and confirms their credibility and objectivity (Ericson, Baranek, & Chan, 1989; Tuchman, 1973). News media are able to continue to function as an unbiased conveyor of what is officially known about crime because it appears that they are being fair and balanced.

Police organizations provide the physical space for news organizations and access to official police documents so that they can control the images that are presented in the news about themselves. The police are institutions frequently under scrutiny and held accountable to the public for their actions. The police go to great lengths to exclude particular crimes or an ineffective police response from public preview because the presentation might adversely affect the public image of the police.

Police organizations increase their opportunity to control by assigning officers to represent the department as police spokespersons. This officer serves public relation functions and is directly responsible for controlling the image that is presented to the public about the police. This spokesperson interacts with news reporters on a daily basis, making decisions about the crimes that should be provided to reporters. The frequent interactions with reporters allows the spokesperson to develop an understanding about the type of information that is considered newsworthy and how to present it in a way that protects the preferred image of the department.

The reliance of the news media on the police affects what can be presented to the public about crime and the mutually beneficial media-source relationship influences how crime is presented to the public. Reporters are less willing to publicly criticize the police for ineffective responses to crime because they fear losing access to police sources and documents. Conversely, police sources are concerned with an image that supports their need for additional resources and manpower.

The Selection of Newsworthy Stories

The access that reporters have to police sources provides them with a range of crimes for selection consideration. The crimes that reporters select must meet an independent set of criteria regarding the newsworthiness of events. Reporters develop an understanding of these criteria over time as they become acculturated in their work. Their interactions with other reporters, sources, and superiors influence their understanding of these criteria. Individual reporters adopt these standardized criteria in order to be rewarded and get their stories displayed prominently. Past research has identified a range of influences on the selection decisions of reporters (Cohen and Young, 1981; Ericson, Baranek, & Chan, 1987; Hartley, 1982).

The first newsworthy factor is the seriousness of the offense. Research has consistently found that violent crimes are significantly more likely to be presented in the news than less serious crimes (Graber, 1980; Marsh, 1988; Sheley and Ashkins, 1981). The presentation of crime is inversely related to the actual number of crimes known to the police in that the crimes least likely to occur (murder, rape) are most frequently displayed (ibid). For example, Graber (1980) reports that murders constituted only .2 percent of offenses known to the police in Chicago in 1976, but accounted for 26 percent of crime stories in the *Chicago Tribune.* Sheley and Ashkins (1981), in a study of media crime coverage in New Orleans, found much the same pattern. Serious crimes predominate in both print and electronic media (Sheley and Ashkins, 1981), although the number of serious crimes that can be presented varies by city size because of access to different types of crime (Chermak, 1993).

Violent crime is news because reporters think that it is what is of most interest to the public. The most serious crime threat to a community is thought to be of most concern to the audience. In addition, police sources are willing to provide access to these types of crime because the image conveyed is consistent with the one that they desire. The threat to the community is perceived as serious and the police are considered the primary agency involved as able to fight this problem.

Second, the individuals involved in an incident can influence decisions about newsworthiness. The victim or the defendant involved can increase the likelihood that less serious crimes are presented in the news. Certain demographic characteristics, such as age and occupation, make a crime more appealing as news. For example, crimes that involve victims or defendants who are very young or old, or those that occupy a position with a high amount of responsibility to the public, such as a police officer, clergy member, or teacher, increases the likelihood that a crime will be prominently displayed in the news.

These characteristics increase the likelihood of presentation because a larger portion of the audience are able to relate to individuals with these characteristics. Children and the elderly are considered deserving of special protections by society. When someone violates either of these protected classes, the public is appalled and react accordingly. Similarly, a large portion of the public has frequent contacts with certain occupations that are expected to protect the public. When someone violates this trust and commits a crime, the seriousness of the event is exacerbated because of the duty to protect.

The third characteristic that has been found to increase the newsworthiness of events is its uniqueness. Crimes that are so extraordinary that they supply an element of shock, humor, or surprise increases the likelihood that the crime will be presented. For example, burglaries are rarely able to fit a reporter's conceptualization of newsworthiness because they are not serious and occur too frequently to be newsworthy on a consistent basis. However, when the burglar commits his crime in order to obtain the underwear of a sleeping, unexpected male victim, then the story is an important one because of its uniqueness. Similarly, victims that are able to defile the odds and show a particular tenacity of survival, such as a security guard shot ten times and survives, increases the likelihood of the presentation of these crimes because his survival was not what was expected.

Another factor that influences which crimes reporters think are newsworthy is the salience of the event. Salience is determined by the location of the event and the frequency of its presentation. News media concerned with attracting a local audience have to rely primarily on crimes that occur within certain audience boundaries. Crimes that affect local individuals or local businesses are of first importance to the news organization because consumers can identify with the street or location where the event occurred, can avoid those areas that might be considered dangerous, and grow concerned with the immediate problems that need to be addressed in their community. Specifically, the public wants to know what local law enforcement agencies are doing to address the problem of crime and violence in their community. News media provide police organizations with the opportunity to justify their response or at least provide a forum to request additional assistance.

The salience of an event as a newsworthy factor can also be illustrated in the selection of certain crimes that fit a particular pattern. If large numbers of a specific type of crime occur, reporters search for similar events to follow through along the same theme. These events are stringed together as a theme because of the public's heightened awareness of these events. Some researchers have discussed how the presentation of crimes within certain themes results in a "moral panic." These moral panics are media generated crime waves that occur independent of the actual occurrence of events. In one of the more carefully documented cases of media distortion, Fishman (1978) reported on a "crime wave" that occurred in New York City. A series of stories pertaining to crimes against the elderly first appeared in a New York newspaper. The theme was picked up in other newspapers and on television, adding to the number of stories over several weeks, showing that the number of stories suddenly rose sharply, remained high for several weeks, and then declined. Police statistics, however, did not reveal any similar pattern in the number of crimes against the elderly. What had occurred was not a crime wave, but rather what Fishman called a "media wave." That is, a journalistic theme—"crimes against the elderly"—had been created, and instances fitting this theme were pulled selectively from the large daily pool of crimes.

The Production of News

Reporters select those crimes made available to them by the police according to these newsworthy criteria. Reporters must then produce the selected stories by relying on sources that are willing to provide comment or go on camera regarding the event. Potential sources will be contacted by telephone or in person to determine whether they will participate or can provide information that help clarify the newsworthiness of an event. Reporters produce the story according to the quality of information that was provided by the various sources used. The ability to cite sources gives a story credibility as well as the impression that the media is only acting as an intermediary funnel providing information.

The most conveniently available and accessible source for crimes recently discovered are representatives from police departments. The heavy reliance of reporters on police sources has been demonstrated by past research. For example, Ericson, Baranek, and Chan (1991, p. 192) found that police officers accounted for nearly 20 percent of the sources used by print and electronic media. A wide range of officers are accessible that can provide comment about a particular case. Patrol officers that are the first responders to a scene, detectives investigating a case, a superior from a particular precinct, or the public relations representative of the department can all provide the necessary information that a reporter needs to write a story. Of course, other sources are cited within stories, but they are used less frequently because of the inherent difficulties of getting in contact with an individual and convincing them to provide comment. This reliance by reporters on police sources for story information exacerbates police control of the image that is presented to the public about crime. Thus, even if the department fails to shield a particular incident from the news media and the crime is presented, police can still control damage to the departmental image by responding directly within a particular news story.

Although the information that is provided by sources determines what can be presented about a particular crime, the production of crime stories is also affected by other factors, such as the time available to produce a story and the space to present, the news organization's need to satisfy format requirements, and editorial scrutiny of the completed product. News space is limited in both print and electronic media and crime stories will be excluded when other stories are thought to be of more interest to the public. Similarly, if a story does not meet the format requirements of a media, such as a television crime story that lacks quality video, then the length of presented news space will either be limited or the story will be eliminated from consideration. In addition, editors exercise a large amount of influence on the reporter's entire decision-making process. Reporters are in constant contact with editors throughout the day, updating them on the status of a story and the willingness of different sources to cooperate. Editors will suggest which stories to pursue, the sources to contact, and the story angle that should be emphasized. In addition, they have the final decision regarding the position of the story within the presented product.

Decisions About the Amount of Space

The crimes that are presented to the public result from a filtering process. Reporters select potential news stories from the pool of crimes made available from police sources. If a reporter decides that a selected story is not newsworthy, then the story is eliminated. Some stories are thought to be news, but are excluded because the reporter did not have the time or resources to produce the story, sources were unwilling to comment, or an editor decided the story was not worthy of news space. However, crimes that pass through each of these obstacles are presented to the public and represent the most important crime events of the day.

The crime stories presented are provided various amounts of news space. Some crimes are especially newsworthy and become important news stories. Others, however, are written simply to satisfy space needs. The estimated level of newsworthiness determines the resources that will be expended to produce the story. Stories that are thought to be particularly newsworthy will be provided with more space, resources, and will be followed over a period of days as it progresses through the criminal justice system.

A story that satisfies a number of the newsworthy criteria discussed previously, has sources that cooperate and provide newsworthy information, and time is available to produce a story, will be presented prominently in the news, and those that do not, will be relegated to the back pages of a newspaper or the end of a broadcast. For example, the capture of serial murderer Jeffrey Dahmer has been one of the most covered crime stories of this decade. Dahmer's crimes were a significant news event because of the large number of victims (17) found in his Milwaukee apartment, the horrific methods used by him to dispose of the remains of his victims (boiled their skulls to preserve them and destroy their dismembered parts by sticking them in a vat of acid), the manner in which his crimes were discovered (a victim barely escaping his wrath), and a police blunder that could have put an early end to his killing spree. The news intensity generated by this story was extraordinary. Conversely, a homicide that results from a drug deal that went bad, involving two youths, might be presented as a news story because of the seriousness of the offense, however, it would be provided a small amount of space and would be excluded if other, more interesting stories could occupy the space.

HOW RACE AFFECTS THE PRODUCTION OF NEWS

The race of the suspect or the victim involved in a crime incident is rarely identified in crime stories. This gives the impression that race is not an important variable that has an impact on the production of news (Hartman and Husband, 1974). Rarely does race impact how reporters evaluate the newsworthiness of events nor does it influence the decision-making of reporters or editors. However, various demographic characteristics of the suspect and the victim are presented as identifiers. Historically, race was the most identifiable demographic characteristic reported in the newspaper. Since that time, however, direct mention of race has been eliminated from most news stories (Chermak, 1993). The demographic characteristics commonly provided are age and occupation. Currently, race is only specifically identified when it provides some explanation for why the crime occurred. For example, a news story about a racially-motivated killing will include a discussion of the race of the parties involved because it explains the cause of the event.

Although race is not identified in news stories directly, it does impact the importance reporters attach to stories. Race influences decisions about whether stories are worthy of news coverage and the amount of coverage and space given to particular stories. Crimes with African American defendants or African American victims are automatically considered to be less significant than crimes involving white defendants and white victims (Sotomayor, 1986). Reporters assume that these crimes are less deserving of space when working through their daily routines. Police reporters typically begin their day by checking police blotter reports and contacting police sources for information about any new crimes that have occurred. These reporters typically follow-up on homicides they come across, but assign low priority status to those involving minority victims and minority defendants.

Race is determined from the information provided on the police report or by the geographic area of the city where the crime occurred (Sotomayor, 1986). Crimes occurring in densely populated African American areas of the city are assumed to be insignificant news stories. The public and reporters are desensitized to the newsworthiness of crimes that occur in these parts of the city. They are assumed to be a normal part of everyday life and not able to meet newsworthy standards. For example, a black-on-black killing occurring in a dilapidated area of the city is considered to be normal and not worthy of newsworthy consideration. Conversely, serious crimes that occur in suburban areas are more newsworthy because these crimes happen less frequently to more "important" members of the community.

Crimes occurring in certain parts of a city are automatically devalued and thought to be less important. Stories are written on crimes occurring in these neighborhoods, but the information provided within them is from the police or other official sources, rarely giving the victim or the victim's family an opportunity to comment and react (Chermak, 1993; Sotomayor, 1986). Although this might be considered a positive benefit in that it allows victims to avoid the traumatizing effects of being questioned by reporters, it does indicate that victims living in these parts of the city are thought to be less important. This is significant because many news stories randomly increase in importance. Reporters may believe, at first, that the crime story they are producing is only deserving of minimal coverage, however, something occurs in the process of production that significantly increases the newsworthiness of these events. For example, a victim, when questioned by a reporter, might provide the reporter with emotional quotes that make a news story more appealing (Chermak, 1993). When this occurs, then the story is provided with more space, time, and resources. Reporters are unable to capture these random newsworthy characteristics from African American or Hispanic victims because reporters rarely give these stories the chance to develop into significant news events.

The majority of crime stories presented in popular news media focus on specific incidents rather than policy issues (Graber, 1980). Specific incident stories are removed from the broader picture of the problem of crime within society, but are frequently produced because they can easily be put into an already established news frame and quickly produced. Stories on larger issues are more difficult to produce because they are time-consuming and resource absorbing. Reporters don't have the time to produce policy-oriented stories because they are expected to contribute stories every day. Although race is an important topic of concern among scholars, rarely are crime stories produced that examine racial criminal justice issues. Issues such as whether the death penalty discriminates against African Americans, the differences of sentences given based on race, and whether the police are more likely to use excessive force, are important concerns, but ignored by the news media. They are unwilling to invest the time and resources to cover these important issues.

Explanations for News Coverage of Racial Crime Issues

According to Ehrlich (1988), special knowledge or training for journalists about subjects they are writing on is seen as irrelevant. For example, a city editor of the *Miami Herald* was interviewed by Ehrlich (1988) and asked whether the reporters who are regularly assigned stories about minority group conflict had any special training; the city editor replied: "No. They are not there to resolve conflicts; they are journalists" (p. 1). Ironically, the

Miami Herald is one of the few major papers that actually has a race relations news beat.

According to Ehrlich (1988), the most knowledgeable writers on any newspaper are those who write about sports. Ehrlich says the reason for this is because, "that's their beat and they work on it year after year" (p. 1). Accordingly, science is another well-defined beat. It would be difficult to imagine sending out a reporter who knew nothing at all about physics or chemistry to cover a story, for example, on a breakthrough in superconductivity. Most major newspapers have a science writer. In fact, these newspapers have specialized writers in music, in film, in cooking, in business, in politics, and even in gossip.

During 1986–1988, the National Institute Against Prejudice and Violence (NIAPV) conducted a survey that included interviews and information about newspaper reporters at many major print and electronic news media in the United States. Of the 200 reporters interviewed, only 10 had any serious knowledge of intergroup relations (NIAPV, 1988).

According to the survey, one reporter from the *New York Times* made four errors in the lead paragraph of a story about race relations, confusing the distinction between prejudice and discrimination. Prejudice refers to people's thinking: their attitudes and beliefs which tend to favor one group over another. Whereas discrimination refers to any behavior on the part of an individual which leads to unequal treatment on the basis of race or ethnicity (Farley, 1988). A second reporter from the same paper was shocked to hear that prejudice was not instinctive. The NIAPV survey reported that 80 percent of the reporters interviewed usually start out asking experts or sources the wrong questions. For example, one reporter described an interview about housing discrimination and move-in violence and was surprised when he learned that financial institutions can play a significant role in perpetuating or minimizing residential segregation. The survey maintains (1988):

> Reporters, like most people in this society, have an implicit theory of prejudice and group relations. This is to say that through their own reading and life experiences they have come to formulate some ideas about race, [about crime], about ethnicity, about how and why people are prejudiced, [about how and why people commit crimes], and so on. It would be naive to expect that journalists, by virtue of their job, should be much different from anyone else. The issue, however, is not that some journalists have an "implicit theory" that is false. The issue is that reporters, because of their job, are expected to "set aside" their preconceived ideas, at least when they write a straight news story. For the institute, there is a fairly simple test of how well reporters have been able to do this. Tell them something they don't want to hear, something that is outside their preconceived mind set, and see whether it makes its way into

print. What we have found, for the most part is that only the news that's fit to hear is fit to print. Tom Wicker, *New York Times* columnist and editor, once commented that reporters who write about what most of their colleagues are ignoring will not be taken very seriously. (pp. 5–6)

Ehrlich (1988) further suggests that there is another dimension to what gets reported and to how well it is reported. He points out that the policies of some major newspapers are not very progressive with regard to intergroup and intercultural relations, especially when crime is involved. Assigning a story to a reporter with no knowledge of the subject is a political decision, Ehrlich maintains, a decision that says that this story doesn't warrant any special concern. When the policies of a newspaper do not give priority to multi-cultural issues or ethnoviolence, the result is a lack of commitment to provide the necessary training for reporters who cover these stories (Ehrlich, 1988). A self-perpetuating cycle of incompetence results. For example, when reporters write about ethnoviolent conflict, it is seldom placed in any social context. According to Raybon (1988), to place it in its social context means doing research and looking carefully at the society, which requires a fair level of knowledge and sophistication. It also requires having the time needed to do research. The National Institute Against Prejudice and Violence (1988) reported that the result of insufficient research because of imposed deadlines is that reporters have to do a less-than-complete job. The shallower job, however, has become the standard of news reports of crime.

Ehrlich (1988) and his associates maintain that partly because of their lack of knowledge and their time constraints, as well as organizational policies, reporters frequently focus on the dramatic and spectacular crime incident. These are so removed from everyday events that their dramatic difference help foster the notion that ethnoviolence is itself an uncommon event. This perpetuates the myth that incidents are isolated instead of pervasive and provides us with an excuse not to act.

Moreover, according to Ehrlich and his associates (1988), another consequence of "reportorial business-as-usual" (p. 5) is that ethnoviolent crime stories are often placed in the wrong frames. The reporter who is rushed, simply accepts some conventional explanation or some participant's definition of the situation. For example, the NIAPV reported that during the 1986–87 school year, as campus ethnoviolent crime was just beginning to be reported, an extraordinary number of stories implied that the cause of these campus incidents was low minority student enrollment. However, not a single story included the NIAPV analysis that low minority enrollments were not the issue. The NIAPV study concluded:

In the reporting of ethnoviolence, the wrong information is frequently conveyed, reporters often communicate their own prejudices, everyday events are being

> transformed into uncommon occurrences, and the wrong interpretive frames are often put around stories. (p. 5)

The media can play an important role in bringing to the public the issues which must be addressed in order for social scientists to respond effectively to ethnoviolence. However, what does not get reported does not get put on the public agenda (Badigkian, 1992).

In summary, according to Johnson (1991), although African American news professionals are more visible than in years past, African Americans are still severely underrepresented among reporters. Managerial positions, those that involve power, remain nearly an exclusively white domain. Cose (1989) reports as recently as 1989:

> Some editors still debate—in the face of overwhelming evidence—whether Puerto Ricans can write good English and whether blacks are too damaged intellectually to compete in the nation's newsrooms. (p. 25)

After 1967, when the National Advisory Commission on Civil Disorders laid partial blame for the urban rebellions on inadequate hiring and reporting within the white-owned print and broadcast media, newspapers and radio and television stations took strides to hire more minority reporters. African Americans began to receive newspaper bylines and often prominent placement at local television station news desks. The hiring boom was short-lived, however. By the mid-1970s, when sympathy for civil rights turned into antipathy for affirmative action, the presence of African Americans in the nation's news media froze at a level higher than during the 1960s but far below proportional representation.

African Americans currently account for about 12% of the U.S. population. During the peak minority hiring period, African Americans comprised only 3% of all network news correspondents (U.S. Commission on Civil Rights, 1979). According to former *Boston Globe* editor Thomas Winship, the majority of the 1,700 daily newspapers in the United States have never employed a single African American, Latino, or Asian-American journalist. Similarly, by 1985 only 5% of all newspaper copy editors and 2% of all reporters were African Americans, many of them on the staffs of African American owned newspapers (Adams, 1985). African Americans are similarly underrepresented in managerial-level media positions in which critically important decisions are made regarding which stories to report, how much space to allocate for them, and what angle to give them.

CONCLUSION

News media select a limited number of stories from the pool of crimes made available to them from criminal justice sources. Some crime stories are selected because news personnel decide that it is newsworthy. Other crimes are thought to be potentially newsworthy, but the organization does not have the resources needed to produce the story. Other crimes are news, but are not presented because of the news organization's concern about damaging their relationship with a source. Some crimes become important news stories and help news media attract consumers, while others are written to simply satisfy organizational space needs.

Crime is an important source of news because of high public interest. News media have institutionalized a process that helps them produce crime stories efficiently. Some crimes are ordinary, and not spectacular. Others, however, are bizarre news stories which are thought to be deserving of more space. Any crime has the potential to be a news story, and how interesting it is determines how the story will be produced. News media rely heavily on criminal justice sources to produce the crimes that occur while expending minimum resources.

Crimes involving minority victims and minority defendants are not thought to be important news stories. Reporters think that murders that occur in inner cities, involving minority victims and minority defendants, are less deserving of a significant amount of news space. Because inner city murders are thought to be common and everyday, the public expect that more minorities will be involved in crime (Sotomayor, 1986). Part of the news formula in deciding what is presentable is whether or not the crime is unique and rare. The public and reporters are desensitized to crimes that occur in certain parts of the city, because they are automatically assumed to be "normal."

In addition, important racial issues are ignored by news media or are covered ineffectively. Sotomayor (1986, p. 11) argues that the "media continue to deal with minority crime victims with inconsistency, insensitivity, often displaying prejudices." He then goes on to discuss how a lack of cultural understanding about gangs and minority culture leads to inaccurate reporting (1986):

> We often portray such groups as "gangs" on the basis of comments by police or witnesses in the neighborhood who have little understanding of youth culture and because they believe that is what minority youths do. We often accept and pass on through our stories the myths that only minority groups form gangs, and that a crime involving a "gang member" constitutes a feud between the gangs. (p. 12)

The problems with news coverage of race and crime issues result, in part, because of the demographic characteristics of those who produce these stories. One can infer that the social background of mass communicators has consequences for the range and substance of the content that is produced, such as news coverage, dramatic themes, portrayal of minorities in television stories, and the like (Bagdikian, 1992; Ehrlich, 1988). To cite an early example, the National Advisory Commission on Civil Disorders (1968), in relating the media's reporting on urban civil disorders to the background of the normal news coverage of race relations in America, expressed the view that the mass media fail to report adequately on race relations and ghetto problems. One means of correcting this oversight, they suggested, is to bring more blacks into journalism and other news organizations. The commission expressed the belief that increased employment of blacks in communication occupations would have a positive impact on news coverage of black activities. Unfortunately, twenty-five years after the Kerner Commission report, minorities still remain greatly underrepresented in news organizations.

A similar belief that greater access to occupations in the communications field would increase the presence of minority ideas, tastes, and values in media content has been expressed by women and various ethnic minority groups. Certainly, access is important, but the overall impact of this access may depend on how important these occupations turn out to be (Johnstone, 1971).

Johnson (1991) presents several provocative solutions for transforming the coverage of race in the media. Of special interest for addressing the problems we have identified, Johnson (1991) suggests that educators should help students become more critical news consumers by (p. 337):

1. Encouraging students to critically analyze news reports.
2. Assigning students to compare coverage of the same story by different news outlets.
3. Teaching students to consider alternative vantage points.
4. From examining the media, students can move to examining themselves.

Students need encouragement to read what is presented in the news. In addition, they need to be taught about newsworthiness, distortion, and news production to understand the limitations of what they read. This encouragement can easily be incorporated into classroom activities. An educator can assign a student to follow the presentation of a course topic across an entire semester within a particular media source. Students can be assigned to a variety of different media sources so that comparisons can be made as the semester progresses. For example, if someone was teaching a course on policing, one of the requirements could be to follow how the police are portrayed in the news media. Students could be assigned to follow the coverage of police in popular press, elitist press, television news, tabloid news, and still others could be assigned the coverage of police in African American owned presses. This will promote discussion, help students understand the bias inherent in the coverage of news, and would provide a base to compare other research material.

The integration of the news media into various topics will help students become critical consumers of news. However, until more African American and other minorities are presented more comprehensively in the mass media, Parenti's (1986) argument will ring true:

> The basic distortions in the media are not innocent errors, for they are not random; rather they move in the same overall direction again and again, favoring management over labor, corporatism over anti-corporatism, the affluent over the poor, private enterprise over socialism, whites over blacks, males over females, officialdom over protesters, conventional politics over dissidence, anticommunism and arms-race militarism over disarmament, national chauvinism over internationalism, U.S. dominance of the Third World over revolutionary change. The press does many things and serves many functions, but its major role, its irreducible responsibility, is to continually recreate a view of reality supportive of existing social and economic class power. (p. 10)

News media will undoubtedly continue to present a steady supply of crime stories for public consumption. They will have to rely on those sources that can provide a large amount of crime information, because of their own organizational concerns, while they search for those newsworthy crimes that they think would be attractive to consumers. However, these factors have limited the racial images received by the public in the news. Reporters need to judge each potential news story on its individual merits. Currently, the assumption is that crimes that occur to minorities living in poverty-stricken areas of the city are less newsworthy and unworthy of public concern, which contributes to the distorted images presented about crime and violence in the news media. News media have to move beyond these stereotypical images, and, should do their part in heightening public concern about race and crime issues. Hopefully, over time, the public will increase their demands on news media to offer a broader perspective on various issues. It is conceivable that the news media will accommodate public demands; forcing mainstream media to offer a more comprehensive and complete picture of society.

REFERENCES

Adams, S. L. (1985). Blackening in Media: The State of Blacks in the Press. *The National Urban League: The State of the Black America: 1985.* New York: National Urban League. (pp. 65–103).

Altheide, D. (1984). TV News and the Social Construction of Justice: Research Issues and Policy. In R. Surette (Ed.). *Justice and the Media.* Beverly Hills, CA: Sage. (pp. 282–304).

Atlanta Constitution. (1964, July 24).
Atlanta Constitution. (1966, August 8).
Atlanta Constitution. (1966, August 19).
Badkikian, B. (1992). *The Media Monopoly.* Boston: Beacon Press.
Chaffee, S. H. & Choe, S. Y. (1981). Newspaper reading in longitudinal perspective: Beyond structural constraints. *Journalism Quarterly. 58*(2), 201–211.
Chaffee, S. H. & Choe, S. Y. (1983). Dimensions of content readership in ten newspaper markets. *Journalism Quarterly. 60*(1), 74–80.
Chermak, S. M. (1993). *Interested Bystanders: An examination of the presentation of crime victims in the news media and how their involvement in the news production process affects the final news product* Ph.D. Dissertation. Ann Arbor, MI: University of Microfilms International.
Cohen, S. (1975). A comparison of crime coverage in Detroit and Atlanta newspapers. *Journalism Quarterly, 52*(4), 726–730.
Cohen, S. & Young, J. (1981). *The manufacture of news: Deviance, social problems and the mass media.* London: Constable.
Cose, E. (1989). Rape in the news: Mainly about whites. *New York Times.* Section 4, p. 27.
Ditton, J. & Duffy, J. (1983). Bias in the newspaper reporting of crime news. *British Journal of Criminology. 23*(2), 159–165.
Dominick, J. (1978). Crime and law enforcement in the mass media. In C. Winick (Ed.). *Deviance and Mass Media.* Beverly Hills, CA: Sage. (pp. 105–128).
Ehrlich, H. J. (1988). Mixed media messages. *Forum. 3*(3), 1–5.
Ehrlich, H. J., Weiss, J., Purvis, R. D., Alatas, S. F., Elias, E. (1988). *The Politics of Victimization.* New York: Oxford University Press.
Ericson, R. V., Baranek, R. M., & Chan, J. B. L. (1987). *Visualizing Deviance: A Study of News Organization.* Toronto: University of Toronto Press.
Ericson, R. V., Baranek, R. M., & Chan, J. B. L. (1989). *Negotiating Control: A Study of News Sources.* Toronto: University of Toronto Press.
Ericson, R. V., Baranek, R. M., & Chan, J. B. L. (1991). *Representing Order: Crime, Law, and Justice in the News Media.* Toronto: University of Toronto Press.
Farley, J. (1988). *Majority-Minority Relations.* Englewood Cliffs, NJ: Prentice-Hall, Inc.
Fishman, M. (1978). Crime wave as ideology. *Social Problems. 25,* 531–543.
Ginsburg, C. (1989). *Race and Media: The Enduring Life of the Moynihan Report.* New York: Institute for Media Analysis, Inc.
Gordon, M. & Heath, L. (1981). The news business, crime and fear. In D. Lewis (Ed.). *Reactions to Crime.* Beverly Hills, CA: Sage. (pp. 227–250).
Gormley, W. (1975). Newspaper agendas and political elites. *Journalism Quarterly. 52*(2), 304–308.
Graber, D. A. (1980). *Crime News and the Public.* New York: Praeger Publishers.
Greenfield, M. (1989, May 15). Other victims in the park. *Newsweek.* p. 86.
Hartley, J. (1982). *Understanding News.* London: Methuen.
Hartman, P. & Husband, C. (1974). *Racism and the Mass Media.* London: Davis Poynter.

Johnson, K. (1990). Media images of Boston's black community. In W. Reed (Ed.). *Racial Stereotyping: The Role of the Media.* William Monroe Trotter Institute, Boston: University of Massachusetts.

Johnson, K. (1991). Objective news and other myths: The poisoning of young black minds. *Journal of Negro Education. 60*(3).

Johnstone, J. W. C., Slawski, E. J., & Bowman, W. W. (1971). *The News People: A Sociological Portrait of American Journalists and their Work.* Urbana, IL: University of Illinois Press.

Marsh, H. L. (1988). *Crime and the press: Does newspaper crime coverage support myths about crime and law enforcement?* Ph.D. Dissertation. Ann Arbor, MI: University of Microfilms International.

McCombs, M. & Shaw, D. (1972). The agenda setting function of mass media. *Public Opinion Quarterly. 36*(2), 176–187.

National Advisory Commission on Civil Disorders. (1968). *Report of the National Advisory Commission on Civil Disorders.* New York, NY: Dutton Books.

National Institute Against Prejudice and Violence. (1988). *Ethnoviolence on Campus: The UMBC Study.* Baltimore, MD: author.

New York Times. (1961, February 28).

New York Times. (1966, August 19).

New York Times. (1967, October 10).

New York Times. (1973, November 16).

Parenti, M. (1986). *Inventing Reality: The Politics of the Mass Media.* New York: St. Martin's Press.

Quinney, R. (1970). *The Social Reality of Crime.* Boston: Little, Brown & Co.

Raspberry, W. (1971). Politics, blacks, and the press. In R. W. Lee (Ed.). *Politics and the Press.* Washington, D.C.: Acropolis Books. (pp. 117–129).

Raybon, P. (1989, October 2). A Case of "severe bias." *Newsweek.* p. 11.

Reed, W. (Ed.). (1990). *Racial Stereotyping: The Role of the Media.* William Monroe Trotter Institute, Boston: University of Massachusetts.

Rhodes, J. (1987, August). Racial coverage of the 1950's print media and the case of Emmett Till. Paper presented at the Annual meeting of the Association for Education in Journalism and Mass Communication. (70th). San Antonio, Texas.

Ryan, M. & Owen, D. (1976). A content analysis of metropolitan newspaper coverage of social issues. *Journalism Quarterly. 53*(4), 634–641.

Sheley, J. F. & Ashkins, C. D. (1981). Crime, crime news, and crime views. *Public Opinion. 45,* 442–506.

Skogan, W. & Maxfield, G. (1981). *Coping with Crime: Individual and Neighborhood Reactions.* Beverly Hills, CA: Sage.

Smith, S. (1984). Crime in the news. *British Journal of Criminology. 24*(3), 289–295.

Sotomayor, E. (1986). A victim's race: Does it make a difference? In T. Thomason and A. Babbili (Eds.). *Crime Victims and the News Media.* A National symposium sponsored by The Texas Christian University. (pp. 11–14).

Swanson, C. (1955). What they read in 130 daily newspapers. *Journalism Quarterly. 32*(3), 411–421.

Tuchman, G. (1973). Making news by doing work: Routinizing the unexpected. *American Journal of Sociology. 79*(1), 110–131.

Turner, P. (1990). Tainted glory: Truth and fiction in contemporary Hollywood. In W. Reed (Ed.). *Racial Stereotyping: The Role of the Media.* William Monroe Trotter Institute, Boston: University of Massachusetts.

U.S. Department of Justice. (1992). Bureau of Justice Statistics. *Criminal Victimization in the United States, 1991.* Washington, D.C.: U.S. Government Printing Office.

United States Commission on Civil Rights. (1979). *Window Dressing on the Set: An Update.* Washington, D.C.: U.S. Government Printing Office.

CHAPTER SEVEN

GAYS AND LESBIANS IN THE CRIMINAL JUSTICE SYSTEM

JAMES S. ARNOTT

INTRODUCTION

Gays and lesbians make a contribution to the criminal justice system as law enforcement professionals. It is uncertain what percentage of police departments' personnel are gay and lesbian. If, however, departments are demographic microcosms of the society they serve, approximately ten percent of officers are homosexual (Kinsey, Pomeroy & Martin, 1948; Kinsey, Pomeroy, Martin & Gebhard, 1953).

Society has not always accepted openly gay and lesbian people as police officers. This has resulted in gays and lesbians leading "double lives," under incredible personal and professional pressure. Police departments are reluctant to change, largely because they are predicated on a paramilitary organizational model. The rank and file believe that change occurs through executive action. Subsequently, changes filter through a chain-of-command structure. If gays and lesbians were open about their sexual orientation, it would be a sudden change to police organizations. The heterosexual norm of police behavior would be violated. The perception is that gays and lesbians should conform to "straight" or heterosexual standards.

Police departments categorically break into two groups: moral leaders and followers. Moral leaders, according to Leinen (1993), comprise about five percent of most police commands. As leaders, this element consequently sets the pattern for acceptable and non-acceptable behavior in police societies. Gays and lesbians are not included in this moral loop.

When gays and lesbians are not tolerated as contributing members in law enforcement, departments face morale and productivity issues. It is devastating to lead a straight life on the job, then switch to a gay or lesbian life when not on duty. What police universally need to do is:

1. Develop an understanding of gays and lesbians as positive contributors to the criminal justice system, especially in law enforcement.
2. Better understand the professional and personal issues gays and lesbians experience as law enforcement professionals.

3. Sharpen personal awareness of the prejudices and stereotypes held toward gays and lesbians, both by members of the criminal justice system and those they serve.

MYTHS ABOUT GAYS AND LESBIANS

Gays and Lesbians are Mentally Abnormal

Several myths are evident about gay and lesbian behaviors. A major stereotype shared by some police and the larger heterosexual public is that gays and lesbians are psychologically or mentally abnormal. The perception is that when a person deviates from the heterosexual norm, that person is subject to being labeled as abnormal. This thought held into the 1950s, even in professional psychiatric and psychological circles.

Dr. Evelyn Hooker, a heterosexual psychologist at the University of California, Los Angeles, challenged the notion that being homosexual is an abnormal behavior. In her work with sixty human subjects, using three projective personality tests she discovered that it is impossible for a psychologist to assess mental disorders directly attributable to being homosexual. The hypothesis intrinsic to the testing process had been that a person taking a projective test, such as the Thematic Apperception Test, would reveal his or her fears, anxieties, and dominant personality behaviors without being consciously aware of the disclosure. In short, the behaviors would surface, resulting in a gay or lesbian identifying their sexual orientation in the test results (Marcus, 1992).

At the 1956 annual conference of the American Psychological Association (APA) in Chicago, Hooker delivered the paper "The Adjustment of the Male Overt Homosexual." Here she argued, gays were as well adjusted psychologically as heterosexual males. Pathology simply balanced out between the homosexual and heterosexual groups. Hooker's study made homosexuality a respectable field for scientific investigation. Her research earned her the Distinguished Contribution Award from the APA, and led to the removal of homosexuality from the list of mental disorders recognized by this leading professional group of psychologists and psychiatrists (Marcus, 1993).

The conclusion to be drawn from Hooker's findings is that while gays and lesbians practice some sexual behaviors, and have affectional preferences which differ from those of heterosexuals, the differences do not constitute a mental disorder. They are simply different. The assumption that gays and lesbians are mentally abnormal is a stereotype well grounded in ignorance; it has no scientific basis for the latest generation of scientific inquiry.

Gays and Lesbians Are Insignificant in Numbers

The exact number of gays and lesbians in the United States is uncertain. Kinsey, however, provided the most comprehensive analysis of what percentage of the population is homosexual. For fifty years, the "Kinsey Scale" has been the most consistently used measure to determine sexual orientation. Despite attempts to improve on the seven-point Kinsey Scale, no researcher has been able to provide an investigative instrument of equivalent value in the field (McWhirter, Sanders, & Machover Reinisch, 1990).

In developing his scale of sexual behavior, Kinsey devised a zero-to-six continuum. Persons who practice heterosexual behavior exclusively are categorized as zero on the scale; whereas, exclusively gay or lesbian behavior is a six, on the opposite end of the scale.

The Kinsey numbers indicate:

0 = Exclusively heterosexual
1 = Predominantly heterosexual, only incidentally homosexual
2 = Predominantly Heterosexual, but more than incidentally homosexual
3 = Equally heterosexual and homosexual
4 = Predominantly homosexual, but more than incidentally heterosexual
5 = Predominantly homosexual, only incidentally heterosexual
6 = Exclusively homosexual (Klein, 1990)

Kinsey and his colleagues argued that sexual behavior crossed between heterosexual and homosexual experiences. They reported that thirty-seven percent of males in their studies experienced homosexual sexual behavior between adolescence and adulthood. This behavior involved males achieving orgasm due to erotic arousal caused by male stimulus. Thirteen percent of Kinsey's subjects experienced more homosexual than heterosexual behavior. Finally, four percent of his participants had exclusively homosexual experiences. Heterosexual women and lesbians reported lower figures for sexual activity, but not significant enough to alter group patterns of sexual behavior (Kinsey, Pomeroy & Martin, 1948; Kinsey, Pomeroy, Martin & Gebhard, 1953).

The general conclusion drawn from the Kinsey studies is that seven percent of women are lesbian, and approximately thirteen percent of men are gay. This has led to the common understanding that about ten percent of the American public is homosexual, and resulted in the use of a ten percent statistic in reporting by scholars, the media and government officials (Voeller, 1990).

In the present author's interviews with more than one hundred subjects from the Minneapolis Police Department, both straight and gay or lesbian, the general conclusion was that lesbians among female officers exceeded the seven percent benchmark. When the finding was shared that a corresponding ten to thirteen percent of male officers were gay, the statistics were often challenged. The consistent pattern seemed to be that gay and lesbian officers are in the department, but often not identified, either by their choice or the failure of straight officers to know who they are, based on performance as an officer. Straight officers consistently assumed that gays are a minimal part of the department's demographics. They often did not realize that this lack of recognition is not a legitimate reason to assume that less than ten percent of the department is gay.

Working in a training capacity with one thousand officers and civilian employees of the same department, the present author was challenged by participants that ten percent seemed an exaggeration, or that they did not know any gay officers. Further, some rejected ten percent, deciding to not be confused by the facts (J. S. Arnott, personal communication, March–April, 1992).

Interviews in the United Kingdom have yielded similar results. Heterosexual officers have relied on "an inherent tendency to accept the common homosexual stereotypes, because they see little in either their home or their work lives which questions them" (Burke, 1993). Police officers assume that gays and lesbians fit stereotypes. Gays should be effeminate, lesbians are masculine women. The reality is that gays and lesbians are difficult to categorize into stereotypes.

Gays and Lesbians Are NOT a Cultural Group

Cultures are defined by common languages, heritage and behavior patterns. When we think about a culture, we look for common patterns. French culture may be determined by considering its language, cuisine, painting, and philosophy. Organizations have cultures that reflect people using common technical terminology, working toward collective goals, dressing alike, and applying different patterns of leadership and employee empowerment strategies to improve productivity and morale.

Gays and lesbians do not share an exclusive ethnic or racial bonding defined in a larger sense as a culture. The collective cultural identity of gays and lesbians is multicultural in one dimension, because gays and lesbians are evident in all cultures on the planet (Bullough, 1990). Therefore, homosexuality is a cultural universal. In another respect, gays and lesbians are a subculture drawn together by similar behavior patterns. They have a specific appreciation of male- and female-specific issues, are urban, mobile (largely due to job availability), use some common language intrinsic to their own social conventions, and have historically found satisfaction in careers that welcome diverse peoples and divergent expression, such as the arts (Browning, 1993).

While gays and lesbians share a subculture, they are often difficult to identify among heterosexuals. In a sample of five thousand homosexuals drawn as study respondents in the San Francisco Bay area, more than half the males and approximately two-thirds of the females reported that their employers and fellow employees did not know or suspect they were homosexual (Leinen, 1993).

Sexual Preference Versus Sexual Orientation

People do not prefer to be homosexual or heterosexual. Sexual behavior is not determined by choice. "Politically, sexual preference is a dangerous term for it implies that if homosexuals choose their preference, then they can be legally forced, under threat of punishment, to choose to be heterosexual" (Money, 1990).

Historically, laws in the United States have been predicated on influences from canon law and English common and civil laws. A major study of laws which dealt with sexual issues reveals that about ten percent of canon law texts during medieval to modern times were concerned with sex, and about six percent of civil law related to issues of sexual behavior. Fornication was the most frequently addressed sexual practice, while sodomy, usually considered a homosexual behavior, was seldom mentioned. The political and religious influences were directed toward the control and prohibition of sexual behaviors other than for the purpose of procreation (Brundage, 1982). If we hold all behaviors to a heterosexual ideal of sexual behavior, centered on male-female unions for procreation, then gay and lesbian relationships and behaviors cannot meet the implied standard, such heterocentricity is commonplace.

Being Gay or Lesbian Is Illegal

Laws restricting gays and lesbians from not having the same freedoms as heterosexuals differ by state. In Illinois, a criminal act for a homosexual occurs only if force or a minor is involved. In some southern states, buggery can result in life imprisonment. Until recently, one could be jailed for twenty years for homosexual activity in Massachusetts. Fortunately, the Massachusetts law was seldom enforced (Ruse, 1988).

The United States Supreme Court, in *Bowers v. Hardwick* (1986), refused to overturn a Georgia state law making sodomy an offense. Further, the court upheld Georgia in that anal intercourse between two men is illegal, even if done in total privacy by consenting adults. The court expressed no dissent on heterosexual intercourse (Ruse, 1988).

The military in the United States for years has been direct in discriminating against homosexuals by stating: "Homosexuality is incompatible with military service" (Ruse, 1988). The Naval Investigative Service (NIS) was legend in its success in expelling gays and lesbians from its branch of the armed forces through intensive interviews of suspected gay and lesbian service personnel. "It was a badge of honor to leave the interview with both a list of fifteen other guys to investigate" (Shilts, 1987). Gays and lesbians until recently had no opportunity to be accepted unless they remained closeted in their sexual orientation and maintained a heterosexual visibility.

Recently, eight states and most cities of the "first class," (100,000 or more inhabitants), have passed legal measures to assure that gays and lesbians share equity with heterosexuals in employment and public treatment. These municipal statutes often govern urban police departments. The California Supreme Court ruled against homosexual discrimination in the private sector in *Gay Law Students Association v. Pacific Telephone and Telegraph* (1979). Further, in federal employment, the United States Civil Service Commission has guidelines forbidding discrimination toward gays and lesbians (Ruse, 1988).

Although the United States Supreme Court decision in *Harris v. Forklift Systems, Inc.* (1993), found a unanimous court ruling for Harris on the specific grounds that she had experienced sex discrimination from her employer, the decision expands the size of the umbrella under which all persons may negatively experience gender harassment in the workplace. Justice Scalia argued that harassment may simply be a hostile work environment. The hostile work environment concept potentially extends the legal umbrella to consider other groups in the workplace who face harassment. Further, the court does not define specific guidelines for determining harassing conduct. Consequently, other legal actions, which could be pilot cases for gay and lesbian rights, may occur in the future (Plevan, 1993).

LIFE EXPERIENCES

San Diego, California

John Graham and Natalie Stone are leaders. They were the first gay and lesbian officers in the San Diego Police Department to come out publicly about their sexual orientation. Consequently, their risk-taking has led to the formation of the Society of Law Officers, or SOLO, which is a gay and lesbian support and professional group dedicated to gay and lesbian issues related to police officers. While the membership of SOLO has political views, the organization is not intended to be politically affiliated. Its membership is largely drawn from San Diego County. In a SOLO focus group conducted by the present author, participants shared several life experiences unique to gay and lesbian officers. They included:

- Living a double life. One as a closeted gay or lesbian. Another as an officer who subscribed to macho standards of physical conditioning. Gay men often attempted to live as heterosexuals to the extent of bringing women as dates to police social functions. They were subjected to gay and lesbian jokes, from roll call to the privacy of a patrol car. They could not show signs of being offended, because they were assumed to be straight.
- Some gay and lesbian officers know other gays and lesbians on the force, but are expected to practice a "code of silence" to protect sexual identities. If you come out, don't expect universal support from other gays and lesbians in the department. They may not choose to have their sexual orientation known.
- Maintaining a silent fraternity about the police. You are expected to support the myth that police are straight, loyal to each other, and must present an image of credibility, competence, and control to their public. There is no room for gays and lesbians in this public image.
- If you do come out, your opportunities for potential promotion may be jeopardized. Discrimination within departments against gays and lesbians has become sophisticated and subtle. You may even risk having another officer not back you up on a call or investigation; their reasons are doubtful but their actions seem short of being grounds for an official report.
- Some officers have been accused of being child molesters, one was even asked to resign from the Boy Scout Explorer Program, despite a long-term commitment to helping youth and a record free of complaints. No legal or other improprieties were proven against Chuck Merino of the El Cajon Police Department, but because he is an openly gay officer, he became the victim of rumors about child molestation. Chuck is an assistant high school football coach, a distinguished police officer of rank, and he has a solid history as an activist for youth programs. The charge that he is a pedophile is unfounded, but being gay is license for slur campaigns.
- A challenge to gays and lesbians as law enforcement professionals is that they are bound together by a cult of sex. Remove sex from their lives and nothing common remains for them. Categorically, gay and lesbian officers identified their sexual orientation at an early age. Sex played a comparable role in their personality development as it would for heterosexuals, but they are linked together with a variety of other interests which are overwhelmingly more important than sex.

They are gay and lesbian; they did not choose to be; it simply is what they are.

- These officers believe they have earned the right to treatment equal to that of their heterosexual police counterparts. Their records as law enforcement professionals are exemplary. It is unfair if they are to be judged only on their sexual orientation. Another's personal moral agenda should not be the criterion by which to assess one's professional destiny (J. S. Arnott, personal communication, February 16, 1994).

United States Military Police

Bill Harris was a military police officer in Germany, serving the United States Army in 1989. He was 19 years old, well trained, committed to the military police motto of "integrity, honesty and courage," intelligent, handsome and gay.

He concealed his sexual orientation for fear of reprisal and eventual dishonorable discharge from the military. A "code of silence" existed in the military. If you were in a gay bar, and were seen by another serviceman, it was assumed that one reported nothing. During his tour of duty, Bill witnessed servicemen being discharged because they were gay lovers. He observed an excessive use of force displayed by military police against servicemen who were alleged to be gay. In one situation, the gay officers were beaten severely. Bill believes that military police characteristically were young, obsessed with power, and psychologically driven to apply physical force over verbal directive.

While in Germany, Harris had a relationship with another serviceman from the medical corps. One evening they returned to their base and took the risk of sleeping together. Other military police apparently had suspected their affectional relationship, had monitored their schedules, and broke into their sleeping quarters. Both young men were interrogated separately; however, they maintained consistent testimony: they were intoxicated, fell asleep together, and were not sharing a gay liaison. Despite persistent efforts to force confessions, the military police were successful only in getting Harris out of Europe. His friend eventually left the military. Bill continued to the East Coast of the United States; there, his German experience preceded him.

Although no written record proving that Harris was officially gay existed, rumor and innuendo caused him to be plagued with hate mail, subtle discrimination, and the silent treatment from other military personnel. Finally, in 1990, Harris left the military at the end of his term of service. He could begin to live openly as a gay person (J. S. Arnott, personal communication, May 22, 1993).

San Francisco, California

San Francisco is, in several respects, one of the most progressive cities in the United States for gays and lesbians. It has a large, well-organized gay and lesbian population; it has a history of being tolerant and open to different cultural and ethnic peoples; and its public agencies have provided a welcoming environment for gays and lesbians unmatched by cities of comparable size.

Gay and lesbian officers have developed a powerful political base in this city, which is reflected through their commitment to a sense of fairness and integrity for the recruitment of other gays and lesbians into their professions. Interviews with officers at the Valencia Street location in the Mission District of San Francisco revealed these collective expressions about gay and lesbian law enforcement personnel:

- Job security is critical to having a sense of confidence in openly owning your sexual identity. The average length of service of the officers interviewed by the author was 14 years. These officers believed that their length of service, distinguished records, and acceptance by other colleagues in the department, both homosexual and heterosexual, all provided them with a comfort factor they did not have when novices in the organization.
- While none of the officers interviewed were strong advocates of being members of a legally "protected class," they categorically argued that the legal protection afforded them by the City of San Francisco, and later by the State of California, offered them an opportunity to function equally with other officers in respect to Equal Employment Opportunity. It also offered a sense of security that they could not be dismissed *carte blanche* on the basis of their sexual orientation.
- Maintaining and building a presence in the department depends on gay and lesbian officers recruiting others like themselves. Additionally, training in respect to gay and lesbian lifestyles, often involving exposure to the gay and lesbian community, is essential to understanding and better communication between heterosexual and homosexual persons. San Francisco's police department conducts training for all recruits in gay and lesbian issues. Gays and lesbians have also found support through professional groups sympathetic to gay and lesbian issues, such as the Golden State Police Officers Association.
- Gay and lesbian officers perceived they are accepted into the organizational culture of their department for various reasons. Gays feel they are accepted because policing is stereotypically a male field. The SFPD has a "gym subculture," according to some officers. Consequently, if you are physically in shape, you are in the police in-group, regard-

less of sexual orientation. Others, both gay and lesbian, argued that San Francisco won hard-fought battles in the 1970s to ensure gay and lesbian parity with straight officers. Consequently, the personality and perceived competence of an officer is more prominent than his or her sexual orientation. Finally, lesbian officers argued that they were accepted because they were not an affectional threat to male heterosexual officers. They also believed that their commitment to professionalism, ranging from superior communication skills to maintaining physical conditioning, contributed to their acceptance on the force.

- Joe Bannon, a San Francisco police officer formerly with the New York Police Department, provided a valuable insight about coming out or revealing sexual orientation to other officers early in a law enforcement career. Coming out is a gradual process for some, especially if they are searching for personal identity in ways ranging from sexuality to whether or not they want to be a career cop. Speaking for himself, he "hid very well, but was dying inside," until he surfaced his sexual orientation. Joe Bannon is confident, articulate and competent, while more youthful officers need time to achieve his level of self esteem (J. S. Arnott, personal communication, February 17, 1994).

Los Angeles, California

Mitch Grobeson was the first gay Los Angeles police officer to publicly identify his sexual orientation. He was dismissed from the department, filed a lawsuit, and, while battling the LAPD in court, assumed assignments with the San Francisco Police Department and the San Francisco State University security force. He was successful in his legal action, has been reinstated in the LAPD, and now conducts gay and lesbian awareness training as an independent consultant, largely to police clientele. He has these suggestions to offer from his experiences.

- In his perception, the San Francisco Police Department is a model for other cities to emulate in respect to accepting and recruiting gays and lesbians for law enforcement careers. The critical factor here is that the city's administration has a firm commitment to tolerance and directly addressing discrimination. Those who exercise intolerance will be held accountable.
- It takes one to three years for a gay officer to personally and professionally identify his sexual orientation in the coming-out process. The majority of gay officers choose to remain in the closet for fears ranging from the social stigma of being gay in a stereotypic, machismo

culture to assuming that officers conceivably would not back them up on police calls.

- Suicide and alcoholism rates are three times as high for gays and lesbians than for their heterosexual counterparts.
- Despite exemplary records, gay and lesbian officers may be rejected from professional positions due exclusively to their sexual orientation. Grobeson was an outstanding Los Angeles police officer who wanted to be a role model, but his career was interrupted simply because he was gay. Currently, Grobeson speaks and organizes with approximately sixty organizations in greater Los Angeles that are sympathetic to gay and lesbian concerns.
- Grobeson's legal action has had an impact on the LAPD. It is now openly advertising for gay and lesbian police candidates (J. S. Arnott, personal communication, March 9, 1994).

Minneapolis, Minnesota

Sharon Lubinski is a professional. She has a record of excellence in law enforcement in two midwestern cities. She is also a risk-taker, the first Minneapolis officer to publicly identify herself as a lesbian to the department and city. Her story about owning sexual orientation for public record needs to be told.

- She tired of living two lives. One was acceptable, when she seemed to act as a heterosexual; the other, as a lesbian, was her real life. Lubinski felt that her coming out would have a positive impact on changing departmental culture by encouraging other gay and lesbian officers to feel secure in openly identifying their sexual orientation. Her public coming out met with mixed reactions. Many police colleagues, regardless of sexuality, offered support. Others practiced avoidance, as if she was seeking media publicity for potential promotion, or pressuring other gay and lesbian officers to come out. Lubinski's public disclosure was predicated on her professional commitment to inclusiveness, that the police department is a microcosm of the community. Therefore, the values we democratically link to pluralism are intrinsic in identifying and valuing all diverse peoples within organizations.
- Being open about sexual orientation not only may pave the way for other officers to come out, but the action may dispel some myths about lesbian officers. Lubinski's experiences, as well as the author's confidential interviews with more than one hundred members of her department, confirmed that lesbians are perceived to be "superwomen" who shoot well, can physically manage law violators like men, and

operate independently on the force. In reality, lesbians are as professional as anyone else in law enforcement (J. S. Arnott, personal communication, March 11, 1994).

Madison, Wisconsin

Alix Olson is an openly lesbian officer in the university town and capitol city of Madison, Wisconsin. She is a detective, an experienced police professional with a no-nonsense approach to gay and lesbian contributions to successful law enforcement. Detective Olson believes that the key to Madison's acceptance of gay and lesbian officers is a commitment by police administration to not tolerate discrimination. If supervisors or officers display bias, they are reprimanded. In 1981, Chief David Couper began building a welcoming environment for culturally diverse groups. This was reinforced when Governor Dreyfus, in 1982, signed into law measures to assure gays and lesbians equal treatment in public employment. Finally, Olson and a gay officer in the Madison Police Department have designed a training curriculum to deal with the professional behavior police officers should demonstrate when dealing with gays and lesbians, both internally and externally. Madison's tolerance of gays and lesbians underscores much of their training experiences (J. S. Arnott, personal communication, March 2, 1994).

HOMOPHOBIA

Homophobia is the irrational fear of gays or lesbians based on stereotypes. It may be inclusive of behaviors that are alleged to be homosexual, such as assuming that effeminate male behavior is equated to being gay. A masculine behavior in a female is assumed to be lesbian. The hypothesis is that the heterosexual standard is not met when behavior is not consistent with the perceptual norm of what is male and female.

Police are as homophobic as other groups in society. Large urban departments are not open to change, primarily because they are structured on paramilitary models. These models are reactive and not oriented to complementary risk-taking. The behavioral norm for a police officer is to fit into the system as a heterosexual (Leinen, 1993).

In the present author's interviews, heterosexual officers reacted to questions about gays and lesbians as contributing members in police departments with ambivalence. Their reactions ranged from positive to negative. They argued that local gay activists are representative of the gay and lesbian community. When pressed, interview subjects were reluctant to identify any homosexual leaders in Minneapolis. Some officers believed that "bizarre street behavior" may welcome violent behavior from straights. Others felt that AIDS is an issue, particularly when considering violence and potential loss of body fluids. Other officers expressed reluctance to investigate domestic abuse calls where gay couples lived for fear of coming in contact with wounds and lacerations. Officers new to an urban department seemed unaware that significant numbers of gays and lesbians lived in cities, such as Minneapolis.

Acquired Immune Deficiency syndrome, or AIDS, is a virus-based disease transmitted between humans by the exchange of body fluids like blood and semen. It is often diagnosed in its initial stages as "HIV positive," which means that the person has been exposed to the virus, though the disease may not accelerate to full-blown AIDS. There is no known cure for AIDS. As a disease, it has devastated communities across the globe. There are also substantial myths and false perceptions about exclusive ways in which the virus is transmitted, as well as to whom. The gay communities of New York City and San Francisco were early centers from which reports about AIDS, this strange virus, began to be reported. These cities have large gay populations, and it was from the gay communities that early reports were received.

Even in the early days of reporting AIDS in the United States, when it lacked an official medical name, it was referred to as "Gay Immune Deficiency syndrome," as if it were a gay disease. As more became known about the medical history of this viral killer, it became evident that its origins were most likely in Africa, and among heterosexual partners, as well as in hospital surgery rooms where antiseptic conditions were not practical. AIDS is not an exclusively gay disease (Shilts, 1987).

Much of the negative stereotyping about gays and AIDS is grounded in societal notions that sex is a dirty business, not to be discussed in public, and approached with trepidation in private. An eminent sex researcher puts it this way: "Consider also that the majority of those who have developed AIDS and died before we really understood the mechanism of transmission, so they had no idea that any disease so deadly was possible. Sexual diseases, in the view of many, carry the special stigma of sin and blame, The Victorian message that comes across is: 'You behaved badly by having sex in an immoral fashion, and so you deserve whatever you get'" (Reiss & Reiss, 1990).

This collective ignorance about how one gets AIDS is a public health issue. Our police officers need to be alert that this virus is evident in all elements of society. Gays and lesbians should not carry the national stigma for AIDS.

Homophobia is grounded in ignorance and stereotypes in suburban departments. In confidential interviews, one police supervisor had all of his officers burn their uniforms following an investigation of a domestic abuse situation involving two violent males alleged to be gay. Another deputy chief reported that when a young man, reported to have died from AIDS, was investigated by a suburban department because of the suspicion of foul play, the officers arrived dressed head-to-toe as if approaching a high-intensity fire. The county public health officials arrived, removed the corpse, and their sole protection consisted of elastic gloves.

Other heterosexual officers the present author visited in the Midwest, as well as in California and the eastern seaboard, believed that having gay officers open about their sexual orientation would be intimidating to the masculine public perception of a police image. Some straight officers perceived that it would be difficult to have conversations with gay officers, especially regarding family-related issues. Bigotry seemed to cut across all lines, regardless of gender, ethnicity or race in the author's confidential interviews. Similar experiences have been reported about bigotry toward gays and lesbians in New York City (Leinen, 1993).

When officers were asked if they could identify gay and lesbian officers or civilians attached to their departments, in the author's case, Minneapolis, most were unable to provide any specific behavioral descriptions. Identifying gay and lesbian officers usually involved knowing them professionally and personally, but not for certain unless they revealed their sexual orientation. When challenged, they admitted that it was nearly impossible to accurately determine who is gay and lesbian. Most gay men are as masculine in appearance as straight males, and lesbians seem no less feminine than their heterosexual counterparts in law enforcement (Leinen, 1993).

Efforts to recruit gay and lesbian officers have been limited. Direct action has been taken against their involvement in police civilian and sworn positions in Houston, Dallas and Los Angeles in the 1980s and on into the 1990s. As of 1992, ten leading American cities directly recruited gays and lesbians, including Atlanta, Boston, Madison, Minneapolis, New York, Philadelphia, Portland, San Francisco, Seattle, Washington, D.C., and, after a change in police administration, Los Angeles (Leinen, 1993).

The Federal Bureau of Investigation (FBI) is frequently perceived as the most professional organization in the criminal justice system. It has more than ten thousand agents; until recently, no gay or lesbian agents were assumed to be within its ranks. On one occasion, former FBI director William Sessions said: "Homosexuality is a factor in whether an agent can properly carry out his or her role as an FBI agent" (Buttino, 1993).

Buttino was the first gay FBI agent to become public about his sexual orientation. Although he was discharged by the bureau, he was successful in obtaining a financial settlement, largely in the form of a pension. The FBI is reassessing its hiring and recruitment policies and procedures toward gays and lesbians.

The life experiences which gay and lesbian officers have shared with the author through extensive interviews are offered as evidence of how much personal and professional risk-taking is taken to end a double life and shift to a more positive sense of personal integrity.

THE HUMAN COST

Gay and lesbian police officers face a dilemma. In one respect, assuming a heterosexual identity removes them from possible intimidation and ridicule. If they act straight, their colleagues will assume that they are straight. In another respect, by posing as straight in the workplace and living as gay or lesbian outside of work, a price is paid in stress. Closeted gay and lesbian officers, in the double life of straight at work, gay or lesbian in other places, are plagued by high rates of suicide, alcoholism and stress-related anxieties (Leinen, 1993).

When one fears to identify who they are due to the societal stigma of being gay or lesbian, the human cost is incredible.

Alcoholism among gays and lesbians is disproportionately higher than for heterosexuals. Alcoholism is nearly pandemic. In comparing samples, Kus (1988) discovered that more than thirty percent of gays and lesbians in Los Angeles were alcoholic. In another study of gay males, in which the Michigan Alcoholism Screening Test was used, it was found that twenty-nine percent were alcoholic. Another study comparing gays and lesbians with heterosexuals analyzed by Kus (1988) revealed that thirty-five percent of lesbians were considered alcoholic, compared to five percent of heterosexual women. The results among men were closer, with gay males at thirty percent, compared to heterosexual males at twenty percent.

Suicide rates are high for gays and lesbians. While no study specific to police suicide is available, data on gay and lesbian suicides among adults and youth is obtainable. Homosexuals of both genders experience suicide rates two to six times higher than heterosexuals. Lesbian and gay youth approach thirty percent of all completed suicides in their age group, annually.

The fear of losing a job is another factor contributing to the measurable human cost. While the United States military is not part of the criminal justice system, it is being legally pressured to open up to gays and lesbians. From 1980 to 1990, 16,919 military personnel were discharged for being homosexual, at an annual cost of twenty-five to thirty million dollars, according to official statistics, as reported by the General Accounting Office (Buttino, 1993).

Another issue facing gay and lesbian police personnel is how they may be subjected to violence, because of their sexual orientation. While they are the protectors of the peace, and may be closeted in their departments, they may also be the victims of violence simply because they are gay or lesbian. Violence against gays and lesbians is a national problem. The National Gay and Lesbian Task Force, or NGLTF, has charted bias crimes against gays and lesbians in eight major American cities for several years. Their sample involved over two thousand homosexuals. In excess of ninety percent of the respondents in 1991 reported some type of victimization due to sexual orientation, and more than one in three had been threatened with violence (Blummenfeld, 1992).

The 1993 report showed a fourteen percent decline in the number of victimization reportings over 1992. The report also showed, however, that severe and violent crimes are rising (NGLTF, 1994). In some cities, gays and lesbians are reluctant to report crimes to the police; either they report them to an agency which is supportive or the incident goes unreported. In St. Louis, Minneapolis, and St. Paul, persons interviewed believed that police were not understanding of a gay or lesbian victimization or that they would have to acknowledge their sexual orientation to the police in order to have a report taken (NGLTF, 1994; Police Community Task Force on Gay and Lesbian Issues, 1994). In assessing statistics on alleged bias crimes for Minnesota, the status of victimization is subject to officer perception (Minnesota Department of Public Safety, 1993). If an officer is homophobic, he or she has considerable control over the initial investigation and reporting of a gay or lesbian victimization or other violent incident.

FUTURE CONSIDERATIONS

Gays and lesbians have become aware of their individual rights. They are becoming open about their sexual orientation. This openness has led to political organizing, which has brought about power gains in major cities and influence causing legislative bodies to pass laws to protect rights. Gays and lesbians have pressed for acceptance and employment in professions which have in the past failed to recruit or hire them. The criminal justice system, particularly law enforcement, is experiencing significant change. Gays and lesbians are being actively recruited, and are assuming leadership roles in police departments. Even the FBI and U.S. military are being forced to be more open to gays and lesbians joining their ranks.

Since June, 1969, when gays and lesbians openly fought the New York City Police Department at the Stonewall Inn, police throughout the nation have developed a degree of respect for gay and lesbian communities in major cities. Gay organizations now deal directly with police regarding social and political issues; the undisciplined raids of gay bars seem to have ended (Tripp, 1987).

More energy should be directed to improve relations between gay and lesbian communities and organizations that represent the criminal justice system. Changes need to be made internally in police departments to provide for a better working climate for gay and lesbian law enforcement professionals.

These future considerations are subsequently discussed:

1. **Develop a welcoming environment.** A welcoming environment involves developing policies and procedures in government agencies which speak against discrimination based on sexual orientation and gender identity. These policies and procedures should be developed cooperatively with gay and lesbian organizations and officers who are out in their departments about their sexual orientation.
2. **Hold supervisors accountable.** Policies, procedures and statutes are meaningless until enforced. Supervisors who apply antidiscrimination processes unfairly or inconsistently need to be disciplined and otherwise held accountable.
3. **Demonstrate commitment from administration.** City councils, mayors, and chiefs of police need to become educated about gay and lesbian issues and rights and subsequently committed to protecting those rights in criminal justice agencies. San Francisco is often held as a model for gay and lesbian police because the City of San Francisco has been committed, since the 1970s, to protecting and recognizing the gay and lesbian community in matters such as public employment. In Madison, Wisconsin, a new chief was instrumental in setting a climate where people, regardless of differences, were welcomed as making valuable contributions to effective law enforcement. Mayors and Chiefs of Police of San Diego have expressed their support of the gay and lesbian community by being supportive of Gay Pride Week. Finally, police chiefs are committed to hiring gay and lesbian officers, and training their department personnel to be culturally aware of diverse groups, particularly gays and lesbians.
4. **Recruit and train.** Gays and lesbians can be recruited for criminal justice positions by advertising in newspapers, trade journals, and gay and lesbian regional publications, and by working collaterally with gay and lesbian community groups and organizations. Field Training Officers (FTOs) who are discriminatory toward gay and lesbian cadets should be removed from their positions. Field training ideally should have a cadet reporting to several FTOs, ensuring that career potential is not subject to the influence of only one FTO. San

Francisco has yielded considerable success with such a program feature. Training in the police academy should include gay and lesbian issue orientation, including gay and lesbian officers being available to discuss their perceptions during training sessions with police cadets. Cultural awareness training for sworn officers, with some focus on gay and lesbian issues, should be ongoing and mandatory.

5. **Support gay and lesbian police organizations.** Gay and lesbian issues hold special interest for police who are homosexual. Support originations, set up by gay and lesbian police, should function as a source of support for fellow officers, as well as a catalyst to crystallize gay and lesbian consensus within a department. Major cities are quickly developing these organizations, such as SOLO in San Diego and GOAL in New York.
6. **Form task forces.** Urban police departments should open channels of communication with gay and lesbian communities, both within and outside their departments. Task forces dealing with policing issues can be an invaluable source of crucial information for police executives. A recent task force effort in Minneapolis has provided Chief John Laux with workable recommendations ranging from recruitment to a unique reporting system where a gay or lesbian victim of bias or violent crime can call a gay or lesbian officer to discuss the incident, prior to officially reporting it. The effort is to encourage the gay and lesbian community to build trust with the police department (Police-Community Task Force on Gay and Lesbian Issues, 1994).
7. **Pay attention to public relations.** Media specialists who are associated with criminal justice agencies should be aware of gay and lesbian policing issues. Their own reporting to the media should reinforce building a welcoming environment for gay and lesbian officers.
8. **Improve crime solving.** The open presence of gays and lesbians in the criminal justice system underscores the commitment of a police department to the gay and lesbian community. Their role helps dispel homophobia while providing an investigative source which may be able to penetrate gay and lesbian networks (Leinen, 1993). Further, Patti Abbott, a Minnesota gay activist, working in collaboration with the Minneapolis Police Department, successfully broke the case of a 1993 series of homicides in Minneapolis, which resulted in the arrest and later conviction of the murderers (J. S. Arnott, personal communication, March 7, 1994).
9. **Use gay and lesbian personnel to their fullest.** From urban police officers to FBI special agents, gay and lesbian law enforcement professionals face career sabotage. Frank Buttino had twenty years of "excellent" and "superior" performance ratings. But an anonymous letter alleg-

ing that he was homosexual cost him his career and the FBI another twenty years of potential crime fighting expertise (Buttino, 1993). In New York City, only forty-two officers are openly out, whereas another two to three thousand officers remain closeted, either out of convenience or fear (Leinen, 1993). This talent can no longer be wasted. Gay and lesbian professionals in the criminal justice system are key to providing quality peacekeeping.

GLOSSARY OF TERMS

Bisexual: A woman or man who forms primary loving and sexual relationships with members of both sexes; someone who has a continuing affectional, emotional, romantic and/or erotic attraction to persons of both sexes.

Gay Male: A man who forms his primary loving and sexual relationships with other men; a man who has a continuing affectional, emotional, romantic and/or erotic attraction to someone of the same sex.

Heterosexism: The societal assumption and norm that the practice of heterosexuality is the only acceptable, sanctioned expression of human sexuality, and that homosexuality and bisexuality are wrong.

Heterosexual: Someone who forms primary loving and sexual relationships with persons of the opposite sex, and who has a continuing affectional, emotional, romantic and/or erotic attraction to someone of the opposite sex.

Homophobia: Consists of those negative feelings, attitudes, actions or behaviors against lesbians, gays, and bisexuals. It is likewise a fear of one's own same-sex sexual or affectional feelings as well as being perceived as gay or lesbian.

Homosexual: A clinical and technical term that is not generally used by lesbians and gays to refer to themselves or their community. For example, Congressman Barney Frank refers to himself as *gay* or *openly gay,* not *admittedly homosexual* or a *practicing homosexual.*

Lesbian: A woman who forms her primary loving and sexual relationships with other women; a woman who has a continuing affectional, emotional, romantic and/or erotic attraction to someone of the same sex. Some lesbians prefer to call themselves *lesbian* and use the term *gay* to refer to gay men; others use the term *gay* to refer to both men and women.

Lover, Partner and **Significant Other:** Terms that lesbians, gays and bisexual people use to identify those people with whom they have romantic or sexual relationships.

Out or **Out of the Closet:** A term which means being open and public about being lesbian, gay or bisexual. A closeted person hides the fact that they are lesbian, gay or bisexual. Some people are *out* in some settings (e.g., with friends) but not *out* in other settings (e.g., at work or with family).

Fag, Dyke, Faggot, Lezzie, Homo, Queer, Fairy, Fruit, Pansy and **Sissy:** All insulting terms to lesbians, gays and bisexual people. They are the equivalent to Wop, Gook, Nigger, Cunt or Retard as insulting terms for Italians, Asians, African Americans, women or people with mental disabilities.

Straight: Gay or lesbian slang expression for a heterosexual male or female.

REFERENCES

Blummenfeld, W. J. (1992). *Homophobia: How we all pay the price.* Boston: Beacon Press.

Bowers v. Hardwick (1986). 478 U.S. 186, 106 S.Ct. 2841.

Browning, F. (1993). *The culture of desire.* New York: Crown Publishers, Inc.

Brundage, J. (1982). Sex and canon law. In V. L. Bullough & J. Brundage. *Sexual practices and the medieval church.* New York: Oxford University Press. pp. 88–101.

Bullough, V. L. (1990). The Kinsey scale in historical perspectives. In D. P. McWhirter, S. A. Sanders & J. Machover Reinisch (eds.). *Homosexuality/heterosexuality.* New York: Oxford University Press. pp. 3–14.

Burke, M. E. (1993). *Coming out of the blue.* London: Cassell.

Buttino, F. (1993). *A special agent: Gay and inside the FBI.* New York: William Morrow and Company, Inc.

Gay Law Students Association v. Pacific Telephone & Telegraph 24 Cal. 3d 458, 595 P.2d 592, 156 Cal.Rptr. 14.

Harris v. Forklift Systems Inc. (1993). 114 S.Ct. 367.

Kinsey, A. C., Pomeroy, W. B., & Martin, C. E. (1948). *Sexual behavior in the human male.* Philadelphia: W. B. Saunders.

Kinsey, A. C., Pomeroy, W. B., & Martin, C. E. (1953). *Sexual behavior in the human female.* Philadelphia: W. B. Saunders.

Klein, F. (1990). The need to view sexual orientation as a multivariable dynamic process: A theoretical perspective. In D. P. McWhirter, S. A. Sanders & J. Machover Reinisch (Eds.). *Homosexuality/heterosexuality.* New York: Oxford University Press. pp. 277–282.

Kus, R. J. (1988). Alcoholism and non-acceptance of gay self: The critical link. In M. W. Ross (Ed.). *The treatment of homosexuals with mental health disorders.* New York: Harrington Park Press.

Leinen, S. (1993). *Gay cops.* New Brunswick: Rutgers University Press.

Marcus, E. (1992). *Making history: The struggle for gay and lesbian equal rights, 1945–1990.* New York: Harper & Row.

McWhirter, D. P., Sanders, S. A. & Machover Reinisch, J. (Eds.). (1990). *Homosexuality/heterosexuality,* Prologue. New York: Oxford University Press.

Minnesota Department of Public Safety (1993). *Bias offense reporting system, summary report.* Saint Paul: State of Minnesota.

Money, J. (1990). Agenda and credenda of the Kinsey scale. In D. P. McWhirter, S. A. Sanders & J. Machover Reinisch (Eds.). *Homosexuality/heterosexuality.* New York: Oxford University Press. pp. 41–60.

National Gay and Lesbian Task Force (1994). *Annual crime and victimization study, 1994.* Washington, D.C.: author.

Plevan, B. B. (1993, December 6). Harris won't end harassment questions. *The National Law Journal.* 19.

Police Community Task Force on Gay and Lesbian Issues (1994). *Police community task force report on gay and lesbian issues.* Minneapolis: Minneapolis Police Department.

Reiss, I. L., & Reiss, H. M. (1990). *An end to shame: shaping our next sexual revolution.* Buffalo: Prometheus.

Ruse, M. (1988). *Homosexuality: A philosophical inquiry.* New York: Basil Blackwell.

Shilts, R. (1987). *And the band played on: Politics, people and the AIDS epidemic.* New York: St. Martin's Press.

Tripp, C. A. (1987). *The homosexual matrix.* (2nd ed.). New York: Meridian.

Voeller, B. (1990). Some uses and abuses of the Kinsey scale. In D. P. McWhirter, S. A. Sanders & J. Machover Reinisch (Eds.). *Homosexuality/heterosexuality.* New York: Oxford University Press. pp. 32–38.

CHAPTER EIGHT

HATE CRIMES: A LEGAL PERSPECTIVE

Lori A. Spillane

INTRODUCTION

In April of 1991, Phillip and Renee Smith, a mixed race couple and their realtor Stacy Litzenberger, visited the house they were purchasing in King County, Washington. The Smiths had recently signed an agreement, and they were visiting the house to measure it for carpets and drapes. David Talley, who lived next door, saw the Smiths and complained to bystanders that "having niggers next door" would ruin his property values. He built a 4-foot-tall cross, planted it in his own yard, set it on fire with gasoline, and began to "hoot and holler." These actions attracted the attention of the Smiths. They noticed that Talley was wearing fatigues, combat boots, a Harley-Davidson t-shirt, and that he had a cleanshaven head. Renee Smith approached Talley and asked if there was a problem. He replied that he did not talk with her "kind" and ordered her off his driveway. The incident disturbed and frightened the Smiths and they opted not to purchase the house. The State charged Talley with six counts of malicious harassment (1993 W.L. 340945 (Wash.) (1993)).

In April, 1991, Daniel Myers, Brandon Stevens, and several other teenagers were at a party at one of the teenagers' homes. Conversation at the party turned to Chris Elion, an African American classmate of the boys. The group decided to burn a cross in the Elion family's yard because some of the boys felt that Chris has been acting "too cool at school." The teens made the cross, which they planted in the Elions' front yard, and attempted to set it on fire. Mr. and Mrs. Elion had just returned from church when Mrs. Elion noticed the group of teenagers outside. She thought they were friends of her son so she opened the door and called out. The group fled. Mrs. Elion saw the cross and screamed to her husband. Mr. Elion ran outside and found the smoldering 8-foot cross. The base of the cross had burned. Myers and Stevens were each charged with malicious harassment (1993 W.L. 340945 (Wash.) (1993)).

On May 29, 1993, David Wyant and his wife rented campsite L-16 at Alum Creek State Park. On May 31, the Wyants' relatives came to join them and rented the adjoining campsite. On June 2, Wyant rerented his site, but released the relatives' site, as they were to leave that day. Later in the day, plans changed and Wyant attempted to rerent the adjoining site. He was told that the site had been rented to someone else, and so he rented L-18. Site L-17 had been rented to the complaining witnesses, Jerry White and his girlfriend Patricia McGowan. White and McGowan are African American; everyone in the Wyant party is white. There was little contact between the groups for most of the evening of June 2nd, but sometime between 10:30 pm and 11:45 pm, White went to park officials to complain of loud music coming from the Wyant campsite. A park official went to site L-16 and asked Wyant to turn off the radio. Wyant complied. Fifteen or twenty minutes later, the radio came on again, and White and McGowan heard racial epithets and threats made in a loud voice by Wyant. Specifically, Wyant was heard to say: "We didn't have this problem until those niggers moved in next to us," "I ought to shoot that black mother fucker," and "I ought to kick his black ass." White and McGowan complained to park officials and left the park. Wyant was prosecuted under the Ohio Ethnic Intimidation statute (597 N.E.2d 450 (Ohio 1992)).

On August 20, 1990, at approximately 2:30 am, Jonathan Ebarb, Christopher Minor, Bill Camilo, Dennis Graff and Christopher McMillan rode in Ebarb's flat bed truck to Little Orphan Andy's, a restaurant in San Francisco. The area was known as the "gay ghetto" and the men in the truck were homosexual. They had just gotten off work and were going to the restaurant to eat breakfast, as they did every Sunday. As they drove along 17th Street, Minor, who along with McMillan, was sitting in the flat bed, heard male and female voices yelling anti-gay epithets, such as "faggot" and "queer." Their tone sounded "hateful." Minor saw two women and two men. All were screaming things like "where are you going, faggot, come here faggot, we are going to kill you. You fucking faggots . . . " Their tone was threatening, and they were walking quickly. After Ebarb parked the truck, the defendants, yelling anti-gay epithets, began physically attacking Ebarb and Minor. The defendants were charged with interfering with the exercise of another's civil rights (1993 W.L. 309596 (Cal.App. 1 Dist.) (1993)).

From cases such as that of Emmit Till, a young African American man lynched in Mississippi in 1955, to that of Allen Schindler, a homosexual Navy sailor beaten to death by his shipmates last year, some of the bleakest moments of our country's memory involve hate crimes. This chapter's focus is on cultural diversity, tolerance, and the violence of "hate crimes." Hate crime legislation and its legal challenges, the offenders and the victims, and the criminal justice system's response to crime spurred by hatred will be examined.

What is a "hate crime"? Hate crimes are directed against members of a specific group merely because of their membership in that group. The basis for the attack may be the victim's age, race, gender, sexual persuasion, religion, or ethnicity. Any physical or cultural aspect of a person separating them from others can serve as the impetus for hate offenses. Significantly, the victim's individual characteristics are irrelevant to the attacker. They are not concerned with the height, eye or hair color or birthplace of their victim.

According to the Federal Bureau of Investigation, hatred need not be the entire motivation for the offense: "A criminal offense committed against a person or property that is motivated, in whole or in part, by the offender's bias against a race, religion, ethnic/national origin group, or sexual orientation group." (emphasis added) (U.S. Department of Justice, 1990a). As long as there is an aspect of the offense which was motivated by bias, the incident may be categorized as a hate crime.

Determining whether hatred motivated a particular offense can be easier depending on the context in which the crime occurred. For example, when the hate offense involves an assault on a person, the perpetrator may make it obvious that the person was attacked for a particular reason. And, in most situations, the attack is remarkably excessive. In Maine, for example, three teenage boys beat a twenty-three year old man whom they believed to be homosexual. After the beating, they threw the young man off a nearby bridge, to his death on the rocks below. The three teenagers later bragged to their friends that they had "jumped a fag and kicked the shit out of him and threw him in the stream." (Center for Democratic Renewal, 1987). The hatred in such a case is demonstrated by the extreme severity of the attack on the individual.

In cases involving offenses to property, however, the bias motive may be obvious for different reasons. In some contexts the hatred is literally illustrated, as in the burning of a cross on an African American family's front yard. During the Gulf War in 1991, a Los Angeles deli owned by an Arab-American was set on fire. Before setting the establishment ablaze, the arsonists left a message on the wall: "You Fuckin' Arab, go home." (American-Arab Anti-Discrimination Committee, 1992). Without such symbols or messages, the motivation for the offense may not be as clear. An absence of this type of evidence may also lead law enforcement away from the possibility that a hate crime has occurred.

In the remaining sections of this chapter, the focus will be on the types of hate crimes, offenders, victims, and the criminal justice response to hate crimes. The significance of community relations, law enforcement priorities, attention to evidence, and the constraints of the United States Constitution will be addressed.

Hate Crime Legislation

Hate crime legislation currently includes reporting statutes, civil rights laws, separate hate crimes, and sentence enhancement laws.

Bias Crimes and Penalty Enhancement Laws

Hate crime laws predominantly are divided into "bias crimes" and "penalty enhancement" laws. Bias crimes are freestanding criminal prohibitions of racially targeted violence. This type of hate crime has encountered the most difficulty under First Amendment scrutiny. In many instances, the criminal prosecution embraces too much of the suspect's speech, encroaching the area protected by the First Amendment. There is a very fine line at which the individual has left the protected area and entered into criminal behavior. For this reason, many states have chosen to attack bias-motivated violence with penalty enhancement laws.

Penalty enhancement laws explicitly rely upon another criminal provision, such as assault, and increase the sentence if the assault was committed with bias motivation. Enhancement laws may increase the sentence by a given length of time, or may increase the "level" of the crime by, for example, increasing a misdemeanor to a felony or a lower felony to one of greater severity. Some penalty enhancement crimes mandate an enhancement of the sentence or provide discretion to the sentencing judge to increase the penalty if appropriate. All penalty enhancement laws are thus derivative of another criminal law. That fact is what has protected such laws from successful constitutional challenge. Pure bias crimes, by contrast, create a freestanding prohibition of some bias-motivated conduct.

Federal Legislation

At the federal level, there are at least five major laws prohibiting bias-motivated violence. The first federal statute forbids conspiracies intended to interfere with an individual's enjoyment of their civil rights. Title 18, USC sec. 241 (1993) "Conspiracy Against Rights." This statute has been widely used in situations in which a neighborhood conspires to keep a minority family from residing there.

The second statute, entitled "Forcible Interference with Civil Rights," was enacted in 1968. This law prohibits interference with an individual who is exercising his or her constitutional rights. It has been used in cases, for example, where an individual by force or threat of force interferes with such constitutionally guaranteed public rights such as eating in a public restaurant. 18 USC Sec. 245 (1993) "Federally Protected Rights."

The third federal statute, entitled "Deprivation of Civil Rights under Cover of Law," targets actions committed by public officials who deprive an individual of their constitutional rights. Most often, the public officials involved are law enforcement officers. The most publicized example of a prosecution under this federal statute is the Rodney King beating incident involving law enforcement officers from the Los Angeles Police Department.

Enacted in 1988, 18 USC sec. 247 (1993), entitled "Damage to Religious Property and Obstruction of Persons in the Free Exercise of Religious Beliefs" makes it unlawful to intentionally deface, damage or destroy any religious real property because of the religious nature of the property. It also makes it unlawful to obstruct, by force or threat of force, any person in the enjoyment of that person's free exercise of religious beliefs.

Finally, the fifth federal statute, "Willful Interference with Civil Rights under the Fair Housing Act," forbids interference with a person's right to buy, rent or live in their own home. This statute has been used to prosecute individuals who, for example, firebomb or fire shots at an individual's home, when such conduct is found to be bias-motivated. 42 USC sec. 3604 (1993).

The United States Congress has made recent attempts at passing the "Hate Crimes Sentencing Enhancement Act of 1993." This act would order the United States Sentencing Commission to adopt guidelines increasing the penalty by a minimum of three offense levels for those crimes that a jury has found beyond a reasonable doubt to be a hate crime. "Hate crime" is defined as:

> a crime in which the defendant intentionally selects a victim, or in the case of a property crime, the property which is the object of the crime, because of the actual or perceived race, color, religion, national origin, ethnicity, gender, or sexual orientation of any person. (Hate Crimes Sentencing Enhancement Act of 1993, 103rd Congress, 1st Session, Report 103–244).

This act is an immediate response to the United States Supreme Court's 1993 ruling which upheld a similar enhancement provision from Wisconsin. *Wisconsin v. Mitchell,* 113 S.Ct. 2194 (1993).

State Legislation

In some states, there is a separate "hate crime" offense. This offense is "any crime for which the motivation was hatred toward another based on race, religion, gender, or nationality." In other states, offenders receive an enhanced sentence for their crime based on proof that hatred motivated the crime. The typical underlying crimes are "crimes against persons" or "crimes against property." For example, murder, arson, assault and battery, property damage, and trespass may be the offense chosen to express the offender's hatred. Instead of being sentenced only for those particular offenses, the offender will receive additional time based upon a finding that hatred toward a particular group or individual motivated the crime.

Before 1980, only five states had any type of bias crime statute. Presently, at least thirty-one states have such laws and federal bias crime legislation has been proposed.

The following is an example of a hate crime law from Wisconsin:
Wis.Stat.Ann. s 939.645 (West 1991) provides:

(1) If a person does all of the following, the penalties for the underlying crimes are increased as provided in sub. (2):

(a) Commits a crime under chs. 939 to 948.

(b) **Intentionally selects the person against whom the crime under par. (a) is committed or selects the property that is damaged or otherwise affected by the crime under par. (a) in whole or in part because of the actor's belief or perception regarding the race, religion, color, disability, sexual orientation, national origin or ancestry of that person or the owner or occupant of that property, whether or not the actor's belief or perception was correct.**

(2)(a) If the crime committed under sub. (1) is ordinarily a misdemeanor other than a Class A misdemeanor, the revised maximum fine is $10,000 and the revised maximum period of imprisonment is one year in the county jail.

(b) If the crime commented under sub. (1) is ordinarily a Class A misdemeanor, the penalty increase under this section changes the status of the crime to a felony and the revised maximum fine is $10,000 and the revised maximum period of imprisonment is 2 years.

(c) If the crime commented under sub. (1) is ordinarily a felony, the maximum fine prescribed by law may be increased by not more than $5,000 and the maximum period of imprisonment prescribed by law for the crime may be increased by not more than 5 years.

(3) This section provides for the enhancement of the penalties applicable for the underlying crime. The court shall direct that the trier of fact find a special verdict as to all of the issues specified in sub. (1).

(4) This section does not apply to any crime if proof of race, religion,

color, disability, sexual orientation, national origin or ancestry is required for a conviction for that crime. (emphasis added).

In addition, the Oregon racial intimidation law is typical of many states, making it illegal for two or more persons to "intentionally, knowingly, or recklessly cause physical injury to another because of their perception of that person's race, color, religion, national origin or sexual orientation." Or.Rev.Stat. s. 166.165(1)(a)(A) (1990). This statute withstands constitutional challenge because it is directed at conduct rather than at the offender's speech.

The largest number of prosecutions of bias-motivated violence occur at the state level. There are various types of state hate crime laws. The first such statute deals with what is referred to as "institutional violence." (Levin & McDevitt, 1993). These laws prohibit the defacing or vandalizing of institutions such as houses of worship, schools, cemeteries, monuments and community centers.

The second type of state hate crime law targets "bias-motivated violence and intimidation." These are the most common of the state hate crime laws. Individuals are prosecuted under these statutes for intimidating, harassing, trespassing upon the property of, or assaulting another person because of that person's race, gender, nationality, religion, or sexual orientation.

There are some state laws that prohibit individuals from burning crosses or other religious symbols. The laws make a distinction between whether the burning occurs on public or private property, recognizing an individual's First Amendment right to burn a cross on his or her own property.

A final type of state hate crime law makes it illegal to interfere with another's religious worship (Levin & McDevitt, 1993). In effect in 18 states, such laws proscribe disrupting a religious service, or theft of religious items used in worship services. These laws are used in cases where, for example, a synagogue is burned to the ground, or a church is firebombed.

All of the above legislation indicate that eliminating hate-motivated violence is a priority at the state level. Despite their valiant efforts, however, many of the states' laws do not survive the scrutiny of the most basic law in our country, the United States Constitution.

Legal Challenges

How is it possible to protect victims of hate crimes while also safeguarding the right of individuals to express racist beliefs? This is the question underlying the hate crime debate occurring in the court system over the past two years. The right to express racist or discriminatory beliefs is grounded in a fundamental constitutional principle. This principle, however, takes on a different shape when the speech turns into violent conduct, threatening the safety of others.

In essence, the United States Constitution guarantees each citizen the right to speak his or her mind—no matter how offensive such speech may be to the listener. The First Amendment provides:

> Congress shall make no law respecting an establishment of religion, or prohibiting the free exercise thereof; or abridging the freedom of speech, or of the press; or the right of the people peaceably to assemble, and to petition the Government for a redress of grievances. U.S. Constitution, Amendment 1.

This constitutionally guaranteed right has never been interpreted as absolute. There are exceptions. The Supreme Court of the United States has chosen the view that in certain contexts, an individual's right to freely express his or her beliefs must be subordinate to society's interests. *Whitney v. California,* 274 U.S. 357, 375–376 (1927) (Brandeis, J., concurring). Bias-motivated violence appears to be one of those contexts in which the individual freedom of expression is pitted against society's interests in multicultural tolerance.

There are two constitutional doctrines that confront hate crime legislation: 1. "clear and present danger" and 2. "fighting words."

States may proscribe speech that presents a "clear and present danger" to the community or society as a whole. The state must establish that (1) the speaker subjectively intended incitement; (2) in context, the words used were likely to produce imminent, lawless action; and (3) the words used by the speaker objectively encouraged and urged incitement. *Hess v. Indiana,* 414 U.S. 105 (1973). If all three elements are established, the speaker's words are deemed to present a clear and present danger to society and may therefore be proscribed. The rationale was detailed by Justice Oliver Holmes in *U.S. v. Schenk,* 249 U.S. 47 (1919):

> The character of every act depends upon the circumstances in which it is done... The most stringent protection of free speech would not protect a man in falsely shouting fire in a theater and causing a panic. It does not even protect a man from an injunction against uttering words that may have all the effect of force.... **The question in every case is whether the words used are used in such circumstances and are of such a nature as to create a clear and present danger that they will bring about the substantive evils that Congress has a right to prevent. It is a question of proximity and degree** (emphasis added).

Government regulation of speech has also been permitted when the target is "fighting words." The basis for this First Amendment exception is that fighting words are predominantly action-oriented rather than containing intellectual worth. They are emotional words designed to incite a violent, immediate response. As such, the state's interest in civil order overwhelms the speaker's right of free speech. *Chaplinsky v. New Hampshire,* 315 U.S. 568 (1942). The Supreme Court has noted that in such situations, "'fighting words'—those which by their very utterance inflict injury or tend to incite an immediate breach of the peace... are not constitutionally protected because their slight social value as a step to the truth is clearly outweighed by the social interest in order and morality." *Chaplinsky v. New Hampshire,* 315 U.S. 568, 572 (1942).

The courts must decide whether the offender's speech was a call to action for others toward violence; whether it was pure violent conduct directed at one individual; or whether it was an expression of one individual's beliefs about the other's race, religion, or other personal characteristic. As the two major United States Supreme Court hate crime cases illustrate, states must walk a very fine line in proscribing hate-motivated behavior.

No law has sought to punish mere belief in racism. Regulation of the succeeding stages of expression has occurred. The current debate over hate crimes began in university speech codes. Concerned over an increase in racial tensions on campuses, many schools adopted policies prohibiting the expression of racial or religious bigotry. None of these codes survived First Amendment challenge in court. Thus far, they have been viewed as prohibitions of speech based solely on the content of that speech. Such a prohibition is considered to be the most violative of the express language and spirit of the First Amendment.

While university speech codes have no direct corollary in general society and there has been no recent attempt by any state to apply a racist speech code to the public, hate crimes are currently viewed as an outgrowth of those speech codes. Frustrated with an increase in racial violence on our cities' streets, state legislatures rush to pass hate crime legislation. As with the university speech codes, however, some states run into difficulty when their legislation prohibits racial or bias-motivated speech, an area protected by the Constitution. It is at that point when the judiciary enter the arena, determining which hate crime laws will survive constitutional scrutiny.

Beginning with the *R.A.V.* case, courts moved beyond the setting of the university and confronted general bias crime laws for the first time. *R.A.V. v. City of St. Paul, Minnesota,* 112 S.Ct. 2538 (1992). The Supreme Court was unanimous in striking down the St. Paul ordinance at issue in *R.A.V.,* but provided no further guidance for the states as to whether motive may be considered at sentencing. Four Justices concurred in the judgment of the Court, but did so solely on the grounds of the ordinance's overbreadth, the statute embraced conduct both outside of and within the First Amendment.

It is safe to assume that some of the Justices would have upheld a narrowly-drawn bias crime statute. In *R.A.V.,* however, other members of the Court reached further and found that the St. Paul ordinance—and presumably any bias crime law—was an unconstitutional content-based regulation of speech. In their view, there was no distinction between the St. Paul ordinance and the historical university speech codes.

The facts of *R.A.V.* are as follows: Robert Viktora, then a minor, was accused of burning a cross on the lawn of Russell and Laura Jones and their children, an African-American family that had recently moved into the neighborhood. Viktora was charged with violating St. Paul's Bias-Motivated Crime Ordinance. In moving to dismiss the indictment, Viktora asserted both that the ordinance was overbroad and that it was an unconstitutional, content-based restriction on speech. The Minnesota Supreme Court rejected the overbreadth challenge because it construed the ordinance's language "arouses anger, alarm or resentment in others" as applying only to "fighting words," and therefore not impacting on any expression protected by the First Amendment. In *R.A.V.*, the United States Supreme Court struck down the municipal ordinance prohibiting cross burning and other actions "which one knows or has reasonable grounds to know" will cause "anger, alarm or resentment in others on the basis of race, color, creed, religion or gender." The Court found that such an ordinance was explicitly directed at protected speech and, therefore, unconstitutional.

In *Wisconsin v. Mitchell,* 113 S.Ct. 2194 (1993), the Supreme Court finally shed some light upon the issue of sentence enhancement due to a hate motive:

> As Blackstone said long ago, 'it is but reasonable that among crimes of different natures, those should be most severely punished which are the most destructive of the public safety and happiness. 4 W Blackstone Commentaries.

In *Mitchell,* a young African American man, Todd Mitchell, had been standing on the street corner discussing the film "Mississippi Burning" with a group of friends. When a white fourteen-year-old boy walked by, Mitchell said, "There goes a white boy. Go get him." Mitchell's friends attacked the boy and beat him unconscious. Mitchell was arrested, tried, convicted and sentenced to four years in prison—two years for aggravated battery and two more years for committing a hate crime.

Mitchell's attorney argued that the sentence was enhanced because of his thoughts and words—clearly violating the First Amendment. The attorney argued the dangerous potential of enhancing punishment because of one's opposition to abortion or to war, or to any other political or moral viewpoint. None of the justices of the United States Supreme Court shared these fears. In fact, the history of the Court indicates otherwise: "Deeply ingrained in our legal tradition is the idea that the more purposeful is the criminal conduct, the more serious is the offense, and therefore, the more severely it ought to be punished." *Tison v. Arizona,* 481 U.S. 137, 156 (1987).

The United States Supreme Court upheld Wisconsin's enhancement law that requires harsher sentences for offenders who "intentionally select" their victims because of race, religion, or gender. The most important distinction is that the Wisconsin law does not formally require judges in hate crime cases to decide whether bias thoughts motivated the offender. Whatever the motive, the offender is liable for selecting his victim because of one of the listed characteristics. The Wisconsin law, unlike that in *R.A.V.,* was directed at conduct not protected by the First Amendment. And, the Court ruled that the state's interest in redressing the harms arising from hate crimes is a sufficient explanation for penalty enhancement and does not in any manner imply disagreement with the offender's beliefs or biases.

> Not everyone has been pleased with the Court's reasoning: Chief Justice Rehnquist wrote that the Wisconsin hate-crimes law is aimed at conduct unprotected by the First Amendment. He offered the rationale that crimes motivated by bigotry are thought to inflict greater individual and societal harm including emotional injury. He treated the First Amendment concern with indifference verging on contempt. (Knoll, 1991).

Since the Wisconsin decision, twenty-six other states have enacted similar laws. A Federal law is in the process of completion as well (Knoll, 1991).

There are arguments on both sides of the hate crime debate. One argument is that cross-burning, defacing property, and other "hateful" conduct is merely an expression of the individual's beliefs. The First Amendment, therefore, affords its speaker protection from criminal prosecution. The criminal justice system, however, disagrees with such a protective argument when the speaker's behavior enters into violence impacting on others.

A question arising from hate crime laws is whether judges and juries should be making pronouncements in these cases. Cases involving direct evidence of a racist motive are easily decided, but what should judges and juries do when the motive is not so easily viewed? One commentator states:

> [I]t is not hard to imagine a hate-crime investigation in which a prosecutor might quite reasonably think himself obliged to look at a defendant's political beliefs, and even at the books he reads. A jury might well be more likely to convict a defendant of a hate crime if his library consisted of a well-thumbed copy of "Mein Kampf"—or, to look down the slippery slope only a bit farther, a tellingly highlighted copy of something by Randall Terry or Pat Buchanan or Malcolm X. (*The New Yorker,* p. 4).

Racism or other destructive attitudes arguably should not be fought with the law for additional reasons. First, forced tolerance does not work. Second, the root of the problems in our country is not racism, homophobia, or prejudice; it is violence.

The hate crime advocates assert that their laws are necessary to prevent a "special evil." One commentator questioned: "Why is it more terrorizing or socially destabilizing to stab someone because he's Jewish . . . than to stab someone for his sneakers?" (Rauch, 1991, p. 18) The second situation is a threat to everyone, while the former is a threat to a particular class of individuals. In addition, by having a unique hate crime, there is an inference created that such crimes are more important than those committed against society as a whole. Finally, there are many critics who doubt that prejudice and hate can be wiped out entirely. The reality may be that such a belief leads to forced elimination of all prejudice but that which belongs to the political majority in the country (Rauch, 1991, p. 20).

In response, advocates of hate crime legislation maintain that hate crimes embrace conduct that may or may not include an element of protected speech. When there is such a combination of speech and conduct, the government may regulate the citizen's behavior. In other words, the goal is not to punish prejudice, but to punish the combination of prejudice and violence.

More importantly, when the conduct or speech presents a "clear and present danger" to society or to a particular individual, the state may proscribe that conduct entirely. Crimes such as cross-burnings, it is argued, are directed at a whole class of individuals, representing a "clear and present danger" to a vulnerable minority class (Rauch, 1991). Laws criminalizing such behavior, therefore, should withstand constitutional scrutiny.

A further rationale for hate crime legislation is that it provides a more severe sanction for a type of offense that has consequences beyond the immediate victim. Hate crimes put others belonging to the victim's "group" in fear of being victims themselves from the perpetrator. This has a dramatic effect upon community relations and society in general (Jacobs, 1992).

Hate Crime Offenders

Who are these people who possess such hatred and disregard for individuals or groups with which they typically have not had any personal contact?

Like most people, hate crime perpetrators are raised in a culture that defines "certain people as righteous, upstanding citizens, while designating others as sleazy, immoral characters, who deserve to be mistreated" (Levin & McDevitt, 1993, p. 21). Often, the hate crime offender may have never had contact as a child with members of the groups for which he or she would later direct their hate. Offenders learn of stereotyping and hating those who are not like themselves. Where do they learn this behavior? Family, school, community, church, television, and mass media contribute to a large extent. The list of influences on each individual is endless. For the hate offender, these influences are grasped tightly and serve to incite violence.

Most observers believe that fewer offenses are being committed by members of organized hate groups, such as the Ku Klux Klan, but that many more are being perpetrated by individuals or small groups of people acting on their own. However, the rhetoric of white supremacist organizations and the failure of many community and national leaders to speak out forcefully against these groups encourages many offenders.

At least half the people arrested for bias crimes are teenagers and young adults between the ages of 16 and twenty-five. This fact has significant influence over sentencing of hate crime offenders. Most of these incidents, unless involving serious bodily injury or death in some states, are handled at the juvenile level. In addition, even if prosecuted as an adult, a lack of any prior criminal record mitigates against the harshest of sentences. As such, boards of probation and parole look for alternatives to incarceration, sending a message to the offender that their conduct was merely poor judgment.

Resentment can be found as a dominant personality characteristic in most hate crime offenders (Levin & McDevitt, 1993). The generalized resentment that often forms the basis for a hate offense is most often targeted toward society as a whole rather than at a particular individual. It is from the wider society that the offender has been separated and it is the wider society that is perceived to have rejected the offender. Because of society abandoning the offender's ideals, the offender has lost all control over his or her future.

In the perpetrator's opinion, the "system" has failed them while it is catering to minorities. Believing themselves to be on the fringes of society because of others, hate offenders lash out at those individuals. The victims in these instances are blamed for the offender's personal or economic plight. For example, disease and lack of economic opportunities for one hate offender may cause him or her to target their hatred upon immigrants or those with foreign nationalities.

In 1982, during the recession, anti-Asian sentiment increased its prominence as many Americans blamed Japanese car manufacturers for massive layoffs in the American auto industry. Capitalizing on this anti-Asian frenzy, automobile dealers sought publicity by providing angry Americans with the opportunity to get even. They placed a Japanese-manufactured car in a prominent area of their car lot and urged citizens to come in and swing at the car with a sledgehammer (Levin & McDevitt, 1993). Such a "campaign of hatred" provides the impetus for many hate crime offenders to act upon their hatred.

The following examples are typical of the character and hatred expressed by hate crime offenders:

—In 1990, in Houston, two skinheads conducted a "boot party" with a 15-year old Vietnamese immigrant named Hung Truong. Just before he was stomped to death, according to a detective on the case, Truong pleaded, "Please stop. I'm sorry I ever came to your country. God forgive me."

–In Salem, Oregon, in September, 1992, three members of the American Front group fire bombed the apartment of an African American lesbian named Hattie Cohens and her roommate, a gay white man named Brian Mock, killing both.

–In 1992, in Birmingham, Alabama, three young skinheads awakened a homeless African American man named Benny Rembert and knifed him to death. It was the killers' idea of celebration; they had been drinking in honor of Hitler's birthday (Van Biema, 1993).

Hate Crime Victims

In many situations, the victim is unable to comprehend why the offender targeted him/her. Victims are left with injuries which are more devastating due to the randomness of the hate attack as well as the fact that they were attacked due to some characteristic over which they have no control. Without immediate confrontation of such incidents by law enforcement, the community itself becomes victimized due to fear of future attacks. Members wonder how widespread the bigotry and hatred is, and how many others in their own neighborhood want them to leave. They wonder how many other teenagers are willing to commit violence just to impress their peers with a racial attack. It is small comfort for victims to believe that they were attacked by one "messed up" individual and that the hatred is not widespread.

Local advocacy groups play an important role in confronting hate crimes. National groups such as the Anti-Defamation League of B'nai B'rith, the National Association for the Advancement of Colored People (NAACP), the National Gay and Lesbian Task Force, and the Asian Society provide victims with assistance at the local level. These groups understand by experience that victims of hate crimes feel particularly vulnerable to future attacks. The advocates may help victims with their contacts with law enforcement, the courts and the media, while also providing sources of support and encouragement.

Most importantly, the advocacy groups provide statistical support and incident reporting in order to educate others as to the prevalence of hate-motivated violence in our neighborhoods. For example, 594 cases of anti-Semitic vandalism and 312 cases of assault, harassment, and threats against Jewish individuals and institutions were reported to the Anti-Defamation League in 1986 (Anti-Defamation League of B'nai B'rith, 1987). The National Gay and Lesbian Task Force recorded reports of 732 cases of physical assaults against homosexuals, 191 acts of vandalism, 10 cases of arson or bombings, and 80 homicides (National Gay & Lesbian Task Force, Anti-Gay Violence, Victimization and Defamation in 1986, 1987).

Finally, many local advocacy groups view themselves as responsible for training law enforcement officers who will deal directly with alleged bias-motivated violence. The Anti-Defamation League has been a major contributor in the area of education concerning hate crimes. In 1990, the League introduced two programs: "A Campus of Difference" and "A Workplace of Difference." Both programs were created to reduce bigotry in the college setting and at the corporate or business levels. The effort stemmed from an earlier League program, "A World of Difference," in which teachers were trained to increase their students' tolerance and awareness of other cultures. The goal has been to encourage discussion of issues relating to racism, discrimination and diversity (Levin & McDevitt, 1993).

A major contribution of the past decade has been the introduction of victim advocate programs in our cities. Victim advocates act as a liaison between law enforcement, prosecutors and victims of crime. The advocates provide information for counseling, court dates and procedures, and information regarding restitution. In the hate crimes context, victim advocates serve a more personal role of demonstrating that someone who does not necessarily share the victim's personal characteristics is concerned about his/her plight.

Beyond victim advocate programs, there are other efforts employed by law enforcement to protect citizens from bias or hate-motivated crimes. One such effort is the emphasis placed on community relations and a sensitivity toward other cultural and racial groups living within the community. Citizens are encouraged to talk with each other and with law enforcement about any difficulties or concerns they are experiencing in their own neighborhood. Citizens must also feel comfortable reporting crimes without fear of retaliation. Law enforcement officers recognize that hate crimes pose a more serious threat to an entire community than many other offenses.

Such a community-sensitive response, however, does not always occur. There are many victims who respond with anger themselves. Their hatred serves to continue the battle over multicultural intolerance. Victims organize parades, marches and demonstrations targeted at those who have violated them. Such demonstrations serve only to divide groups even more against each other. The responsibility for controlling such activities falls upon law enforcement and the criminal justice system.

Law Enforcement and Hate Crimes

Law enforcement officers are the individuals who have the initial contact with hate crime offenders and victims—either during commission of the crime or immediately thereafter. Progressive police departments have appreciated the significance of hate crimes in their areas and their role in prevention.

These departments recognize the need for aggressive investigation and sensitive handling of hate offenses.

One way in which this is accomplished is by department policies established specifically for hate crime incidents. Requiring certain investigative steps for all officers to whom an incident is reported enables consistent handling of all cases. Some of these policies require personal contact between supervising officers and victims. Others require continuous follow-up with the victim and community education. Such policies provide officers with guidance as to the proper handling of a bias crime. From a community viewpoint, the manner in which a local police department handles hate crimes shows the level of importance that department places upon such offenses. An aggressive department may provide more reassurance to a community than a department that doesn't make an effort to address bias-motivated crime.

Training officers to recognize hate crimes is also an important step in the process of confronting hate offenses. There may be specialized training in the area of victimology, evidence collection, and investigation. Identifying hate offenses, however, is an area for which all law enforcement officers must be trained. The Federal Bureau of Investigation has provided a guide as to how to recognize a hate crime. These factors suggest that the offense may be bias-motivated and thus requiring further or specialized investigation:

- that the offender and victim were of different racial, religious, ethnic/national origin, or sexual orientation
- that oral comments, written statements, or gestures were made by the offender that show his/her bias
- that bias-related drawings, markings, symbols or graffiti were left at the crime scene
- that the victim is a member of a racial, religious, ethnic/national origin, or sexual orientation group that is overwhelmingly outnumbered by members of another group in the neighborhood where the victim lives and the incident took place
- that the victim was visiting a neighborhood where other hate crimes had taken place or where tensions are high against his/her group
- that most people in the community where the crime occurred perceived that the incident was motivated by bias
- that the incident coincided with a holiday relating to, or a date of particular significance to, a racial, religious, or ethnic/national origin group
- that the offender was previously involved in a similar hate crime or is a member of a hate group. (U.S. Department of Justice, 1990b, pp. 172–173).

The initial contact with law enforcement is where a hate crime investigation begins. The first officer taking the hate crime report must be able to determine whether the incident is potentially a hate crime.

Investigative Techniques

There are three areas deemed crucial to proper investigation of hate crimes: 1. interviewing the victim; 2. searching the crime scene; and 3. investigating the neighborhood.

Interviewing the Victim. Of the three investigative techniques, this is the most important because it is the point at which the investigating officer develops a rapport with the victim. The victim must feel that their experience is important to law enforcement. As with any crime, the victim needs the security of knowing that the officers will attempt to apprehend the person who committed the hate crime.

Additionally, there is a stark deficiency in the area of data collection due to underreporting. Many victims do not report bias-related incidents because they distrust law enforcement. Some believe that the incident is of no significance or that the police would be unable to do anything about the incident. Other victims keep the crime to themselves because they have a language barrier, fear retaliation, or desire to avoid public scrutiny of their minority status. If a victim has the courage to bring the matter to law enforcement, the investigating officer's techniques during the initial interview and handling of the matter are crucial.

One important area that applies in certain hate crimes contexts is the offender's language. The victim's recollection of the offender's language is essential to establishing a bias motive. A prosecutor must prove that hatred motivated the offense and the best evidence is that which the offender provides. Investigating officers must interview the victim as to the gestures and words used by the offender that suggested to the victim that the attack was bias-motivated. The exact language is necessary to a successful hate crime prosecution. Sensitivity toward the victim who must relive the incident in order to assist law enforcement is extremely important during these interviews.

Searching the Crime Scene. Hate crimes often include the use of physical evidence in the commission of the offense. As such, it is important for law enforcement to make a thorough search of the crime scene for fingerprints or other indicators linking the offense with a suspect. Law enforcement officers must be trained to identify hate symbols and messages which may have been overlooked in the past. There is a substantial likelihood that the perpetrator wants society to know that this was a crime motivated by hatred and will make that obvious by the nature of the attack and the surrounding crime scene. The location of the offense or the type of instrument used may lead investigating officers toward a particular group or individual.

Investigating the Neighborhood. As part of their duties, law enforcement officers find out whether there were any eyewitnesses to an offense. In the area of hate crimes, neighborhood investigation provides the investigators with information relating to cultural or racial conflicts in the neighborhood as well as eyewitnesses to the crime. Developing a rapport with the neighborhood residents is as important as that developed with the victim. There must be open communication between the residents and the local police so they feel secure in notifying law enforcement officers of incidents in the area. Hostility between law enforcement and local residents does not benefit either party. Both need each other to prevent the occurrence of hate crimes. The local police may organize forums in various neighborhoods to explain to the residents how they will handle hate crimes. Contact with minority residents in their neighborhoods provides those individuals with more security that the police will attempt to minimize hate-motivated violence.

A thorough investigation enables the police to present the case to the next level of the criminal justice system—the prosecutor.

Criminal Justice System and Hate Crimes

For all of the previously discussed laws to be of any consequence, law enforcement, prosecutors, judges and juries must use them to convict hate crime offenders.

If law enforcement can determine who committed the hate crime, the next step lies in the prosecution of the suspect. The prosecuting attorney at the state level and the United States Attorney at the federal level make decisions to prosecute. The decision to prosecute will also have an effect upon the community as a whole due to the nature of hate crimes. Similar to law enforcement, the prosecutor's attitude toward hate crimes significantly influences community reporting of such incidents. In addition, the prosecutor's choice of charges affects the amount of punishment a convicted offender will receive.

To prosecute hate crimes, the prosecution must establish the defendant's motive. That is the basis by which the state charges the individual with committing a hate crime. This is extremely difficult. The nature of the crime may provide a motive, for example, painting a swastika on the side of a Jewish family's house. Clearly, common understanding interprets this action to be a direct assault upon the fact that the family is Jewish. This, in turn, implies that the offender engaged in this conduct because of what the swastika symbolizes. From this evidence and the defendant's statements to others, the prosecutor can form the bias-related motive. Of particular importance is the language used by the offender during the commission of the offense. It is crucial, therefore, that victim interviews occur at the earliest point possible.

Some indicators used by prosecutors in determining whether a crime is bias-motivated:

- common sense (as in the swastika example)
- language used by suspect (racial slurs etc.)
- severity of the attack (particular types of mutilation)
- lack of provocation
- contact or prior history between victim and suspect
- previous history of similar incidents in the same area
- absence of any other apparent motive (e.g. battery without robbery)

The prosecutor, on behalf of the government, is charged with the role of proving a hate crime beyond a reasonable doubt. There are difficulties with evidence in terms of convincing a jury of exactly what biases or prejudices motivated this offender. It is also the role of the prosecutor to alert the court to a situation in which "hatred" or "bias" is involved, in order for the court to fully assess the case before sentencing. Finally, the prosecutor represents the victims' interests by asking that the court order restitution for any damage caused to the victim. The court may also order the defendant to successfully complete a cultural or interpersonal sensitivity program through local probation and parole offices.

Prosecutor offices in Massachusetts and New York have been particularly active in targeting hate crimes. In April of 1987, the Queens County (New York) District Attorney established an Anti-Bias Bureau staffed with four assistant district attorneys. The bureau works with the Police Department's Bias Incident Investigating Unit, a separate unit consisting of three sergeants, sixteen investigators, and four police administrative agencies. The officers monitor and investigate racially, religiously, and ethnically motivated acts and hate violence committed against homosexuals. Officers must report suspected bias incidents to precinct commanding officers who confirm motivation and then report the crime to the Bias Unit for follow-up investigation.

The Bias Unit contacts the District Attorney's Anti-Bias Bureau and, if warranted, a bureau prosecutor may go to the scene or to the police station to interview witnesses. The bureau verifies that the incident is bias-related. Few cases are plea bargained (Levin & McDevitt, 1993).

The Manhattan District Attorney's office has selected a paralegal as liaison to the homosexual community. The liaison meets with community groups to encourage victimized residents to report incidents. In addition, the liaison provides sensitivity training to the prosecutors in the office to understand the reluctance of the residents to report incidents and the importance of not blatantly disapproving of a victim's lifestyle. Training also includes practical issues such as conduct of jury selection, questioning of defendants, and argument techniques to neutralize jurors' potential prejudice toward homosexuals. It is the office policy to charge the highest offense possible for bias crimes and to recommend that the judge take the hate component into account at sentencing (Levin & McDevitt, 1993).

Boston established a Community Disorders Unit similar to that of New York. Intensive investigation by the unit includes ride-alongs with the victim, surveillances, door-to-door interviews with potential witnesses, and undercover operations.

The courts have the important role of impressing upon hate crime offenders that their conduct is against the law. The courts do this by using their resources to teach offenders to refrain from criminal behavior when confronted with hate feelings or beliefs. The court has the power to add time onto an offender's sentence if hatred motivated the crime. Most important, however, the court is the most powerful means of setting a societal tone about what types of behavior will and will not be allowed.

Society and the media directly influence sentencing decisions in many hate crime cases. In society's viewpoint, the crime was committed against the community as a whole and it is within the judge's power to prevent these types of crimes from occurring by harsh punishments. At the same time, the media may have followed the case from the initial incident to the sentencing hearing. They will scrutinize any lack of vigilance upon the prosecutor or judge's part to address such violence. The prosecutor and judge, as elected officials, naturally are sensitive to public opinion. The resulting effect of both media and public pressure may be toward treating hate crimes as very serious offenses for which the most severe sanctions available are warranted.

CHAPTER SUMMARY

As time passes, the successes and failures with respect to hate crimes will become more apparent. Is hate crime punishment effective law enforcement or merely an instrument of forced tolerance of others? If viewed as such an instrument, should society accept this as necessary due to the increasing problems of tolerance of other cultures, races, genders, sexual preferences, and nationalities? Is there an alternative?

One of the most significant arguments supporting hate crime legislation is based upon the idea of deterring hate offenses. This is accomplished in two ways. First, stiffer penalties serve to discourage potential hate crime perpetrators from committing such crimes. Second, the legislation provides an impetus for law enforcement to be more vigilant in the context of hate crimes. There are new methods of apprehension, more contact within the community, and an increased sensitivity toward hate crime victims.

In more and more communities in the United States, after a bias-motivated crime has been committed, citizens are urging law enforcement to make arrests, prosecutors to convict and judges to sentence the offender to the maximum allowable by law. Media publicity about hate crime offenses increases the public's awareness of the severity of these incidents and their long-term impact on communities. Law enforcement officials have communicated to the community that such violence will not be tolerated.

An example of the progress occurring over the past decade occurred in 1989 when members of a fraternity at the University of Vermont, expelled a student from the fraternity after discovering that he was a homosexual. A student judicial board ruled that the fraternity had discriminated against the student based upon sexual orientation. The board ordered the fraternity to apologize to the student, to refund his pledge fee, and to organize in-house educational programs discussing homosexuality. More than four hundred students and the mayor of Burlington, Vermont, participated in a parade against hate on campus. Soon after, the mayor approached the local aldermen and requested that they amend the city's housing discrimination code so that college fraternities would be legally prohibited from discriminating on the basis of sexual orientation (*The New York Times,* 1990).

These are all responses to an increasing tide of intolerance in our country. The progress has quickened over the past few years due to the increase in violence and the passage of state laws increasing penalties for committing hate crimes. The United States Supreme Court will, no doubt, continue to be a major influence in the area of hate crimes as states become more creative in their legislative responses.

REFERENCES

Chaplinsky v. New Hampshire, 315 U.S. 568 (1942).
Hess v. Indiana, 414 U.S. 105 (1973).
Ohio v. Wyant, 597 N.E.2d 450 (Ohio 1992).
R.A.V. v. City of St. Paul, Minnesota, 112 S. Ct. 2538 (1992).
State v. M.S. and A.G., 1993 W.L. 309596 (Cal.App. 1 Dist.) (1993).
State v. Myers, 1993 W.L. 340945 (Wash.) (1993).
State v. Talley, 1993 W.L. 340945 (Wash.) (1993).
Tison v. Arizona, 481 U.S. 137, 156 (1987).
U.S. v. Schenk, 249 U.S. 47 (1919).
Whitney v. California, 274 U.S. 357, 375–376 (1927) (Brandeis, J., concurring).
Wisconsin v. Mitchell, 113 S. Ct. 2194 (1993).
18 USC s. 241 (1993) "Conspiracy Against Rights."

18 USC s. 247 (1993) "Damage to Religious Property and Obstruction of Persons in the Free Exercise of Religious Beliefs."

18 USC s. 245 (1993) "Federally Protected Rights."

42 USC s. 3604 (1993) "Willful Interference with Civil Rights under the Fair Housing Act."

Hate Crimes Sentencing Enhancement Act of 1993, 103rd Congress, 1st Session, Report 103-244.

Or.Rev.Stat. s 166.165(1)(a)(A) (1990).

Wis.Stat.Ann. s 939.645 (West 1991).

American-Arab Anti-Discrimination Committee, (1992, February) *1991 Report on Anti-Arab Crimes.* Washington, D.C.: American-Arab Anti-Discrimination Committee.

Anti-Defamation League of B'nai B'rith, (1987) *1986 Audit of Anti-Semitic Incidents.* New York: Anti-Defamation League of B'nai B'rith.

Center for Democratic Renewal. (1987) *They don't all wear white sheets: A chronology of racist and far right violence – 1980–1986.* Atlanta: Center for Democratic Renewal.

Jacobs, J.B. (1992, September) Hate crime legislation: Challenging intolerance. *Current* p. 16.

Knoll, E. (1991, August) A matter of intent. *The Progressive* p. 4.

Levin, J. & McDevitt, J. (1993) *Hate crimes: The rising tide of bigotry and bloodshed.* New York: Plenum Press.

National Gay & Lesbian Task Force, Anti-Gay Violence, Victimization and Defamation in 1986. (1987) (Washington, DC: National Gay & Lesbian Task Force.

New York Times. (1990, April 11) Fraternity stirs whirlwind in Vermont. p. A17.

The New Yorker. (1993, June 21) Bad motives. p. 4.

Rauch, J. (1991, October 7) Thought crimes. *The New Republic,* pp. 18, 20.

United States Constitution, Amendment 1.

U.S. Department of Justice. (1990a) *Hate crime data collection guidelines.* Washington, DC: Federal Bureau of Investigation.

U.S. Department of Justice. (1990b) *Training guide for hate crime data collection.* Washington, DC: Federal Bureau of Investigation.

Van Biema, D. (1993, August 9) When white makes right. *Time Magazine,* pp. 40–43.

ADDITIONAL READINGS

Anti-Defamation League of B'nai B'rith. (1989) *Combatting bigotry on campus.* New York: Anti-Defamation League of B'nai B'rith.

Anti-Defamation League of B'nai B'rith. (1989) *Hate crimes: Policies and procedures for law enforcement agencies.* New York: Anti-Defamation League of B'nai B'rith.

Anti-Defamation League of B'nai B'rith. (1990) *Liberty lobby: A network of hate.* New York: Anti-Defamation League of B'nai B'rith.

Anti-Defamation League of B'nai B'rith. (1990) *Neo-nazi skinheads: A 1990 status report.* New York: Anti-Defamation League of B'nai B'rith.

Berrill, K. (1986) Anti-gay violence: Causes, consequences, responses. Washington, D.C.: National Gay and Lesbian Task Force pp. 1–26.

Clark, F. (1991) Hate violence in the united states, *F.B.I. Law Enforcement Bulletin* p. 60.

Coates, J. (1987) *Armed and dangerous: The rise of the survivalist right.* New York: The Noonday Press.

Comstock, G. (1991) *Violence against lesbians and gay men.* New York: Columbia University Press.

Dugo, D. & Aragon, L. (1991, May–June–July) Alert eyes spot hate crime evidence. *Law Enforcement Quarterly.*

Herek, G. Berrill, K. (1992) *Hate crime: Confronting violence against lesbians and gay men.* Newbury Park, CA: Sage.

Hodge, J., Struckmann, D. & Trost, L. (1975) *Cultural bases of racism and group oppression.* Berkeley, CA: Two Riders Press.

Keen, S. (1986) *Faces of the enemy.* San Francisco: Harper & Row.

Levin, J. & Fox, J. (1985) *Mass murder: America's growing menace.* New York: Plenum Press.

Mohr, R. (1988) "Anti-gay stereotypes." *Gays/justice: A study of ethics, society and law.* New York: Columbia University Press.

Schuman, H., Steeh, C. & Bobo, L. (1988) *Racial attitudes in america.* Cambridge, MA: Harvard University Press.

Siegelman, L. & Welch, S. (1991) *Black americans' views of racial inequality.* Cambridge: Cambridge University Press.

Singular, S. (1987) *Talked to death: The life and murder of alan berg.* New York: Morrow.

Tobin, G. & Sassler, S. (1988) *Jewish perceptions of anti-semitism.* New York: Plenum Press.

Cal. Penal Code s. 422.6 (West 1991) ("Interference with exercise of civil rights," enacted 1987); Cal. Penal Code s 422.7 (West 1991) ("Aggravating factors for punishment," any racially motivated crimes not covered by s 422.6 have the penalty increased, enacted 1987).

Colo.Rev.Stat.Ann. s. 18-9-121 (West 1990) ("Ethnic intimidation–injury, fear or property damage," enacted 1988).

Conn.Gen.Stat.Ann. s. 53-37a (West 1991) ("Deprivation of civil rights by person wearing mask or hood," enacted 1982); Conn. Gen. Stat. Ann. s. 46a-58 (West 1991) (criminalizing "[d]eprivation of rights" through the use of a burning cross, enacted 1949).

D.C.Code Ann. s. 22-3112.2 (1991) ("Defacing or burning cross or religious symbol; display of certain emblems," enacted 1983).

Fla.Stat.Ann. s. 775.085 (West 1990) ("Evidencing prejudice while committing offense," enacted 1991); Fla. Stat. Ann. s. 876.20 (West 1991) (criminalizing wearing a mask or placing an exhibit for the purpose of intimidation, enacted 1951).

Ga. Code Ann. s. 16-11-37(b)(1) (Michie 1990) (criminalizing the burning of a cross with the intent to terrorize, enacted 1968); Ga. Code Ann. s. 16-11-38 (Michie 1990) (criminalizing the wearing of a hood or mask which conceals one's identity, enacted 1986).

Idaho Code s. 18-7902 (1991) (harassment based on race, color, religion, etc., enacted 1983).

Ill.Rev.Stat. ch. 38, para. 12-7.1 (1991) (commits assault, battery, etc., based on race, enacted 1983).

Iowa Code Ann. s. 708.2C (West 1992) ("Assault in violation of individual rights," lists penalties, enacted 1992); Iowa Code Ann. s. 712.9 (West 1992) (penalty enhancement statute, enacted 1992); Iowa Code Ann. s. 729A.2 (West 1992) (defines hate crimes for use in this and other statutes, enacted 1992).

Me.Rev.Stat.Ann. tit. 17, s. 2931 (West 1989) ("Harassment based on characteristics," interference with free exercise of rights, enacted 1987).

Md.Crim. Law Code Ann. s. 470A (1989) ("Crimes against religious property, institutions, or persons," enacted 1988).

Mass.Gen.L. ch. 265, s. 39 (1989) ("Assault or battery for purpose of intimidation," enacted 1983).

Mich.Comp. Laws s. 750.147b (1991) ("Ethnic intimidation"—causes or threatens harm to person or property motivated by race, color, religion, gender, or national origin, enacted 1988).

Mo.Rev.Stat. s. 574.090 (1989) ("Ethnic intimidation in the first degree," enacted 1988); Mo.Rev.Stat. s. 574.093 (1989) ("Ethnic intimidation in the second degree," enacted 1988).

Mont. Code Ann. s. 45-5221 (1992) (malicious intimidation or harassment relating to civil or human rights, enacted 1989); Mont. Code Ann. s. 45-5-222 (1992) (sentence enhancement for offenses committed because of victim's race, enacted 1989).

N.C.Gen.Stat. ss. 14-12.7 to 14-12.10 (1991) (criminalizing the wearing of hoods or masks, enacted 1953); N.C.Gen.Stat. s 14-12.12 (1991) (criminalizing cross-burning, enacted 1953).

N.H.Rev.Stat.Ann. s. 65:6(I)(g) (extended terms of imprisonment for crimes motivated by hostility to race, religion, etc., enacted 1990).

N.J.Rev.Stat. s. 2C:33-11 (1982) ("Defacement or damage of property by placement of symbol," enacted 1981); N.J.Stat.Ann. s. 2C:44-3(e) (West 1992) (criteria for sentencing defendants acting with ill will, hatred, or bias due to race, color, religion, sexual orientation, or ethnicity, enacted 1990).

N.Y. Penal Law s. 240.31 (McKinney 1989) ("Aggravated harassment in the first degree," commits personal or property damage based on race, etc., enacted 1982).

Ohio Rev. Code Ann. s. 2927.12 (Anderson 1987) ("Ethnic intimidation," committing other crimes motivated by race, enacted 1987).

Okla.Stat. tit. 21, s. 850 (1990) ("Malicious intimidation or harassment because of race," etc., enacted 1987).

Or.Rev.Stat. s. 166.155 (1990) ("Intimidation in the second degree," tampers with property due to race, etc., enacted 1981).

18 Pa.Cons.Stat. s. 2710 (1991) ("Ethnic intimidation," commits any crime with malicious intent due to race, enacted 1982).

R.I.Gen. Laws s. 11-42-3 (1991) ("Ethnic or religious intimidation," enacted 1982); R.I.Gen. Laws s. 11-53-2 (1991) ("Threat by terror," burning crosses, displaying

Nazi swastikas, etc., enacted 1981); R.I.Gen. Laws s. 11-53-3 (1991) ("Threats to immigrants," enacted 1983).

Tenn. Code Ann. s. 39-17-309 (1991) (intimidation due to race, religion, etc., enacted 1988).

Utah Code Ann. s. 76-3-203.3 (1992) (committing a "primary offense" (assault, trespass, etc.) with the intent to intimidate or terrorize, enacted 1992).

Va. Code Ann. s. 18.2-422 (Michie 1991) (prohibiting wearing masks or hoods in specific circumstances, enacted 1950); Va. Code Ann. s. 18.2-423 (Michie 1991) (criminalizing cross-burning, enacted 1950).

Vt.Stat.Ann. tit. 13, s. 1455 (1991) ("Hate motivated crimes," increases penalties for violations of other crimes if committed with a racist motivation, enacted 1989).

Wash.Rev. Code Ann. s. 9A.36.080 (West 1991) ("Malicious harassment," intimidation because of race, includes cross-burning or defacing with swastika etc., enacted 1981).

W.Va.Code s. 61-6-21 (1991) ("Prohibiting violations of an individual's civil rights," injury or intimidation, based on race, religion, etc., enacted 1987); W.Va. Code s. 61-6-22 (1991) ("Wearing masks, hoods or face coverings," enacted 1988).

Wis.Stat.Ann. s. 939.645 (West 1991) ("crimes committed against certain people or property," enacted 1988).

CHAPTER NINE

JUVENILE JUSTICE: MULTICULTURAL ISSUES

CHARLES J. CORLEY AND GENEVA SMITHERMAN

INTRODUCTION

There are primarily three broad areas of interest to be addressed regarding multicultural issues and juvenile justice. These areas include: assessments of racial/ethnic disparity in processing and sanction; cross-cultural examination of rates of offending (this includes an examination of the processing and sanctioning patterns of Anglos, African-American, Hispanics, Asians, and Native Americans); and multicultural sensitive system response/treatment alternatives that could empower the juvenile justice system to better meet the needs of youths of color.

Unlike its' adult counterpart, the juvenile court has been empowered to act as a parent for juveniles appearing before it. Since its inception in the latter 1800's, the primary objectives of the juvenile justice system has been to prevent juvenile crime and rehabilitate juvenile offenders (Siegel & Senna, 1991). Through its philosophy of parens patriae (*in the child's best interest*) the juvenile court intervenes in the lives of adolescents who have been either neglected and/or adjudicated delinquent with the objective of providing individualized corrective treatment. To achieve its goal of individualized treatment, the juvenile justice system (*unlike the adult criminal justice system*) has never used a decision-making model requiring formal rationality (Platt, 1969; Horwitz & Wasserman, 1980). To do so would eliminate consideration of extra-legal and/or social factors that might provide insight into the adolescent's behavior and further suggest the court has abandoned its attempt to provide individualized treatment not punishment. Instead, the court operates on a model of substantive justice in which it is acceptable to use social background variables (such as school attendance, peer relations, and family characteristics) as a means to personalize treatment (Horwitz & Wasserman, 1980).

Thus, while the juvenile justice system has been called upon to administer justice, it has also been required to temper its administration of justice in an effort to act in the best interests of adolescent offenders. To that end, the President's Commission on Law Enforcement and the Administration of Justice (1967) suggests that:

> there should be a response to the special needs of youths with special problems. They may be delinquent, they may be law abiding but alienated and uncooperative, they may be behavior or academic problems in school or misfits among their peers or disruptive in recreation groups. For such youths, it is imperative to furnish help that is particularized enough to deal with their individual needs but not separate them from their peers and label them for life.

However, recent trends in juvenile court dispositions suggest a shift away from a protective and rehabilitative posture taken towards adolescents who violate the law. Barry Feld (1990) suggests recent changes in juvenile courts' sentencing policies and practices reflect more of a punitive "just desert" model whereby the amount of punishment is reflective of the juvenile's prior criminal record and seriousness of the offense rather than the best interest of the offender. Feld cites the waiving of more serious juvenile offenders to adult court, inclusion of minimum mandatory sentencing guides, and exposure of juveniles to the death penalty as evidence that the juvenile justice system has become more punitive.

However, if the just deserts model were strictly implemented throughout juvenile justice, racial disparities relative to disposition should not exist. The juvenile court would be utilizing a decision making model predicated on a form of formal rationality whereby extra-legal and/or social factors such as race should not have an impact. Yet, several state level studies show higher rates of incarceration for Black and Hispanic juveniles compared to whites. Perhaps Feld's (1988) finding that most juvenile courts' sentencing provisions continue to follow the "progressive origins" (on which the juvenile court was founded), explains some of the disproportionate representation of juveniles of color and racial disparities found among recent state-level assessment of juvenile justice. That is, if juvenile courts are shifting towards more punitive sanctioning of juveniles perhaps this, combined with perceptions of minority juveniles as in need of more intense supervision and control, contributes to the over-representation of minority juveniles within the system.

The debate concerning the impact of race on criminal justice processes has been waged for decades. On the one hand, there are the supporters of a nondiscriminatory system of criminal justice who suggest that if minorities are disproportionately represented in the system, it is in part due to a higher commission of crime or more serious crimes by minority youth and/or other factors associated with the behaviors and attitudes of minorities. Conversely, there are those who would point to more recent empirical research (e.g., state level juvenile justice assessments) and seek to understand how a criminal justice system can function in a capitalistic sociopolitical environment such as ours and not be affected by such factors as race, socioeconomic status, gender, and age. The latter, (proponents assert that bias exists in the criminal justice system) adopt a more conflict-oriented theoretical approach and suggest that it would be improbable that our criminal justice system could operate in a vacuum unaffected by the larger social system in which it exists. They would assert that even the definition of criminal behavior is biased against those who occupy more marginal positions and lack power/resources to manipulate the criminal justice system on their behalf. Moreover, it is suggested that more marginal status members of society are more likely than those in positions of wealth and power to have their deviance detected, labeled, and sanctioned. This would be applicable to minority group members who often occupy less powerful positions in society. However, the conflict perspective and its application to the juvenile justice will be discussed in more detail below.

The former, (proponents of a more fair and equitable criminal justice system) assume somewhat a functionalist theoretical approach. This approach suggests there is consensus among a society's members on what constitutes illegal behavior. In accordance with the consensus model, it becomes the purpose of the law to differentiate legal from illegal behavior, control the behavior of the local citizens, punish those who violate the law, and deter others from commission of illegal acts (Siegel, 1992). Moreover, the consensus model implies that the law is applied uniformly across all segments of society (Sutherland & Cressy, 1966). There are laws that regulate the behaviors of both the poor and wealthy.

However it is the conflict/labeling perspective that points to a process that is more likely to view the behaviors of persons in marginally less powerful positions in society as deviant, and therefore, more likely to come to the attention of the criminal justice system.

The Conflict/Labeling Perspective

Conflict theory draws many of its theoretical postulates from Marxist ideology which suggests that within a society there are essentially two classes of people. First, there are the bourgeoisie who are the owners of the means of production. Second, there are the proletariats or the workers. The bourgeoisie, or ruling class, are powerful individuals who influence the economic, legal, and other systems to operate in a manner that supports their class interests. However, as societies continued to evolve, another class of individuals emerged. While these individuals do not meet the strict criterion of bourgeoisie status (they do not directly own the means of production), they are in a status higher than the proletariat. These "middle persons" have a stake in maintaining the status quo of society, in part, because the status quo supports their perceived economic interests.

Conflict theorists maintain that the fabric of society is held together by conflict and/or competition for scarce resources. In this competition over scarce resources (i.e., wealth, status, and power) all members of society are not equal. Members of the lower classes are more disadvantaged than others. For instance, psychologist Kenneth B. Clark (1965) observed that in the United States class and race merge in such a way that blacks are at the bottom of society whereas whites are at the top. In brief, this interaction of class and race merge in a manner that contributes to the depiction of people of color as members of an outgroup who are regulated to a lower social status in American society.

Thus, conflict theorists such as Richard Quinney (1970) suggest the legal system best represents the interests of those who hold power in a society. The legal system becomes a method of regulating and controlling the behaviors of the poor (of which a disproportionate percentage in America are minority).

In addition, labeling theorists argue that it is the aforementioned members of the outgroup who are more likely to have their behaviors detected, defined as illegal, and sanctioned by an official agency more so than persons occupying higher social positions (Tannenbaum, 1938; Lemert, 1951). Specifically, Lemert suggests that while numerous persons have engaged in primary deviant acts (behavior for which there is the possibility of sanction), it is the more marginal persons who are likely to have their behavior labeled as deviant. Further, the assignment of a deviant label can set into motion a self-fulfilling prophecy whereby additional deviant acts are committed in reaction to being labeled. That is, once a person is labeled deviant, others perceive and respond to the individual as a deviant (Becker, 1963). Thus, the deviant stigma can influence individuals, so labeled, to continue their deviant actions.

The merging of conflict theory with the labeling perspective describes how the criminal justice system may be used as an oppressive instrument. In short, these perspectives describe how it is that in a society such as ours (where social inequality exists), members of the outgroup (poor, minority and disadvantaged) are perceived to be a threat to the general order and, as a result, are more likely than others to be defined as criminals.

DISPARITY IN JUVENILE JUSTICE PROCESSES AND SANCTIONS

Empirical assessments of the impact of social variables on the juvenile justice process have been undertaken by numerous researchers since the decade of the sixties and have yielded varied results. While some studies have indicated that race has an impact (Arnold, 1971; Brown, Sagan & Greenblatt, 1980; Fisher & Doyle-Martin, 1981; Lundman, 1978; Marshall &

Thomas 1983; Poole & Regoli, 1980; Thomas & Cage, 1977; Thomas & Sieverdes, 1975; Thornberry, 1979); others suggest that social characteristics such as race has no impact on juvenile justice processes (Carter, 1979; Cohen & Kluegel, 1978 and 1979; Hohenstein, 1969; Horwitz & Wasserman, 1980; Huryn, 1982; Keiter, 1973; Kowalski & Rickicki, 1982; Kramer & Steffensmeier, 1987; Mann, 1980; Mead, 1973; Pawlak, 1977; Phillips & Dinitz, 1982; Sheldon & Horvath, 1987; and Walter & Ostrander, 1982).

Several explanations have been offered to make clear the aforementioned contradictory results. First, many of the earlier studies that examined the impact of social characteristics on juvenile justice processes and found race to be influential were thought methodologically flawed. These studies were criticized for only comparing sanctioning patterns of black and white juvenile offenders. Few studies examined the experiences of other minority groups (i.e., Hispanics, Asians and Native Americans) relative to the juvenile justice system.

Additionally, many of these studies focused on rather limited components of the juvenile justice process (e.g., referral and/or disposition). Yet, it should be noted that juvenile justice decision making is a process and since bias can occur at any stage of the process, multiple decision points should have been examined (Pope & Feyerherm, 1990a). Multivariate assessments of referral, intake, adjudication, and sanctions should be undertaken to better understand the possible effects of race at each stage.

Many earlier studies failed to utilize multivariate statistical techniques and/or implement appropriate statistical controls (Hindelang, 1978). Researchers should consider the possible interaction of race with other sociodemographic variables such as age, social class, familial background, school attendance, and performance, as well as characteristics of the victims on juvenile justice processes and sanctions. Inclusion of the previously mentioned variables with appropriate statistical controls would enable researchers to determine the single and contributory effects of each variable at each stage of the juvenile justice process. For instance, it may be that older minority juveniles from non-intact families are sent through formal adjudication more so than other juveniles. A multistaged analysis of juvenile justice decision making with appropriate statistical controls would be better able to detect such an effect. Moreover, if such an analysis were inclusive of juveniles from other minority groups, researchers would be able to determine whether all youths of color are treated similarly.

However, the higher volume of criticism leveled at earlier studies that found a race effect in juvenile justice compared to studies that found no such effect is, itself, a concern. For instance, Thompson and Zingraff (1981) noted, "In the past, research which found no discrimination demanded little, if any, explanation or re-analysis, while research which found discrimination was subjected to scrutiny" (p. 879). Studies that found no race effect in juvenile justice also suffered from many of the same shortcomings of studies that detected discrimination. Yet, they too may have been flawed. For instance, it may be that the lack of a multivariate analysis and proper statistical controls could not discern the direct effects of race on referral and/or disposition because "race surrogates" were operating. That is, variables so closely related to race such as social class and familial structure (two parent households) were so inter-related with race that they were found to affect juvenile justice processes instead of race. However, given that a disproportionate percentage of the lower class are minority and single parent homes are more common among juveniles of color, race is still having an impact through these variables. Nonetheless, earlier studies that did not report a race effect on juvenile justice sanction and/or referral were not exposed to a great deal of scrutiny.

Since the decade of the sixties many of the studies that reported racial bias have overcome some of the aforementioned methodological shortcomings. For instance, Bortner and Reed, (1985) in a five year assessment of juvenile court sentencing reported that black juveniles were more likely than whites to be detained, have formal hearings, and receive severe dispositions (especially Black females). Thus, Bortner concluded that his analysis revealed systematic differential treatment premised on race.

In addition, more recent state level assessments of racial bias suggest that racial and/or gender bias is operative within the juvenile justice system in America (Bishop & Frazier, 1990; Bynum, Wordes & Corley, 1993; Kempf, Decker & Bing, 1990; and Leiber, 1992). More specifically, empirical investigations of state level juvenile justice systems in Missouri, Florida, Iowa and Michigan indicates that race and/or gender impacted various components of the juvenile justice process.

These more recent state level assessments of juvenile court processing are in response to the Federal Office of Juvenile Justice and Delinquency (OJJDP) 1989 mandate that states receiving federal funds determine whether minority youths are disproportionately represented in their juvenile justice system. Moreover, the mandate required that states whose minority youth were over-represented (particularly in secure institutions) take appropriate measures to reduce their presence in the system.

These more recent assessments of juvenile justice practices overcome many of the limitations of previous research. In particular, more recent studies incorporate a multistage juvenile justice assessment. That is, many of these studies tracked youths from their initial entry into the system until final disposition of their case (Bishop & Frazier, 1988 and 1990; Bynum, Wordes & Corley, 1993; Fagan, Slaughter & Hartstone, 1987; Kempf, Decker & Bing, 1990; Leiber, 1992; and McCarthy & Smith, 1986). A number of these multijurisdictional studies identified an "amplification effect" (Bishop & Frazier, 1988; Fagan, Slaughter & Hartstone, 1987; and McCarthy & Smith, 1986). These studies indicate that differential treatment of youth of color increased as they progressed through the system. For instance, if minority youths were more likely to be detained at intake than other youths, their detention status contributed to more formal and/or punitive responses from the court.

In addition, inclusion of multijurisdictions in these state level assessments showed that justice practices vary across and within jurisdictions. All jurisdictions within the same state, city or county did not process their youth uniformly. Rural, suburban and urban differences exist and contribute to the differential processing of youths appearing before the court (Bishop & Frazier, 1990; Bynum, Wordes & Corley, 1993; Kempf, Decker & Bing, 1990; and Leiber, 1992).

The aforementioned geographical variations also affect police arrest decisions. Thus, it is important to examine police encounters with juveniles across jurisdictions since that encounter may likely be the youth's initial contact with the juvenile justice system and judicial responses vary across urban, suburban, and rural jurisdictions. However, if bias exists at the police phase it marks the beginning of what has been described as the "amplification effect" of race.

Police Responses To Juvenile Delinquency

Unlike encounters with adult suspects where police interactions are guided by the letter of the law; police encounters with juveniles are not as well defined and allow greater use of police discretion. Yet, the arrest phase is the most important stage because it marks the entry point of a youth into the criminal justice system (National Council of Family Court Judges, 1990). If minority youth are over-represented within the juvenile justice system, the beginning of that over-representation would likely be at the stage of arrest.

Unlike interactions with adults, where specific police guidelines and procedures are to be followed, police have a broad realm of discretion in their encounters with juveniles. Siegel and Senna (1991) identify several factors that can affect police discretion in terms of the decision to arrest. Among them are: seriousness of the alleged offense, presence of a victim, social status of the victim, attitude of the community towards crime, policies, customs and practices of the police department, and availability of community alternatives for police intervention.

More specifically, police are more likely to take a youth into custody for a serious offense. That is as offense seriousness increases so does the likelihood of arrest (Corley & Dickinson, 1993). The arrest decision can also be conditioned by the presence of a victim who may be insistent upon referring charges. In fact, some research suggests that black youths are more likely to be arrested than white youths because there is often a victim who seeks to file charges against them (Bynum Wordes & Corley, 1993).

The community's attitude, as well as its available resources impacts the decision to arrest. For instance, in communities where there is a low tolerance for criminal behavior, police officers may be more inclined to take a youth into custody. Moreover, in some larger urban municipalities, police officer discretion may be limited whereby presumably all under age law violators are taken into custody as a standardized response (Bynum et al., 1993).

It was also noted that the decision to arrest a juvenile is conditioned by the availability of community resources and alternatives. That is, communities that have resources for alternatives for youths in trouble with the law, (e.g., diversion programs, youth run courts, etc.) are more likely to take a non-arrest posture (Corley & Dickinson, 1993). However, many urban municipalities (where a larger percentage of blacks and other minorities reside) do not have resources that enable it to offer programs that deter arrest. This may subsequently contribute to the greater likelihood of arrest for youths of color.

Yet, many of the aforementioned factors that affect police decisions to arrest juveniles are further influenced by the characteristics of the juvenile. Specifically, the juvenile's demeanor, attitude of the parent(s) and/or family situation can affect the decision to arrest. Piliavin and Briar (1964) observed that youths who displayed a more hostile demeanor towards the police were more likely to be arrested than youths who exhibited a more pleasurable disposition. Moreover, uncooperative parents as well as juveniles perceived to be from non-traditional or dysfunctional families can contribute to a more formal and/or punitive judicial response (Corley, Bynum & Wordes, 1993).

The impact of the characteristics of juveniles may have more of a negative affect on arrest decisions for blacks and other youths of color than majority youths. Historically, majority citizens have maintained better relations with the police than members of the minority community. Working and lower-class minorities in particular are less likely to possess favorable attitudes towards the police. This may contribute to the negative and even hostile demeanor youths of color at times display during encounters with the police. Moreover, when the attitudes of the parents and juvenile's living situation enter in the decision to arrest it invariably disadvantages youths of color. In addition to the already discussed attitudinal differences between majority and minority citizens towards the police, family patterns among minority families are more non-traditional than those found among whites. For instance, a youth from a single parent home may be perceived to be more in need of a formal juvenile justice intervention than a youth from a traditional two parent home (Corley, Bynum & Wordes, 1993). Since single parent homes are disproportionately found more often among minorities than the majority, it disadvantages minorities when such factors as family living situation impact the decision to arrest. While it is generally thought that the aforementioned social factors affect police discretion and the decision to arrest, it is difficult to record the occurrences of such phenomenon.

Contrary to juvenile court proceedings where a record of decisions and factors that contributed to these judicial decisions are documented, the decision to arrest and/or investigate has a lower degree of visibility and less documentation (Piliavin & Briar, 1964). Therefore, it is difficult to determine the affects (if any) that race have on the police decision to arrest. This, in part, also explains why research on police interaction with juveniles has been limited in number. There are few research methodologies (*that would not require and enormous expenditure of time and money*) that enable a researcher to assess police interaction with all juveniles encountered and discern differences between those juveniles arrested and those not arrested. A thorough analysis of police decision making would, at the very least, require observations of police work. However, given the time demands and low levels of replicability of observational research, a researcher would need to balance this method with a more empirically objective, statistically rigorous, and less time consuming approach.

Once an officer encounters a youthful suspect, a diverse range of options become available. These options usually range from an outright "warn and release," to arrest and/or referral to juvenile court. Police discretion empowers officers to act in the perceived "best interest" of the child (Siegel & Senna, 1991). However, it is the application of police discretion that has prompted researchers to examine police encounters with juveniles to determine if there is a selection bias in the arrest and referral of youth to the juvenile court. A review of the research on discretion lead Siegel and Senna (1991) to conclude that law enforcement officers have a great deal of discretion at their disposal and apply it without uniformity and clear guidance.

Although it has been estimated that nearly forty to sixty percent of all juvenile suspects who have contact with the police are handled informally (Goldman, 1963), the majority of youth who appear in court are referred by the police. However, it is the characteristics of those who are released that researchers have not been able to profile.

Nonetheless, arrest trends in the Uniform Crime Report show that for the year 1987 black juveniles were arrested at a rate five times that of white youths (UCR, 1987). It would appear then, that youth of color are either: committing more crimes (which explains their over-representation in the juvenile justice system), or they are victims of a racist system.

In perhaps the most frequently cited "differential processing article," Piliavin and Briar (1964) found that blacks and boys whose appearance matched the delinquent stereotype were more frequently stopped and interrogated by patrol officers, even in the absence of evidence that a crime had been committed. Additionally, it should be noted that more recent research suggests that minority youth are more likely to be arrested and referred to court than white youths (Bishop & Frazier, 1988; Black & Smith, 1981; Fagen, et al., 1987; and Thornberry, 1979).

On the other hand, it has been suggested that in cases involving black suspects there is a greater likelihood of a complainant seeking justice. In addition, it has been suggested that police consider the nature of the offense and demeanor of the suspect before making an arrest decision (Lundman, 1974; Griswold, 1978). Thus, it remains to be empirically determined whether social characteristics such as race affect police decisions to arrest and/or refer juveniles for further processing.

Yet, it should be noted that there are more than two sides to this debate. There exists yet another group of studies that suggest race has a more select impact on juvenile justice processes and varies accordingly. For instance, more recent studies suggest that race is context specific and interacts with a number of other variables to produce differential juvenile justice outcomes (Pope & Feyerherm, 1990b).

Thus, issues surrounding the impact of race on juvenile justice processes are more complex than once thought. It is not simply a question of whether black and white youths are sanctioned differently. Rather, it is more specifically a question of determining how race interacts throughout various stages of the juvenile justice process. However, it is the more recent state level empirical assessments of the impact of race that more thoroughly explore its interactive effects with other legal and extra-legal factors on juvenile justice processes.

Race and Juvenile Justice Processing

Whereas, it has been difficult to moniter and critically evaluate police decision making relative to juveniles, the tracking of youths once they have entered the system following arrest can be painstakingly done. More specifically, cases may be traced from the point of arrest through the dispositional stage. For instance, Johnson and Secret (1990) used juvenile court statistics data from Nebraska for the years 1982 through 1987 to examine the influence of race on detention, petition, adjudication and dispositional decision making. Johnson and Secret (1990) found that black juveniles were more likely than whites to be detained. Moreover, blacks were two to three times more likely, than comparable white juveniles, to have a petition filed against them. While Johnson and Secret found that whites were more likely to be adjudicated guilty, blacks received more severe sentences than did whites. Their research also revealed an amplification effect of race. That is, Johnson and Secret noticed significant interaction effects between race, detention, and the petition decision at various points in time. Thus, it would appear that juveniles, who are detained, are more likely to have a petition filed against them. However, if race contributed to the detention decision and the detention decision influences the filing of a petition, then it is possible that the effects of detention will influence judicial decisions throughout. This would suggest that race is impacting decisions throughout the juvenile justice process.

Similar results were observed using multijurisdictional data from the state of Michigan. In particular, Bynum et al., (1993) found that detention decisions were influenced by race and socioeconomic status. Black juveniles were more likely than whites to be detained. Moreover, Bynum et al., commented on the apparent cumulative effects of detention on later juvenile justice decision making. In brief, youth who were detained were more likely to have petitions filed, receive formal treatment and be adjudicated (Bynum et al., 1993).

Using juvenile justice system records for 1983 Fagen et al., (1987) examined extra-legal factors and their impact on apprehension, detention, prosecutorial charging, adjudication, probation and final disposition. Although it was suggested that type of counsel (public defender) may explain why black juveniles are more often adjudicated than whites, Fagen et al., (1987) found that minority youth adjudicated for minor offenses were sentenced to correctional facilities more often than their white counterparts. Thus, Fagen et al., (1987) concluded that race influenced juvenile justice decision making. This was found in the decisions to apprehend, detain, adjudicate, and sentencing practices of the juvenile justice system.

Similarly, Bishop and Frazier (1988) examined case records from the state of Florida over a three year period. Specifically they examined the impact of legal and extra-legal variables on court referral, intake, detention, and adjudication. They concluded that while the impact of legal factors was pronounced, race also influenced decisions.

In summary, more recent state level assessments of juvenile justice show that minority youth are over-represented. Moreover, these studies show that while legal variables impact juveniles justice processes, race also influences decision making. It should be noted that most of the aforementioned studies do not suggest that minority over-representation in the juvenile justice system is caused by discrimination. These studies merely showed that race was a factor in juvenile justice decision making. However, they fall short of determining motives for the racial patterns described throughout the juvenile justice process.

On the other hand, there are those who postulate that minority juvenile over-representation is reflective of the volume and seriousness of crime committed by youths of color. Their position seems to contradict information contained in nationwide self-reported delinquency data.

Self-reported delinquency studies consist of asking youths about their law violating behavior over a specific period of time. That is, youths are asked to report their involvement in illegal activities over the previous twelve months. Data derived from self-report studies usually contradict information contained in official crime statistics. In short, self-report data suggest that delinquency is more widespread than is reported in official statistics. Youths from various social backgrounds and races report involvement in at least one violation of the law, although most of these violations are petty and/or status type offenses (Flowers, 1990). That is, official statistics show delinquency to be a lower class phenomenon, whereas, self-report delinquency studies shows that youths from all walks of life have at some point, engaged in illegal behavior.

Nonetheless, official statistics have primarily been used to assess the level of crime that occurs in American society. The following discussion focuses upon the extent of crime, especially crime among minority youths, as measured by the Uniform Crime Reports.

The Uniform Crime Report

In order to explore whether minority youths commit more crimes than majority youths, there has to be an examination of the indices of crime. The Uniform Crime Report (UCR) is the most commonly used set of official statistics used to examine reported crime. The UCR consists of arrest data compiled by the Federal Bureau of Investigation (FBI) and has been published on an annual basis since the early 1930's. The data compiled by the FBI are derived from more than fifteen thousand law enforcement agencies nationwide that voluntarily report crimes brought to their attention. However, the statistics compiled by the FBI are summary data on reported crime and are not incident-based statistics (however, the FBI is currently phasing in the newer National Incident-Based Reporting System, the NIBERS). This will be illuminated as a shortcoming later when our discussion focuses upon limitations of the Uniform Crime Report.

The UCR is divided into Part I and Part II offenses. Part I offenses include murder and nonnegligent manslaughter, forcible rape, robbery, aggravated assault, burglary, larceny-theft, motor vehicle theft, and arson. Part II offenses are inclusive of less serious offenses such as other assaults, forgery and counterfeiting, fraud, embezzlement, stolen property (buying, receiving, and possessing), vandalism, weapons (carrying, possessing), prostitution and commercialized vice, sex offenses (except forcible rape, and prostitution), drug abuse violations, gambling, offenses against family and children, driving under the influence, liquor law violations, drunkeness, disorderly conduct, vagrancy, all other offenses (except traffic), suspicion, curfew, and loitering violations, runaways, and truancy.

There are several concerns and limitations regarding the usage of the UCR as a depiction of crime trends. First, it is important to remember that the UCR contains data on crimes reported to the police and does not reflect the actual number of crimes committed, solved or suspects found guilty (Savitz, 1978). It should be noted that the UCR is a non-weighted index of crime. That is, as a summary index it does not distinguish serious crime from less serious offenses. All crimes are treated equal. Thus, when it is reported that the UCR shows an increase in criminal activity for a given year, it is not often shown where the increase occurred. However, given that the majority of offenses committed are not the most serious offenses such as murder, rape and/or robbery (Savitz, 1978), it is likely that the reported increase reflect changes in the commission of less serious offenses.

Moreover, the number of arrests does not accurately reflect the number of persons arrested. A large volume of juvenile crime is committed by a small percentage of juveniles (Cernkovich Giordano & Pugh, 1985). These more chronic offenders may be arrested multiple times during the course of a given year. However, this will not be captured in the UCR. Thus, the number of arrests does not reflect the number of persons arrested.

The UCR is also inhibited by reporting trends and police practices. For instance, motor vehicle theft tends to be one of the more reported offenses to the police, whereas it is estimated that approximately three times as many rapes occur than are reported (Siegel, 1992). Mann (1993) also suggests that victims of robbery, burglary and/or larceny may view the crime as trivial especially if the amount taken is small and may therefore not report the crime. Additionally, Mann indicates that persons who have had negative experiences with the police, particularly minorities, are less likely to report crimes to the police. The reasons why victims may not report an offense are many; but regardless of the reason, the UCR contains only offenses reported and not those unreported to the police.

Police reporting practices also affect data contained in the UCR. In particular, police presence and discretion can influence whether an incident is recorded and how the crime is categorized. Higher crime rates in urban areas reflect the larger police presence in such areas (Hagan, 1993). Moreover, through police discretion officers determine whether a complaint is worth filing in a particular case. In cases where the victim is of lower social status, officers may be less willing to record an incident compared to instances where the complainant is a person of higher social standing (Grove, Hughes, & Geerken, 1985).

Finally, it should be understood that the UCR records crimes through use of a hierarchical rule. That is, only the most serious offense committed during an illegal act is included in the UCR. The fact that it is a non-incidence based measure means that the other elements of an illegal (*less serious crimes committed while in commission of a more serious crime*) act are not recorded. Although several crimes may have been committed during one particular incident, only the most serious offense will be included in the UCR. Moreover, incident-based data provide more details of offenses and may be superior to UCR data.

CRIME AMONG MINORITY JUVENILES

Examination of the Uniform Crime Report for 1989 shows that 11,224,528 arrests were made. Approximately 16% of those arrested (N = 1,740,461) were juveniles. In particular, Table 1 shows that 69.5% of juvenile arrests in 1989 were white, 28.1% black, 1% American Indian or Alaskan Native and 1.4% Asian or Pacific Islander. It is unfortunate that an analysis of Hispanic arrest trends cannot be performed because the Uniform Crime Report (UCR) does not include Hispanic as a racial/ethnic category in their juvenile data collection efforts. Therefore, our examination will be restricted to whites, blacks, American Indians and Asians.

While the majority of youths arrested in 1989 were white, the numbers of black juveniles arrested are higher than should be given their proportion in the youthful aged population. Thus, black juveniles are over-represented in the arrest statistics. Proponents of the non-discriminatory criminal justice system assert that minority youths are over-represented in the juvenile justice system because of their criminal behaviors and not as a result of discriminatory practices by elements of the criminal justice system.

Analysis of the arrests of juveniles in 1989 charged with Part I offenses displayed in Table 1 appears to lend support to the argument that black juveniles commit more serious criminal offenses than whites. Larger percentages of black juveniles were arrested for murder and/or nonnegligent manslaughter and robbery than white juveniles. On the other hand, larger percentages of whites were arrested for aggravated assault, burglary, larceny-theft, motor vehicle theft, and arson. However, a larger percentage of black juveniles (53.5%) were arrested for violent offenses than white juveniles (44.8%).

Inter-group comparisons between black and white juveniles reveal that the top eight offenses for whites for 1989 were alcohol related offenses, arson, runaway, vandalism, burglary, curfew violations, larceny-theft, and overall property crime whereas; the top eight offenses for blacks were robbery, gambling, murder and/or non-negligent manslaughter, rape, drug abuse,

Table 1. Uniform Crime Report—Arrests Under 18 Total Arrest Distribution by Race, 1989.

Offense Charged	*Total*	*% White*	*% Black*	*% American Indian*	*% Asian*
Total	1,740,461	69.5	28.1	1.0	1.4
Murder & Nonnegligent Manslaughter	2,202	37.0	61.2	.5	1.3
Forcible Rape	4,696	49.3	49.1	.3	.8
Robbery	30,776	32.7	65.7	.3	1.2
Aggravated Assault	46,899	52.6	45.6	.7	1.0
Burglary	113,489	74.3	23.2	1.0	1.6
Larceny/Theft	359,206	71.6	25.4	1.2	1.8
Motor Vehicle Theft	74,658	55.2	41.7	1.1	2.0
Arson	6,349	82.3	16.0	.9	.8
Violent Crime	84,573	44.8	53.5	.6	1.1
Property Crime	553,702	70.0	27.0	1.2	1.8
Crime Index Total	638,275	66.7	30.5	1.1	1.7
Other Assaults	112,427	58.7	38.9	.8	1.6
Forgery/Fraud	15,534	68.0	29.9	.6	1.4
Stolen Property	35,347	54.5	43.8	.6	1.1
Vandalism	97,188	80.0	18.1	.7	1.1
Weapons	31,541	57.6	40.7	.5	1.3
Sex Offenses	14,876	68.5	29.9	.7	.9
Drug Abuse	89,900	50.5	48.5	.4	.6
Gambling	952	26.8	64.2	—	9.0
Alcohol	149,769	93.1	4.6	1.6	.6
All Non-traffic	252,360	69.1	28.4	.8	1.7
Curfew	64,922	72.8	24.8	.8	1.9
Runaway	129,585	81.1	15.8	1.2	1.8

Source: Uniform Crime Reports, 1989.

aggravated assault, stolen property, and overall violent crime. This inter-group analysis shows that black juveniles were arrested for more serious and/or violent offenses than white juveniles. For example, consider that the percentage of black youths arrested for robbery (65.7%) is more than twice the percentage of white youths arrested for robbery (32.7%). However, Coramae Mann (1993) points that inter-group comparisons between racial groups identified in the UCR does not reveal the true essence of criminal behaviors among minorities. More specifically, Mann (1993) suggests that studies of minority crime, that also draw upon inter-group analysis, demonstrate an emphasis on certain types of crime that may be reflective of researcher and/or public interest, but are not always indicative of the most frequent crimes committed by members of minority groups. Rather, Mann (1993) suggests that intra-group analysis offers a more accurate depiction of criminal behaviors and trends among minority groups.

Table 2 displays juvenile arrest data derived from the 1989 Uniform Crime Report through an intra-group analysis. In particular, Table 2 shows the top ten offenses for which white, black, Native American, and Asian youths were arrested. Thus, comparisons can be made relative to the frequency of the types of crimes for which the aforementioned groups were arrested.

When the data are displayed in this manner a different picture emerges. First, it should be noted that the last row of statistics displayed in Table 2 shows that Part I offenses account for less than half of the arrests among each of the groups. While Asians were the highest with 42.9% of their arrests attributed to violent offenses, less than half of the Asians arrested were charged with violent offenses. Thus, the more serious types of crimes that the general public fears most, do not constitute the majority of offenses for which juveniles were arrested. This point is also made in self-reported delinquency statistics.

The majority of juveniles arrested (within each of the racial groups) were charged with Part II crimes or less serious offenses. In fact, intra-group analysis reveals that violent offenses account for rather small percentages of arrests among juveniles. Among white juveniles, violent offenses accounted for 4.9% of their arrests. Blacks were the highest, whereby 9.3% of black juveniles arrested were charged with violent offenses. American Indians were lowest with only 2.9% of their arrests attributed to violent offenses. While these data still show that arrests for violent offenses are highest among black juveniles, it perhaps more accurately reflects the frequency of arrest for such acts. Moreover, there exist socio-historical reasons that yield insight into this higher level of violence exhibited among younger blacks. This will be further explored following the conclusion of our intra-group examination of crime.

Further examination of Table 2 shows that the largest within-group proportions of white, black, American Indian and Asian arrests were for larceny-theft offenses. In fact, the groups seem comparable on their tendencies to be arrested for larceny-theft. The top offenses for which white juveniles were arrested include larceny-theft, non-traffic related offenses, alcohol offenses, running away from home, and burglary. Black juveniles were arrested most

Table 2. Within Racial Group Percentages of the Uppermost 1989 Arrest Offenses for Juveniles.

Offense	*% White*	*Offense*	*% Black*	*Offense*	*% Native American*	*Offense*	*% Asian*
Larceny	21.3	Larceny	18.6	Larceny	26.4	Larceny	26.0
Non-Traffic	14.4	Non-Traffic	14.7	Alcohol	14.8	Non-Traffic	17.5
Alcohol	11.5	Other Assaults	8.9	Non-Traffic	11.4	Runaway	9.2
Runaway	8.7	Drug Abuse	8.9	Runaway	9.6	Other Assaults	7.3
Burglary	7.0	Motor Vehicle	6.4	Burglary	6.9	Burglary	7.1
Vandalism	6.4	Burglary	5.3	Other Assaults	5.6	Motor Vehicle	5.9
Other Assaults	5.5	Agg. Assault	4.4	Motor Vehicle	4.7	Curfew	4.9
Curfew	3.9	Runaway	4.2	Vandalism	4.3	Vandalism	4.2
Drug Abuse	3.8	Robbery	4.1	Curfew	3.3	Alcohol	3.2
Motor Vehicle	3.4	Stolen Property	3.2	Drug Abuse	2.3	Drug Abuse	2.3

Source: Uniform Crime Reports 1989.

often for larceny-theft, non-traffic related offenses, other assaults, drug abuse, and motor vehicle theft. The largest percentages of American Indians were arrested for larceny-theft, alcohol offenses, non-traffic related offenses, running away from home and burglary; whereas, the largest percentages of Asians arrested were charged with larceny-theft, non traffic related offenses, running away from home, other assaults, and burglary.

The intra-group analysis of arrest trends suggests the groups are more comparable in the commission of offenses that lead to their arrest than the inter-group comparisons generally displayed in the UCR. These intra-group data show that white, American Indian, and Asian juveniles are perhaps more comparable in the commission of illegal acts that lead to their arrest than black juveniles. However, the differences in the proportion of group members who are arrested for certain offenses are not as large as those depicted in the inter-group comparisons. For instance, Table 1 showed that black youths constituted 65.7% of the juveniles arrested for robbery; intra-group analysis showed that robbery accounted for 4.1% of the black juveniles arrested in 1989. Moreover, larceny-theft was the alleged offense that accounted for most of the arrests among white, black, American Indian and Asian juveniles. Thus, the groups appear to be more similar in the types of crime alleged that lead to arrest via intra-group analysis than inter-group comparisons. This would suggest that race as well as other social factors (e.g., urban residency, social class, unemployment, etc.) operate in a manner that makes the illegal behaviors of youth of color more visible than others. Thus, their disproportionate numbers in the juvenile justice system are reflective of a number of social factors that place them at a higher risk of arrest than others.

The prevalence of violence in the black community is one force that makes the indiscretions of minority youth more visible. Crime tends to be an urban phenomenon. One popular theory used by some social scientists to explain the higher levels of violence found in some urban and poor communities is the subculture of violence thesis. However, others (Hawkins, 1986; Mann, 1993; Silberman, 1979; and Staples, 1975) believe that the higher incidences of violence in the black community reflects the social and historical experiences of the group.

Proponents of the former believe there exists a subculture of violence in many minority, urban, and poor neighborhoods that encourages a lifestyle of violence through socialization processes (Wolfgang & Ferracuti, 1967; Comer, 1985). More specifically, Comer (1985) points to the following subcultural analysis of black violence.

> In reaction to failure, the most vibrant and reactive often become disrupted and violent in and out of schools, both individually and in groups or gangs. Neighborhoods and communities of adequately functioning families are then overwhelmed by the reactive and most troubled individuals and families. Models of violence and other troublesome behavior for children abound in relatives, friends, and neighbors unsuccessful in previous generations (p. 80).

Thus, for Comer, at least the subculture of violence is reflective of failure and despair. It seems similar to Albert Cohen's strain theory whereby frustrated youths lash-out at society because of their inability to compete successfully for society's valuable resources. However, there are several concerns regarding the subcultural violence thesis. First, and perhaps foremost, is the inability of researchers to provide adequate documentation that such a subculture exists (Haft-Picker, 1980). Moreover, the theory is not empirically testable (Hawkins, 1983).

However, social scientists who point to the socio-historical experiences of blacks in America often gain insight into the higher level of violence found among the group. These social scientists conduct research inclusive of the social, economic and political conditions that may propel black youths towards violence. Black Psychologist, Alvin Poussaint (1983) argues that "Many of the problems in the black community are related to institutional racism, which fosters a chronic lack of black self-respect, predisposing many poor blacks to behave destructively and with uncontrollable rage" (p. 163).

In addition, research conducted by Blau and Blau (1982), Robert Sampson (1987) and Wiltz (1985) identify ways in which structural inequality, unemployment, and poverty influence rates of offending among blacks. For instance, in an analysis of violence committed by blacks, Sampson (1987) observed that black male unemployment impacted family dissolution which, in turn, predicted robbery and homicides among black juveniles.

Moreover, similar factors interact in such a manner that marginalization, and even isolation, are enhanced among youth residing in many inner city areas. This in part, contributes to the attractiveness of juvenile gang membership among adolescents. However, gangs are not a new phenomena, they have existed for decades in many poor urban communities. In addition, it should be understood that not all crime committed by youths is gang related. Yet, youth gangs, and gang related illegal activities have become a focal concern of law enforcement officials across the country.

Since the earlier gang research of the 1930's, research has consistently concluded that the gangs of today are much more violent than the gangs first studied in Chicago (Miller, 1982; Bensinger, 1984; Kornblum, 1987). However, it should be noted that the media presents an overestimated and distorted image of gangs and gang related activities (Harris, 1985). Nonetheless, the presence of gangs in urban communities contribute to the violence that occurs at the local level. One factor that can propel gang membership is fear of victimization. Campbell (1984) noted that many of the Puerto Rican girls she studies joined fighting gangs as a result of a perceived need for protection. Thus, becoming a gang member offered protection in the sense that they were the family who would protect their members from harm and/or offer retaliation against those who challenged them.

Then again, non-fighting gangs have become involved in illegal money-making activities where violence may be needed to conduct business. These entrepreneurial gangs may become involved in a quasi-mafia styled organization in order to make money from illegal drug and other activities (Taylor, 1990). However, violence is not a necessary pattern in their business affairs. Moreover, National Crime Survey data does not show an increase in offenses committed by multiple offenders between 1978 and 1987. An increase of offenses by multiple offenders would be an indication of gang activity. However, no increase has been officially documented. Thus, while media and others (local politicians) have exacerbated the gang phenomenon, there is little evidence that the problem is as widespread as indicated.

Gangs and gang membership were introduced as one plausible factor that may explain the higher incidence of violence perpetuated by black juveniles. However, official crime data does not show that gangs in and of themselves are responsible for the higher level of violence found in the black community. Moreover, examination of previous research suggests that social, political, and economic factors operate in a manner that further marginalize black youth and contribute to an escalation of violence among them. Thus, it remains to be seen whether an actual subculture of violence can be shown to exist, or the socio-historical experiences of blacks as a whole better explain patterns of violence found among black youths.

DELINQUENCY TREATMENT AND PREVENTION

There has been an increase over the last ten years in the number of juveniles placed in some form of correctional facility. There are primarily six types of facilities that house juveniles. These include: (1) detention centers—secure holding facilities used to detain juveniles awaiting final disposition or placement; (2) Training schools—long-term secure facilities that house juveniles who have been adjudicated delinquent; (3) Diagnostic centers—short holding facilities that evaluates adjudicated juveniles for appropriate custody level assignments; (4) Shelters—short term nonsecure community based facilities holding less serious offenders; (5) Camps/Farms—long-term facilities holding adjudicated juveniles in either secure or non-secure environments where youth enhancement/behavioral modification programs are implemented; (6) Halfway houses/Group homes—nonsecure or less secured community based facilities that treat juveniles through continued interaction within the community.

One of the primary multicultural concerns is that youth of color are placed more often in public and secured facilities such as the aforementioned detention centers, and or training schools such as boot camps than their white counterparts. Public facilities are more likely to be designated secure facilities that house youths adjudicated for delinquency offenses whereas, private facilities are more likely to house juveniles sentenced for status offenses or neglected youths. Nationwide, there are more than 11,000 facilities that can house juveniles (this is inclusive of adult jails). The majority of these institutions are public facilities. However, both private and public facilities process more than 800,000 juveniles annually (OJJDP, 1990). Moreover, the majority of youths taken into custody are held in public facilities, and most of these are short-term detention holdings. It should also be noted that the majority of youths detained are youths of color.

This short-term detention of youths of color more often than majority youths, is particularly troublesome given their disproportionate numbers in the overall system. Moreover, if the detention decision is a racially biased decision it has further negative impacts of the disposition decision. That is, detained youths are more likely to receive more severe dispositions than youths who are not detained. This may contribute to the disproportionate out-of-home placements among minority youths. Consider that:

> In 1989, for the first time, minorities accounted for more than half (52%) of all juveniles in public and private facilities. Between 1985 and 1989, the proportion of minority youth in public custody by race (black, Hispanic, or other) increased 13 per cent. By 1989 black youth represented the largest group of youths in public facilities. Hispanic youths experienced a four per cent increase, whereas the proportion of white youths detained declined 13% between 1985 and 1989 (OJJDP, 1990).

The increased detention of youths of color may have further detrimental consequences for them as justice processing proceeds. That is, since detention occurs relatively early in the processing of juveniles, the biased decision to detain them is amplified at other stages throughout the process. Youths who are detained often receive more severe dispositions than juveniles who are not detained. Hence, the detention decision further exposes minority youths to more restrictive sanctions than white juveniles (Bynum, et al., 1993).

Our discussion of culturally sensitive system responses to delinquency begins with a theoretical overview of classical and positivist explanations of the causes of crime. It is important to start with an examination of classical and positivist approaches to criminal behavior because prevention strategies should be premised on the causes of delinquent behavior (Albanese, 1993).

Classical and positivist theory vary in their explanations of criminal behavior. Classical criminologists argue that humans are free willed and rational beings. As such, motives for their behavior are governed by attempts to seek pleasure and avoid pain. Thus, Cesare Beccaria suggests that given alternatives, humans would rather seek pleasure than pain. Jeremy Bentham expanded upon Beccaria's work and suggests that laws set proscribed punishments for crime in proportion to the act committed. This would likely assist in deterrence of more serious offenses since the punishment for the more serious crimes could result in more punishment (pain) inflicted upon the perpetrator.

On the other hand, positivists such as Cesare Lombroso, asserted that crime is produced by factors outside of the individual's control. These factors can be biological, social/environmental, and/or psychological. Thus, crime is caused by multiple factors over which the individual has little or no control. However, delinquency prevention strategies based upon this approach presume that these factors can be eliminated or the response to them changed. Programs that seek to rehabilitate offenders have been primarily based upon a positivist approach.

There are primarily two types of delinquency programs; primary prevention programs and secondary or rehabilitative programs. Primary prevention programs seek to stop delinquency before it occurs or becomes a serious problem. Secondary or rehabilitative programs seek to intervene in the lives of youths who have engaged in officially reported delinquent behavior with the goal of stopping the behavior and preventing escalation to more serious delinquent acts.

Albanese (1993) identifies three main issues to be addressed relative to delinquency prevention programs. In particular, Albanese (1993) recognizes that:

> (1) prevention programs be based on the causes of delinquency, (2) primary and secondary prevention programs may require different types of strategies and (3) people commit crimes for different reasons, so it may be that a single prevention strategy will not work for everyone.

To that end, Hawkins, Pastor, Bell and Morrison (1980) developed a typology of twelve delinquency prevention strategies. Each strategy is related to a theory of delinquency causation:

A. *Deterrence* strategies presumes that delinquency is resultant of perception of a low degree of risk or difficulty associated with committing delinquent acts.... They seek to increase the cost and lower the benefit of criminal acts through limiting opportunities and minimizing incentives for engaging in criminal behavior.

B. *Education/Skill Development* strategies presume that delinquency results from a lack of knowledge or skills needed to exist in society without violating laws. This strategy seeks to provide youths with personal skills than can help them lead delinquency free lives.

C. *Social Network Development* strategies assume delinquency stems from weak attachments to conforming members of society. They attempt to increase contacts and interactions with nondeviant others.

D. *Power Enhancement* strategies assume that delinquency stems from a lack of power or control over environmental factors. These strategies attempt to increase the youth's ability to influence or control their environment.

E. *Activities or Recreation* strategies suggest that delinquency is the result of idle time the youth has. They seek to provide nondelinquent activities as alternatives.

F. *Role Development/Role Enhancement* strategies presume that delinquency results from a lack of opportunity to engage in legitimate activities as a source of gratification. They attempt to provide such opportunities.

G. *Criminal Influence Reduction* strategies suggest delinquency stems from interactions with individuals who either directly or indirectly promote participation in delinquent acts. These strategies seek to reduce the influence of those who may encourage delinquent behavior.

H. *Economic Resource* strategies assumes that delinquency stems from a lack of adequate resources at one's disposal. These strategies attempt to provide such resources as a method to alleviate delinquent behavior.

I. *Clear and Consistent Social Expectations* strategies suggest that delinquency results from conflicting and/or confusing demands placed upon youths by legitimate institutions and organizations. These strategies seek to increase the level of consistency in expectations from these institutions and organizations.

J. *Psychological/Mental Health* strategies suggest that delinquency stems from intrinsically maladaptive or pathological conditions. This strategy seeks to alter such conditions.

K. *Abandonment of Legal Control/Social Tolerance* strategies suggest that delinquency stems from social responses that label the juvenile's behavior as delinquent. These strategies try to remove the delinquent label from certain behaviors.

L. *Biological/Psychological* strategies suggest that delinquency stems from physiological, biopsychiatric or biological conditions. These strategies attempt to eliminate, control or weaken these conditions.

Although a number of these strategies have been utilized over the years, Trojanowicz and Morash (1992) note that many programs do not have a clear theoretical basis. Moreover, there has been a tendency to combine primary with secondary intervention strategies and overlap various combinations of the aforementioned strategies. Thus, it is not always clear whether such programs were intent upon preventing delinquency or rehabilitating the offender. Yet, in terms of youths of color, many of the aforementioned strategies lacked a multicultural component whereby youths of color could feel comfortable with the program and other participants.

These primary and secondary prevention strategies should be modified to operate within the social and cultural system in which they exist. For example, many of the substance abuse programs (e.g., Alcoholics Anonymous) do not initially consider that drinking patterns vary among racial/ethnic groups. In fact, groups vary in terms of how they perceive and react towards alcohol. Yet, only a limited model of alcohol treatment is offered. This contributed to a lower number of minorities seeking treatment for the disease of alcoholism. This lack of cultural sensitivity on the part of Alcoholics Anonymous (once identified as a problem), contributed to the establishment of more varied and culturally specific treatment programs in minority urban communities.

Delinquency prevention or rehabilitation programs must also be made aware of the culture of the clientele they are to serve. For instance, they should understand that much of the destructive and violent behavior to which a number of young urban males subscribe is actually a coping strategy. That this over-emphasis on masculinity is associated with what has been described as playing it "cool." The slang, dress, verbal abusiveness, baggy pants, untied shoes, defiant attitudes, threatening looks and provocative walking exhibited by black males is an attempt to display their pride, coolness and/or self-esteem (Foster, 1986). These are the obtainable definitions of masculinity to which many urban males aspire. This focus on masculinity has been attributed in part, to the emasculation of black males within American society. In short, the inability of black males to serve as providers, protectors and in otherwise traditional male roles contributed to a re-definition of manhood. To many of these young males, the aforementioned is a definition of masculinity that a poor male can attain.

Attempts to offer youths of color non-delinquent activity alternatives, skill development, power enhancement and/or other delinquency prevention without knowledge of cultural specifics may further alienate diverse group members. While a number of programs designed to assist black youths have used an Afrocentric perspective (a cultural ideology based on unity stemming from African philosophy), not all successful programs fully embrace this particular model. Many of the successful programs such as the The Door, The Urban League's Black Male Responsibility Program and mentoring programs seek to provide impulse control, life skills, education, counseling and linkages with a black culture to which many African American youths feel separated from (Majors, Tyler, Peden, & Hall, 1994).

However, it is likely these programs would not be as successful had they not been sensitive to the needs of the group they intend to serve. Mentoring programs are especially interesting given the informal expansion of black and other urban families to include non-blood related family members. This suggests that persons outside of the traditional nuclear family may be capable of reaching and impacting the lives of urban youths. Yet, it should be understood that programs must vary because the reasons youths commit criminal acts vary (Albanese, 1993). The lack of culturally diverse delinquency prevention and treatment programs ignores the reality of the previous statement.

SUMMARY

This chapter examined multicultural issues relevant to juvenile justice. More specifically, this chapter focused upon: racial/ethnic disparity in juvenile justice processing and sanction; cross-cultural comparisons of rates of offending among Anglo, African-American, Hispanic, Asian, and Native American youths; and alternative culturally sensitive system responses that could enable the juvenile justice system to better address the needs of minority youths. It has been the goal of the juvenile court to address the needs of youths appearing before it. This includes youths who have been either neglected or abused, and/or status, and criminal offenders. Because it is the role of the court to act in the "best interest" of the child (*and not necessarily punish the youth*), the juvenile court operates within a substantive model of justice. This model enables the court to consider a youth's particular background and other social circumstances when considering treatment. It is the inclusion of these social characteristics that enables the court to tailor its responses to meet the specific needs of adolescents appearing before it.

However, it has been suggested that the waiving of juvenile offenders to adult courts and their exposure to the death penalty is evidence that the court has become more punitive. Moreover, this more punitive philosophy when combined with a substantive model of justice decision-making, and perception that minority youths are in need of more supervision and control than other youths contributes to the over-representation of minority youths within the juvenile justice system.

Yet, there are primarily two schools of thought regarding the over-representation of minority youths in the juvenile justice system. For instance, one suggests that minorities are over-represented because they commit more crimes or more serious offenses and/or possess attitudes and behaviors that contribute to their more frequent exposure to the juvenile justice system. Supporters of this school of thought draw heavily from functionalist/consensus theorists who assert that the purpose of law is to differentiate legal from illegal behavior. Moreover, consensus theorists suggest there is widespread agreement throughout society in terms of what constitutes illegal behavior and that the law is applied equitably to everyone within society. Thus, if minorities are over-represented in the criminal justice system, it is because of the actions of the group.

However, the other school of thought regarding the over-representation of minorities suggest their disproportionate representation reflect biases within the criminal justice system and society as a whole. Supporters of this approach lean towards theoretical orientations that encompass a conflict/labeling approach. In short, conflict theorists assert that the legal system best represents the values and interests of the elites within a society. That is, not only are the laws applied differentially (with poorer individuals receiving more scrutiny and punishment), but definitions of illegal and legal behavior is primarily decided by these members of the ruling class who look out for their own best interests in their inactment of laws.

In addition, labeling theorists suggest that it is the poor or more marginal members of a society who are more likely than others to have their deviance detected, labeled, and sanctioned. Because, in American society blacks and other persons of color are relegated to a lower social status than whites, labeling theorists argue that members of these groups are more likely to have contact with the criminal justice system.

Research on disparate treatment of minorities in the criminal justice system has yielded mixed results. Earlier research conducted in the decades of the 1960s and 1970s that found biases were often highly criticized, whereas, studies that found no effects of race and other social variables on sanctions were less scrutinized. However, more current state level juvenile justice assessments (*performed because of OJJDP's mandate that requires states to assess their juvenile justice systems for over-representation of minorities*) overcame many of the shortcomings of earlier research. In particular, these state level assessments examined multiple decision-making points throughout the justice process and implemented statistical controls so as to detect the separate effects of social variables on juvenile justice processes and sanctions. The majority of these assessments indicates that social factors such as race impact juvenile justice processes and sanctions.

Yet, proponents of the consensus model of justice persist that over-representation of minorities in the criminal justice system occurs because of the actions of members of the group. Therefore, data from the Uniform Crime Reports for 1989 was examined in an attempt to determine whether minority juveniles were disproportionately arrested. However, the UCR could not provide direct information on the amount of crimes committed across racial groups. The UCR contains data on the numbers of arrests. It only reports deviant acts reported to the police. Moreover, it does not depict convictions, only the numbers of youths arrested.

Initial examination of the UCR shows that the majority of crimes committed by juveniles are the less serious Part II Index offenses. The crimes the public fears most, occur less often. However, inter-racial group comparisons indicate that African-American youths commit more violent offenses than others. Notwithstanding, intra-racial group analysis of the same data revealed that these crimes constitute a small percentage of arrests for African-Americans. Moreover, intra-racial group comparisons suggest that Anglo, African-American, Native American, and Asian youths commit similar types of offenses. However, it is the youths of color who are over-represented in official arrest statistics. Yet, the question remains to be answered. Are African-Americans and other minorities over-represented because they commit more serious crimes and/or criminal acts? The fact that a larger percentage of African-Americans were arrested for violent offenses was in part explained by the environmental factors and socio-historical circumstances of the group. Gang membership can become attractive for many of these young males because it offers them some social support. The level of violence found in many urban black communities has lead some criminologists to believe that there exists a subculture of violence in these communities that defy nullification and treatment. However, the subculture of violence hypothesis has yet to be proven and there are some programs in poor urban communities that lessen the involvement of black youths in gangs and violent crime. Unfortunately, the question of whether minorities are over-represented in juvenile justice because of their own actions cannot be answered empirically. However, more recent state level assessments suggest that social characteristics of youths such as race, impact juvenile justice processes and sanctions.

In regard to delinquency treatment, and prevention one of the primary concerns articulated by minority group members is access to treatment alternatives. There is a great concern that their children (those who commit delinquent acts) will be institutionalized and not recommended for community level alternative treatment programs. Reports published on the characteristics of youths held in custody show that minority juveniles are disproportionately placed out of home more often than their white counterparts. Moreover, police responses to minority youth often differ from their interactions with majority youths. This seems to at least suggest that these youths will be brought to the station for further questioning. This entry level interaction is important because it is at this phase that the potential amplification of race may begin. The end result of this continued amplification of race is the out of home placement, and/or incarceration of minority youths. Minority youth like many others can be found in primary prevention programs or secondary rehabilitative programs. However there is concern that minority youths may not be able to identify with the programs to which they have been referred. Culturally sensitive programs attempt to understand who the youth feels about their particular culture and attempts to link that adolescent with persons and/or resources that strengthen that bond. Although Afrocentrific programs were discussed, not all programs beneficial to black males adopt the perspective. However, it should be understood that the primary objective of programs (*that have been successful with Black adolescents*) has been to make black youths feel proud of themselves, create an atmosphere of unity and not individualism, and expose youths to alternative non-detrimental reactions to the frustrations (particularly racism) they encounter in their daily lives. Moreover, it should be recognized that even the emphasis that young African-American males and others place on the demonstration/portrayal of masculinity or manhood suggest that they like others desire to be treated with respect. It should be further understood, especially by those providing treatment, that much of the "acting out" and even violence displayed by minority youths represent a form of coping. However, even the development of culturally sensitive delinquency treatment and prevention programs will not have a significant impact if youths of color are not diverted and/or referred for treatment.

REFERENCES

Albanese, J. (1993). *Dealing with Delinquency: The Future of Juvenile Justice.* Chicago: Nelson Hall.

Arnold, W. R. (1971). Race and ethnicity relative to other factors in juvenile court dispositions. *American Journal of Sociology, 77*(2), 211–227.

Becker, H. (1963). *The Outsiders: Studies in the Sociology of Deviance.* New York: MacMillan.

Besinger, G. (1984). Chicago youth gangs: a new old problem. *Journal of Crime and Justice, 7,* 1–6.

Bishop, D. M., & Frazier, C. S. (1988). The influence of race in juvenile justice processing. *Journal of Research in Crime and Delinquency, 25*(3), 242–263.

Bishop, D. M., & Frazier, C. S. (1990). *A study of race and juvenile justice processing in Florida.* Report, University of Florida.

Black, T. E., & Smith, C. P. (1981). A preliminary national assessment of the numbers and characteristics of juveniles processed in the juvenile justice system. Reports of the National Juvenile Justice Assessment Centers.

Blau, P., & Blau, J. (1982). The cost of inequality: Metropolitan structure and violent crime. *American Sociological Review, 47*(1), 114–129.

Bortner, M., & Reed, W. (1985). The preeminence of process: An example of refocused justice research. *Social Science Quarterly, 66*(2), 413–425.

Brown, M., Sagan, R., & Greenblatt, E. (1980). Juvenile Bindovers: 1979. Prepared for the office of Commissioner of Probation (Joseph P. Foley, Commissioner).

Bynum, T., Wordes, M., & Corley, C. (1993). *Disproportionate Representation in Juvenile Justice in Michigan: Influence of Race and Gender.* Research supported by funding from the Michigan Committee on Juvenile Justice through the office of Contract Management—Grant Management Division.

Carter, T. J. (1979). Juvenile court dispositions: A comparison of status and nonstatus offenders. *Criminology, 17*(3), 341–359.

Cernkovich, S., Giordano, P., & Pugh, M. (1985). Chronic offenders: The missing cases in self-report Delinquency research. Journal of Criminal Law and *Criminology, 76,* 705–732.

Clark, K. B. (1965). *Dark Ghetto.* New York: Harper and Row.

Cohen, L., & Kluegel, J. (1978). Determinants of juvenile court dispositions: Ascriptive and achieved factors in two metropolitan courts. *American Sociological Review, 43*(2), 162–176.

Cohen, L., & Kluegel, J. (1979). The detention decision: A study of the impact of social characteristics and legal factors in two metropolitan juvenile courts. *Social Forces, 58*(1), 146–161.

Comer, J. (1985). Black violence and public policy, in Lynn Curtis (Eds.) *American Violence and Public Policy.* New Haven: Yale University Press.

Corley, C., Bynum, T., & Wordes, M. (1993). Assessing the impact of family variables on juvenile justice processes. Paper presented at the *American Society of Criminology* meeting in Phoenix.

Corley, C., & Dickinson, B. (1993). *Disproportionate Representation and Processing of Juveniles by Race and Gender: Detroit Police Department—Ninth Precinct.* Research supported by funding from the Michigan Committee on Juvenile Justice through the office of Contract Management—Grant Management Division.

Fagen, J., Slaughter, E., & Hartstone, E. (1987). Blind justice? The impact of race on juvenile justice process. *Crime and Delinquency, 33*(2), 224–258.

Feld, B. (1988). The juvenile court meets the principle of offense: Punishment, treatment, and the difference it makes. *Boston University Law Review, 68*(5), 821–915.

Feld, B. (1990, October 4). The punitive juvenile court and the quality of procedural justice: Disjunctions between rhetoric and reality. *Crime and Delinquency, 36,* pp. 443–466.

Fisher, G., & Doyle-Martin, S. (1981). The effects of ethnic prejudice on police referrals to the juvenile court. *California Sociologist, 4*(2), 189–205.

Flowers, R. (1990). *Minorities and Criminality.* New York: Praeger.

Foster, H. (1986). Ribbin', Jivin', and Playin' the Dozens: The *Unrecognized Dilemma of Inner City Schools.* Cambridge, MA: Ballinger.

Goldman, N. (1963). The differential selection of juvenile offenders for court appearance. Washington, D.C.: National Council on Crime and Delinquency.

Griswold, D. (1978). Police discrimination: An elusive question. *Journal of Police Science and Administration, 6,* 65–66.

Grove, W., Hughes, M., & Geerken, M. (1985). Are Uniform Crime Reports a valid indicator of index crimes? An affirmative answer with minor qualifications. *Criminology, 23*(3), 451–501.

Haft-Picker, C. (1980). Beyond the subculture of violence: An evolutionary and historical approach to social control. In Newman, G. (Ed.), *Crime and Deviance: A Comparative Perspective.* Beverly Hills: Sage.

Hagan, F. (1993). *Research Methods in Criminal Justice and Criminology.* New York: MacMillan.

Harris, M. (1985). *Bikers: Birth of a Modern Day Outlaw.* London: Faber and Faber.

Hawkins, D. (1983). Black and white homicide differentials: Alternatives to an inadequate theory. *Criminal Justice and Behavior, 10*(4), 407–440.

Hawkins, D. (1986). *Homicide Among Black Americans.* Lanham, MD: University Press of America.

Hawkins, J., Pastor, P., Bell, M., & Morrison, S. (1980). *A Typology of Cause-Focused*

Strategies of Delinquency Prevention. Washington, D.C.: U.S. Government Printing Office.

Hindelang, M. (1978). Race and involvement in common law personal crimes. *American Sociological Review, 44,* 995–1014.

Hohenstein, W. F. (1969). Factors influencing the police disposition of juvenile offenders. In T. Sellin, & M. E. Wolfgang (Ed.), *Delinquency: Selected studies.* New York: John Wiley & Sons.

Horwitz, A., & Wasserman, M. (1980). Formal rationality, substantive justice, and discrimination. *Law and Human Behavior, 4*(1/2), 103–115.

Huryn, J. S. (1982). Factors in juvenile intake decisions. In V. L. Swigert (Ed.) *Law and legal process.* Sage Publications.

Johnson, J., & Secret, P. (1990). Race and juvenile court decision making revisited. *Criminal Justice Policy Review, 4*(2), 159–187.

Johnstone, J. (1981). Youth gangs and black suburbs. *Pacific Sociological Review, 24,* 355–375.

Keiter, R. (1973). Criminal or delinquent? A study of juvenile cases transferred to the criminal court. *Crime and Delinquency, 19*(4), 528–538.

Kempf, K., Decker, S., & Bing, R. (1990). *An analysis of apparent disparities in the handling of Black youth within Missouri's Juvenile Justice Systems.* Technical Report. St. Louis, University of Missouri—St. Louis.

Kornblum, W. (1987). Ganging together: helping gangs go straight. *Social Issues and Health Review, 2,* 99–104.

Kowalski, G. S., & Rickicki, J. P. (1982, January). Determinants of juvenile post-adjudication dispositions. *Journal of Research in Crime and Delinquency,* 65–83.

Kramer, J. H., & Steffensmeier, D. J. (1987). The differential detention/jailing of juveniles: A comparison of detention and non-detention courts. *Pepperdine Law Review, 5*(3), 795–807.

Lemert, E. (1951). *Social Pathology.* New York: McGraw Hill.

Lieber, M. (1992). *Juvenile justice decision making in Iowa: An analysis of the influence of race on case processing in three counties.* Technical Report. The University of Northern Iowa.

Lundman, R. (1974). Routine police arrest practices, *Social Problems, 22,* 127–141.

Lundman, R. (1978). Shoplifting and police referral: A reexamination. *Journal of Criminal Law and Criminology, 69*(3), 395–401.

Majors, R., Tyler, R., Beden, B., & Hall, R. (1994). Cool pose: A symbolic mechanism for masculine role enactment and coping by black males. In R. Majors and J. Gordon (Eds.) *The American Black Male: His Present Status and Future.* Chicago: Nelson Hall.

Mann, C. (1980). Courtroom observations of extra-legal factors in the juvenile court dispositions of runaway boys: A field study. *Juvenile and Family Court Journal, 31*(4), 43–52.

Mann, C. (1993). *Unequal Justice: A Question of Color.* Bloomington: Indiana University Press.

Marshall, I., & Thomas, C. (1983). Discretionary decision-making and the juvenile court. *Juvenile and Family Court Journal, 34,* 47–60.

McCarthy, B. R., & Smith, B. L. (1986). The conceptualization of discrimination in the juvenile justice process: The impact of administrative factors and screening decisions on juvenile court dispositions. *Criminology, 24*(1), 41–64.

Mead, A. (1973). Seriousness of delinquency, the adjudicative decision and recidivism—A longitudinal configuration analysis. *Journal of Criminal Law and Criminology, 64*(4), 478–485.

Miller, W. (1982). *Crime by Youth Gangs and Groups as a Crime Problem in Major American Cities.* Washington, D.C.: Heath.

National Council of Family Court Judges (1990). Minority youth in the juvenile justice system: A judicial response. *Juvenile and Family Court Journal, 41* (3A).

Office of Juvenile Justice and Delinquency Prevention. (1990). *Juveniles Taken Into Custody: Fiscal Year 1990 Report.* Washington, D.C.: U.S. Department of Justice.

Pawlak, E. J. (1977). Differential selection of juveniles for detention. *Journal of Research in Crime and Delinquency, 14*(2), 152–165.

Phillips, C. D., & Dinitz, S. (1982). Labelling and juvenile court dispositions: Official responses to a cohort of violent juveniles. *Sociological Quarterly, 23*(2), 267–278.

Piliavin, I., & Briar, S. (1964). Police encounters with juveniles. *American Sociological Review, 51*(1), 101–119.

Platt, A. (1969). *The Child Savers: The Invention of Delinquency.* Chicago: Chicago University Press.

Poole, E., & Regoli, R. (1980). An analysis of the determinants of juvenile court dispositions. *Juvenile and Family Court Journal, 31*(3), 23–32.

Pope, C. E., & Feyerherm, W. F. (1990a). Minority status and juvenile processing. *Criminal Justice Abstracts, 22*(2), 327–336.

Pope, C. E., & Feyerherm, W. F. (1990b). Minority status and juvenile processing. *Criminal Justice Abstracts, 22*(2), 327–336 and *22*(3), 527–542.

Poussaint, A. (1983). Black on black homicide: A psychological-political perspective, *Victimology, 8,* pp. 161–169.

President's Commission on Law Enforcement and the Administration of Justice. (1967). *The Challenge of Crime in a Free Society.* Washington, D.C.: U.S. Government Printing Office.

Quinney, R. (1970). *The social reality of crime.* Boston: Little, Brown.

Sampson, R. (1987). Urban black violence: The effect of male joblessness and family disruption. *American Journal of Sociology, 93*(2), 348–382.

Savitz, L. (1978). Official police statistics and their limitations. In L. Savitz and N. Johnson (Eds.) *Crime in Society,* New York: Wiley.

Sheldon, R. G., & Horvath, J. A. (1987). Intake processing in juvenile court: A comparison of legal and nonlegal variables. *Juvenile and Family Court Journal, 38*(3), 13–19.

Siegel, L. (1992). *Criminology.* New York: West Publishing Co.

Siegel, L., & Senna, J. (1991). *Juvenile delinquency: Theory practice and law.* St. Paul: West Publishing Co.

Silberman, C. (1979). *Criminal violence, criminal justice.* New York: Random House.

Staples, R. (1975, March). White racism, black crime and American Justice: An application of the Colonial Model to explain crime and race. *Phylon,* 14–22.

Sutherland, E., & Cressey, D. (1966). *Principles of Criminology.* New York: J.P. Lippincott Co.

Tannenbaum, F. (1938). *Crime and the Community.* New York: Columbia University Press.

Taylor, C. (1990). *Dangerous Society.* East Lansing: Michigan State University Press.

Thomas, C., & Cage, R. (1977). The effect of social characteristics on juvenile court dispositions. *Sociological Quarterly, 18,* 237–252.

Thomas, C., & Sieverdes, C. (1975). Juvenile court intake: An analysis of discretionary decision-making. *Criminology, 12*(4), 413–432.

Thompson, R., and Zingraff, M. (1981). Detecting sentencing disparity: Some problems and evidence. *American Journal of Sociology, 86*(4), 896–880.

Thornberry, T. (1979). Sentencing disparities in the juvenile justice system. *Journal of Criminal Law and Criminology, 70,* 164–171.

Trojanowicz, R., & Morash, M. (1992). *Juvenile Delinquency: Concepts and Control.* New Jersey: Englewood Cliffs.

U.S. Department of Justice (1992). *Survey of Youth in Custody, 1990.* Ann Arbor, Michigan: Inter-University Consortium for Political and Social Research.

U.S. Department of Justice (1989). *Federal Bureau of Investigation Uniform Crime Reports: Crime in the United United States.* Washington, D.C.: U.S. Government Printing Office.

U.S. Department of Justice (1987). *Federal Bureau of Investigation Uniform Crime Reports: Crime in the United United States.* Washington, D.C.: U.S. Government Printing Office.

Walter, J. D., & Ostrander, S. A. (1982). An observational study of a juvenile court. *Juvenile and Family Court Journal, 33*(3), 53–69.

Wiltz, C. (1985). *Poverty, Family Structure and Black Homicides.* Paper presented at the annual meeting of the Academy of Criminal Justice Sciences.

Wolfgang, M., & Ferracuti, F. (1967). *The Subculture of Violence.* London, England: Social Science Paperbacks.

Zatz, M. (1984). Race, ethnicity and determinate sentencing: A new dimension to an old controversy. *Criminology, 22*(2), 147–171.

CHAPTER TEN

INVISIBILITY AND MARGINALIZATION OF WOMEN OF COLOR

Helen Eigenberg and Agnes Baro

INTRODUCTION

Introductory texts are important because these texts play a crucial role in education. They provide an overview of a particular subject matter. They legitimize paradigmatic assumptions about the nature of a discipline, provide synthesized overviews of topics, familiarize students with basic concepts, establish disciplinary parameters, and review the body of knowledge associated with a discipline (Kuhn, 1974; Rothman, 1971). However, before textbooks reach students, they must be reviewed by colleagues and selected by faculty who require students to read these texts. Thus, "members of the discipline act as 'gatekeepers' for the types of knowledge incorporated into introductory textbooks" (Rothman, 1971). For all of these reasons then, empirical analyses of textbooks provide insight into the social construction of a discipline.

Prior research suggests that racial and gender bias is not uncommon in textbooks. Previous *textual* analyses reveal that racial and ethnic minorities are excluded from high school social science (Dhand, 1988) and history (Banks, 1976) texts. These biases are also evident in college textbooks in the areas of psychology (Brown, Goodwin, Hall, & Jackson-Lowman, 1985) and marriage and the family (Bryant & Coleman, 1988). Likewise, analyses of college textbooks imply that women are excluded in texts in a variety of fields including criminology (Wilson & Rigsby, 1975; Wright, 1987), sociology (Ferree & Hall, 1990; Hall, 1988), law (Erickson, 1990), and economics (Feiner & Morgan, 1990). Thus textual analyses suggest that some disciplines are constructed in ways that render women and other minorities invisible.

Introductory textbooks, however, also provide a *visual* portrayal of a discipline. Through pictures, authors and publishers are able to translate abstract concepts and data into more concrete images. For example, texts may discuss the increasing number of women entering policing as an occupation but use pictures which only display male officers. Thus, the written discussion may provide some (limited) coverage of female police officers but the pictures may reinforce the idea that policing is "men's work." Therefore, visual analyses also provide insight into the social construction of a discipline. And while the majority of research on gender and racial biases has focused on textual material, some prior research (Baro & Eigenberg, 1992; Dorworth & Henry, 1992; Ferree & Hall, 1990; Whatley, 1988) suggests that visual images in textbooks also marginalize women and people of color.

This chapter reviews the literature and argues that people of color have been marginalized in criminology. We contend that discrimination is additive and interactive and that women of color are particularly ignored in criminology because they experience many types of discrimination.[1] This chapter also asserts that visual images in textbooks reinforce traditional stereotypes about race and gender. It presents the results of our study on the visual images of women of color in introductory criminology and criminal justice textbooks by examining whether textbook illustrations provide socially constructed images of women of color which mirror social reality. We conclude by discussing ways to make women of color more visible in the discipline and argue that curriculum transformation plays an important role in achieving this goal.

RESEARCH ON THE MARGINALIZATION OF WOMEN OF COLOR

Whites in our culture, see themselves as the prevailing standard of what it looks like and means to be human. People of color are "others" who are accorded some separate meaning and space. As Adrienne Rich says, whites tend to think and act as if whiteness describes the world (1979, p. 299). It is interesting that whites have managed to retain this view in a world that is populated mostly by people of color.

With the help of scientists, academicians, and religious and political leaders, white people have constructed and maintained a vision of humanity that perpetuates racism and oppression. By making it normal to see people of color as fundamentally different, it is then quite easy to take the argument one step further and argue that "they" also are inferior. Definitions of race control how each of us think and act, and are a product of our social structure. And while race, gender, and class are experienced by all people, not all people receive similar benefit or harm because of our social organization. Our society is built upon powerful hierarchies, and if one is rich, male, and white there are benefits that generally are not available to poor, female, people of color.

These biases also are evident in scientific research. For example, criminology has failed to acknowledge its Eurocentric biases. Most of the knowledge base of the field has been developed by economically priviledged white men. There is very little literature which examines this bias, and when exclusion is discussed it most often focuses on the marginalization of African-Americans. Most literature fails to examine the invisibility of scholarship by, on, and for other minorities (e.g., Hispanics, Native-Americans, Asian-Americans).

Several authors, however, have specifically examined the exclusion of work by African-American criminologists (Barak, 1991; Caldwell & Greene, 1980; Greene, 1979; Mann, 1989; Young & Sulton, 1991). These scholars contend that there is a relatively large body of African-American literature which is generally ignored by mainstream journals and texts. In addition, these critiques also note that African-American scholars rarely serve on editorial boards of journals and that they infrequently serve on important committees in professional organizations.[2]

This same body of literature also discusses the ways in which women of color are excluded or marginalized in criminology. Barak (1991) observes that there is a particular need for a black feminist perspective which would facilitate the development of theories and the implementation of policies which are relevant to the experiences of African-American women. Other literature also suggests that criminology and criminal justice have failed to attend to the double bind experienced by minority female offenders (Caldwell & Greene, 1980; Greene, 1981; Mann, 1989; Young, 1986). Mann (1989) concludes that "little attention is devoted to the Black, Hispanic, or Native American female offender." Young (1986) states that literature on African-Americans concentrates on black men, while information about women concentrates on white women. As a result, "black women have not been perceived as a group worthy of study." (p. 322). Furthermore, Greene (1981) points out how difficult it is to find data on black, female offenders. Therefore, criminology has ignored race in general and obscured the interactive effect of race, gender and class in particular (Barak, 1991; Chambliss, 1988; Daly, 1993; Daly & Chesney-Lind, 1988; Messerschmidt, 1994; Young & Sulton, 1991).

Daly (1993) confronted this issue at the 1991 meeting of the American Society of Criminology. During a special session wherein relatively new criminologists had the opportunity to ask questions of well known theorists, Daly asked "When you are writing statements about crime—and when you are thinking about the person, the actor, or the lawbreaker, does that person have a specific class, race or gender?" (p. 66). One of the responses came from Travis Hirschi who is a well known, social control theorist. Daly reports that Hirschi said, "I really do think that the image I have is a person without any of these qualities. The offender is everyone—they have no qualities of class, race, or gender" (Daly, 1993, p. 66). Since one can not find a picture of a person without class, race, or gender in any criminology text, one wonders what "it" might look like and how a late, twentieth century social scientist came to have such a vision.

Perhaps the image that Hirschi has is a product of extreme positivism. Positivism is a way of "seeing" the world. It is based on the assumption that the scientist can and should separate himself/herself from the human world of values, politics, and emotion. The rule of positivism is that one must be absolutely neutral and in order to do so, a profound separation must occur. Daly charges that modern positivists have so distanced themselves from the real world of class, race, and gender that they can "deny the particular social relations and histories" of the people and events they study (1993, p. 65). Race, class, and gender are reduced to "variables" to be counted and they are treated as separate phenomenon and little attention is paid to their interactive effects. In other words, researchers look at relationships using race, sex, and income as variables, but they lack a complex theoretical understanding of the concepts, and they rarely examine how these variables intersect. For example, crime rates are examined by race or by class or by gender, but rarely by two or three of these variables. Thus, one can examine how race may influence crime rates but not how race and gender affect these rates. Therefore, it is difficult to determine rates of criminality and victimization for women of color. This problem is only magnified when class is also considered.

This problem also is evident in theoretical works. For example, Marxist literature too frequently ignores race and gender. Feminist literature has concentrated on the effects of gender, but it focuses on the concerns of white, middle-class women (Anzaldua, 1990; Collins, 1990, 1993; Hooks, 1981, 1989, 1990; Smith, 1982; Zinn, M., Cannon, L., Higginbotham, E., & Dill, B., 1986). In addition, women of color also are isolated from scholarship which focuses on race. Collins (1990) discusses how the literature on race often maintains a "prominent masculinist bias" (p. 8). She states that:

> The assumptions on which full group membership are based—whiteness for feminist thought, maleness for black social and political thought, and the combination for mainstream scholarship—all negate a black female reality. Prevented from becoming full insiders in any of these areas of inquiry, black women remain outsiders within, individuals whose marginality provides a distinctive angle of vision on the theories put forth by such intellectual communities (p. 12).

There is a small, but growing body of literature which examines the intersections of race, class, and gender, and this literature explores the marginalization of women of color. However, we are only just beginning to understand how difficult it is to make these intellectual connections when doing so requires dismanteling a great deal of scientific tradition within criminology.

In sum, then, our social structure determines that whiteness is the norm and that people of color are "others." As such, whites tend to believe that only "others" have race and ignore the powerful discriminatory factors in our culture that perpetuate inequality. Criminologists also have grounded their research using these same fundamental assumptions. As such, criminology, as a discipline, ignores race as a theoretical concept; however, it also ignores class and gender. Hence, women of color are marginalized and rendered invisible in the discipline. Therefore, we predict that visual images will reflect the same patterns and that women of color will lack a visual presence in introductory textbooks on crime. The following section of the chapter discusses why visual images are important and reviews other studies on images of women of color.

RESEARCH ON VISUAL IMAGES

In an important essay on the relationship between visual images and human development, Berger (1987) contends that "seeing comes before words" (p. 7) in two ways; we see before we learn to speak and what we see establishes our place in the world more profoundly than the language we learn to explain our vision. Furthermore, educational researchers express concern that the United States is one of the few countries that does not incorporate visual literacy into the curricula (Shapley, 1991). Thus, in a world that is becoming increasingly dominated by visual messages, students in this country may be the least capable of interpreting and critically assessing images that shape their attitudes and influence their behavior (Goldstone, 1989).

Prior research on visual images of racial minorities suggests that they frequently are excluded from the popular media. For example, Sentman (1983) finds that depictions of African-Americans engaged in everyday life activities were excluded from "Life Magazine" for the entire 35 years of its initial publishing history (i.e., 1937 to 1972). Williams and Condry (1989) find that television images of minorities primarily represent people who lack status or importance. Within academe, Whatley (1988) finds that photographic images of blacks in sexuality texts are rare and that, when present, they are portrayed in a negative way. Likewise, Ferree and Hall (1990) report that visual images in introductory sociology texts reinforce stereotypes about women of color. Their research is reviewed in more depth because the current research project relies heavily upon it (1990).

Ferree and Hall (1990) report that minorities are proportionately represented as individuals in textbook photos when compared to their numbers in the general population. However, the number of men and boys (64%) in pictures significantly exceeds their representation in the general population and women are underrepresented in photos regardless of their race (averaging about 36% of the individuals, p. 511). Therefore, because of gender imbalances and unrealistic portrayals of racial minorities, women of color have very little visual presence in these textbook illustrations. Furthermore, pictures in sociology texts almost never show women of color without the accompaniment of minority men or whites (both men and women). And finally, photos of women are most apt to appear in chapters on gender while pictures of minorities (including women of color) tend to be located in chapters on race. As Ferree and Hall note, this type of presentation gives the impression that only women have gender, only minorities have race, and women of color have race but not gender.[3]

Other studies suggest that women and African-Americans are underrepresented in criminology and criminal justice textbooks (Baro & Eigenberg, 1992; Dorworth & Henry, 1992). Baro and Eigenberg (1992) conducted a content analysis of photographs in 22 introductory criminology and criminal justice textbooks published between 1988 and 1991. They report that males visually dominate images in introductory texts. This dominance is reflected by the overrepresentation of males in the photos as well as the tendency to depict men in pictures which are devoted exclusively to men (i.e., pictures which fail to include women). In addition, illustrations of men are most apt to appear in those substantive areas which are central to the discipline (e.g., areas focusing on theory or key institutions in the criminal justice system). Furthermore, women are portrayed in stereotypical ways. Women are least apt to be portrayed as criminals and professionals and most apt to be pictured as victims or as peripheral persons. Thus, Baro and Eigenberg conclude that women are invisible in the photographs in introductory criminology and criminal justice textbooks. As such, they convey the impression that who men are and what they do is of greater sociological significance.

Dorworth and Henry (1992) report similar findings. They analyzed visual portrayals of women and African-Americans in 22 introductory criminal justice textbooks published between 1984 and 1989. They report that males and whites have a dominant visual presence in these textbooks and that women and blacks are underrepresented as authorities (employees of the criminal justice system). In addition, women and whites are more likely to be portrayed as victims than are men and blacks. Furthermore, blacks and men are most often portrayed as offenders. The authors conclude that the "distorted representation and the underrepresentation of blacks and females in introductory criminal justice textbooks" contributes to a chilly climate for women and blacks in the field (Dorworth & Henry, 1992, p. 257).

It is important, however, to note some limitations of this study. Dorworth and Henry fail to clearly specify how they defined and coded individuals in photos according to their main categories of authorities, victims, and offenders. The presentation of their data also is somewhat confusing. They appear to compare the actual representation of authorities, victims, and offenders in society to the number of individuals portrayed in these categories in pictures which depict only men or only women and only whites or only blacks. For example, they compare official crime rates of women to the number of women in textbook illustrations who are pictured in photos which contain only women. Thus, their data on female criminals in textbook photos fails to include women who are portrayed as criminals in gender integrated pictures (those which contain both men and women). This problem also occurs with their comparisons by race. Most importantly, the authors fail to tabulate their data by both race and gender, thus the interactive effects of race and gender cannot be evaluated.

Thus, the limited body of research on visual images in textbooks suggest that both racial and gender biases operate to marginalize the presence of women of color. Research also indicates that people of color, especially women, are excluded and/or marginalized, both as authors and as subjects of inquiry. As a result, we are interested in empirically examining the extent to which women of color have a visual presence in introductory criminology and criminal justice texts and whether these illustrations challenge or conform to popular stereotypes.[4]

Specifically, this study addresses four broad research questions:

1) Are women of color proportionately represented in terms of the total number of individuals portrayed in pictures?
2) Are women of color, as individuals, proportionately represented in terms of various status categories (e.g., victims, criminals, and professionals)?
3) Are pictures containing only women of color as common as pictures which portray only whites or only women?
4) Are women of color proportionately represented in portraits (pictures of single individuals)?

Based on prior research on texts, critiques which argue that discipline is androcentric and Eurocentric, and literature which discusses the marginalization of minority women, we predict that women of color will lack a visual presence in textbook illustrations.

METHODOLOGY

Drawing from Ferree and Hall's (1990) method, the current study uses two levels of visual portrayal: 1) the depiction of individuals and 2) the social composition of illustrations.[5]

Individual Level

The first level of visual portrayal includes an examination of the race and gender of individuals to determine whether the number of women of color in textbook illustrations is proportionate to their representation in the population (*Research Question Number One* [***RQ#1***]). Examination at this level captures inclusiveness or the degree to which women of color are represented as a proportion of the total number of individuals portrayed. In other words, *it offers a description of the overall visual presence of women of color* in texts. We hypothesize that women of color will be underrepresented when compared to their numbers in the general population.

Expanding upon the method suggested by Ferree and Hall, individuals in photos also are classified using four status categories: criminals, professionals, victims, and peripheral persons (persons who are either unrelated or peripherally related to the criminal justice system). These status categories are included because it is important to understand the relationship between visual presence and the picture's symbolic content. For example, women of color could be well represented as a proportion of all individuals depicted but this would not be a fair representation if portrayed mainly as victims. Because of this possibility, the race, gender, and status of individuals in each picture are examined to determine whether women of color are proportionally represented in each of the various status categories (*Research Question Number Two* [***RQ#2***]). We predict that women of color will be more apt to be portrayed in those status categories with the least prestige in the discipline (as victims and peripheral persons); although, we anticipate that they will be more apt to be depicted as criminals than will white women. We also hypothesize that women of color will be proportionately underrepresented with respect to their involvement in various occupations in the criminal justice system (e.g., police officers, attorneys, judges, and correctional officers).

Social Composition

The second level of analysis concentrates on the social composition of the pictures. Using the picture as the unit of analysis, we examined illustrations and classified them into five groups: exclusively white male; exclusively minority male; exclusively white female; exclusively minority female; and racially and gender integrated illustrations.

The exclusive portrayal category is important because these types of pictures "are a form of visual dominance and suggest greater sociological significance" (Ferree and Hall, 1990, p. 506). While analysis at the individual level provides a measure of overall visual presence, *analysis of the social composition of photos allow us to determine the extent to which women of color are given a visual presence of their own,* independent of white males, minority males, and white females (*Research Question Number Three* [***RQ#3***]). For example, different meanings are sent when a picture portrays an African-American, female police officer in the presence of five white, male officers and one white, female officer compared to an illustration which portrays only female police officers of color.

We do not expect the majority of the pictures to be integrated by race and gender as such a portrayal is not a realistic depiction of society, the discipline, or the criminal justice system. However, given the Eurocentric and androcentric nature of our society, we predict that white males will dominate the exclusive category. Specifically, we predict that the percent of exclusive portrayals of women of color will be less than their representation in the general population as well as their representation at the individual level of portrayal. We also anticipate that white men will be most likely to be depicted in exclusive portrayals while women of color will be least likely to be portrayed as such.

We also expanded on Ferree and Hall's (1990) method by concentrating upon a special type of exclusive portrayal: the portrait. Portraits are pictures which contain only one individual and constitute a sub-category of exclusive portrayals. Portraits are important because the exclusive visual dominance is magnified when only one person is presented in the illustration. Portraits, like exclusive portrayals, may be positive because they provide members of a particular group with "a room of their own" (Ferree & Hall, 1990, p. 506). Conversely, when portraits are used to define group members in stereotypical ways, they can be negative. For example, a portrait of a woman of color who is a criminal does not carry the same connotation as does a portrait of a judge who is a woman of color (*Research Question Number Four* [***RQ#4***]). We predict that portraits of women of color will be underrepresented when compared to their representation in the general population, at the individual level of portrayal, and in the exclusive portrayal category as a whole. We also anticipate that portraits of women of color will represent similar status categories as depicted by individual women of color as a whole; i.e., we predict that portraits of women of color will reinforce stereotypical definitions of minority women and their roles in criminology and the criminal justice system.

Textbook Selection

Texts were included in our sampling frame if they were published between 1988 and 1991, and if they were introductory texts.[6] This time frame was used because the purpose of this study is to examine the current state of the discipline. The sample is also limited to introductory texts (in both criminology and criminal justice) because these books provide a comprehensive overview of the discipline. Texts were included if they used the word introduction in the title or if the title suggested that the text was an overview of the subject matter (e.g., Conklin's [1988] *Criminology*).

To select our sample, we reviewed all titles listed under "Crime and Criminals" and "Criminal Justice Administration" in the *Subject Guide to Books in Print: 1990–91.*[7] We initially identified 35 textbooks which met our criteria; however, eight texts were eliminated because they contained no pictures[8] and we were unable to locate a copy of five other texts.[9] As a result, 22 textbooks are analyzed in this study.

Coding

Detailed coding information is discussed in Table 1; however, because subjectivity is often considered a weakness of content analysis, it is important to briefly discuss inter-coder reliability. Illustrations were coded by three students (two white females and one white male) and by one of the co-authors of this paper (a white female). Student coders received four hours of initial and two hours of follow-up training on the study methods and the coding scheme. Using five of the texts, data from coding conducted by the students were compared to data from coding conducted by the co-author. These cross-checks suggest that inter-coder reliability is acceptable (98% agreement for the social composition category, 98% for gender, 92% for race, and 88% for the status category as a whole). Detailed coding information is presented in Appendix A.

FINDINGS

The 22 texts in this study gleaned 1,465 pictures which portrayed 4,986 individuals;[10] however, 217 (14.7%) pictures were excluded from the analyses because the social composition could not be determined.[11] In addition, we were unable to decipher gender and race for 378 (7.6%) individuals. As a result, 1,248 pictures and 3,994 individuals are analyzed in this study. After excluding pictures with missing data, the average number of pictures per book is 57 and the average number of individuals is 182.

The Representation of Women of Color as Individuals (RQ#1)

Consistent with our hypothesis, women of color are underrepresented when compared to their representation in the population. Table 1 shows that men of both races are overrepresented when compared to their numbers in the population; white men are 61% of the individuals in photos yet they

Table 1. Race and Gender of Individuals by Status Categories.

Race and Gender of Individuals	Criminals n	%	Professionals n	%	Victims n	%	Peripherals n	%	Total n	%
Minorities	382	(35)	235	(16)	34	(26)	291	(23)	942	(24)
Females	26	(2)	38	(3)	8	(6)	82	(6)	154	(4)
Percent of All Females		(3)		(5)		(1)		(11)		(20)
Percent of All Minorities		(3)		(4)		(1)		(9)		(16)
Percent of Total Individuals		(1)		(1)		(0)		(2)		(4)
Males	356	(33)	197	(13)	26	(20)	209	(16)	788	(20)
Percent of All Males		(46)		(6)		(1)		(6)		(24)
Percent of All Minorities		(38)		(21)		(3)		(22)		(84)
Percent of Total Individuals		(9)		(5)		(1)		(5)		(20)
Whites	704	(65)	1265	(84)	98	(74)	985	(77)	3052	(76)
Females	93	(9)	140	(9)	52	(39)	335	(26)	620	(16)
Percent of All Females		(12)		(18)		(13)		(43)		(80)
Percent of All Whites		(3)		(5)		(3)		(10)		(20)
Percent of Total Individuals		(2)		(4)		(1)		(8)		(16)
Males	611	(56)	1125	(75)	46	(35)	650	(51)	2432	(61)
Percent of All Males		(19)		(35)		(1)		(20)		(76)
Percent of All Whites		(20)		(37)		(2)		(21)		(80)
Percent of Total Individuals		(15)		(28)		(1)		(16)		(61)
Total	1086	(27)	1500	(38)	132	(3)	1276	(32)	3994	(100)

represent only 41% of the population in the United States (Bureau of the Census, 1991, p. 18). Likewise, men of color comprise 20% of the individuals in photos, yet they represent about 8% of the population (Bureau of the Census, 1991, p. 18). Meanwhile, white women account for 16% of the individuals in illustrations, which is far below their representation in the population (43%; Bureau of the Census, 1991, p. 18). Women of color are only 4% of the total individuals in photos, while census data indicate that they are about 8% of the general population (Bureau of the Census, 1991, p. 18). Furthermore, only 16% of all minorities in pictures are women of color, compared to white women who represent 20% of all whites in pictures. Thus, at the individual level of portrayal, gender imbalances in the illustrations result in the marginalization of all women, but racial imbalances also serve to render women of color invisible in these photos.

Women of Color as Individuals in the Various Status Categories (RQ#2)

The data in Table 1 also shows that women of color (and white women) are least likely to be portrayed as criminals and professionals, while white males are most apt to be depicted as professionals and men of color are most likely to be shown as criminals. Thus, consistent with our hypothesis, women of color are most apt to be portrayed in those status categories which have the least status in the discipline: victims and peripheral people.

Victims

Women of color are underrepresented as victims in textbook illustrations. According to National Crime Survey data, African-American women represent 22% of the victims of violent crime as well as 22% of the victims of theft (Whitaker, 1990). And while both minority and white women are most apt to be portrayed as victims, pictures of female, minority victims represent only 1% of the illustration of all minorities while photos of female, white victims account for 3% of the photos of whites.[12] Thus, both race and gender imbalances contribute to the underrepresentation of women of color as victims.

Peripheral People

Gender imbalances appear to account for the overrepresentation of women of color in the peripheral person category. While women account for 32% (N=451) of the peripheral people in photos, these portrayals represent 53% of all females in illustrations. In other words, over half of the women in pictures are portrayed as peripheral persons. In contrast, only about one-fourth of males are portrayed as such. However, racial imbalances do not appear to contribute greatly to the overrepresentation of women as peripheral persons. Women of color and white women represent about the same proportion of their respective racial categories (9% for women of color and 10% for white women).

Criminals

As predicted, women of color are least apt to be portrayed as professionals and criminals. Contrary to our prediction though, women of color are not portrayed more frequently as criminals than are white women. Table 1 shows that both women of color and white women represent about 3% of their respective racial categories. However, women of color are underrepresented as criminals in textbook illustrations.

Minority women represent 2% (N = 26) of the criminals in textbook photos. And while it is difficult to find data which is divided by BOTH race and gender, we were able to ascertain that 4% of jail inmates are African-American women (Bureau of Justice Statistics [BJS], 1990, p. 30). In addition, 40% of females in state prisons are white, non-Hispanic women, yet white women account for 78% (N = 93) of the illustrations of female criminals in texts (BJS, 1991, p. 2). Based on these figures, it appears that women of color are underrepresented as criminals; although, these figures clearly over-represent "street crime" and underrepresent white collar and corporate crime. This issue will be discussed in more depth below.

Professions

Table 2 provides a breakdown of individuals by professions. While women of color are infrequently portrayed as professionals, they are most apt to be portrayed as professional "others". This pattern also holds true for white women. Interestingly, women in the "other" professional category are portrayed as court reporters, counselors, and probation or parole officers. Men in the "other" category are more likely to be shown as academicians or theorists and law makers or politicians.[13] Thus, even in the other composite category, men are portrayed in professions with more status.

Contrary to our prediction, women of color appear to be adequately represented or only slightly underrepresented as police officers. Two percent of police officers depict women of color, while data suggest that between 2.6% (Bureau of Justice Statistics, 1992a, p. 5) and 3.5% (Police Foundation, 1990, p. 29) of sworn police officers are minority women. Furthermore, 3.5% of sworn personnel in sheriffs' departments are women of color (Bureau of Justice Statistics, 1992b, p. 6).

Consistent with our hypotheses, minority women are clearly underrepresented in the remaining professional categories: as correctional officers, judges, and attorneys. Only 1% of the correctional officers in illustrations include minority women; although, this percentage exaggerates the visual presence of women of color in this category (n = 2) because the total number of correctional officers portrayed in the photos is small (n = 84). Nonetheless, this figure suggests that minority women are underrepresented in photos

Table 2. Race and Gender of Individuals by Status Category Professions.

	Professions											
	Police Officers		*Correctional Officers*		*Attorneys*		*Judges*		*Other Professions*		*Total*	
Race and Gender of Individuals	*n*	%	*n*	%	*n*	%	*n*	%	*n*	%	*n*	%
Minorities	165	(19)	17	(20)	9	(7)	19	(10)	25	(10)	235	(16)
Females	24	(2)	2	(1)	1	(1)	0	(0)	11	(4)	38	(3)
Percent of All Female Professionals		(3)		(0)		(1)		(0)		(6)		(5)
Percent of All Minority Professionals		(10)		(1)		(0)		(0)		(3)		(16)
Percent of Total Professionals		(1)		(0)		(0)		(0)		(1)		(3)
Males	141	(17)	15	(18)	8	(6)	19	(10)	14	(6)	197	(13)
Percent of All Male Professionals		(11)		(1)		(1)		(1)		(1)		(15)
Percent of All Minority Professionals		(60)		(6)		(3)		(8)		(6)		(84)
Percent of Total Professionals		(9)		(1)		(1)		(1)		(1)		(13)
Whites	685	(81)	67	(80)	117	(83)	173	(90)	223	(90)	1265	(84)
Females	55	(8)	12	(14)	17	(13)	19	(10)	37	(15)	140	(9)
Percent of All Female Professionals		(31)		(7)		(10)		(11)		(21)		(79)
Percent of All White Professionals		(4)		(1)		(1)		(2)		(2)		(11)
Percent of Total Professionals		(14)		(1)		(1)		(1)		(3)		(9)
Males	630	(74)	55	(65)	100	(79)	154	(80)	186	(75)	1125	(75)
Percent of All Male Professionals		(48)		(4)		(8)		(12)		(14)		(85)

Percent of All White Professionals		(50)		(4)		(8)		(12)		(15)		(89)
Percent of Total Professionals		(42)		(4)		(7)		(10)		(12)		(75)
Total	850	(57)	84	(6)	126	(8)	192	(13)	248	(17)	1500	(100)

when compared to their numbers in the field; 9% of officers in adult facilities and 16% in juvenile facilities (American Correctional Association, 1991, p. xii, xiii). *Remarkably, there is not one single picture of a minority female judge and there is only one female minority attorney depicted.* Thus, on the whole, women of color are underrepresented in the various professions.

Exclusive Portrayals (RQ#3)

The next level of analysis addresses the social composition of the photos. As Table 3 demonstrates, 39% of the pictures are integrated in terms of either race or gender, or both. About 61% of the illustrations are exclusive portrayals; of these, almost two-thirds (69%) depict exclusive portrayals of white men. In contrast, 16% of the exclusive portrayals depict minority males, while 11% portray white women only and a mere 3% concentrate exclusively on women of color. When these figures are compared to levels in the population (41% white men, 8% minority men, 43% white women, 8% minority females; Bureau of the Census, 1991, p. 18), males are overrepresented (both minority and white), while women (both minority and white) are underrepresented. Furthermore, women of color are underrepresented in exclusive portrayals (3%) when compared to their depiction as individuals in pictures (4%). Thus, the data confirm both hypotheses in this area.

Table 3. Social Composition of 1,248 Pictures.

Social Composition	*Number of Pictures*	*Percent of Category*	*Percent of All Pictures*
Integrated in Terms of Race and/or Gender	490	100	39
Exclusive Portrayals	758	100	61
Minority Females Only	24	3	2
Minority Males Only	124	16	10
White Females Only	83	11	7
White Males Only	527	69	42

Portraits (RQ#4)

The data on portraits also confirm the visual dominance of white men and the marginalization of women of color. Over one-half (59%) of the exclusive portrayals are portraits, but women of color account for only 5% of these portraits (see Table 4). White males represent 63% of the portraits, while minority men are 17%, white females are 15%, and women of color account for a mere 5%. Thus, representation of women of color in the portrait category is less than their representation in the general population (8%), but just slightly higher than their level of inclusion at the individual level of portrayal in illustrations (4%) and the exclusive portrayal category as a whole (3%).

However, the percentage of minority women as a portion of all minorities presents a different image when compared to the percentage of white women as a portion of all whites. Using these figures, women of color are more apt to be depicted as criminals and professionals while white women are more likely to appear as victims. *Surprisingly, not a single woman of color appears in any of the portraits of victims.* Furthermore, the percentage of portraits depicting women of color (5%) is lower than the percentage of portraits of both white women (15%) and minority men (17%). Moreover, portraits of women of color represent 21% of the minority portraits which is similar to white women who make up 19% of the portraits of whites.

The data offer support for most of our hypotheses. While women of color approach proportional representation with respect to their portrayal as police officers, they are either underrepresented or rendered totally invisible in all other areas (as professionals, victims, and offenders). The dominant visual image of white males is that of professionals, while minority males are most apt to appear as criminals, and both white women and women of color are portrayed as victims and peripheral persons. Males, especially white males, visually dominate images in introductory texts at the individual level and in terms of exclusive portrayals (including portraits). Thus, men in general and white men in particular have a dominant visual presence that is exclusively their own. In contrast, women, especially women of color, are rendered invisible. Hence, gender and racial imbalances serve to marginalize the visual presence of women of color.

DISCUSSION OF FINDINGS

Overall, we expected minority women to be underrepresented because they are impacted by both racism and sexism; however, the level of exclusion is astounding. Ferree and Hall (1990) find that white males account for 45% of the individuals in sociology texts. They also report that 26% of the

Table 4. Race and Gender of Portraits by Status Categories.

Race and Gender of Portraits	*Criminals* n	*Criminals* %	*Professionals* n	*Professionals* %	*Victims* n	*Victims* %	*Peripherals* n	*Peripherals* %	*Total* n	*Total* %
Minorities	53	(28)	31	(16)	7	(25)	7	(16)	98	(22)
Females	6	(3)	13	(7)	0	(0)	2	(5)	21	(5)
Percent of All Minority Portraits		(13)		(13)		(0)		(2)		(21)
Percent of All Female Portraits		(15)		(15)		(0)		(2)		(24)
Males	47	(25)	18	(9)	7	(25)	5	(12)	77	(17)
Percent of All Minority Portraits		(48)		(18)		(7)		(5)		(79)
Percent of All Male Portraits		(13)		(5)		(2)		(1)		(21)
Whites	136	(72)	159	(84)	21	(75)	36	(84)	352	(78)
Females	21	(11)	18	(9)	17	(61)	12	(28)	68	(15)
Percent All White Portraits		(6)		(5)		(5)		(3)		(19)
Percent All Female Portraits		(24)		(20)		(19)		(13)		(76)
Males	115	(61)	141	(74)	4	(14)	24	(56)	284	(63)
Percent All White Portraits		(33)		(40)		(1)		(7)		(81)
Percent All Male Portraits		(32)		(39)		(1)		(7)		(79)
Total	189	(42)	190	(42)	28	(6)	43	(10)	450*	(100)

*Total does not include 28 portraits where gender is identifiable but where race is unknown (24 males and 4 females).

individuals are white females, 19% are minority males, and 11% are women of color. In contrast, we find that white males represent 61% of the individuals in criminology and criminal justice texts. Furthermore, white females are 16% of the total individuals, 20% are men of color, and 4% are women of color. Thus, when compared to sociology texts, criminology and criminal justice texts portray a considerably higher proportion of white males, approximately equal number of minority males, and much fewer women (both white and of color).

It is clear that gender and racial imbalances serve to give white men a dominant visual presence; however, gender imbalances appear to be more pronounced. Individual women of color, on the whole, represent a slightly smaller proportion of their racial category than white women do as a proportion of all whites in illustrations (16% for minority women and 20% for white women). However, these figures are quite similar when compared across status categories. For example, as a percent of all minorities, individual minority women are 3% of offenders, 4% of professionals, 1% of victims, and 9% of peripheral persons. In comparison, as a percent of all whites, individual white women account for 3% of criminals, 5% of professionals, 3% of victims, and 10% of peripherals. Furthermore, women of color and white women represent a similar proportion of their race in terms of their representation in the various professional categories (police officers, correctional officer, judges, attorneys, and "others").

Gender imbalances are demonstrated by the overwhelming visual dominance of males. Men represent 81% of the individuals in these texts and at least one man is present in 90% of the illustrations. Furthermore, 87% of the exclusive portrayals in the texts portray only men which means that men are about seven times as likely to be depicted in exclusive portrayals than are women. Thus men clearly have a dominant visual presence in introductory criminology and criminal justice texts. *Hence, proportionate representation of minorities coupled with the underrepresentation of women serves to marginalize women of color.*

This trend is also evidenced when examining exclusive portrayals. White males in particular dominate the exclusive portrayal category; 42% of all illustrations in texts. This figure exceeds the percentage of photos devoted exclusively to white males in sociology texts (30%; Ferree & Hall, 1990). Furthermore, we find that 7% of the illustrations are exclusive portrayals of white females, 10% of minority males, and 2% of minority females. In sociology texts, 13% of the photos are exclusive portrayals of white females, 10% minority males, and 5% minority females (Ferree & Hall, 1990). Thus we conclude that providing white males such a large, disproportionate, exclusive visual presence sends out the message that who they are and what they do is of greater significance. We also contend that gender imbalances in criminology are more profound than they are in sociology.

The data also suggest that women of color are underrepresented as criminals, but only if the definition of crime is restricted to "street crime." Another study (Wright & Ducaji, 1992) find that textbooks write about the serious nature of white collar crime but that visual images concentrate on street crime. Thus, textbook illustrations appear to reinforce traditional definitions of crime which support the notion that street crime is more dangerous and harmful than white collar and corporate crime. If we had accurate figures about the relative amount of street crime versus white collar crime, and if these data were broken down by race and gender, we suspect that women of color would be overrepresented in current textbook illustrations.

This study also finds that women of color are underrepresented as professionals and victims. Thus, criminological texts fail to acknowledge the contributions of workers in the field, but also refuse to recognize the victimization of women of color. Thus, gender imbalances render all women invisible, but the interactive effects of race and gender serve to marginalize the presence of women of color in the discipline. In other words, visual images in these texts place white men at the center of interest in terms of disciplinary inquiry and reflect both Eurocentric and androcentric assumptions about crime and criminals.

POLICY IMPLICATIONS

The findings of this study suggest that women of color who have any interest in criminology or criminal justice will, at the very beginning of their academic careers, be confronted with a discipline that has rendered them invisible. For some, this type of experience may become a challenge to remain and work toward curriculum transformation. Other disciplines have inspired similar reactions. For example, Ronald Takaki is an Asian-American who has become a leading scholar in the transformation of history. Takaki insists that he became a historian largely because "the traditional historians had offered me, and many people like me, a mirror which had rendered us invisible" (Aronson, 1994, p. 12). Similarly, African-American feminists are seeking to transform disciplines as diverse as theology and biology. In what Winkler calls "a steady stream of publications," black feminist scholarship has advanced to the point where a recent announcement of a new, interdisciplinary newsletter titled "The Womanist" rapidly drew expressions of interest from approximately 100 scholars across the academic disciplines (Winkler, 1994, p. A12).

However, all too many women of color may also walk away from their criminology or criminal justice introductory courses to pursue studies in other disciplines such as sociology that appear to be more inclusive if only in textbook visual portrayals (Ferree & Hall, 1990). What is suggested here is that women who cannot even find textbook pictures that reflect their own identities, concerns, and aspirations, may get the impression that they are simply not welcome in the discipline or the related professions. Thus, the first step in retaining and encouraging women of color in criminology and criminal justice may well be to (at least) give them an appropriate and considerable visual presence in the textbooks.

This is not just a question of proportional representativeness or of making sure that whatever percentage of the population might be women of color in any given census period is also the percentage visualized in textbook photographs. Nor is it just a question of making sure that women of color are proportionately represented as police officers, correctional officers, judges, and attorneys. Instead, we are suggesting that publishers and textbook authors impose upon themselves a policy of using photographs to encourage women of color to remain in the discipline and/or to enter related professions. One way of providing this type of encouragement could be to increase the numbers of exclusive portrayals of women of color. For example, texts should include photographs of groups of attorneys who are all women of color and portraits of black feminists such as Patricia Hill Collins who address crimes against women by writing about the ways in which class, race, and gender interact (Collins, 1993). In other words, photographs can and should be used to draw women of color into the center of interest, focus, and disciplinary inquiry. However, we do not advocate increasing the number of photos of minority, female offenders. Minorities, as a group, are more likely to be portrayed as criminals while whites are more likely to be portrayed as professionals. These images support stereotypical definitions about the nature of crime and law enforcement.

Publishers might also adopt a policy of asking those whom they employ to review textbooks to pay attention to the photographs and to provide analyses of visual content. In order to do this, publishers may have to reach out beyond criminology and criminal justice and add reviewers from media and communication disciplines who are experts in interpreting visual images. A good way to start locating such people might be to obtain a copy of Messaris's (1994) new text on visual literacy. Similarly, those who serve as book review editors for criminology and criminal justice journals could also ask for critiques of visual content.

On a national level, opportunities to develop and publish introductory textbooks that provide women of color with both a visual and textual presence might be found in a current proposal for a gender equity in education law. If this law is passed, an office of gender equity will be added to the U.S. Department of Education and grant funds will become available for the development of model curricula and curricula materials (Kaplan & Aronson, 1994, p. 25). Within the disciplines of criminology and criminal justice, policies should also be developed to encourage those who seek sabbaticals, research grants, or release time to write multicultural, introductory textbooks or to produce more inclusive curricula materials.

Meanwhile, those who teach introductory criminology and criminal justice courses can also have an important impact by including visual portrayal as a criterion for textbook selection. Before deciding to adopt a particular text, an instructor might review it in terms of the visual impressions she or he obtains about women of color. Even more importantly, one might also ask minority female students to conduct similar reviews. Most importantly, publishers must be told about the visual portrayal criterion and about the related reasons why instructors decided to adopt or not adopt particular textbooks.

Alternatively, instructors might also simply decide to abandon the use of introductory criminal justice and criminology textbooks. Using journal articles, special topics monographs, library, "on reserve" readings and incorporating audio-visual materials are tactics that can eliminate the need for a textbook. Students can also be assigned to locate relevant written and visual material about Native Americans, Asian-Americans, African-Americans, Hispanics and other minorities. Admittedly, this type of approach does involve a lot more preparation but the rewards can include higher levels of student interest and interaction and a greater ability to encourage and retain women of color who are or might become interested in careers in criminology or criminal justice.

CONCLUSION

Additional research should examine the publication process in more depth. It would be interesting to survey authors and editors to gather more information. For example, how much input do authors have into the selection of photographs. Who selects these photos and what sort of options are available? For example, are authors forced to select from a small pool of photos on file? If so, do authors have the power to insist upon a more diverse group of photos? Do publishers prefer certain types of photos? Why do some texts use photos while others do not? Do editors and/or authors believe that photos are important to the overall presentation of a text? Why or why not? Are reviewers asked to examine and comment upon the photos when texts are sent out for peer review?

We acknowledge that textbook authors may not have exclusive control over the production of texts and that structural limitations such as the availability of pictures may constrain even the most conscientious author from producing a textbook which is gender balanced in terms of illustrations (Ferree & Hall, 1990). However, in the final analysis, the selection of illustrations is an ideological process and we cannot ignore the outcome of such a process simply because authors lack exclusive control. As Ferree and

Hall (1990) emphasize, we must attend to the racial and gender composition of illustrations in texts because it is an issue of fundamental fairness.

It is important that textbook authors and editors consciously pursue diversity by increasing the number of illustrations of women of color and by placing these illustrations in such a way as to challenge rather than reinforce traditional social definitions of gender and race. However, in the final analysis, it appears reasonable to assume that textbook illustrations mirror the Eurocentric and androcentric biases which are embedded in the scholarship itself.

Our scholarship, in general, and our texts, specifically, must become more inclusive. Otherwise, "by teaching a curriculum that is centered in the lives of whites and men, we legitimate a view of the world for our students which sees men's experience as central, women's as peripheral, white experience as the norm, and all 'others' as deviant or exceptional" (Anderson, 1988, p. 123).[14]

We challenge scholars to begin the onerous, but critically important, task of re-conceptualizing the discipline. Anderson (1988), for example, has called for an entire reconstruction of the field of sociology. She asks how sociology might be different if women of color were placed at the center of the discipline. She envisions this transformation as a process. Using a conceptual scheme presented by McIntosh (cited in Anderson, 1988), she argues that there are five stages which occur in curriculum evolution.

In the first phase, women and minorities are totally absent from the discipline which revolves around white males. In the second stage, women and minorities are added to the existing curriculum, although the links between race and gender are rarely a focus of concern (sometimes referred to as the add women and stir approach). In the third phase, women and men of color are seen as problematic because they fail to fit into the existing theories or paradigms—they are still viewed as "the other". In this stage, the exclusion and invisibility of disenfranchised groups (such as women and men of color) is documented. Racism and sexism become important topics of inquiry. In stage four, women and minorities become the focus of research. As a result, new ideas and theories are brought to the discipline while old paradigms are challenged. In the fifth and final phase, white males cease to provide a normative standard and all groups are viewed in relation to each other. Toward this end, sociologists have attempted to move toward a discipline which explores the intersections between race, class, and gender.[15] In other words, the new focus is on "interlocking systems of oppression" (Collins, 1990, p. 225). Thus, oppression and privilege are viewed in relation to one another, as overlapping categories, rather than hierarchal and additive in nature.

It appears that criminology is somewhere between stage two and four of

Anderson's classification scheme. In some cases, information on women and people of color is still relatively invisible, although there is some literature which is beginning to discuss and document omissions of literature on these groups (Barak, 1991; Daly & Chesney-Lind, 1988; Baro & Eigenberg, 1992; Caldwell & Greene, 1980; Simpson, 1989; Young & Sulton, 1991). Likewise, there appears to be a growing interest in research on, by, and for women and people of color;[16] however, there is much work to be done in these areas.

Class, race, and gender are not just three separate "variables." Instead, these three characteristics of our social structure and additional conceptual work needs to be done before we can truly begin to understand the interactive effects of these social phenomenon. It is not easy to try to re-invent criminology and the terrain is not always clear. As Daly notes, this way of thinking is "a way of analyzing or theorizing about inequality, but it is not a perspective or a paradigm or a theory. It is an idea, a claimed set of interrelationships" (1993, p. 66). It is a powerful orientation. "For women of color, the construct establishes a ground from which to articulate experience, theory, and politics" (Daly, 1993, p. 64). *In other words, the class-race-gender construct has the power to facilitate visibility and to lift the barriers that silence black women.*

However, asking criminologists to employ this construct is also asking them to undo most of their intellectual heritage. This type of paradigmatic revolution is complex. Major theories and methods will have to be torn apart and rebuilt. Teaching will also be more difficult and much more complex. We cannot assume that faculty are prepared or willing to face these demands (Platt, 1993, p. 77). Even if they are, it will require either abandoning existing textbooks which are extremely important especially in introductory classes or waiting for the production of new texts which may or may not be forthcoming. And even if this type of change seems overwhelming, the current race, class, gender construct is not yet broad enough (Platt, 1993). If criminology is to truly become multicultural, there are other areas of structural oppression that also need to be integrated into the conceptual framework (sexual orientation for example).

None the less, we believe that the current race/class/gender discussions are encouraging and suggest movement in terms of curriculum transformation. Several anthologies in sociology are organized around race, class, and gender (Rothenberg, 1992; Zinn & Dill, 1994). A national conference in the field (Academy of Criminal Justice Sciences) made race, class, and gender its' annual program theme in 1993. Anthologies such as the current one indicate that we are making progress.[17] However, there is a great deal of work that remains to be done before criminal justice can claim to be inclusive.

Perhaps someday the field will have evolved to the point that we can pick up introductory texts and find that race, class, and gender are central organizational features of every text and hopefully these texts will include illustrations which challenge stereotypical notions of crime and criminology. At that point, perhaps we will have moved toward the final evolutionary phase envisioned by McIntosh—the phase where white males cease to be the normative standard and all groups are viewed in relation to each other.

APPENDIX A: CODING INFORMATION

Coding of Individuals

Illustrations which did not contain any individuals were not coded for analysis. Pictures of 20 or more people were coded as crowds and deleted from the study unless they clearly depicted individuals in some part of the picture. If these individuals were obviously the focal point of the picture, the picture was coded with respect to individual traits of the focal person or persons; however, other categories such as social composition may have been coded as undecided. For example if two police officers were shown arresting a person in front of a large crowd of demonstrators, only the gender, race, and status of the police officers and the criminal were coded.

Coding of Gender and Race

Clothing, hairstyle, and physical characteristics were used to identify males and females. Race was determined by examining skin color, hairstyle, and physical characteristics. Race was coded according to two categories: white and minority. Individuals were coded as members of a minority group if they were African-Americans, Hispanics, Asians, or "others" such as Native Americans or Pacific Islanders. Coders also used captions and surrounding text to assign both gender and race. If gender or race could not be ascertained, the individual was coded as undecided.

Status Category

Criminals: Individuals who were depicted as someone who had violated the law (e.g., a suspect under arrest, a defendant before the court, or a person under some type of correctional supervision) or who was depicted in the process of committing a legal violation (e.g., someone using drugs, robbing a store, or shoplifting).

Victims: Individuals who were portrayed as having suffered some loss or injury due to criminal activity. We included pictures of individuals directly victimized (e.g., person who is being robbed by another) as well as indirect victims (e.g., parents, partners, or friends of victims—the most common portrayal being friends or relatives of murder victims). (The use of the concepts direct and indirect victims derives from literature in the field of victimology: see Karmen, 1990.)

Professionals: Individuals who appeared in photos as employees of the criminal justice system. Using data from a pre-test, more detailed information was obtained on those professions which visually dominated texts: police officers; correctional officers; attorneys; and judges. A composite "other" professional category was also used which includes: employees of the criminal justice system who are rarely in photos (court reporters; probation or parole officers; counselors or therapists; and police or correctional administrators) and professionals in other occupations associated with the discipline (academicians, theorists, lawmakers, and politicians).

Peripheral People: This composite category encompasses several types of individuals who are not central to the criminal justice system. Individuals were coded as peripherals if they were portrayed as people who provide occasional assistance or supportive services (e.g., jurors, paramedics, witnesses, members of the Guardian Angels, and fire fighters). Likewise, people on the street or bystanders were coded as peripheral as were people who were used to portray a concept (e.g., pictures of poor people used to illustrate a conceptual relationship between poverty and crime). In addition, people whose status could not be determined were coded as peripheral because if the reader could not determine the status of individuals, those individuals are, by definition, peripheral in terms of their relationship to the discipline. For example, pictures frequently portrayed a criminal escorted by a police officer on the street surrounded by several other individuals; however, it was rarely possible to determine whether these other individuals were police officers, attorneys, fellow criminals, or by-standers. As a result, the image constructed was one of a peripheral person.

APPENDIX B: INTRODUCTORY CRIMINOLOGY AND CRIMINAL JUSTICE TEXTBOOKS

Abler, F., Mueller, G. and Laufer, W. (1991). *Criminology.* New York: McGraw Hill.

Bartollas, C. and Dinitz, S. (1988). *Introduction to criminology.* New York: Harper and Row.

Beirne, P. and Messerschmidt, J. (1991). *Criminology.* New York: Harcourt, Brace and Jovanovich.

Brown, S., Esbensen, F. and Geis, G. (1991). *Criminology: Explaining crime and its context.* Cincinnati: Anderson.

Chambliss, W. (1988). *Exploring criminology.* New York: Macmillan.

Cole, G. (1989). *The American system of justice.* (5th Edition). Monterey, California: Brooks/Cole.

Conklin, J. (1989). *Criminology.* (3rd. Edition). New York: Macmillan.

Cox, S. and Wade, J. (1989). *The criminal justice network* (2nd Edition). Dubuque, Iowa: Wm. C. Brown.

Hagan, F. (1990). *Introduction to criminology.* (2nd. Edition). Chicago: Nelson Hall.

Inciardi, J. (1990). *Criminal justice.* (3rd Edition). New York: Harcourt, Brace and Jovanovich.

Meier, R. (1989). *Crime and society.* Boston: Allyn and Bacon.

Newman, D. and Anderson, P. (1989). *Introduction to criminal justice.* New York: Random House.

Pursley, R. (1991). *Introduction to criminal justice.* (5th. Edition). New York: Macmillan.

Reid, S. (1990). *Criminal justice.* (2nd Edition). New York: MacMillan.

Reid, S. (1991). *Crime and criminology.* (6th Edition). Chicago: Holt, Rinehart and Winston.

Samaha, J. (1991). *Criminal justice.* St. Paul: West.

Schmalleger, F. (1991). *Criminal justice today.* New York: Prentice-Hall.

Senna, J. and Siegel, L. (1990). *Introduction to criminal justice.* (5th Edition). St. Paul: West.

Siegel, L. (1989). *Criminology.* (3rd. Edition). St. Paul: West.

Territo, L., Halsted, J., and Bromley, M. (1989). *Crime and justice in America.* (2nd Edition). St. Paul: West.

Travis, L. (1990). *Introduction to criminal justice.* Cincinnati: Anderson.

Wrobleski, H. and Hess, K. (1990). *Introduction to law enforcement and criminal justice.* St. Paul: West.

ENDNOTES

1. Women of color is an inclusive term which refers to women of various racial and ethnic groups including African-Americans, Hispanics, Asian-Americans, Native-Americans.

2. Young and Sulton (1991) report that only 2 of 157 members of the editorial boards of the top 10 journals in the field are African-Americans.

3. The authors also report that women are over represented in pictures representing the institutions of family and sexuality, although White women visually dominate these areas. In contrast, women of color dominate sections on population leading Ferree and Hall (1990, p. 528) to conclude that "White women have sex and women of color have babies". White men visually dominated the institutions of politics and economy. Minorities visually dominated sections on education and the authors hypothesize that this presence is best explained by the high proportion of minorities portrayed in racially integrated classrooms.

4. Young and Sulton (1991) state that they believe that empirically documenting claims of Eurocentrism distracts researchers from the more important task of researching the more important issues (i.e., those associated with crime causation and policy implementation). Fundamentally, we agree with their perspective; however, we also believe that empirical documentation of biases in the discipline may make it more difficult for those individuals who are grounded in androcentric and Eurocentric perspectives to dismiss other perspectives as biased. Furthermore, we believe that ALL knowledge is socially constructed and that empirical investigations help us understand *how* this construction affects our basic understanding of topics including crime causation and policy implementation.

5. We have borrowed these two levels of analysis from Ferree and Hall (1990). However, we have eliminated a third level: placement of illustrations. This third level examined where photos were placed in a variety of substantive areas. We collected this data, however, there were too few photos of women of color to make this analysis meaningful when the data was broken down by substantive areas.

6. If there were several editions of a text in this time frame, we used only the most recent edition.

7. The *Books in Print Supplement 1990-91* was also used for this project. However, we found that several texts that we personally owned were not listed in either of these sources. We cannot explain these omissions. As a result, we used texts that we owned

as well as texts of our colleagues. We also consulted a list of texts published by Wright and Ducaji (1992). These authors conducted an analysis of criminology texts to examine pictorial representation of white collar crime. We were able to locate all but two texts listed in this article; however, these authors do not discuss their sampling frame. And finally, we called all major publishers and asked for copies of their introductory criminology and criminal justice texts. Thus we have attempted to be as thorough as possible in collecting texts published during the identified time frame.

8. These books are by the following authors: Germann, Day and Gallati, 1988; Galliher, 1989; Gilsinan, 1990; Jeffery, 1990; Mannie and Hirschel, 1988; Massey and Talarico, 1989; Shelley, 1990; Timmer and Eitzen, 1989; Williams and McShane, 1988.

9. We were unable to locate two texts which contain pictures (Barlow, 1990; and Masters and Roberson, 1990) (based on information in the Wright and Ducaji [1992] article) and two other texts which may or may not have pictures in them (Ellis and Ellis, 1989; Lilly, 1989).

10. It is important to note, however, that the texts varied quite a bit in terms of both the number of pictures per book ranging from 12 to 218.

11. Social composition was coded as missing in cases where the race or gender of some individuals in the picture were determined but where the gender or race of another person (or persons) could not be established. For example, a picture containing one African-American male and one individual whose race was undetermined made it impossible to determine whether the photo was racially integrated or not.

12. We were unable to locate data on victimization of other minority women. The NCS has published a special report on Hispanic victims (Bastian, 1990), but the data are not broken down by BOTH race and gender. We could not locate information on the victimization of other women of color (e.g. Native American women or Asian women).

13. Males as individuals make up 100% of the illustrations of lawmakers or politicians and 97% of the academicians or theorists.

14. In fact, we have become so frustrated with textbooks that we are contemplating abandoning them all together. We have found it virtually impossible to use these books without reinforcing the notion that the "supplemental" material is additional and less important than what students read in their texts.

15. These are the three intersections which appear to be receiving the most attention. However, in the tradition of feminist scholarship, we believe that the field will also (eventually) push beyond these three systems of oppression (e.g., sexual orientation, age, ethnicity, religious orientation).

16. For example, *Justice Quarterly, Journal of Criminal Justice Education, Quantitative Criminology, and Research on Crime and Delinquency* all have recently published special issues on women and crime or race and crime or have plans to publish such an issue in the near future.

17. A possible exception is a forthcoming edition (2nd Edition) of Price and Sokolof's, *The Criminal Justice System and Women.* The proposed manuscript is organized around the interactive effects of race, class, and gender.

REFERENCES

American Correctional Association. (1991). *Directory of juvenile and adult correctional department, institutions, agencies and paroling authorities.* Laurel, Maryland: American Correctional Association.

Anderson, M. (1988). Moving our minds: Studying women of color and reconstructing sociology. *Teaching Sociology, 16,* 123–132.

Anzaldua, G. (1990). *Making face, making soul: Haciendo Caras.* San Francisco: Aunt Lute Foundation.

Aronson, D. (1994). Reflections from a different mirror. *Teaching Tolerance, 3* (1), 11–15.

Banks, J. (1976). A content analysis of the Black American in textbooks. In M. Golden (Ed.), *The Research Experience.* Itasca, Ill: F.E. Peacock.

Barak, G. (1991). Cultural literacy and a multicultural inquiry into the study of crime and justice. *Journal of Criminal Justice Education, 2* (2), 173–192.

Barlow, H. (1990). *Introduction to criminology.* Glenview, Illinois: Scott, Foresman/Little, Brown.

Baro, A. & Eigenberg, H. (1992). Images of gender: A content analysis of photographs in introductory Criminology and Criminal Justice textbooks. *Women and Criminal Justice, 5* (1), 3–36.

Berger, J. (1987). *Ways of seeing.* London: British Broadcasting Corporation and Penguin Books.

Bastian, L. (1990). *Hispanic victims.* Washington, D.C.: U.S. Department of Justice.

Brown, A., Goodwin, B., Hall, B., & Jackson-Lowman, H. (1985). A review of psychology of women textbooks: Focus on the Afro-American woman. *Psychology of Women Quarterly, 9*(1), 29–38.

Bryant, A. & Coleman, M. (1988). The black family as portrayed in introductory marriage and family textbooks. *Family Relations, 37*(3), 255–259.

Bureau of the Census. (1991). *Statistical abstract of the United States: 1991.* Washington, D.C.: U.S. Department of Commerce.

Bureau of Justice Statistics. (1990). *Jail inmates 1990.* Washington, D.C.: U.S. Department of Justice.

Bureau of Justice Statistics. (1991). *Women in prison.* Washington, D.C.: U.S. Department of Justice.

Bureau of Justice Statistics. (1992a). *State and local police departments, 1990.* Washington, D.C.: U.S. Department of Justice.

Bureau of Justice Statistics. (1992b). *Sheriffs' departments, 1990.* Washington, D.C.: U.S. Department of Justice.

Caldwell, L. & Greene, H. (1980). "Implementing a Black perspective in criminal justice." In A. Cohn and B. Ward (Eds.), *Improving Management in Criminal Justice.* Beverly Hills: Sage.

Chambliss, W. (1988). *Exploring Criminology.* New York: Macmillan.

Collins, P. (1990). *Black feminist thought: Knowledge, consciousness, and the politics of empowerment.* Boston: Unwin Hyman.

Collins, P. H. (1993). The sexual politics of black womanhood. In P. Bart and G.

Moran (Eds.), *Violence Against Women: The Bloody Footprints* (pp. 85–113). Newbury Park, Ca.: Sage.
Conklin, J. (1988). *Criminology* (3rd Edition). New York: Macmillan.
Daly, K. (1993). Class-race-gender: Sloganeering in search of meaning. *Social Justice, 20* (1–2), 56–71.
Daly, K. & Chesney-Lind, M. (1988). Feminism and criminology. *Justice Quarterly, 5* (4), 497–535.
Dhand, H. (1988). "Bias in social studies textbooks: New research findings." *History and Social Science Teacher, 24,* (1), 23, 25–27.
Dorworth, V. & Henry, M. (1992). "Optical illustrations: The visual representation of blacks and women in introductory criminal justice textbooks." *Journal of Criminal Justice Education, 3* (2), 251–260.
Ellis, R. & Ellis, C. (1989). *Theories of criminal justice: A critical reappraisal.* Longwood Academic.
Erickson, N. (1990). "Final report: Sex bias in the teaching of criminal law. *Rutgers Law Review 42,* 309–604.
Feiner, S. & Morgan, B. (1990). "Women and minorities in introductory economics textbooks: 1974 to 1984." *Women's Studies Quarterly, 3&4,* 46–67.
Ferree, M. & Hall, E. (1990). "Visual images of American society: Gender and race in introductory sociology textbooks." *Gender and Society, 4* (4), 500–533.
Galliher, J. (1989). *Criminology.* Englewood Cliffs, New Jersey: Prentice-Hall.
Germann, A.C., Day, F. & Gallati, R. (1988). *Introduction to law enforcement and criminal justice.* Springfield, Illinois: Charles C Thomas.
Gilsinan, J. (1990). *Criminology and public policy: An introduction.* Englewood Cliffs, New Jersey: Prentice-Hall.
Goldstone, B. (1989). Visual interpretation of children's books. *Reading Teacher, 42* (8), 592–95.
Greene, H. (1979). *A comprehensive bibliography of criminology and criminal justice literature by Black authors from 1895 to 1978.* Hyattsville: Ummah Publications.
Greene, H. (1981). "Black women in the criminal justice system." *The Urban League Review, 6* (1): 54–61.
hooks, b. (1981). *Ain't I a woman: Black women and feminism.* Boston: South End Press.
hooks, b. (1989). *Talking back: thinking feminist—thinking black.* Boston: South End Press.
hooks, b. (1990). *Yearning: Race, Gender, and Cultural Politics.* Boston: The South End Press.
Jeffery, C. (1990). *Criminology: An interdisciplinary approach.* Englewood Cliffs, New Jersey: Prentice-Hall.
Kapplan, J. & Aronson, D. (1994). The numbers gap. *Teaching Tolerance, 3* (1), 21–27.
Karmen, A. (1990). Crime victims: An introduction to victimology. (2nd Edition). Monterey, CA: Brooks/Cole.
Kuhn, T. (1974). *The structure of scientific revolutions.* Chicago: University of Chicago Press.
Lilly, J. (1989). *Criminological theory: Context and consequences.* Beverly Hills: Sage.

Mann, C. R. (1989). "Minority and female: A criminal justice double bind." *Social Justice, 16* (4), 95–114.
Mannie, H. & Hirschel, D. (1988). *Fundamentals of Criminology.* Englewood Cliffs, New Jersey: Prentice-Hall.
Massey, J. & Talarico, S. (1989). *Explorations in crime and justice: A casebook.* Boston: Allyn and Bacon.
Masters, R. & Roberson, C. (1990). *Inside criminology.* Englewood Cliffs, New Jersey: Prentice-Hall.
Messaris, P. (1994). *Visual "literacy": Image, mind and reality.* N.Y.: Westview Press.
Messerschmidt, J. (1994). *Masculinities and Crime.* Lanham, Maryland: Rowman & Littlefield.
Platt, A. (1993). Beyond the canon, with great difficulty. *Social Justice, 20* (1–2), 72–81.
Police Foundation (1990). *On the move: The status of women in policing.* Washington, D.C.: Police Foundation.
Pfohl, S. (1994). *Images of Deviance and Social Control: A Sociological History* (2nd ed.). New York: McGraw-Hill.
Rich, A. (1979). *On Lies, Secrets, and Silence.* New York: Norton.
Rothenberg, P. (1992). *Race, class, & Gender in the United States: An integrated study.* (2nd Ed.). New York: St. Martins Press.
Rothman, R. (1971). "Textbooks and the certification of knowledge." *American Sociologist, 6* (2): 125–127.
Sentman, M. (1983). "Black and white: Disparity in coverage by 'Life Magazine' from 1937 to 1972." *Journalism Quarterly, 60* (3), 501–508.
Shapley, B. (1991, May 15–17). Integrating mass media instruction: Connecting NIE and TV programs for the 21st century. Paper presented at the annual conference on newspapers in education and literacy (New Orleans, La.).
Shelley, J. (1990). *Criminology: A contemporary handbook.* New York: Wadsworth.
Simpson, S. (1989). Feminist theory, crime, and justice. *Criminology, 27* (4), 605–631.
Smith, B. (1982). Racism and women's studies. In G. Hull, P. Scott, and B. Smith (Eds.), *But some of us are brave.* (pp. 48–51). Old Westbury, NY: Feminist Press.
Timmer, D. & Eitzen, S. (1989). *Crime in the streets and crime in the suites: Perspectives on crime and criminal justice.* Boston: Allyn and Bacon.
Whatley, M. (1988). "Photographic images of Blacks in sexuality texts." *Curriculum Inquiry, 18* (2), 137–155.
Whitaker, C. (1990). *Black victims.* Washington, D.C.: U.S. Department of Justice.
Williams, M. & Condry, J. (1989). "Living color: Minority portrayals and cross-racial interactions on television." Paper presented at the Kansas City, Mo., April 27–30, 1989 meeting of the Society for Research in Child Development.
Williams, F. & McShane, M. (1988). *Criminological theory.* Englewood Cliffs, New Jersey: Prentice-Hall.
Wilson, N. & Rigsby, C. (1975). Is crime a man's world? Issues in the exploration of criminality. *Journal of Criminal Justice, 3,* 131–140.
Winkler, K. (1994). The rise of black feminist thought. *The Chronicle of Higher Education, XL* (30), A12 & A17.

Wright, R. (1987). Are 'sisters in crime' finally being booked? The coverage of women and crime in journals and textbooks. *Teaching Sociology, 15,* 418–422.

Wright, R. & Ducaji, C. (1992). "When pictures lie: Photographs of crimes and criminals in introductory criminology textbooks. *Teaching Sociology, 20,* 36–43.

Young, V. (1986). "Gender expectations and their impact on black female offenders and victims." *Justice Quarterly, 3,* (3), 305–327.

Young, V. & Sulton, A.T. (1991). "Excluded: The current status of African-American scholars in the field of criminology and criminal justice." *Journal of Research in Crime and Delinquency, 28* (1), 101–116.

Zinn, M., Cannon, L., Higginbotham, E. & Dill, B. (1986). "The costs of exclusionary practices in women's studies." *Journal of Women in Culture and Society, 11* (2), 290–303.

Zinn, M. & Dill, B. (1994). *Women of Color in U.S. Society.* Philadelphia: Temple University Press.

CHAPTER ELEVEN

CRIMINAL JUSTICE CURRICULA

Michael P. Brown

INTRODUCTION

A college education has long been recognized for its value in most professions, but it has only been recently recognized as contributing to the quality of performance for those in the criminal justice field. That is not to say that criminal justice education has been absent from college campuses. On the contrary, the study of crime and its causes have been part of undergraduate curricula since the 1920s (Gibbons, 1979); and in 1930, criminal justice was offered as an associates degree (Kuykendall, 1977).

Traditionally, many roles in the criminal justice system have been filled by those who have less than an undergraduate education. The call for post-secondary educational requirements for criminal justice practitioners can be traced to the results of a survey conducted by the American Bar Foundation in the 1960s. This study attempted to gain insight into everyday justice system practices—the "discretion . . . exercised by police officers, prosecutors, judges and correctional agencies" (Remington, 1990, p. 13). The results of the survey, according to Remington, " . . . demonstrated that incredibly important and complex decisions were made at every stage of the criminal justice system, particularly at the law enforcement stage, and that improvement in these decisions required an increase in knowledge and in sophistication" (p. 14).

At the time the results of the American Bar Foundation's survey were being published (Dawson, 1969; Lafave, 1965; Miller, 1970; Newman, 1966; and Tiffany, McIntyre & Rotenberg, 1967), a series of reports were issued by the President's Commission on Law Enforcement and Administration of Justice (1967a, b). These reports recommended that police officers earn, at minimum, a baccalaureate degree to be considered for employment. It was believed that the " . . . complexity of police tasks, coupled with police officers' need for a strong foundation on which to base many critical decisions . . . " necessitated a college education (Carter & Sapp, 1990, p. 60).

However, the National Advisory Commission on Higher Education of Police Officers (1979) expressed skepticism about the relationship between a college education and police performance. Perhaps more importantly though was the Commission's belief that undergraduate criminal justice education was woefully lacking, both in the quality of courses taught and in the faculty teaching them (National Commission on Higher Education of Police Officers, 1979).

Despite this skepticism, the 1970s were marked by significant growth in post-secondary criminal justice education (Durham, 1992). A number of factors, including the expansion of the educational system and a reaction to unparalleled crime rates in the 1960s, brought about the establishment of criminal justice programs throughout the country (Greene, Bynum & Webb, 1982). Furthermore, the creation of the Law Enforcement Assistance Administration (LEAA), and especially the Law Enforcement Educational Program (LEEP), provided the economic foundation upon which criminal justice programs flourished (for discussions, see Durham, 1992; Fletcher, 1975; Weirman & Archambeault, 1983).

However in the early 1980s both LEAA and LEEP were terminated, and consequently the economic foundation of many programs crumbled (Durham, 1992). Several programs were impacted by declining enrollments (Weirman & Archambeault, 1983); "A number of these programs eventually closed" (Durham, 1992, p. 37).

Weirman and Archambeault (1983) point out, however, that not all programs were negatively affected. In fact, many programs which had primarily traditional students were not effected at all and some even increased in size. Furthermore, if the number of criminal justice programs and departments throughout the United States is an indication of the stability of criminal justice education in college curricula, it would appear to be more stable than ever. Whereas "by the late 1970s [there were] more than 600 institutions . . . offering associate, baccalaureate, master's, and doctoral degrees in criminal justice or related fields" (Durham, 1992, p. 37), there are more than 1000 today (Nemeth, 1991).

The increase in the number of programs over the past decade appears to suggest that the belief that a college education benefits justice system practitioners continues today. Ernest L. Boyer may have provided insight into the issue when he wrote in *College: The Undergraduate Experience in America* (1987, p. 1):

> The undergraduate college in America, with its long and venerable tradition, has a unique mission to fulfill, one that will enrich and, at its best, transform . . . Why else provide college for those who otherwise could be trained on the job or in a corporate classroom? It can only be because of the conviction that something in the undergraduate experience will lead to a more competent, more concerned, more complete human being.

Similarly, Lynch (1987) asserts that "a college education, regardless of the area of study, can help crystalize raw experience, dispel prejudice and heighten tolerance for ambiguity" (p. 274). A similar belief also exists among practitioners in the field. In the words of one police chief: "The better educated [police officers] tend to stand out in analytical, communications, problem-solving ability, and to display more initiative, less prejudice, and be more global oriented" (Carter & Sapp, 1990, p. 83).

Despite the generally positive beliefs about the value of a college education for justice system practitioners, we are again witnessing a resurgence in questions about the quality of criminal justice education. Critics argue for fundamental changes in the curricula, justified on the grounds that: American society is becoming increasingly culturally diverse (Barak, 1991), there exists a disparity in the number of racial and ethnic minorities under the supervision of the criminal justice system (Flowers, 1990), females have a significantly lower crime rate than males (Garrison, McClelland, Dambrodt & Casey, 1992; Wonders & Caulfield, 1993), the feminist perspective has rapidly developed and risen to prominence in criminological thought (Koser Wilson, 1991; Wonders & Caulfield, 1993), and females and racial/ethnic minority group members are marginalized (Moyer, 1985). In short, the call for change is characterized by the inclusion of multicultural perspectives in criminal justice curricula.

Although the discussion of these issues may lead to future developments in criminal justice education, it is imperative that we digress momentarily from this pedagogical debate and take a practical look at curricular change. Hence, this study does not examine the relative merits of multiculturalism in undergraduate criminal justice education. Rather, its objective is to describe the attitudes and perceptions of criminal justice educators about multicultural education for undergraduates. To date, there has been no such study.

Four general areas are explored. An attempt is made to:

- gain insight into the level of support criminal justice educators have for the inclusion of multicultural perspectives in undergraduate criminal justice education.
- gain insight into the justifications for the inclusion of multicultural perspectives in criminal justice education.
- gain insight into the process perceived as helping to bringing about the inclusion of multicultural perspectives into traditional criminal justice curricula.
- locate where (or determine at what stage) criminal justice education is in the process of curricular transformation.

UNDERGRADUATE CRIMINAL JUSTICE EDUCATION AND MULTICULTURALISM: A REVIEW OF THE LITERATURE

Support for the Inclusion of Multicultural Perspectives

At least two issues arise when one asks whether there is support for the inclusion of multicultural perspectives in undergraduate criminal justice education. On the one hand, an educator may recognize the need to address these perspectives in the classroom and therefore support their inclusion. This level of support may be described as an attitude or belief. On the other hand, an educator may not only believe that multicultural perspectives should be addressed, but also discusses them in the classroom. At this level of support, the belief that multicultural perspectives should be addressed inspires the teaching of the subject matter.

By reviewing the literature, it is difficult to determine the actual level of support existing among educators. This is especially true of attitudinal support. And while research exists to give insight into the extent to which multicultural perspectives are addressed (i.e., support displayed by teaching the subject matter), there has been no direct measure of either level of support.

One may extrapolate from previous research to gain insight into these issues. To do so, however, requires the use of indirect measures of support. And as we are all aware, indirect measures can be misleading and provide conflicting results.

For example by examining the results of content analyses of textbooks (Wright, 1987), one might conclude that since female and racial/ethnic minority perspectives are paid little attention that there is likewise little attitudinal support and scant coverage of the material in the classroom. On the other hand, one may attempt to gauge level of support by examining the depth and breadth of the subject matter. It has been pointed out elsewhere that the feminist (Heindesohn, 1987) and the racial/ethnic perspectives literatures (Barak, 1991) are large. This might lead one to the conclusion that there is wide-spread support.

It is important to make the distinction between attitudinal support and supporting multicultural perspectives through instruction. For if the literature continues to expand and the perspectives are not finding their way into the classroom, where one would hope they are being taught, multicultural literature serves the purpose of "trying to convert the converted." Let us turn our attention to the literature on teaching multicultural perspectives—i.e., the current state of criminal justice education.

The State of Undergraduate Criminal Justice Education

In recent years a great deal of change has taken place in criminal justice education. Among the more noteworthy changes is the shift in focus from vocational education to a more liberal arts orientation (Loewenthal, 1980). And while this shift is applauded by most educators, many believe that there is much more to accomplish. Specifically, there is the need to fully include multicultural perspectives in the curricula.

However, the path, according to Dorworth and Henry (1992), is not free of obstacles.

> "Criminal justice as a field of study in higher education offers special challenges regarding the inclusion of females and blacks because it is traditionally dominated by white males" (p. 251).

White males are the gatekeepers of the field. Consequently, they define "legitimate knowledge," attempting to pass off white "men's studies... as general knowledge" (Geselthorpe & Morris, 1988, p. 94).

And when multicultural perspectives are covered in the classroom, they tend to be presented in a format which marginalizes females and racial/ethnic minorities. Speaking specifically to the manner in which feminist perspectives are addressed, Geselthorpe and Morris (1988) indicate that occasional lectures on female criminality and their experiences with the criminal justice system "... highlight... the failure not the success of feminists to permeate the discipline. The lectures are insertions, addenda, and therefore, marginal" (p. 2). Furthermore, Moyer (1985) notes that although courses on women and crime are being offered, few criminal justice faculty are willing "... to make these courses part of the required core curriculum" (p. 199).

Textbooks, a traditional source of information for most students, have the tendency to also marginalize females and minority group members. Wright (1987), for example, notes that despite substantial growth in the literature feminist perspectives have consistently comprised about three percent of the content in standard texts. In addition, Dorworth and Henry (1992) note that pictures in textbooks tend to marginalize and stereotype African Americans. Whereas African Americans were portrayed as authority figures in two percent of the pictures, they were portrayed as offenders in sixty-six percent of the pictures (Dorworth & Henry, 1992).

This review suggests that the current state of criminal justice education is appalling. On the one hand, multicultural perspectives are rarely addressed; and on the other hand, when they are addressed, they tend to marginalize females and racial and ethnic minorities.

Justifications for Multicultural Perspectives in Criminal Justice Education

A review of the literature reveals several reasons why it is important to include multicultural perspectives in the curricula. The following are some of the more commonly cited justifications for including multicultural perspectives within traditional courses.

Improved Classroom Environment: The literature asserts that covering multicultural perspectives in the classroom will have a positive affect on females and racial/ethnic minorities. A curriculum devoid of multicultural perspectives leads females and minorities " . . . to question their intellectual ability, their career choice and major, their relationship with fellow students, and their interaction with the instructor . . . " (Garrison, McClelland, Dambrot & Casey, 1992, p. 207).

Goodstein (1992) contends that a multicultural approach benefits all students, fostering critical and analytical thought. It makes classrooms places of effective learning for all students. Koser Wilson (1991) makes a similar assertion when she describes the benefits of a gender balanced curriculum.

> "A curriculum that affirms women's experiences as well as men's will give to our women students a sense that change for the better is possible—a sense of fun, excitement, challenge. Women need to feel competent, hopeful, at peace with themselves and their world. This open approach to life should be stimulated in **all** of our students, but it will be systematically denied to female students unless the curriculum is opened up to their experience of life" (pp. 88–89; emphasis mine).

Diversity of American Society: The increasing diversity of American society is well documented throughout the literature (see, for example, Barak, 1991; Takaki, 1987). This trend has resulted in culturally diverse classrooms, highlighting the importance of transforming criminal justice curricula (Garrison, McClelland, Dambrot & Casey, 1992). For educators, this diversity can be used to enhance and expedite the integration of multicultural perspectives into the curricula (Garrison, McClelland, Dambrot & Casey, 1992). The result will be students bringing multicultural understanding into daily life experiences, thus enhancing their quality of life.

Better Prepare Students for Employment in Criminal Justice: It is readily recognized that " . . . the goal of most criminal justice programs . . . [is the] prepar[ation] of students for entry-level jobs in the official criminal justice system" (Koser Wilson & Moyer, 1992, p. 281). This is an important point to remember because in classrooms across the country are those aspiring to be law enforcement officers, prosecutors, corrections officers and judges. These persons will assume the responsibility of social control and will confront cultural diversity daily while performing their occupational duties. It is, therefore, essential that criminal justice students receive a multicultural education.

Theory has Developed Significantly: Most of the multicultural literature is authored by feminist scholars who assert that mainstream criminal justice education can benefit from increased analysis of female crime (Goodstein, 1992; Koser Wilson, 1991; Lynch, Huey, Santiago, Close & Johnston, 1992; Mahan & Anthony, 1992; Wonders & Caulfield, 1993). On the whole, feminist scholars point to the potential benefits of better understanding why females are less criminally active and commit less severe crime than males. Moreover, it is only through the application of feminist theory that one can understand these issues. However, Heindensohn (1987) indicates that feminist perspectives have not been fully integrated into traditional criminological theory and methodology.

Substantial work has also been done in the development of racial/ethnic perspectives. Barak (1991) asserts that the inclusion of racial and ethnic minority perspectives in criminal justice education would enhance theoretical power, thus providing insight into crime rate differences between the races and the reasons behind the disproportionate number of incarcerated minorities. Barak (1991) correctly points out that while race, ethnic, and class issues have traditionally received considerable coverage in criminal justice curricula, they are predominately based upon white male perspectives.

It is perhaps Goodstein (1992) who best summarized the importance of including multicultural perspectives in criminal justice curricula.

> Efforts to include all peoples' experiences will lead inevitably to changes not only in the manner in which the formerly underrepresented groups are studied and taught, but also in how we look at material dealing with those who previously had been at the core of the conventional curriculum . . . Fundamental transformations may be needed in every discipline in which the starting point for theory and analysis has not included the perspectives of women and other underrepresented groups (p. 167).

Bringing About Change

How are multicultural perspectives to be brought to the center of criminal justice curricula? And, what factors need to be present to bring about this process? To date, there is no consensus on the most effective and efficient method to bring about the desired change. Furthermore, according to Goodstein (1992), criminal justice education has not witnessed significant strides toward a multicultural curricula.

Drawing from other academic fields and from the criminal justice literature presently available on curricular change, however, provides insight into the factors needing to be present for successful change to take place (Koser Wilson, 1991). In general, these factors tend to fall within two general categories (for thorough reviews, see Garrison, McClelland, Dambrodt & Casey, 1992; and Goodstein, 1992):

- **Ongoing Departmental/University Support:** e.g., provisions for release time, funding and educational seminars for the educators.
- **Commitment on the Part of the Educator:** this would involve, among other things, the desire to bring about change, willingness to devote the time needed to become familiar with and keeping up-to-date with the relevant literature.

THE PRESENT STUDY

Research Questions

Broadly defined, the objective of the present study is to describe the current state of multicultural perspectives in undergraduate criminal justice education. From the review it is clear that while the multicultural literature is burgeoning, there is wide-spread agreement that it is not making its way into the classroom. In an attempt to gain insight into this issue, answers to several questions are pursued.

First, to what extent is there attitudinal support for the inclusion of multicultural perspectives in undergraduate criminal justice education? Currently, there is no direct measure of this dimension of support. Relatedly, the second question is: how should multicultural perspectives be addressed within the curricula (i.e., in specialty courses only, integrated into traditional courses only, or a combination of specialty courses and integrated into traditional courses).

Third, to what extent is there support in teaching multicultural perspectives among educators? The literature provides indirect measures of this issue. What is needed is a measure of course content devoted to addressing multicultural perspectives. The present research reports the percentage of total course content devoted to teaching these perspectives.

Fourth, what justifies the inclusion of multicultural perspectives in traditional course work? Several justifications have been offered in the literature. The present research asks educators what they believe are the reasons why it is important to address multicultural perspectives in their classes.

Finally, what is the process by which multicultural perspectives are brought into the core of criminal justice education? Central to this question is the process by which educators believe curricular transformation takes place. Respondents were asked to rank a number of items in one of four categories: initial stage, middle stage, final stage, and never part of the process of curricular transformation. This question also provides an opportunity to assess the extent to which curricular transformation has taken place.

METHODS

Data Source

To obtain the information necessary to gain insight into issues relevant to the present research, an attempt was made to identify professionally active educators. To do this, the names of participants at the 1993 meetings of the Academy of Criminal Justice Sciences and American Society of Criminology were combined into a master list. Duplicate names were removed, as were those whose mailing address indicated that they: (1) did not reside in the United States and (2) were not educators (e.g., an address of a private research firm or a probation department).

Five hundred names and addresses were randomly selected from the master list. With the financial support of a grant from Ball State University (1994), a survey questionnaire, cover letter and postage-paid return envelope were mailed to those selected. The cover letter briefly explained the purpose of the survey and promised anonymity. The cover letter also provided a definition of multiculturalism as "looking at the world from more than one cultural perspective." Also, since the present study focused on feminist and racial/ethnic perspectives, definitions were provided for these concepts. Feminist perspectives was defined broadly to include women's criminality and experiences with the criminal justice system, as well as feminist theories and methodologies. Racial/ethnic minority perspectives was likewise broadly defined to include criminality, experiences with the criminal justice system and theories formulated by racial and ethnic minorities.

Approximately two weeks after the initial mailing, a postcard was sent to those who had not yet returned their survey. The postcard stressed the importance of their participation and requested that they return the survey.

Response Rate

Of the 500 surveys mailed, 4 were returned because the educator was no longer employed at the address indicated on the master list. Additionally, 7 surveys were returned by graduate students who were not teaching. Hence, the response rate—defined as the number of completed surveys (214) divided by the number of eligible (or locateable) respondents (489)—is 43.8 percent.

Sample Demographics

As can be seen in Table 1, the sample is composed mostly of males (65.9 percent) and whites (89.7 percent), and is indicative of the characteristics of criminal justice educators as cited above. Ages ranged from 24 to 65. The mean (and median) age is 43. Nearly all sample respondents had earned either a doctorate (80.2 percent) or master's degree (14.6 percent). Nearly 3 percent were lawyers. The others had not yet finished their doctorate (2.4 percent); they are classified ABD.

Table 1. Demographics (n = 214).

Characteristic	*N*	%
Gender		
Female	73	34.1
Male	141	65.9
Race/Ethnicity		
African American	10	4.7
Asian	5	2.3
White	192	89.7
Hispanic	3	1.4
Native American	4	1.9
Age[1]		
Mean	42.8	
Median	43	
Range	24–65	
Educational Attainment[2]		
Doctorate	170	80.2
Master's	31	14.6
JD	6	2.8
ABD	5	2.4

1. Three respondents did not provide their age. Mean and median ages were calculated based on n = 211.
2. Two respondents did not provide educational information (n = 212).

FINDINGS

Support for Multicultural Perspectives

A likert scale was utilized to determine the level of attitudinal support for the inclusion of multicultural perspectives in undergraduate criminal justice curricula. Of the 214 respondents, nine (4.2 percent) indicated that they were "strongly unsupportive" or "unsupportive" of including multicultural perspectives in the curricula. Twelve (5.6 percent) were "uncertain." But of the remaining 193 (90.2 percent) respondents, 115 were "strongly supportive" and 78 were "supportive" of including multicultural perspectives in the curricula.

Restricting the analysis to those who were "uncertain," "supportive" and "strongly supportive" (n=205), respondents were asked to indicate the method by which they believed multicultural perspectives should be addressed (see Table 2). Three options were offered: (1) specialty courses only (e.g., women and crime or race and crime classes), (2) integrated into traditional courses only and (3) both specialty courses and integrated into the traditional courses.

Sixty-nine percent indicated that multicultural perspectives should be covered both in specialty courses and in traditional courses. Twenty-seven percent did not support the use of specialty courses. For these respondents, multicultural perspectives should be addressed solely in traditional courses. The use of specialty courses as the only method by which multicultural perspectives are addressed is supported by few of the respondents (3.9 percent).

Table 2. Methods of Addressing Multicultural Perspectives[1]

Method	*N*	%
Specialty Courses:	8	3.9
Integrated into Traditional Courses:	55	27.0
Both Specialty Courses and Integrated into Traditional Courses:	141	69.1

1. One respondent did not provide a response to this question (n = 204).

Extent of Coverage

The 205 respondents who are supportive or uncertain as to whether multicultural perspectives should be included in criminal justice curricula teach a variety of courses. Table 3 contains a list of courses taught by the respondents. It also includes, in the first column of the table, a ratio: the number of courses which address multicultural perspectives to the total courses taught; by extension the table presents the percentage of courses which address multicultural perspectives (column 2). Furthermore, column 3 contains information which provides insight into the extent to which multicultural perspectives are addressed in each course (i.e., the percentage of course content). No attempt is made to distinguish among the perspectives addressed in each course. Excluded from the table are specialty courses (e.g., women and crime), since they are specifically designed to cover multicultural perspectives. Twenty-four respondents (12%) indicated that they teach specialty courses.

As can be seen, of the 431 courses taught (an average of 2.1 courses per respondent) 384 address multicultural perspectives. Overall, then, about 90 percent of the courses have multicultural subject matter. And of these

Table 3. Extent of Coverage: Ratio of Courses Covering Multicultural Perspectives to Total Courses Taught, Percent of Course with Multicultural Content and Percent of Multicultural Perspectives in Total Course Content.

Course Title [1]	*Ratio: Multicultural Perspectives Covered/Total*	*Percent of Courses with Multicultural Content*	*Percent of Total Course Content*
Victimology	3/3	100.0	38.0
Law	16/18	88.9	24.0
Violence	3/3	100.0	23.7
Other	76/84	90.5	22.7
Seminar	8/10	80.0	20.0
Juvenile Justice	22/24	91.7	18.8
Institutional Corrections	42/45	93.3	17.3
Ethics	3/3	100.0	17.0
Independent Study	2/2	100.0	16.2
Criminology	54/54	100.0	15.3
Introduction to Criminal Justice	42/46	91.2	15.0
Policing	33/40	82.5	14.0
Community Corrections	13/15	86.7	13.7
Deviance	6/6	100.0	10.7
Corporate and White Collar Crime	5/6	83.3	10.6
Statistics	3/9	33.3	10.6
Methods	29/39	74.4	7.1
TOTAL	384/431	89.1	16.9

1. See Appendix A for description of courses.

courses, multicultural perspectives comprise 17 percent of the total course content.

Several course types (e.g., victimology, ethics and deviance) are consistently reported as covering multicultural perspectives. It might be argued that the foci of these courses are compatible with multiculturalism. However, while this may be true it does not predict the percentage of course content devoted to such topics. In fact, the extent to which multicultural perspectives permeate course content varies considerably, from 38 percent for victimology courses to 17 percent for ethics courses to 11 percent for deviance courses. Research methods courses are reported as having the least coverage of multicultural perspectives: 7 percent of the total course content.

Justifications for Including Multicultural Perspectives in the Curriculum

At this point in the analysis it is clear that there is wide-spread support for including multicultural perspectives in undergraduate criminal justice education. Moreover, most respondents believe that these perspectives should be addressed in both specialty and traditional courses. It is also evident that multicultural perspectives are addressed in all courses. However, the extent to which they permeate course content varies considerably. The next issue to be addressed is, on what grounds are multicultural perspectives justified for inclusion? In other words, why is it important for students to be exposed to these perspectives? Table 4 contains the justifications offered to respondents.

Table 4. Justification for Including Multicultural Perspectives in Undergraduate Curriculum (n = 205).

Item	*N*	%
They would Improve the Classroom Environment for Females	102	49.8
They would Improve the Classroom Environment for Ethnic/Racial Minorities	103	50.2
The Diversity of American Society Necessitates a Broader Approach to the Study of Criminal Justice	181	88.3
They would Help to Better Prepare Students for Working in the Justice System	175	85.4
Theory has Developed Significantly and Students Should be Exposed to Differing Perspectives	123	60.0

As can be seen, about half of the respondents believe that multicultural perspectives should be addressed because they would improve the classroom environment for females and racial/ethnic minorities. Furthermore, one respondent indicated that addressing these perspectives

> ... would [also] improve the classroom environment for white males.

However, some of the respondents were strongly opposed to using "an improved classroom environment" as justification for inclusion. One respondent argued that while multicultural perspectives may improve the classroom environment for females and minorities,

> if used as rationales it has the potential to make it seem that women [and] minorities are lesser students and they are not.

In a much stronger statement, one respondent indicated:

> I see multicultural perspectives as nonsense. I don't see any use in the idea of multicultural education—**It hurts the academic process and marginalizes women and racial minorities.** [emphasis mine]

Somewhat more support (60 percent) is given for the inclusion of multicultural perspectives on the grounds that theory has developed and students need to be exposed to it. As one respondent noted, presenting a . . .

> variety [of] perspectives helps to develop analytical/critical thinking skills.

For most respondents, however, the inclusion of multicultural perspectives is justified on two grounds. First, multicultural perspectives would help to better prepare students for working in the criminal justice system (85.4 percent); and second, the diversity of American society necessitates a broader approach to the study of criminal justice (88.3 percent). The comments of two respondents suggest that the magnitude of support for these justifications may be based on an orientation for the future. In their words, addressing multicultural perspectives:

- exposes the criminal justice system to more possibilities for change.
- . . . would better prepare the criminal justice field to deal with crime control in the future.

Several respondents offered other justifications for the inclusion of multicultural perspectives in undergraduate curricula. Among them are that multicultural perspectives:

- . . . should be simply considered a fundamental part of any curriculum.
- . . . provide a platform for students to critically assess the world around them.
- . . . will enhance individual growth that can apply to all aspects of life in general.

Bringing About a Multicultural Curriculum

Respondents were asked to rank a list of items in the order they believe would help bring about the inclusion of multicultural perspectives into undergraduate criminal justice curricula. Most of the respondents ranked the items as being in the initial stage, middle stage, final stage or never being a part of the process. The results of the ranking are found in Table 5. Others ranked the items in another fashion. All of the responses, including those shown in Table 5, can be found in the Appendix B.

Upon close inspection, trends are revealed in the ranking of these items. For example, a majority of respondents considered (a) educating Ph.D. candidates in multicultural perspectives (72.9 percent), (b) hiring women

Table 5. The Process of Integrating Multicultural Perspectives into Undergraduate Criminal Justice Education.

Item	*Initial Stage*	*Middle Stage*	*Final Stage*	*Never Part of Process*	*Total*
Educate PhD candidates in multicultural perspectives:	137 (72.9)	31 (16.5)	17 (9.0)	3 (1.6)	188 (100)
Publish high quality multicultural literature:	75 (40.1)	65 (34.8)	43 (23.0)	4 (2.1)	187 (100)
Establish specialty courses:	80 (42.8)	61 (32.6)	27 (14.4)	19 (10.2)	187 (100)
Departmental policy, multicultural perspectives taught in all courses:	49 (26.5)	22 (11.9)	18 (9.7)	96 (51.9)	185 (100)
Hire women/minority faculty:	139 (77.2)	30 (16.7)	7 (3.9)	4 (2.2)	180 (100)
Integrated textbooks:	131 (71.6)	43 (23.5)	9 (4.9)	0 (0.0)	183 (100)
Actively recruit women/minorities into graduate school:	140 (76.1)	33 (17.9)	7 (3.8)	4 (2.2)	184 (100)
Actively recruit women/minorities into undergraduate school:	141 (76.2)	32 (17.3)	7 (3.8)	5 (2.7)	185 (100)
Specialty courses, required:	46 (24.6)	57 (30.5)	43 (23.0)	41 (21.9)	187 (100)
Use professional meeting to discuss methods of inclusion:	109 (58.9)	49 (26.5)	26 (14.0)	1 (.5)	185 (100)

and racial/ethnic minority faculty (77.2 percent), (c) making available textbooks which integrate multicultural perspectives with traditional perspectives (71.6 percent), (d) actively recruiting women and racial/ethnic minorities into (e) graduate (76.1 percent) and (f) undergraduate (76.2 percent) criminal justice programs, and (g) utilizing professional meetings to discuss methods of inclusion (58.9 percent) as the initial stage of curricular transformation.

Some of the respondents were unconvinced that hiring women and racial/ethnic group members would help bring about the inclusion of multicultural perspectives. For example, one respondent indicated:

> Mere membership in a particular group does not automatically promote multicultural understanding. My preference would be to recruit *anyone* who was open-minded to multicultural perspectives, regardless of gender or race/ethnicity.

The middle stage is characterized by (a) the publishing of quality multicultural literature (34.8 percent), (b) the establishment of specialty courses (32.6 percent), and (c) requiring specialty courses as part of the required core curriculum (30.5 percent). A respondent recounted a salient point related to this middle stage.

> This year marks the first year our department (which is five years old) formulated and requires a race and gender class. Although the faculty strongly support the course there has been some resistance on the part of the students—an indication that they are in need of such a course.

Unlike the initial and middle stages of the process, the data reveal no clear trend for the final stage. However, it is clear that passing a departmental policy which required multicultural perspectives to be taught in all courses is considered inappropriate; fifty two percent of the respondents indicated that this should never be part of the integration process. Many respondents indicated that such a policy would infringe on their academic freedom. Moreover, in the words of one respondent:

> [a] policy requiring people who don't want to [teach multicultural perspectives] . . . may [mean that they will] do a lousy job at it—worse than nothing.

Another respondent added:

> Sell the concepts, don't jam it down peoples throat. Orders and mandates don't promote social equality. Grassroots approaches do.

Still another respondent argued:

> Multiculturalism as an addition is useful, but it is often presented as an alternative. Indeed, traditional subject matter is often devalued. But no amount of multiculturalism can replace core skills in statistics, quantitative analysis, computer skills, writing, analytical thinking, etc. . . .

Diagram 1 (below) depicts the process of curricular transformation described above. It is important to point out that several respondents mentioned that they had difficulty designating the items to a particular stage—that is, "These items would be found throughout the integration process." In fact, one respondent stated:

> Integration is probably not a linear process. Some things done at the start of the process will also be [found throughout]...

Several respondents suggested additional items to help with the integration process. Some of the suggestions were:

- Provide professional development opportunities for present faculty on multicultural education in criminal justice.
- Establish [a] resource center.
- Show successful minority professionals to students.
- Develop teaching seminars/programs for faculty. [Also] fund faculty development in these areas.

Diagram 1
The Curricular Transformation Process

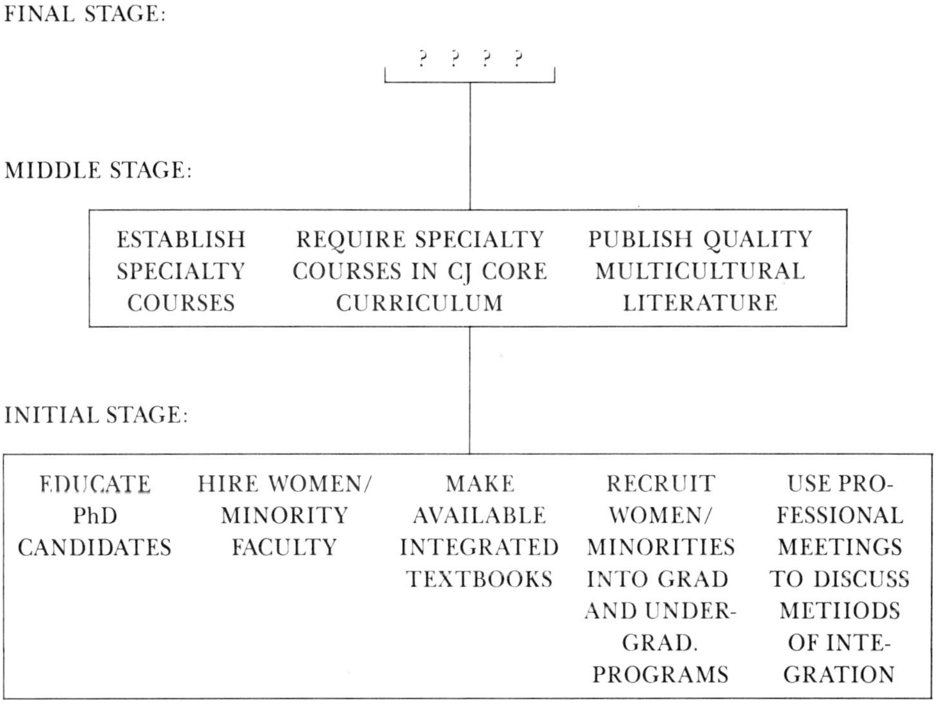

Although imposing a structure on the process of bringing multicultural perspectives into the center of criminal justice education may not be appropriate, Diagram 1 appears to suggest that the stage is set for the inclusion of multicultural perspectives into traditional curricula. Surely there are many obstacles that yet need to be confronted. Nevertheless:

- many doctoral programs are educating future educators on the most current multicultural perspectives;
- females and minority group members are being hired to teach in criminal justice programs and departments;
- integrated textbooks are becoming increasingly available;
- female and minority group members are being recruited into undergraduate and graduate criminal justice programs;
- professional meetings are utilized by the traditionally under-represented as support groups and as opportunities to share ideas;
- specialty courses have been established;
- in at least one program (see comment by respondent above), a specialty course has been made a requirement for graduation;
- and there is an abundance of quality multicultural literature.

SUMMARY AND CONCLUSIONS

Criminal justice education has been sharply criticized twice in recent history. The first time was from outside the academy, by the National Advisory Commission on Higher Education of Police Officers (1979). Most recently, however, criticism has come from within the academy by those who contend that the curricula is not sufficiently culturally diverse and marginalizes females and racial/ethnic minorities. There is also the criticism that traditional theory lacks explanatory power when applied to female offenders.

To date, the literature calling for the inclusion of multicultural perspectives in the curricula has been pedagogical. The present study departed from this tradition by examining issues previously unexplored. Specifically, the research reported here attempted to gain insight into the attitudes and perceptions of criminal justice educators regarding their (1) support for including multicultural perspectives in the curricula, (2) why it is important that these perspectives are addressed in the classroom, (3) how the process of inclusion is conceptualized and (4) at what stage in the process of inclusion is the curricula.

Data indicate that about 96 percent of the respondents were not opposed to including multicultural perspectives in the curricula (90.2 percent were strongly supportive or supportive and 5.6 percent were uncertain). Also, these educators were in favor of including the subject matter not only in specialty courses, but also integrated within the traditional curricula (69.1 percent). Only 4 percent of the respondents wanted to restrict multicultural perspectives to specialty courses.

This support was reflected in the fact that all of the respondents reported that they address multicultural perspectives in the classroom. However, the extent to which multicultural perspectives permeate course content varied considerably across course type. Several questions arise with this finding. However, the central question relates to how one can determine whether multicultural perspectives are being given appropriate coverage in a course. The extent to which multicultural perspectives permeated course subject matter ranges from 38 percent in victimology courses to 7 percent in research methods.

Does it mean that for a course to be fully integrated that 50 percent of the subject matter must pertain to multicultural perspectives? If this is the measure by which the results are compared, then none of the classes would be considered appropriately integrated. Other researchers may wish to address this issue.

Respondents were also asked why it was important that multicultural perspectives are included in the curricula. The findings suggest that most believed that a better understanding of crime and the criminal justice system can be achieved from a broader perspective (88 percent). Likewise, it was believed that students would function more effectively upon entering the criminal justice field (85 percent).

These findings seem to suggest that the respondents recognize the limitations of traditional perspectives. They likewise suggest that there is a recognition among educators that their students need to be knowledgeable and appreciative of cultural diversity upon entering the work force. Several of the written responses also indicate that multicultural perspectives would extend into and improve one's personal life.

The development of feminist theory and theories written from the perspective of racial/ethnic minorities received noteworthy support (60 percent) as a reason for including multicultural perspectives in the curricula. Some of the respondents speculated that by covering these theories, it would promote analytical and critical thinking skills.

Improving the classroom environment for females (50 percent) and minority group members (50 percent) received the least support as justifications for including multicultural perspectives in the curricula. This finding may be surprising since as educators we strive to provide the "best" learning environment possible for all our students. However, the relatively low rating may reflect a genuine concern expressed by one respondent: if used as rationales it has the potential to lower the status of females and minorities. Finally, respondents appear to largely agree on what needs to be accomplished to bring about an integrated curricula. Data suggest that initially what needs to be accomplished is the education of future educators (PhD candidates), diversifying faculties (i.e., hiring traditionally under-represented persons), making available textbooks which take a multicultural approach, recruiting females and racial/ethnic minorities into both undergraduate and graduate programs, and utilizing professional associations to promote and assist with diversification efforts. Then, building upon these advancements the next step to take would be to publish quality literature, establish specialty courses and require specialty courses as a requirement of the core curricula.

Clearly, the distinction between the stages should not be considered absolute. After all, quality multicultural literature (indicated at the middle stage) must be present before students can be effectively educated (indicated at the initial stage) in the perspectives. Forcing the integration process into a static model over-simplifies the dynamic nature of bringing multiculturalism into the curricula. Consequently, it might be best to conceptualize the inclusion of multicultural perspectives as an interactive process. A process in which developments in one area differentially impact upon other areas.

This analysis suggests that movement toward bringing multicultural perspectives into the classroom has been noteworthy. All of the components of the model are being accomplished. Yet there is more to be done. Based upon the comments of respondents, it appears that wide-spread commitment of individuals to transforming his or her courses is perhaps the best predictor of curricular change. Criminal justice programs and universities need to provide support services and resources, but without individual commitment significant transformation is unlikely to occur.

There are two limitations of the present research that require mentioning. First, data for the analysis were derived from a self-report survey. And while the respondents demonstrated great care in the responses provided, there is the possibility for over- or under-reporting. Also, the reader is cautioned not to generalize the results of this research to all criminal justice educators. At best, one can only generalize these findings to those who share the characteristics of the respondents.

Future research might build from this study by surveying justice system practitioners to determine whether salient issues encountered in the field are addressed in the classroom. It may also be instructive to survey students about the presentation of multicultural perspectives in the classroom. The successful inclusion of multiculturalism will certainly be influenced by how students react and how multicultural education is presented to them. Knowing why students are supportive and not supportive of the material are related to effective learning. Therefore, this may be a fruitful area for future research.

APPENDIX A

Course Descriptions

Course Title(1)	Description
Law	criminal law, procedural law, constitutional law
Violence	family/domestic violence
Other	administration of criminal justice organizations, psychology and the criminal procedure, practicum, sociology of law
Seminar	senior/capstone courses
Independent Study	no indication of topic(s) studied

(1) The remainder of the courses were reported by the title indicated in Table 5. No other information was reported.

APPENDIX B

The Process of Integrating Multicultural Perspectives into Undergraduate Criminal Justice Education (n = 205)(1)

		Stages			Not	All
Item	Initial	Middle	Final	Never	Selected	Stages
Educate PhD candidates in multicultural perspectives:	137 (66.8)	31 (15.1)	17 (8.3)	3 (1.5)	10 (4.9)	7 (3.4)
Publish high quality multicultural literature:	75 (36.6)	65 (31.7)	43 (21.0)	4 (1.9)	11 (5.4)	7 (3.4)
Establish specialty courses:	80 (39.0)	61 (29.8)	27 (13.2)	19 (9.3)	15 (7.3)	3 (1.5)
Dept'l policy, multi cultural perspectives taught in all courses:	49 (23.9)	22 (10.7)	18 (8.8)	96 (46.8)	18 (8.8)	2 (1.0)

Hire women/minority faculty:	139 (67.8)	30 (14.6)	7 (3.4)	4 (1.9)	16 (7.8)	9 (4.4)
Integrated textbooks:	131 (63.9)	43 (21.0)	9 (4.4)	0 (0.0)	16 (7.8)	6 (2.9)
Actively recruit women/ minorities into graduate school:	140 (68.3)	33 (16.1)	7 (3.4)	4 (1.9)	12 (5.8)	9 (4.4)
Actively recruit women/ minorities into under graduate school:	141 (68.8)	32 (15.6)	7 (3.4)	5 (2.4)	12 (5.8)	8 (3.9)
Specialty courses, required:	46 (22.4)	57 (27.8)	43 (21.0)	41 (20.0)	16 (7.8)	2 (1.0)
Use professional meeting to discuss methods of inclusion:	109 (53.2)	49 (23.9)	26 (12.7)	1 (.5)	12 (5.8)	8 (3.9)

(1) Percentages are presented in parentheses.

REFERENCES

Ball State University (1994). New Faculty Research Grant, Internal Grants Program. Muncie, Indiana.

Barak, G. (1991). Cultural Literacy and a Multicultural Inquiry into the Study of Crime and Justice. *Journal of Criminal Justice Education, 2*(2), 173–192.

Boyer, E. L. (1987). *College: The Undergraduate Experience in America.* New York: Harper and Row Publishers.

Carter, D. L., & Sapp, A. D. (1990). The Evolution of Higher Education in Law Enforcement: Preliminary Findings From a National Study. *Journal of Criminal Justice Education, 1,* (1), 59–83.

Dawson, R. (1969). *Sentencing.* Boston: Little, Brown.

Dorworth, V. E., & Henry, M. (1992). Optical Illusions: The Visual Representation of Blacks and Women in Introductory Criminal Justice Textbook. *Journal of Criminal Justice Education, 3*(2), 251–260.

Durham, A. M. (1992). Observations on the Future of Criminal Justice Education: Legitimating the Discipline and Serving the General Population. *Journal of Criminal Justice Education, 3*(1), 35–50.

Fletcher, T. H. (1975). The Criminal Justice System and the Role of Education. *Southern Quarterly, 13,* 119–130.

Flowers, R. B. (1990). *Minorities and Criminality*. New York, New York: Praeger.
Garrison, C. G., McClelland, A., Dambrodt, F., & Casey, K. A. (1992). Gender Balancing the Criminal Justice Curriculum and Classroom. *Journal of Criminal Justice Education, 3*(2), 201–220.
Geselthorpe, L., & Morris, A. (1988). Feminism and Criminology in Britain. *British Journal of Criminology, 28*(2), 93–110.
Gibbons, D. C. (1979). *The Criminological Enterprise*. Englewood Cliffs, NJ: Prentice-Hall.
Goodstein, L. (1992). Feminist Perspectives and the Criminal Justice Curriculum. *Journal of Criminal Justice Education, 3*(2), 165–181.
Greene, J. R., Bynum, T. S., and Webb, V. J. (1982). *Crime Related Education: Faculty Roles, Values and Expectations*. Washington, D.C.: U.S. Department of Justice.
Heindensohn, F. (1987). Women and Crime: Questions for Criminology. In P. Carlen & A. Worrall (Eds.), *Gender, Crime and Justice* (pp. 16–27). Philadelphia: Open University Press.
Koser Wilson, N. (1991). Feminist Pedagogy in Criminology. *Journal of Criminal Justice Education, 2*(1), 81–94.
Koser Wilson, N., & Moyer, I. (1992). Affirmative Action, Multiculturalism and Politically Correct Criminology. *Journal of Criminal Justice Education, 3*(2), 277–291.
Kuykendall, J. L. (1977). Criminal Justice Programs in Higher Education: Courses and Curriculum Orientations. *Journal of Criminal Justice, 5*, 149–164.
LaFave, W. (1965). *Arrest*. Boston: Little, Brown.
Loewenthal, M. A. (1980). The Crisis in Criminal Justice Education: Constructive Reappraisal or Intellectual Masochism? *Criminal Justice Review, 5*(1), 25–41.
Lynch, G. W. (1987). Cops and College. *America, April*, 274-275.
Lynch, M. J., Heuy, J., Santiago Nunez, J., Close, B. R., & Johnston, C. (1992). Cultural Literacy, Criminology and Female-Gender Issues: The Power to Exclude. *Journal of Criminal Justice Education, 3*(2), 183–202.
Mahan, S., & Anthony, A. M. (1992). Including Women in Corrections Texts. *Journal of Criminal Justice Education, 3*(2), 261–276.
Miller, F. (1970). *Prosecution*. Boston: Little, Brown.
Moyer, I. (1985). Academic Criminology: A Need for Change. *American Journal of Criminal Justice, 9*(2), 197–212.
National Advisory Commission on Higher Education for Police Officers (1979). *Proceedings of the National Symposium on Higher Education for Police Officers*. Washington, D.C.: The Police Foundation.
Nemeth, C. P. (1991). *Anderson's 1991 Directory of Criminal Justice Education*. Cincinnati, OH: Anderson Publishing Co.
Newman, D. (1966). *Conviction*. Boston: Little, Brown.
President's Commission on Law Enforcement and Administration of Justice (1967a). *The Challenge of Crime in a Free Society*. Washington, D.C.: U.S. Government Printing Office.
President's Commission on Law Enforcement and Administration of Justice (1967b). *Task Force Report: Police*. Washington, D.C.: U.S. Government Printing Office.

Remington, F. J. (1990). Development of Criminal Justice as an Academic field. *Journal of Criminal Justice Education, 1*(1), 9–20.

Takaki, R. (1987). *From Different Shores: Perspectives on Race and Ethnicity.* New York: Oxford University Press.

Tiffany, L., McIntyre, D., & Rotenberg, D. (1967). *Detection of Crime.* Boston: Little, Brown.

Weirman, C., & Archambeault, W. G. (1983). Assessing the Effects of LEAA Demise on Criminal Justice Higher Education. *Journal of Criminal Justice, 11,* 549–561.

Wonders, N. A., & Caulfield, S. L. (1993). Women's Work? The Contradictory Implications of Courses on Women and the Criminal Justice System. *Journal of Criminal Justice Education, 4*(1), 79–100.

Wright, R. A. (1987). Are Sisters in Crime Finally Being Booked? The Coverage of Women and Crime in Journals and Textbooks. *Teaching Sociology, 15,* 418–422.

CHAPTER TWELVE

CULTURAL SENSITIVITY TRAINING

Stephen M. Hennessy

INTRODUCTION

The study and understanding of differing cultures is a critical part of living in a world that is rapidly becoming multicultural. Law enforcement agencies face an added challenge in understanding the ever changing cultural diversity of the communities they are sworn to serve, as well as the diversity of the employees in the departments themselves. The challenge for law enforcement, more unique than in any other service profession, creates a special need for understanding a pluralistic, multicultural society. The very success of the many facets of community policing is dependent on this understanding.

Every law enforcement agency is struggling with these issues. The importance of understanding these problems gained a new and important emphasis after the Rodney King assault in California. Not only did the incident bring racial issues and concerns back into focus, it also awakened the concern for understanding the changing demographics of our populations.

One mistake often made when teaching cultural awareness and racial sensitivity is to condemn the culture of the United States as colonialist, racist, sexist, and exploitive while holding other cultures up as superior in structure and belief. When this is done, everyone sees the true ignorance of human nature throughout history. All cultures are, or have been exploitive and violent to minorities in one way or another. There is not a piece of land anywhere on this earth that belongs to its rightful guardian. The North American Anglo-Saxon culture of the United States, the one that people often rush to condemn, is one of the few that openly discusses and debates these issues and concerns for all to see in an attempt to strive towards truth and equality.

Cultural awareness training and attempts to educate police officers to be more sensitive to different races, began to proliferate in the early 1960's. Many courses were structured in such a way to afford various minority representatives an opportunity to address rookie trainees or in-service officers. The usual setting, in the form of a panel, often became one way monologues or confrontational dialogues between both minority representatives and attendees in an attempt to induce learning and a change of attitude. Such a style typically was marked by a strident and emotional challenge to participants which could, and often did, result in deep anger and resentment on the part of the participants (Work, 1989). In these sessions there was no opportunity to discuss issues in an adult learning environment which would include an intellectual exchange of thoughts and ideas.

The concern for understanding the importance of differences in culture and what the role of the police in society play is not new. During the first three decades of this century, the police in the United States were often perceived by the public as corrupt and inefficient. In fact, negative attitudes by police regarding race and culture were evident and noted by police researchers in the early 1900's. According to C. Simon (1929), there was a belief held by many American police officers during the earlier years of this century that the immigrant population was largely composed of "the mentally and morally unfit of Europe" (p. 27). Jordan (1972) claimed that police officials did not raise the issue in criticizing this attitude because recent immigrants were becoming police officers and they thought such criticism would damage morale and cause dis-array.

According to Walker (1980), "Special training in race relations was virtually unthinkable in an era when most police departments offered no formal training of any sort" (p. 166). There was little or no tolerance for diversity on the part of police, even though many of the police were immigrants themselves, or the sons of immigrants. As the nation grew, so did the troubling racial problems. In 1944, Gunnar Myrdal, a Swedish social scientist and a Nobel Peace Prize winner, published *An American Dilemma,* a study of Black-White relations in a cross section of areas in both the northern and southern United States. D. W. Suthen (1987) commented that even though Myrdal's work contained more than fifteen hundred pages with vast amounts of data and numerous hypotheses, a common theme emerged (p. xiii). Myrdal asserted that "White Americans experienced a troubling dilemma because of the discrepancy between the hallowed American Creed whereby they think, talk, and act under the egalitarian and Christian precepts, and the oppressive way they treat Afro-Americans."

Historically we've been struggling with cultural and racial issues and often seem to be no further along than many years ago. Human nature being what it is, we have a tendency to look for quick and simple solutions to problems that are deeply rooted in the human psyche.

As Bickham and Rossett (1993) noted, there are no "Silver Bullet" solutions to these concerns, but involve a planned, structured response organizationally from the top down. The strongest challenge is to determine what our profession is attempting to accomplish by becoming involved in teaching these issues to its employees. The goals of these programs are critically important and reflect the very essence of community policing and should include:

- Understanding the importance of power and image in maintaining a professional reputation for our law enforcement organizations.
- Understanding contributions and life styles of the various racial, cultural, and economic groups to our communities;
- Recognizing and dealing with our biases, discrimination and prejudices that effect both our organizations and the citizens we serve;
- Understanding professional behaviors which contribute to the self esteem of the residents of our communities and to positive interpersonal relations within our organizations; and
- Respecting diversity and personal rights.

Law Enforcement agencies often begin these programs when forced to as a "knee jerk" reaction to community pressure. Often the courses are the result of perception by outside groups that officers in the department have not been sensitive enough to the differences of the various cultures residing in the city. These programs should not be seen as a "punishment" for a wrong, but an opportunity to respond positively to the future.

In designing training content for programs, trainers should conduct a needs assessment if at all possible. This process, which does not have to be long and involved, identifies training needs and priorities as well as defines objectives. It introduces trainers to the organizational communication climate of the organization. Usually, several main themes arise from a "needs analysis" point of view. These typically are:

- The organizational need to adhere to affirmative action goals, educate executives and employees regarding human and civil rights legislation, and to deal with institutional racism as represented in policy and procedure issues.
- How law enforcement can better understand the changing and diverse nature of our communities and how we can best serve them.

We often tend to use the term "cultural diversity" or "cultural awareness" in the narrow sense of dealing with and understanding the various cultures that are fast becoming political and economic forces in this country, such as the African/Americans, Asian/Americans, Chicanos, Latinos, American Indians and others. Becoming a culturally competent professional is much more complex than just learning differences in various cultures. Anyone who has struggled to understand and comprehend another person, even one that is closest, can appreciate the immensity of the challenge of intercultural understanding. Concentrated exposure to other cultures may result in the ability to use the same dictionary, but it by no means guarantees understanding or empathy. Just to learn complexities of differences in culture or race is difficult enough and obviously doesn't address differing values of the young or old, rich or poor, pro-government or anti-government, or preferences we have about physical appearance and attractiveness. What may often appear as an overwhelming task must be broken down into small parts for us to even begin to understand. Many discussions about issues involving culture and race in this chapter may seem simplistic. There is neither time nor space for complete discourse. One could say that complete and accurate discourse may be impossible because of the changing and ever developing nature of culture itself. It is difficult enough for the human mind to grasp these issues individually, leave alone be able to be involved in a comprehensive written discussion of them in their entirety. With those parameters in mind, lets begin to examine the nature and complexity of issues between police and the community.

Part of this complexity and paradox has to do with the nature of police work itself. Many recruits may enter the profession with a distorted view of what they, as police officers, represent and what the job is all about. Ask a newly commissioned officer as to where they got the idea of what their job was all about and you will probably hear something like prime time television. Television glorifies action oriented policing, emphasizing the "call to call" action on the power shift. Movies constantly glorify police independently taking matters into their own hands with amazing results against the "bad guys." Often new officers do not have an understanding of the power they have over all citizens and what is expected of them out on the street. Society holds law enforcement officers to a higher standard of behavior in everything that they do, but many officers may not realize why or what that responsibility entails.

The culture of the United States is a young, action oriented culture that emphasizes individual rights above all else. The police forces in this country are the only readily identifiable governmental representatives of power. The United States Constitution has various safeguards to insure the military cannot be used arbitrarily to control the country so law enforcement becomes the ever present reminder that individual freedom can be taken away. This is an awesome responsibility law enforcement officers have. The majority of the public supports the police, but in a silent, non-demonstrative way. They realize that law enforcement is a necessary part of society and people are relieved to see officers when they call and need them. However, they are not necessarily happy to see them when they pull in behind them in a marked squad on the street and are relieved when the squad turns off.

Often issues that may be thought of involving race may be more related to power. When an Anglo officer pulls over a Black teenager for speeding, often as not the teenager may say "you are only stopping me because I am Black." The Anglo officer may state "no I didn't" or sarcastically says "you're right!, I did," and the verbal battle is on. This may be viewed as a race issue, but consider the following. When a Black police officer pulls over a Black youth, that officer gets the same sort of comments but from a different point of view. The teenager may say "Cut me some slack, Brother," or "you're selling me out, Uncle Tom." In doing this, the youth is using the only power he or she has left, that is the power of verbal protest. Understanding that many violators will naturally use verbal challenges to challenge power is part of the job. The law enforcement officer's understanding of the power they represent in the community is much of the rest.

Police cadet training in rookie schools emphasizes order, discipline, and strict adherence to rules and regulations, as it should. Controlling the situation becomes synonymous with good enforcement. The need for action becomes the byword. The paramilitary socialization process emphasizes an action oriented, macho approach to problem solving. This is not to say that the paramilitary approach is the wrong one, quite the contrary. Academy settings are absolutely necessary to develop a sense of camaraderie and spirit in addition to instilling discipline and the importance of following orders. Few recruits entering law enforcement today have military backgrounds and some have never understood the rationale for, nor have had to follow orders. However, the old military model of cadet training may emphasize the how-to-do's of arrest, search and seizure, and proper patrol techniques, over other areas of education equally as important in this changing world such as diversity, sociology, psychology of communication, and understanding power. Recent studies (Ness, 1991) continue to reflect that academies do prepare officers to perform police tasks, however, not necessarily adequately.

The communities are changing fast. Law enforcement agencies often don't understand many of these changes and try to conduct business as usual using the same tools and rules that have worked before and find they don't work now. Ask many seasoned officers as to where they think the community is going and often you will hear that "we have lost it." Their main concern is to last through each shift and go home in one piece. This only serves to reinforce a macho, force oriented culture that serves to drive them more together as a group and further from the community they serve.

We often do ourselves a disservice by failing to continually redefine, and put back into perspective, the role we have as individuals in a law enforcement agency and the role that agency has in the community. The community expects officers to act like and to be paragons in a world full of mortals. We need to give officers more and better tools to help them begin dealing with the changing communities of the twenty-first century.

Understanding Ourselves and Our Culture

First, law enforcement needs to put itself back into perspective by understanding social roles and the Anglo-Saxon, North American culture. The study of our roles in law enforcement means not only going back to the basics of understanding the nature of law enforcement, the nature of power, what we represent in the community and what the community wants, but in understanding the nature of our American culture itself. This may sound like "Sociology 101," but to understand the full impact of culture, it should be revisited. As an example, law enforcement agencies in the United States are primarily White, male, and Anglo-American. In 1990 ninety-two percent of sworn officers were men and eighty-three percent were White. Blacks comprised ten and one half percent, Hispanic officers represented slightly more than five percent and other minorities, such as Asians and American Indians, about one and one-third percent (Reaves, 1992). Anglo-American or the American culture is considered a lower context culture emphasizing facts, with logical progressions in communication (Samovar and Porter, 1994). As an example, we can simplify this information into an easily understood structure as follows:

The primary immigrants to this country during its early formation were from the Scandinavian countries, Germany, England, and Ireland. These countries are considered to be a lower context in nature. In these cultures, most of communication and intent of the message as being sent from one person to another are imbedded in the words themselves, with little outside meaning or inference.

In his classic research on communication and context, Edward T. Hall (1977) specified general assumptions that can be made about low context cultures in the following areas. Among those he mentioned concerned:

- **Verbal Communication:** Words send most of the message and are extremely important. They detail the specifics and details with explicit meanings. Linear thinking, based on Socratic thought, is structured and direct, with less emotion.
- **Monochronic Time:** The passage of time is critical. The schedule is as important as the completion of the task. Process is not as important as content. Time can be saved, wasted, lost, made up, and can crawl.

Other areas that can be considered characteristic of Low Context cultures involves Proxemics, or the use of personal space. Typically, those from lower context cultures prefer more space between themselves and others when communicating socially or in business settings and others can threaten if they move into their personal space.

The above can be broadly equated with many North American Cultural Values. As mentioned previously, the largest groups of immigrants to this country, as the culture originally formed, were from lower context cultures such as Germany, Northern Europe, the Scandinavian counties, and England. Some of the major cultural values that we have in the United States may tend to reflect the strengths of low context cultures such as the following:

–Respect for Independence.
–Rugged individualism: The individual is critically important.
–Constitutional rights, laws and responsibilities.
–The centralized government is often more important than family values.

Some additional mainstream American cultural values that can also be equated with some of the characteristic of low context cultures are:

–Individualism and personal achievement is encouraged.
–Individual competition is a strong value.
–Conversations are usually direct and to the point.
–Individual opinions are encouraged and valued.
–The more you personally achieve, the more you learn.
–Risk taking and individual initiative is encouraged.
–Personal recognition is important.
–Emphasis is on facts and being objective.
–Social relationships are informal.
–Open expressions of personal confidence are encouraged.
–Completion is more important than the process of getting there.
–Nuclear family structure is common (Mother, Father, 2.8 Kids).

Comparing and Contrasting Cultures

Understanding the basis of our own culture becomes paramount to beginning to understand how other cultures differ. Realizing that all human beings are ethnocentric and believe that their own way is best gives officers an opportunity to believe in the strengths of this culture as well as trying to understand why others may believe as strongly in the value of their own culture. Keesling (1965), in his classic study of cultural anthropology, noted that ethnocentrism is the "Universal tendency for any people to put its own culture and society in a central position of priority and worth" (p. 46). It is critically important that the worth and benefits of this United States culture are articulated to those involved in learning about other cultures.

Several common and general themes regarding the differences between the culture in the United States and that of many other countries and cultures can be discussed, those of use of language, emotion and voice volume, (high context communication with implicit meanings) and that of extended family and nuclear family. The United States can be considered a low context culture with a general nuclear family structure. The primary language spoken in the United States is English, the structure of words sending most of the message. Often the way we communicate as police officers, expecting each and every word to have meaning, spoken logically and directly, usually without emotion, sends an explicit message. If you were to ask law enforcement officers to list values and job tasks, they would specify of keeping order, relative quiet, and controlling the situation as primary.

In higher context cultures, such as those of Japan, Korea, or Southeast Asia, words mean less and the environment or "context" in which they are spoken, means more. Communicative behavior is governed by rules that define conduct and procedure. These rules include both verbal and non-verbal components and determine not only what is being said but how it is being communicated. Non-verbal rules apply to kinesics, proxemics, haptics, olfactory issues and appearance and dress. Hence, other cultures, which may be higher in context, may view this logical progression as insincere and impersonal. In our police culture, we use a more direct communication style with the low context, Anglo-American cultural use of more personal space than many other cultures along with the need to control the situation. It's no wonder we have cultural clashes when we combine the preceding with research (Hennessy, 1992) showing the vast majority of police officers having cognitive, perceptive and judgment styles which tend to make them appear cold, condescending, and matter-of-fact. Many other cultures in our communities, whether they are African, Asian, or Hispanic, or American Indian, have higher context societies and communication styles which can be more complex, with more emotion, verbiage, and have indirect or assumed meanings. The speech and communication dynamics of Anglo culture can be vastly different when compared to others. Weber (1994) states that many African-Americans culturally have a different command of language than other English speaking Americans or others in this country. A specific language developed as a result of Africans' contact with Portuguese, French or English in the early 1600's, prior to the slave trade. Weber speaks of other studies of African Languages that demonstrate the grammatical, phonological, and rhythmic similarities between these and Black English. Hence, Black Americans may be typically more verbal, more rhythmic in speech and intonation, and can be louder in conversational volume. In all cultures, speech, language, context, and persuasion style differences, when combined with differences in male hierarchy, concern for loss of face, and lack of respect for the role of police makes for extremely complex interactions between individuals and the police.

Again, several generalizations can be made about those cultures that are considered higher context, such as various Asian, Hispanic, Italian, African, and American Indian groups.

—Verbal Communication: Process and content are equally important. Words send only part of the message. The message that is spoken has to be understood in the whole context of the conversation or discussion.

—Emotion, connections, and posturing with implicit meanings often are buried in words. Individuals may be much more verbal and less direct with less logic and a more complex structure to discussions.

– **Polychronic Time:** Completion of the task is more important than schedule. In many of these high context cultures, the issue of "being late for an appointment" or "being late for work" is a non-issue, or the terms or words don't even exist. Time flows and is non-specific. The wristwatch and importance of timekeeping is a western culture and industrial revolution issue.

Contrast the additional characteristics equated with a higher context culture with lower context cultures.

– Family unit more important than the individual. Extended Family.

– Collectivists.

– Saving face, and dignity are important.

– Centralized government is less important.

– Family, Tribe, Village rules more determinate of Values, Ethics and Laws.

If you examine many Asian, Hispanic, African, and Native American cultures, you will find the communication patterns more complex and more emotional with less concern for direct meanings. This is true even if an individual of a different race or culture was born here or is affiliated with a culture has been in the United States for generations (Samovar, et al., 1994). All cultures or peoples attempt to create a method of discourse through which they can convey their experiences to each other. These messages about "who we are and how we do things" are transmitted, part consciously and part unconsciously to each generation. As a classic example of the complexities in culture, the following law enforcement situation personifies the issues between low context–high context culture communication, power of the police and the state, individualism, and extended family. The above issues are complex enough before you add in the realities personal ego, individual experience, economic issues, and personal values of the officers involved.

Ask law enforcement officers what usually happens when they stop a car in some Hispanic or African/American neighborhoods. They will say that people will gather around the scene to see what is going on. They are interested in one thing and that is information and they are often not quiet in demanding it. The concern for extended family and concern for race and culture are paramount. They are also reacting to the issues of the power that the police represent in their community. All minority cultures feel powerless at times and will act to protect themselves. The conversational level may be louder than in other neighborhoods, with more macho behavior or emotion displayed. It is macho for some young males to try to challenge that power in one way or another. Often power is the greater theme in these interactions, rather than race. Race is often only used as an excuse. As mentioned previously, a Black officer often gets more of a challenge than some White officers in a Black neighborhood.

To help officers put the importance of other cultures' concern for extended family members and own race into perspective, discuss the issue of how they feel when an officer is shot down, or is hurt in an accident. Even if they don't know that officer, or if they are from a different department, they still feel and have concern for that person and will band together to express solidarity for and to protect that person. That same feeling is the concern that other individuals whose cultures involve extended family structure feel when a member of their culture or race gets into any sort of trouble with the police.

General Cultural Differences

The following are general characteristics that can be observed and may be characteristic of different groups. Before beginning this discussion, one must remember the offense that may be caused by the very nature of discussing characteristics of various cultures. By the very nature of the discussion, we may be stereotyping different cultures. Some may resent the very idea and insist that we are all individuals, which, of course we are. However, the very issue of discussing culture, sociology, and anthropology calls for a starting point somewhere. By discussing definitive and quantifiable differences, we are able to gain insight into these differences and how they affect us as individuals. Learning cannot take place by refusing to discuss or acknowledge differences and similarities. Remember that everyone is an individual and may not share those differing traits characteristic of certain cultures.

Traditional Hispanic Cultures

These cultures are expansive and multi-faceted, generally meaning anyone sharing Spanish ancestry, spreading from the Lesser Antilles in the Caribbean through Mexico and Central America to the tip of South America. Contained within the term "Hispanic" are many races and cultures. Most Hispanics do share some general characteristics, though. The term "Hispanic" is an umbrella term used to identify people who claim Spanish-speaking ancestry. Some Mexicans prefer the term "Chicano," while Puerto Ricans may prefer "Latino." If ever in doubt, mention the different terms to the class and ask those of Hispanic ancestry what they would prefer to be called.

—Higher value is placed on interaction with others rather than individualism. Relationships with others may be more important than the eventual outcome or finished product. Generally other characteristics may be:

—Greater concern about family expectations.

—Concern about opinions of others and "saving face."

—Diplomacy and tactfulness is important.

–Communication is indirect in the interests of courtesy.
–Time is more free flowing rather than specific.
–High value placed on honor of family and personal reputation. The family and religion are more important than central government. Communication may be more vocal, emotional, and centered around process rather than the content of the words. The extended family (aunts, uncles, grandparents, cousins) is important.

Traditional Asian Cultures

In comparing this higher context culture with that of Hispanic origins one can see common themes throughout. Again, the term "Asian" reflects those individuals with Asian heritage including China, Southeast Asia, Japan, Korea, Thailand, the Philippines, the Pacific Islands, and some peoples from mainland Asia. Each culture is different from each other, but again, they may share some of the following common characteristics.
–Cooperation is important and competition is avoided. Sharing with the group is important. The individual is less important than the group and value is placed in what the individual can contribute to the group.
–A high value is placed on harmony with others.
–There is a sense of obligation to the group and organization.
–Formality is respected in social interactions.
–Conversation is complex and process is as important as content.
–Planning is long term and can involve more than one lifetime.
–Conversation is usually quiet, formal, and extended over long periods of time prior to business or other important subjects that are discussed.
–Interactions are polite and may be tentative with much discussion.
–Time is free flowing and less structured. Business negotiations with Asians can take a longer time as the process is as important as the content. Asians usually place a high value on patience and indirectness.
–Asians may tend to be more spiritual and less materialistic than other cultures.

Traditional African/American Culture

Several key issues must be taken into consideration from the onset when discussing African-American culture which includes the fact that the vast majority of African Americans were initially brought to this country as slaves which affected their treatment then, and continues to affect it to this day. Institutional racism, which involves the systematic, and often unconscious, exclusion of many African Americans from the mainstream of American society because of inaccurate stereotypes and folklore has persisted since the early 1700's. Because of that experience, "Black American Culture" is somewhat different than "African Black Culture".

"Black language" and "Soul" are expressions of an experience, feelings, pride, and intentions.

–Extended families and kinship are important.

–Language can be spoken loudly, with emotion and complexity and that process can be as important or more important than content.

–African cultures are considered to be High Context, more so than Anglo culture, meaning much unstructured communication patterns.

–Stereotypes of Blacks as only excelling in sports, for example, has overshadowed the accomplishments of Black lawyers, scientists, professors, doctors, and other mainstream African Americans who have contributed to American growth and greatness.

–The media has often depicted African-Americans in a negative light, focusing only on the smaller percentage of people that are struggling in crime ridden inner cities, and not depicting successes and deep strengths represented by self-determination, loyalty, and kinship of the majority of Blacks for each other.

–"Black Power" may be considered by most African-Americans as a positive reinforcement of esteem, pride, and accomplishment.

It's hard not to rely on culture-specific guidebooks or the "cookie-cutter" approach to understanding culture, but it's important to become familiar with the specific cultures that reside in our communities. As an example, "Hispanic" is a cultural term that has been used to "label" people of Spanish descent. It is a confusing and somewhat controversial term that is used here because of its widespread use. There are some shared characteristics of many Hispanic cultures such as the importance of extended families which affects policing in those neighborhoods. Knowing this generality, it is also important to know the cultures of various Hispanic groups, i.e. Mexicans, Puerto Ricans, Cubans, or citizens of Argentina are vastly different and should be learned individually if they are a significant part of your community. Individuals of different cultures that immigrate to this country also change as they are exposed to our culture here in the United States. As an example, some Asian cultures maintained a direct male hierarchy with strong family control in their own country, but when they come to the United States and their children begin to attend American schools, that family structure may quickly disintegrate. Young Asian males who may have a propensity for criminal activity quickly learn the idiosyncracies of the Anglo-American legal structure that emphasizes stringent proofs of guilt and use them to their advantage. They may not appreciate one Anglo-American cultural strength of respect for individual rights calling for individual use of personal responsibility and control.

Law enforcement professionals should understand the dynamics of cross-cultural communication, and, more than awareness, need to develop communicative, analytical, and interpretive skills to help them deal with the ever changing population base of the United States. If one considers the characteristics of a lower context culture such as the United States along with Jungian cognitive styles of police officers, it's no wonder that culture clashes occur.

Cognitive Learning Styles of Police

Recent research into Myers-Briggs Cognitive Styles, based in Jungian Personality Type Theory and data from other cognitive studies indicate the greater majority (65 percent) of law enforcement officers prefer to take in information and process it through their five Senses rather than Intuition, which means they are "bound in reality." It should also be noted, that law enforcement officers (80 percent) prefer to make decisions through Thinking, or pure logic. Other personality measures with police populations are consistent with these results (Hennessy, 1992). Some general descriptors of those that prefer to take in and process information are:

Concrete	Logical	Traditional
Decisive	Thorough	Observant
Practical	Matter-of-Fact	Impersonal
Service-Oriented	Structured	Factual
Sensible	Pragmatic	Direct

These officers are generally very good at detail and can absorb a great number of facts. They like to be sequential, taking one step at a time. They enjoy working under a structured plan and like established ways of doing things. They reach a conclusion through careful analysis and are generally patient with routine tasks. They are practical and analytical. They are naturally brief and businesslike and if forced to choose between tact and truthfulness, they usually choose truthfulness. They may appear to others as being serious and very literal.

They are not likely to be convinced by anything but reasoning based on solid facts. This is one reason that appeals to the heart such as "valuing diversity," "celebrating diversity," or other caring and sharing programs that may appear to be too "touchy feely."

Contrast the above cognitive styles of police with other occupations such as the helping professions, media, ministry, nursing, arts, and social work. Only twenty (20) percent of law enforcement officers prefer to make decisions through social value; however, the vast majority of individuals in the above professions prefer to make decisions or judgments through Feeling or social value. They tend to be aware of people and their feelings. They appear more sympathetic and value subjective considerations.

This group of officers comprises only twenty percent of the law enforcement population compared to fifty-five percent of the general population. They are referred to as being the "uncommon types" in the profession. They prefer to process information through sensing or intuition and then decide through Feeling, or social value. Some general descriptors are:

Global	Compassionate	Gentle
Creative	Idealistic	Committed
Intense	Devoted	Empathetic
Perceptive	Friendly	Diplomatic
Congenial	Charismatic	Conceptual

If they are in the police profession, they tend to be involved in personnel oriented issues and serve as chaplains, employee representatives, psychologists, or in community oriented or juvenile projects. They are responsive to people's needs most of all, feeling concern for what others think and want, and attempt to provide due regard for other people's feelings.

In view of the above, when teaching cultural awareness or gender issues to those in the law enforcement profession, the information presented needs to be factual, realistic, concrete, and practical. This stresses the importance of a pragmatic rationale for these classes at the on-set. The cognitive style of making decisions through objective logic does not necessarily emphasize a value for issues of compassion, empathy, congeniality, and the rationale of valuing diversity for the sake of social value and humanity over truth, justice, ethics, and fairness. Police need to know pragmatically, logically, and objectively, why it's important for them to spend time learning about these issues. With this profession, the appeal needs to be directed to the head, not the heart. Understanding the importance of becoming culturally competent needs to have a rational basis such as making their jobs safer, or gaining the respect of the community.

The Issue of Power

The United States was founded by individuals who were trying to escape from the tremendous power of the church and state, primarily in England and northern Europe. Its earliest inhabitants were strong individualists who felt personal rights were paramount with the rights of the state second. There exists a general distrust and dislike of power by the residents of the United States.

Police agencies are the most powerful organizations in our communities and often the position of chief of police is more powerful than the mayor. Power is a significant theme for those in the law enforcement profession. Most law enforcement officers haven't really taken a hard look at the tremendous amount of power they have on the street.

Understanding the nature of the power that is connected to the uniform and the squad car is important. Many officers don't understand that the ways we behave or present ourselves to our communities during our daily activities can facilitate or inhibit communication between them and the citizens they serve.

Power and the Police:

Often individuals in the media appear as though they are specifically trying to put law enforcement agencies in a negative light. To us, many of the stories are lacking in facts. They interview people they consider community leaders that are not representative of the community at all. To help understand some of this apparent conflict, the following should be noted.

Since law enforcement agencies have and represent the power they do, the media will put them in a "fishbowl" to be sure to note any alleged abuses of that power. Their business is to report on stories of human interest, and police agencies are those dealing with human interest situations all of the time, even though most of the contact has to do with maintaining the public safety which has negative consequences for many.

As is mentioned during the discussion of cognitive styles of police officers, research has shown that the majority of police officers prefer to take in information and make decisions in vastly different ways than those in the media and helping professions (Hennessy, 1992). This research explains that the two professions look at the same situation from two completely different points of view. Both are valid, but reflect each group's different view of the situation as reality.

Power can also be viewed as personal power, that formal and informal power we have by virtue of being part of a particular agency or organization. Many officers feel powerless on the street because of rules, regulations, laws and other components of the criminal justice system such as the courts, prosecutors, and correction that seem to work at cross purposes when they are trying to do their job. This feeling of powerlessness is not new; Walker (1980) stated that in the 1930's, officers were stating that they were alone as the primary defenders of justice and that the other components of the criminal justice system did not contribute and were working at cross purposes with the police.

When police can begin to understand the personal power they and others have and how it can be used in a positive manner, changes in a culture will occur. To use the phrase "to do the right thing" can often be threatening when peer pressure exists to do just the opposite.

In a police organization, change can be difficult. The culture is predominately masculine, macho, action oriented. It's a "we against they" mind set. Because of the power that police forces have, law enforcement officers have often been rather isolated from the general community. Their daily work experience is dealing with those who are usually breaking some law or ordinance, and, realistically, most of their work takes place in the more economically disadvantaged areas of the city, where their exposure to minority populations usually results in negative consequences, both literally for the person arrested, and socially and attitudinally with the officers involved.

This, in and of itself, results in the creation and the maintenance of a very strong in-group—that of the members of the department themselves. Every officer is a member of this group and under the subtle or not so subtle influence of those who are the informal leaders of that group. They are all under the direct influence and control of those who are the formal leaders and policy setters, whether they realize it or not. It is not enough to tell people that they must change and how this change is to be achieved. They need to understand the "why" of the change and to be continually reinforced as to the importance of the change. As an example of this personal and peer power, recent studies have shown that a small minority of officers are responsible for the majority of complaints about specific instances of police brutality. These same officers continue to act with little sanctions against them even though their actions are well outside the acceptable norm of response to a specific situation. Yet, as fellow officers, we do little to discourage them through use of peer power.

The vast majority of law enforcement officers have a good idea of the professional way their jobs should be performed. If an officer is seen treating a citizen, prisoner, or a co-worker with verbal or physical abuse or violence that is not really responsive to the situation, others may not speak up because of the peer pressure which they feel may go against them. They value the relationships with their peers and others in their in-groups and that fear of being placed outside of the group is strong. What they may fail to realize is that taking human nature into consideration, most other officers, although they may appear to subscribe to the "macho" police image, don't condone that activity either, but are remaining silent for the same reasons others do.

To break this culture takes the courage to speak up against the derogatory comments and actions that bring discredit to the profession. An officer who does take the plunge to speak out against harassment may be surprised to find that when speaking up, the majority of the other officers have been feeling the same way but didn't have the courage to speak up first. It takes courage to break away from the group. To do so, however, even though it may appear risky, is really an exercise in leadership.

Much can be done to change the negative responses we get as a result of our behavior in uniform by paying attention to the image we portray while on the job. As an example, when an officer tells someone to do something such as "You need to get out of the street" and they don't respond, they may re-state the order in a more forceful tone such as "I said get out of the fucking street." What has happened in that exchange is the citizen remembers the "fucking" part of the message and professionalism suffers.

The same is true when a crowd gathers during an incident. The agency is then "on stage." The crowd does not know what has occurred, but only that "one of their brothers or sisters" is being taken downtown and emotions fly. The officers want to get in and get out and may use inappropriate language or use of force to accomplish the task.

The issue that is important lies in the fact that law enforcement officers need to understand the difference between intentions verses behavior. We intend to perform our jobs with the least risk and danger to ourselves and others. Those bystanders though, see us as we behave. It may not be fair nor true to our intentions, but it is the way it is. Additionally, understanding non-verbal communication is as important as understanding words in communicating the intent of a message and the attitude of the sender. Dr. Mehrabian's (1987) well known studies on non-verbal communication reflected the body sends 55% of the message, the tone of voice sends 38% of the message, while actual words account for only 7% of the message.

It is important to realize that if police do not act professional, they won't be treated as professionals, and if they don't treat all people with respect, they will not receive respect in exchange. People need to be treated with common courtesy and consideration.

Changing the Status Quo

Attitudes, as we all know, are extremely difficult to change. This training can, however, succeed in changing people's behavior as a result of various classes dealing with these subjects in several ways. Asking people to examine their closely held beliefs and prejudices can be emotion-negative. People may not initially appear to receive and discuss the information in a positive manner. Class attendees may need to think about it for a while. The process of changing our minds about these issues is long and difficult. One shot training sessions on any subject do little to change behavior. That is why a long term, commitment organizationally to these values we have been discussing is important. If an instructor has succeeded in causing the officers to think about the issues, the goal has been reached. As participants hear and struggle with some of the concepts brought to their attention, one can be sure that when their thoughts reform, they reform towards more tolerance and understanding. That usually causes a behavioral change. When they behave in a way that is more positive towards various groups of diversity, they will immediately see positive actions coming back to them, which, in turn can change attitudes.

When people are asked to change their behavior, sometimes they do it easily without question, if the change requested is one that doesn't cost them anything one way or another. Generally, if one is asked to change a procedure, fill out a form they haven't had to fill out before, or switch shifts with someone when it causes them no inconvenience, they'll do it without question. If, however, as is the case of asking participants to analyze their attitudes about certain minority groups and different cultures with the goal in mind of improving or modifying their behavior towards those groups, often you are asking for change with a capital "C."

Change regarding behavior and attitude is a complex and long-term effort. Most agree that an attitude cannot be changed easily, but behavior can be changed. If a change in behavior brings enough positive result over an extended period of time, often an attitude change then follows. Understanding that this effort is going to be an extended and continual process from now on is the first critical issue to realize.

Education is the second issue. Sometimes informing people as to why the change is necessary is sufficient. However, when asking people to examine closely held biases that were formed early in their lives and to reevaluate their method of dealing with some people will be no easy matter, particularly if they have no historical perspective on trends and future projections. Information must be provided on a continual basis as to cultural diversity in the community and what demographers expect to occur in the future. These changes cannot be seen as cold, abstract facts, but must be explained by integrating them into what police officers do on a day-to-day basis. Education and training must be primary and continual.

Demand performance standards. People need to be held responsible for their actions. One can talk often about changing the culture, but if that change is not reinforced through action, it will not happen. Clear, enforceable policy regarding the exercising of bias and prejudice within the department and in the way we treat citizens of the community must be vigorously enforced and supported throughout the ranks.

Recognize independent action. As we have mentioned before, power is a significant theme in the law enforcement profession both within the department and in the community. Law enforcement has immense power in the community which sets itself apart from all of the other governmental functions. This power is a perfect formative agent for creating a powerful in-group, where a "protecting of each other" philosophy is very strong.

Officers need to understand that the organization is committed to taking action away from any prejudice, bias, and discrimination of the past. It is moving toward a new direction of dealing positively with diversity. If the administration, up through the ranks to the chief or director strongly supports the new direction, change will occur. The change is made attractive to those potentially impacted if the direction is clear and consistent throughout the organization.

TRAINING METHODOLOGIES

There is a significant difference between teaching children and adults. Unfortunately, we tend to use the same methodology in teaching both, particularly in teaching police recruits or in-service officers. Malcolm S. Knowles (1984), a well known expert in adult education, speaks of the use of student centered methodology or Andragogy as obviously more effective than Pedagogy, which is teacher centered. There are many excellent theories and approaches to adult learning that, because of space, cannot be discussed in this chapter, but I will attempt to synthesize the major issues involved in teaching cultural awareness and racial sensitivity to the law enforcement profession. William E. Arnold and Lynn McClure (1994) are an excellent source of many excellent key principles of adult learning all of which tie into the major theories of adult education.

The Nature of The Subject Matter

Teaching classes dealing with racial prejudice, gender fairness and multicultural issues is unique and challenging. Facilitating an opportunity for people to examine deeply held personal values and beliefs is difficult and emotionally involving. Cultural awareness training has been called emotion negative which should provoke participants into examining the causes for their own professional and personal behavior. The trainer's motives should be to assist participants to examine and consider their perceptions about people of different cultures and races that have shaped their behavior through most of their life (Work, 1989).

Many police and criminal justice trainers and educators have been involved in leadership, motivation, communications, and team building types of training which are positive in nature. They have dealt with hands-on training regarding pursuit driving, handling weapons, operating computers, and other types of "how to" training which are neutral as far as emotions are concerned. At the conclusions of these courses reviews and critiques as to teacher performance and subject matter retention and relevance are usually excellent, or at least satisfactory. Dealing with racial, cultural, and gender issues in training sessions will, however, most likely elicit less positive feelings about the subject matter, and, most probably, less positive appreciation for the instructor. The teaching methodology, by the very nature of the subject matter, requires provocational techniques. Warren Bennis (1968) discussed the importance of the process of (1) unfreezing, (2) changing, and (3) refreezing a change in attitudes and institutionalized behavior. This is accomplished through furnishing logical information that does not confirm an attendee's preconceived knowledge about issues of prejudice gender, and race discrimination. Any change in behavior or attitudes, however, tends to be emotionally resisted because to even admit that the instructor may be right means that one's attitudes and beliefs about an issue(s) may have been wrong. Rarely will participants admit that they have been wrong. Herein lies the challenge. Many participants will end the sessions with varying degrees of animosity towards the instructor. The consequences of this attitude can be reflected by giving low ratings to the instructor. Teaching these courses takes much reading, thought, planning, understanding human nature, and a tolerance for critical review. The additional challenge is the need to examine our own personal values as trainers and assist others in examining theirs. Educators have an outstanding opportunity to grow in intellect and understanding as they aid others in understanding the complexities of these issues. By helping people to gain insight into their prejudices, we make a contribution to the community of human beings. These courses are completely different from any others educators will ever teach. They can be the most rewarding, but also the most difficult. Trainers are dealing with attitudes that have been ingrained through lifetimes of adult experiences and relationships. The following are some additional general comments that are characteristic of courses such as these.

Trainers need to be committed to these issues and must be willing to dedicate time to personally expand their knowledge in these complex areas. The need to study human behavior, keep current on new research, and study trends is paramount to success. Gordon Allport's classic *The Nature of Prejudice* along with Samovar and Porter's *Intercultural Communication, A Reader,* are outstanding books to begin that study.

In planning, trainers need to be acutely aware of what each exercise is designed to accomplish, and be willing to adjust and insure the objectives of the exercises are met. Each activity should be structured to build on the ones preceding. There are several sample exercises towards the end of this chapter that will give trainers and educators some direction in exercise methodology.

The trainer must be willing to challenge participant's thinking in ways that may cause hard feelings. Trainers must realize they are challenging the life long images and values that people individually, and families collectively, may have held for generations. We are dealing with law enforcement officers and civilian employees whose behaviors for years have been reinforced through experience. Many of us are reluctant to let these images go. Much of it has to do with ego and the feeling of looking less than bright in the classroom in front of other officers and employees. Some of it has to do with the strong, powerful image that some officers and others have about their jobs. People will go to great lengths to avoid losing face, and will argue at length about specific issues that are core to their view of the world. The emotion and arguments should not be a real concern, nor should the trainer be concerned about getting his or her specific point across. Just the mere indication that emotional discussions are going on indicates that the personal values of various participants are being examined or challenged. Bear in mind that the other members of the class are listening to the discussions and examining their own values as to the topic at hand, even though they may say nothing about it at the time.

One area that may be disconcerting to trainers involved in prejudice, bias, and gender issue education is that often the subject matter may not "flow" as well as that of other subjects. The discussing of these various issues can be highly emotionally charged and some topics may seem to lead off in tangents. The job of the instructor is to let the emotion come out and to direct the discussions back toward the subjects at hand as smoothly as possible.

Additionally, trainers should realize that the participants will not necessarily voice agreement with what is being said or come to the front of the room at the conclusion of class and discuss the class content in a positive manner with the instructor(s). However, you can be assured they are thinking about their behaviors and the nature of the subject matter.

One must trust in the intellectual level of the group. The rationale of placing attendees in teams, or groups of five or six, allows the trainer to facilitate discussion by asking the group to consider a question or issue. Those participants who react immediately to an emotionally or value laden issue can be balanced by those that will give the issues considerable thought and speak later. It should be remembered, even though attendees may not state it directly, participants are listening and may be modifying their own biases and thoughts on what they hear.

Even though the groups may come from the same organization or department, one group may be very receptive while the next can be difficult. Understand that this is generally the rule and not the exception. In fact, facilitating discussions of this nature may make you feel rather "beat up" at the conclusion of one session while others really seem to click to your satisfaction.

Don't be concerned if the discussions become so involved and intense that the class outline or schedule is not maintained. The discussions between the group participants are an important learning phase of the course. The discussions, however, should be relevant to the topic. Some venting may be appropriate, but if they wander too far from the subject, the important teaching points may be lost. Sometimes exercises may "flop." Be assured it rarely is the result of the instructor's style, but in the composition of the group and their willingness (or lack thereof) to discuss the issues. If little reaction from one exercise is noted, move on to the next without much comment. Some exercises work well with some groups and may not effect others in quite the same way.

Adults Bring Experience into the Classroom

One of the critically important issues deals with the fact that adults bring personal experiences to the training session. Police officers bring critical and important experiences to in-service cultural awareness training sessions and should have the opportunity to discuss and comment on these experiences with other officers and instructors. The lecture (pedagogical) method of instruction with attendees facing the instructor in an auditorium or classroom setting does not encourage this interaction nor optimizes learning when dealing with these critical subjects. It also will tend to "set up the facilitator as an expert" encouraging officers to play mental games with highly emotional issues. In the case of law enforcement officers, that experience in dealing with minorities or those of other cultures is often negative. Effective training must rely on the bringing of those experiences into the process and discussion. Failure to access that experience can almost guarantee polite, but unbelieving acceptance of the information or outright hostility to the message being conveyed. One excellent way to encourage the exchange of information is to situate officers in small groups of four or five. They can easily deal with case studies, role plays, practice sessions, and pen and paper exercises that will stimulate thought and discussion. Officers learn from each other through discussion and comment while instructors can validate their "street sense" points of view. Giving officers an opportunity to articulate both their positive and negative experiences with individuals of various minority groups gives the instructor an opportunity to link certain behaviors police may interpret as challenging their control or safety to cultural differences.

Adults Must Have a Clear Motivation to Learn

They need to know, "What's in it for me?" The Message regarding these issues has to be Pragmatic and Job Related. The training has to be job specific, logical, and to the point. The importance of understanding the changing population structure in the United States must be integrated into all of the curriculum, from cadet academy settings through in-service training. Trainers need to make the information specific, logical, and to the point. As mentioned before, the vast majority of police officers in this country are Anglo-American males. We can couple this understanding with cognitive learning styles of the vast majority of police officers and should design these courses to be concrete, practical, logical, and pragmatic. Police generally tend to be practical and analytical and are naturally brief and businesslike. They need to know why these issues are important to them and how they can use the information to better perform their job. With this profession, the appeal needs to be made to the head, and not to the heart.

Stressing police officers' safety is of paramount importance here. Validating their personal concern for their own safety, but giving them additional insights into their own cultural viewpoints and those of others different from themselves can give them additional insights to dealing with complex problems. Law enforcement officers exercise broad discretion on the street and additional knowledge regarding cultural implications in human behavior can go a long way in reducing tensions for both them and the community.

Many officers have a pre-conceived notion of what is being taught and come into the class with prejudices and stereotypes intact. Classes on cultural awareness in the past have been mandatory and often the result of some "deficiency" or incident that has caused the concern in the first place. Many officers may feel the classes are a form of punishment. They often don't want to discuss or take a close look at their own biases or prejudices. Some may actually believe they have no biases and treat everyone the same, and may consider the classes to be an insult to their personal integrity. Keeping the subject matter focused on how additional insights and knowledge into different cultures can make their job easier rather than insisting they have to act or feel certain ways towards others can give them much to think about.

TRAINING LOGISTICS

Class Size and Structure

The class size for general sessions dealing with passing information regarding statutes, human rights violations, gender issue complaints, and EEO data can be large (50 or more participants). The rationale here involves the need to acquaint people with a lot of information that is fairly pragmatic and does not involve a whole lot of discussion. Classes that involve discussions and the examining of closely held personal values should be smaller groups of 20 to 30 participants. It is important to discuss these issues and a large group may make it virtually impossible to constructively exchange ideas. In a larger group, the instructor has a much greater chance of losing control, resulting in chaos and irrelevant discussion, making the program an exercise in futility.

Douglas F. Warring (1994) states experience has shown that, when teaching emotion laden topics such as cultural or gender issues, smaller groups of attendees, specifically arranged in teams of five or six at tables suitable for small group discussion, is optimum. The greatest effect of these programs is realized when attendees are able to discuss various issues among themselves as a group as well as with the instructor(s). Seating attendees to small groups affords optimum learning to take place. If students are in a "seats facing forward" classroom or auditorium, the instructor is set up as "The Expert." Those sitting in the audience have several choices in addition to learning which include sitting it out or trying to trip up the instructor, the latter sometimes being an entertaining option to the attending groups. A lecture method of instruction with this cognitive style does not optimize learning in these courses.

Attendees should be engaged in active dialogue and exercises during most of the training sessions. The small group settings gives them the opportunity to continually interact with each other. They learn best through discussions with each other, performing various pencil/paper exercises, an addition to interaction with the instructor. Much of the learning in courses of this type, takes place through the interaction between others. No matter what someone says about an issue or how pragmatically they may disagree, they will hear and consider other points of view from their peers, which is all we can ask.

The instructor's role is that of a facilitator rather than a teacher, calling upon various groups and individuals for comments and opinions as often as possible. This keeps attention focused on the subject and stimulates thought, which affords the attendees an opportunity to express themselves. The use of case studies and role plays also affords them opportunities to contribute their experience and points of view.

Using Civilian Members of the Minority Communities as Presenters

When you bring up the issue of "Cultural Diversity Training" or "Sensitivity Training," some police officers bristle, particularly those veterans who feel they have experienced the result of "being more sensitive" as the streets become more violent. Many veterans have attended more than a few of these cultural training sessions over the years. These sessions may have often included comments from representatives of the various minority communities which, though intended to be helpful in understanding cultural differences, have quickly become "cop bashing sessions." The minority representatives from the community and the police are both human and seldom are these issues discussed without the use of personal examples of wrong on both sides. The minority communities harangue the police about treating them "better" while the police tell the representatives they don't understand the parameters the police have to work under. They quickly become one way monologues where both presenter and attendees lose and little learning takes place, except perhaps to reinforce stereotypes held about each other.

It is important for members of the minority communities to have continual, open dialogue with police officials to deal with numerous problems. Open communication to deal with specific issues is critical to the success of community policing. The opportunity for having spokespersons from various minority communities address officers in certain circumstances may be an excellent experience for both the speaker and officers to broaden their horizons. As an example, if a specific cultural group resides within the boundaries of a certain precinct, it would be important for the police to contact that group and make an attempt to institute a dialogue for mutual benefit. However, we need to exercise caution here. First, the person(s) volunteering to speak or be spokespersons for the specific community may not represent the community in question and may use the forum to bring up specific instances of police maltreatment. Secondly, allowing representatives of one specific group access to police without allowing access to all minorities, can encourage accusations of bias that may cause additional misconceptions and concern.

The present author highly recommends placing emphasis on the experience, ability, and intellect of the officers themselves in discussing community concerns and the police response to their issues. There is a vast amount of untapped knowledge within the law enforcement community in both sworn and civilian employees. Give them an opportunity to express themselves and become a part of this process. They are the ones that have the most to gain and probably the most to lose.

White, Male, Police Trainers Need to Get Involved

One of the issues sure to stimulate comments, discussion, and research in the future is the need for more white male instructors to become involved in teaching cultural issues. In the past, police administrators looked primarily to people of color or women to teach cultural diversity or gender issues based on the presumption that these individuals could teach the subjects best. Much of this presumption is based on the erroneous assumption that those who have experienced bias and discrimination can best teach it. In discussing this issue, several considerations must be considered at the onset.

As mentioned before, the vast majority of police personnel in law enforcement agencies throughout this country are white males. We may be "setting up" minority instructors for failure by recommending they handle the classes to the exclusion of white males and females. Officers may not discuss personal biases or make comments to the instructor because of not wanting to appear prejudiced to the instructor or the rest of the attendees. In-service officers may choose to "sit this one out" and take the training as a mandated and necessary process to go through. Other officers may use the situation as an opportunity to make a personal statement, placing the presenter on the defensive and in a "no-win" situation seeming to defend the actions of others of the same race or culture as the instructor. Generally, all minorities in police agencies have suffered from discrimination to one extent or another. It is very difficult for any individual who is a minority from keeping their own personal issues out of the discussion. Learning may not be maximized in this situation.

Additionally, we are making an assumption that because a person is a minority or person of color, that by virtue of their minority status or skin color alone, they are capable of, knowledgeable about, or even want to teach these issues. As was mentioned before, teaching cultural awareness can be referred to as emotion negative training and often is more demanding on the instructor than any other type of training. The same need for competence in teaching methodology applies even more so in these courses than others. One who supervises or teaches these courses will quickly realize that fewer instructors will choose to teach these subjects and even more, after being exposed to trying to mediate and deal with the confrontational nature of the subject matter, will opt to remove themselves from the task.

No matter what the instructor's race or ethnic origin, to be successful, they must be credible, respected by the rank and file, know how to facilitate and instruct, as well as a strong advocate of the issues they are teaching.

By including white males and others to teach or team teach these issues with minority instructors often will refocus participants' attention to discussing these critical issues with instructors appearing to have no "personal axe to grind." In paying attention to the importance of instructor selection, group and human dynamics will come into play, causing a more of an open dialogue between participants and make a statement that these cultural and racial concerns are a departmental commitment involving everyone and not just a passing phase.

SAMPLE EXERCISES

Stereotypes

One of the basic functions of any culture is to lay out a predictable world in which a person is firmly oriented. Stereotypes do what Ernest Becker (1962) asserts they must do, make the world understandable, whether or not the preconceived beliefs are true or not. Stereotypes are positive or negative pictures or images we hold of certain people, races, or ethnic groups within various categories. They are defined as an exaggerated belief associated with a category. The stereotype's function is to justify or rationalize our own conduct in relation to ourselves as compared to others in those categories.

Some stereotypes are totally unsupported by facts while some have somewhat of a "kernel" of truth to them, but may be overgeneralized, causing a gross distortion of fact.

People use stereotypes as a justification for their actions in accepting or rejecting various people or groups of people. Psychologically, it serves as a screening device to enable people to maintain a simplicity of perception or thought. They are also used to justify hostility towards groups or serve as a conduit for our own personal inner conflicts.

As an example of stereotypes having a grain of truth to them, if one were to look at the probability of certain groups being prone to alcoholism more than others, one might say that the Irish are more prone to alcohol abuse than Moslems. This is potentially a provable generalization. Yet if we say, "Typical Irishmen, they're drunk all of the time," or "Moslems always refrain from drinking alcohol," we are exaggerating the facts concerning both issues and making generalizations that are not true.

Another stereotype people talk about is that "The Jews control all of the banks" or "All Jews are strongly religious." In truth, per capita, there are fewer Jews in the banking industry than gentiles, and Jews observe religious holidays in much the same percentages as those people of other religions.

We know that stereotypes exist as a legitimate way of simplifying our lives. They may or may not represent a grain of truth. The problem is that the stereotypes continue to exist, even though they may not be true. They are supported through our media and mass communication. Most of our written records contain bias that contributes to continuing the stereotypes. Older persons are depicted as being feeble, Blacks are depicted as unintelligent, slow and lazy, Irish are pictured as drunks, Poles as stupid, Asians as sly, Italians as crooks, and women as helpless. The importance of discussing stereotypes in exercises concerns the need to discuss information we have about other races and cultures that may or may not be true. All people hold negative stereotypes in their minds. Unless they have an opportunity to discuss these negative stereotypes or experiences, they will not listen to positive information or put their negative experiences into perspective (Hennessy, Warring, and Arnott, 1994). Police often deal with the underclass in tough neighborhoods daily and, because of this, may fail to realize that the vast majority of people in those neighborhoods support the police and their actions. Have the participants discuss these experiences in their groups and then report their discussions to the rest of the class. You will hear some negative information from some group members that will be discussed and put into perspective by others in the group or class along with many positive experiences that will move the discussion to a positive learning experience. Many trainers are reluctant to use this exercise for fear that it will just reinforce negative stereotypes. The present author believes that the thoughts already exist in individual's minds and need to be brought out. You will be able to direct the discussion and help put all of their comments into perspective.

One effective method is to ask participants in groups to discuss their positive and negative experiences they have experienced with members of one cultural or racial group or another. Also ask them to indicate whether the members in those groups are either higher context or lower context and if that culture has more of an extended or nuclear family structure.

By structuring the exercises this way, a facilitator accomplishes several things. The participants' knowledge base and experience is valued and can be discussed in a group setting. Other members of the group will naturally serve as monitors insuring the discussions stay on course. As people speak their minds, they listen to what they are saying and become aware of their own mis-statements and over simplifications. Others in the groups also hear these emotional outbursts, if they occur, and serve to moderate the comments. Once the negative emotions have been expressed, they seem to moderate. This is called Catharsis, or a mental clearing. Once the tension is released, often a person can see a different and more moderate perspective and can gain additional insight. Allport (1979) stated that even though catharsis alone is not a curative, it does however, clear out some negative emotion and allows opportunity for the other side to be heard. If the original statements regarding race, culture, religion, or other stereotyping have been exaggerated, slanted, or unfair, as they usually are, the resulting understanding of how one sided they are after being said out loud, often induces a person to seek a more balanced point of view.

These exercises allow the educator as well as the participants the opportunity to add additional positive knowledge about a culture or race that may be unknown to the participants along with negative experiences. It also helps put those negative experiences into the perspective of police work.

The list of groups to be discussed in this manner should be mentioned prior to the exercise being begun. It is important to also include Anglos as a culture (white, non-Hispanic) to allow those members of the training group that are not white an opportunity to express their view of dealing with white motorists, or other violators on the job. An instructor may also want to add White, male police officers, if internal gender issues are to be discussed. There is not a woman in any male dominated workplace or occupation that has not really felt she was not held to a higher standard.

CASE STUDIES

Many law enforcement officers enjoy working on case studies as they involve the real world of work. As a facilitator, you are again respecting their ability and experience as adult learners. Often we are surprised at the results of the discussions that can lead to a better understanding of the issues. The following case study is an example of possible conflicts with a culture:

THE HMONG DOMESTIC CALL

"Two officers are called to a home where a Hmong male is alleged to have beaten his spouse. Neighbors heard her screams and reported their concerns by dialing 911. A male and female officer investigate the incident.

When they arrive, an elder male opens the door and ushers the officers into the living room where a woman is seated. She appears to be physically harmed. Her husband is in the next room. When questioned, she says nothing. The elder is of no help because he seems unfamiliar with English. Her husband is fearful of the officers. When they attempt to question him, they get nowhere because of his anger and evasiveness. The woman continues to ignore them.

What should the officers do?

Are there grounds for arrest? For whom?

Do you need a translator?

Can you remove the woman from the home?

Did police uniforms or nonverbal behavior have an initial negative impact?"

Even though the issue may seem simple, the different teams will come up with many alternative issues to discuss. If the trainer is an effective facilitator, he or she can elicit the best possible answer while the group learns several things, one of which is that they, as police officers, do not all look at the issue in the same way, even though they may believe they do. There are a myriad of examples of what one would or wouldn't do in this situation. The participants learn that they share differing values, as well as the fact that there are several ways to handle the situation. Additionally, some may privately have felt they may have handled the situation poorly, but have learned from others in the group what to do if the situation should arise.

Gender Related Issues

This topic is one of the most relevant yet may be the most difficult topic of all to deal with. Depending on the time frame or focus, gender issues should also be included in the exploration of cultural and racial issues because of the fact that males and females transcend all races and cultures. It is and can become more of a critical issue in and of itself. Additionally it has the dimension involving the human psyche of sexual attractiveness, which is one of the most powerful motivational forces and stimuli existing among human beings. Various pencil and paper tests are important tools to use in gender issue discussions. The difference between these discussions compared to those dealing with cultural clashes are important. Cultural issues are broad concerns with much latitude involved in the discussion. Gender issues are more definitive as to what one can or can not do, as well as the existence of case law clearly defining limits of harassment and inappropriate work behavior. Case studies regarding these issues are also excellent ways to get into the real discussion phase of the situation. Often, when the role players are selected for these exercises, one might assume they were type cast for the role. The Christine Harper case is one example:

> "Christine Harper is a new patrol officer assigned to the night shift. She is 23 years old, physically attractive, serious minded, a little officious, and very eager. She is fresh out of rookie school and really wants to do a great job and move up in the organization. During her first several weeks with the shift she notices and points out to supervisors several procedures that were being violated by other officers. She does everything "by the book." Male officers, many of who initially wanted to team with her because of her looks, are shying away from her. Several of the other female officers who are more senior to her feel she is a time bomb ready to go off.
>
> Today at shift break, someone taped a Playboy magazine centerfold to the steering wheel of her squad just before she picked it up for duty. Her name had been penned in under the photo and a set of automatic pistols had been drawn over the fairly ample hips of the model. When Christine got into the squad, she saw the centerfold, ripped it off the wheel, and marched into the squad room, heading right for the shift supervisor's office . . . yours.
>
> You have been aware of the disruption she has caused over the past weeks and hoped she would just settle down after kicking around a bit. You even pulled a couple of officers aside and casually suggested they approach her and tell her how things really work around here. This was not really what you had in mind.
>
> You notice her approaching your office, knock and request a meeting with you, "immediately sir." She is not smiling. You are her superior. How do you plan to deal with this situation? What are some of the implications here?
>
> You need to follow the sexual harassment policies of the department. You must also supervise veteran male officers whose behavior was not to offend. Be prepared to ask the right questions."

The above case study is complex and can lead to much discussion as to what should be done. It can also be made into a role play. As mentioned before, the vast majority of women working in a male dominated workplace have been the victims of harassment of one sort of another. A woman officer role playing Christine Harper, will, within several minutes of the start of the role play, appear to have been type cast for the role.

Dealing With Homophobia

Phobia is defined in Webster's dictionary as "an exaggerated and often disabling fear." "Homophobia" is not yet found in many dictionaries, but the meaning is quite clear. It is a real fear of homosexuals.

To even raise the subject of homosexuality in discussions with law enforcement officers is certain to elicit some outrage. Some people feel that any consideration of or discussions regarding homosexuality without condemning it outright as being "unnatural" is wrong. These discussions can and often do evoke fear and strong emotion. But if we are to deal with discrimination, racism, and other "ism's," we must consider all other issues involving discrimination including discriminating against gay men and lesbians.

It is important to not be trapped into taking a moral position regarding the "rightness" or "wrongness" of any sexual orientation issue. Also it is important to avoid justifying the legitimate existence and right of any one sexual orientation over another. It is important, however, to discuss some possibilities of misinformation that we all have been exposed to throughout our lives in an attempt to understand some of the issues.

First, we must be wary of justifying oppression or discrimination in any way through the use of religion. Similar arguments have been used by various religious groups to try to justify and legitimize slavery, racial segregation, anti-semitism, and male domination. It is also important to note that many religious groups strongly advocate the civil rights of lesbians and gay men, and various caucuses of differing faiths are working toward increasing rights for gays and lesbians within religious communities.

Secondly, we all have personal opinions and deeply held beliefs. Our perceptions of what is "natural," however, is often the product of socialization. What has long been proscribed, legislated, and condemned can come to be seen as "unnatural." It is instructive to note, for example, that homosexuality was considered "natural" for a small percentage of individuals in most European societies until the 13th century when religious groups who controlled governments, began an attempt to declare it "unnatural" on religious grounds.

Additionally, we also need to discuss the question of "proselytizing," since this is usually raised when efforts are made to discuss homosexuality in an open forum. Many people fear that such discussions will somehow "lure" youngsters into homosexuality from heterosexuality. People do not want to be accused of influencing people to become gay so they usually try to avoid discussing the subject altogether. This, of course, makes he assumption that being a gay male or lesbian is a matter of free choice. People erroneously imagine or assume they really have the power to guide children to the "right" choice.

Though the direction of one's sexuality may be a matter of choice for a small percentage of adults, the majority of gay men and lesbians become aware that they are somehow "different" from the heterosexual norm when quite young. This awareness generally occurs in a profoundly anti-gay social setting and in spite of a heterosexual society that continually reinforces the superiority of heterosexuality over homosexuality. Given the issue that gay men and lesbians succeed in discovering their sexual identity in the pervasiveness of heterosexual influences provides a strong argument that sexual orientation is not influenced by "proselytizing."

To date, science has not positively determined how sexual orientation develops; however recent research has begun to point to genetic factors other than free choice. We only know that homosexuality, like heterosexuality, has existed in all types of families, in all societies, throughout history. According to current research, approximately ten percent of individuals in the population are either gay men or lesbians. They face discrimination daily, particularly in jobs and housing. They also face name calling, taunting, hatred, and violence.

The critical issue is that gay men and lesbians, as legitimate and productive citizens of our communities, are entitled to the same rights as the other citizens of our communities; and that is to be free from harassment and discrimination.

ADDITIONAL ISSUES OF IMPORTANCE

Process Versus Content: The Importance of Dialogue

As professionals are all acutely aware, the issues of prejudice, bias, gender, and racial discrimination are extremely emotional issues. Rarely can most individuals restrain themselves to deal with the logic of the situation when the rage and violence involved has offended individual sensibilities to such an extent as to make quiet logic seemingly impossible at times.

This is often the case when dealing with advocate groups or various commissions. Representatives may make powerful assertions for instance "that the time for waiting is over, and the need for action is long overdue." They comment that they have suffered enough injustices to last many lifetimes. As this occurs, an interesting phenomenon is playing out. When the mind is dealing with thoughts that are extremely negative or if the person is full of emotional rage, and these feelings are not allowed out, the mind has a hard time opening itself up for other ideas or for constructive discourse. This means that people, particularly those that are or feel aggrieved, need to be able to express this emotion. Understanding this is important for two reasons, both in and out of the classroom.

Those in the minority communities need to be heard. Many of their members are feeling real rage at real or perceived injustices. Dialogue must be allowed to happen, and the comments of these individuals, no matter how illogical, emotional, or off base they may sound to us, need to be heard. Even though their demands may seem inappropriate or impossible to meet, we all need to understand that they must be listened to and taken seriously. If the demands or solutions are not possible to meet, they will fall of their own weight anyway, but if they are not allowed to be placed on the table, they will fester and serve as a barrier to real discussions. People have honest, real concerns along with a sense of self tied up in many of these issues. If they are given the respect of a forum with which to express themselves, they often will move from what we perceive as emotion into more of a problem solving dialogue. Usually, if you fail to give them that opportunity or even the respect of a comment, you can expect no real movements toward solutions.

Often in teaching classes of this nature, people may make comments either as an aside to other participants or to the instructor that are insensitive or racist. The instructor needs to keep from counter arguing and listen as the hostile outbursts come. As people say what they feel needs to be said, they usually become aware of their own mis-statements and oversimplifications. Often, other members of the class will be quick to challenge the individual making the comments. The negative emotions, once expressed, seem to moderate. If the original statements regarding race, culture, or stereotyping have been exaggerated, slanted, or unfair as they usually are, the resulting understanding of how one sided they really are after being said out loud often induces a person to seek a more balanced point of view.

During these types of discussions, much emotion will be apparent. Don't lose sight of the fact that as you are hearing emotion driven, biased, one sided characterizations and comments, others in the class are hearing them too. Be assured that the majority of the other class members are aware of the exaggerations and even though they may be struggling with their own personal prejudices, they can often be called upon to modify the comments to be more balanced. Be sure not to neglect this excellent resource by asking "How about a comment about this from other members of the class. What do the rest of you think?" It also gives you more time to reflect on your reply.

This same situation exists when advocate groups and commissions wish to critique the content of various courses you may teach on Prejudice, Racial Discrimination, Bias, and Gender Issues. A department may feel strongly about the direction they are going and are not looking for additional input, but allowing outside individuals to observe, offer recommendations and comments also helps to solidify relationships within the community. You may not wish to use the recommendations, which is your right, but allowing critique and comment only makes the program stronger and more acceptable to the minority communities you are trying to serve.

Getting the "Buy-in" From Management

While departments talk about management involvement and support, many programs seem only to receive "permission" from top management to spend money and take employees' time. Real support from management in many organizations is lacking. Support for pro-active multi-cultural diversity programs means more than a "Letter from the Chief" or a speech regarding these issues at morning roll call. It means that ranking officers attend various sessions along with other officers. It comes from executives attending the graduations, or making introductory remarks at the beginning of each session. It comes when managers are making sure their people are attending the sessions. Real involvement comes from inquiring as to the results of the training, what has been learned, and recommending attendance. All of the attention from top management contributes to reinforcing the culture of the agency that respects, enhances, and fully supports multicultural diversity.

As trainers and educators the need to market the importance of these subjects needs to be emphasized. Many of us are put off by the idea of having to market these ideas when their benefits are so obvious. However, it is critically important that the top administration is in full support of these efforts. Several ways you can help achieve a top level buy-in are:

- Form a high level affirmative action advisory committee including the chief and senior operations officers. The committee should meet regularly to determine policy, recommend allocation of resources towards goals, and, by their very presence, strongly affirm the direction the department is taking with these issues; and
- Depending upon department size, it is recommended a newsletter is put together that speaks to the issues of affirmative action, differences in culture and the effect they both have on team or community policing. A column can be added to a department's existing publications. If a scheduled newsletter would tend to deemphasize the importance through overkill, at least keep command officers advised through frequent correspondence as to what is happening in the training sessions.

Another issue that must be recognized is the nature of the training function in many law enforcement agencies. Often the appointment of a trainer or commander of the section is a promotional step which means that eventually the officer may be promoted out after a specific tour of duty in the training section. This may lead to an interesting situation in that the officer, who has been teaching these subjects, will find himself or herself back out on the street working with the same officers they were challenging in the classroom. Even though individuals realize the importance of these subjects, it is human nature to try to remain part of our peer group or organization, realizing they will be returning to it. The situation is not unlike the first time individuals start to seek promotions and found it difficult to "add the stripes to their uniform." They wanted the people they supervise to treat them exactly like they did before promotion. They soon found that being an effective supervisor meant having to treat and be treated differently by their subordinates. The same is true with teaching these subjects. Instructors not only need to be committed to the subject matter, but need to resist the racial or gender humor that will arise in the classroom as peers make subtle, but derogatory remarks. Instructors cannot allow ourselves the luxury of trying to play both sides of the fence. Laughing at racial humor and then teaching racial discrimination obviously will send double messages that will do nothing to help change the culture.

All must realize that in the context of the subjects taught, there are no real answers, except the ones that contribute to the dignity of human beings.

CONCLUSION

We are all aware of the fact that the issues of prejudice, racial differences, and gender fairness are important to the law enforcement profession in insuring a safe and appropriate workplace for our employees along with concern and respect for the ever changing culture of the citizens that we serve. In addition to these humanitarian issues are the pragmatic ones of the obvious heavy cost of lawsuits when we fail to recognize problems and then have to pay judgments when we have not done as well as we could have. Most of our law enforcement agencies and our communities are self-insured, and when they have to pay, this money usually comes right out of operating budgets which means less equipment and resources to serve our communities.

When departments pro-actively take steps to design specific programs within their own agencies, they are taking responsibility in raising the consciousness of their organizations. They are also demonstrating a good faith effort in dealing with potential problems that effect the dignity of the employee and the workplace.

Much emphasis has been placed on the importance of community policing in recent years. Understanding and respecting the differences of the members of our communities is paramount to the success of those programs. We are all aware of various "fads" in the training areas that tend to come and go. The issues for becoming a culturally aware professional are here to stay. If you are successful in helping people to understand why they form opinions with scant information, form stereotypes, and hold values that are not based on true information, we have all been successful.

Law Enforcement Organizations that work pro-actively with Multicultural, Prejudice, Discrimination, and Bias issues demonstrate leadership that will be necessary to survive into the next century. Those that do not will suffer consequences within their departments and in the communities and citizens they serve. They will face organizational disharmony, greater labor-management tensions, high discrimination suit costs, loss of productivity, as well as becoming reactively ineffective with public safety issues in a multicultural community.

Our communities are growing much more diverse. The criminal justice system cannot afford to ignore these changes in the community and in their own work forces. Other cultures and races have different ways of doing things and it is imperative we learn about and understand our own culture and those of others in order to do our jobs better. Organizations that pro-actively begin this educational process are demonstrating sound and enlightened leadership as they move towards the twenty-first century.

REFERENCES

Allport, G. (1979). *The Nature of Prejudice.* Reading, Maine: Addison-Wesley.

Arnold, W. E. and McClure, L. (1994). *Communication Training And Development.* Prospect Heights, Ill.: Waveland Press.

Becker, E. (1962). *The Birth and Death of Meaning.* New York: Free Press.

Bennis, W., Schein, E. H., Steele, F. I., and Berleu, D. E. (Eds.). (1968). *Interpersonal Dynamics, Essays And Readings On Human Interactions.* Homewood: The Dorsey Press, Rev. Ed.

Bickham, T., and Rossett, A. (1993, November). "Diversity Training, Are We Doing The Right Thing Right?" *Police Chief,* pp. 43–47.

Hall, E. T. (1977). *Beyond Culture,* Garden City New York: Anchor Doubleday.

Hennessy, S. M. (1992). *Thinking Cop-Feeling Cop, A Study in Police Personalities.* Scottsdale, Arizona: Leadership Press.

Jordan, K. (1972). *Ideology and coming Professionalism: American Urban Police in the 1920's and 1930's.* Unpublished doctoral dissertation, Rutgers University.

Keesling, F. M. (1965). *Cultural Anthropology: The Science Of Custom.* New York: Holt, Reinhart and Winston.

Knowles, M. S. (1984). *Andragogy In Action.* San Francisco: Jossey-Bass.

Mehrabian, A. (1987). Communication Without Words. In G. Weaver (Ed.). *Readings in Cross-Cultural Communication.* 2nd ed. Lexington, Mass.: Ginn Press.

Myrdal, G. (1964). *An American Dilemma.* (Twentieth Anniversary Edition). New York: Harper and Row.

Ness, J. J. (1991). The Relevance of Basic Law Enforcement Training. Does The Curriculum Prepare Recruits For Police Work: *Journal Of Criminal Justice.* Vol. 19, 181–193.

Reaves, B. A. (1992). *State and Local Police Department, 1990.* Washington, D.C.: Bureau of Justice Statistics.

Samovar, L. A., and Porter, R. E. (1994). *Intercultural Communication: A Reader* (7th ed.). Belmont, California: Wadsworth.

Simon, C. (1929, August). "Basic Causes of Crime." *The Police Journal.*

Suthen, D. W. (1987). *Gunnar Myrdal and Black-White Relations.* Baton Rouge, LA: Louisiana State University Press.

Walker, S. (1980). *Popular Justice: A History of American Criminal Justice.* New York: Oxford University Press.

Warring, D. F. (1994). *Human Relations and Multicultural Educational Manual.* Scottsdale, Arizona: Leadership, Inc.
Weber, S. N. (1994). The Need To Be. The Socio-Cultural Significance Of Black Language. In L. S. Samovar and R. E. Porter (Eds.). *Intercultural Communication, A Reader.* Belmont, California: Wadsworth.
Work, J. W. (1989). *Toward Affirmative Action and Racial/Ethnic Pluralism.* Arlington, Virginia: Belvedere Press.

POSTSCRIPT

Multicultural Perspectives in Criminal Justice and Criminology merges the companion areas of cultural diversity, criminal justice, and criminology. In so doing, this anthology introduces the reader to multiculturalism and the fields of criminal justice and criminology with special emphasis on policy implications and criminal justice system responses. Additionally, the volume allows for a convergence of theory and practice when examining the role and function of multiculturalism and diversity with criminal justice and criminology. Moreover, we present, through the fine work of the criminal justice and criminology scholars assembled herein, various perspectives with a focus on multiculturalism in criminal justice theory, practice, and research.

The perspectives presented allow the reader to evaluate the role, value, utility, and implications of a multicultural focus within the complimentary and companion fields of criminal justice and criminology. The volume does not attempt to provide any conclusive answers concerning the role and function of multiculturalism for criminal justice and criminology. Rather, we wish merely to introduce this area of study as completely and comprehensively as possible given the current state of knowledge within this domain.

Our three objectives for the volume are realized. First, and through the work of the anthology authors, the reader is introduced to various multicultural perspectives. The authors, while not always representing consensus, do converge on one issue. There is a tremendously important role for an understanding of multiculturalism in practice, theory, and research within criminal justice and criminology. Second, the volume demonstrates the important role and function of multiculturalism for criminal justice and criminology. Each author, while addressing a different dimension of this topic, clearly made a strong case for the inclusion of a multicultural understanding of issues related to crime and justice. Whether the author was writing on empirical research, training issues, or diverse groups in society, this theme surfaced. Third, and finally, the anthology represents different perspectives on crime and justice while concentrating on cultural diversity. The editors wished to provide the reader with a collection of multicultural perspectives which demonstrates the diversity within the field which is as diverse as society itself.

It is our belief that the volume may be delineated based on four key topical themes. These include (1) the significance and inclusion of diverse groups within criminal justice, (2) inclusion of, and the analysis of, diverse groups in reference to criminal justice practice and criminological scholarship, (3) emerging diversity issues within criminal justice practice, and finally (4) the importance of education and training with a multicultural focus.

The inclusion of, and significance of, multicultural perspectives in addressing specific groups within society is clearly demonstrated in Chapter 1 through Chapter 3. Wynkoop and Kiselica (Chapter 1) discuss the dynamics of inclusion, exclusion, prejudice, discrimination, and definitional issues often present within a multicultural society. Chapter 2, by Eigenberg, Scarborough and Mullings, deals with the issue of gender and criminology and provides the reader with a clearer understanding of gender within this context via feminist perspectives. McKean in Chapter 3 addresses the conceptual and methodological issues often present in race and crime data which is important to our recognition of the influence of race, or lack thereof, in the commission of crime.

Second, Chapters 4 through 7 address the inclusion of, and the analysis of, diverse groups in reference to criminal justice practice and criminological scholarship. Siedschlaw and Gilbert discuss the ever present, yet often neglected, issue of Native American justice and provide the reader with a perspective on criminal justice within a multicultural context. Myers, Cintron and Scarborough in Chapter 5 share with the reader an important, and also neglected, area within criminological scholarship. This would be the question of the conceptualization of race and ethnicity when addressing Hispanics in research. Chapter 6, by Chermak and Rome, also deals with a conceptualization issue but from the vantage point of reality construction within the news media as the media has often been accused of distorting the role of race in crime stories. Finally, Chapter 7 by Arnott introduces the reader to the important, and not yet recognized, contribution gays and lesbians may make within criminal justice practice.

Third, Chapters 8 and 9 address emerging diversity issues within the criminal justice system. Spillane in Chapter 8 takes a legal perspective on the issue of hate crime which is motivated by racial, ethnic, religious, and sexual orientation insensitivity, bias, and prejudice. Corley and Smitherman in Chapter 9 also address an important and emerging issue for criminal justice. Taking a multicultural perspective in relation to juvenile justice issues, the authors bring together important and critical information for understanding diversity and juvenile delinquency.

The final trilogy of Chapters, 10 through 12, also address a common theme; education and training issues. Chapter 10 by Eigenberg and Baro addresses the important, and often taken-for-granted, images of women of color in criminal justice and criminology textbooks and make the argument that such depictions have social and policy consequences. Brown in Chapter 11 also addresses an issue of education from a multicultural perspective by attempting to uncover the patterns and practices of the inclusion of diversity within criminal justice pedagogy. Finally, Chapter 12 by Hennessy places education in the context of criminal justice practice by highlighting the important role that cultural sensitivity training has in law enforcement.

Together, the authors, through their contributions, allow the reader to see the significance of multiculturalism for criminal justice and criminology. The perspectives presented herein, we hope, will encourage others who have an interest in the criminal justice system and the field of criminology to pursue this avenue of scholarship and practice. American society is becoming more diverse on a macroscopic level with regard to population changes. American society is also becoming more diverse in reference to the inclusion of new voices, ideas and perspectives. It is our hope that *Multicultural Perspectives in Criminal Justice and Criminology* will provide a beginning for the criminal justice system and the field of criminology within this new direction.

James E. Hendricks, Ph.D.
Bryan Byers, Ph.D.

AUTHOR INDEX

Q

R

S

Y

Z

SUBJECT INDEX

D

E

H

K

L